Liquid Land

ALSO BY TED LEVIN

Backtracking: The Way of a Naturalist (1987)

The Curious Naturalist (Ted Levin and others, 1991)

Blood Brook: A Naturalist's Home Ground (1992)

Everglades National Park (1995)

with Frank Asch

Sawgrass Poems: A View of the Everglades (1996)

Cactus Poems (1998)

Song of the North (1999)

A JOURNEY

THROUGH

THE FLORIDA

EVERGLADES

Liquid Land

BY TED LEVIN

The University of Georgia Press
Athens

Published by the University of Georgia Press

Athens, Georgia 30602

© 2003 by Ted Levin

All rights reserved

Set in 11/13.5 Adobe Garamond

Printed and bound by Maple-Vail

The paper in this book meets the guidelines for
permanence and durability of the Committee on
Production Guidelines for Book Longevity of the
Council on Library Resources.

Printed in the United States of America

07 06 05 04 03 C 5 4 3 2 1

Library of Congress Cataloging-in-Publication Data

Levin, Ted, 1948–
Liquid land : a journey through the Florida
Everglades / by Ted Levin.
       p. cm.
Includes bibliographical references (p.).
ISBN 0-8203-2512-0 (alk. paper)
1. Natural history—Florida—Everglades.
2. Restoration ecology—Florida—Everglades.
I. Title.
QH105.F6L47 2003
508.759'39—dc21

2003001891

FOR ANNIE

Since the days of the earliest explorations, the herpetological fauna of Florida has evoked spirited comment. Hardly a mosquito-bitten Spaniard writing home for supplies or a French sea captain recording in his log the adventures of a shore party but mentions "vipers" or "crocodiles," or the shocking noise the frogs made, or the Indian who tried to feed him snake. Colonizing Florida was such a strenuous matter, however, that zoological observation was considerably tainted with emotion, and only those forms of life which bit people, or which people could eat, elicited any enthusiasm.

ARCHIE CARR, 1940

A Contribution to the Herpetology of Florida

Contents

The South Florida wilderness is a study in
halftones, not bright, bold strokes of a full brush
. . . there are lonely distances, intricate and
monotonous waterways, birds, sky, and water.

DANIEL BEARD, 1938

Preface

For more than a century people have been lured to Florida's edges by the
siren song of winter warmth. There we created a theme park of the sun, and
then slowly converged on its wild interior. We bent the land to suit our needs
and fancies to such a ludicrous extreme—canals, levees, artificial ponds, golf
courses, a latticework of roads—that we extinguished the essence of Florida
that captured us in the first place. What was once a gorgeous yet inhospitable
and threatening landscape has been drained and shackled to such an extent
that the fragile pockets that survive call to us more sharply.

Is it possible to restore the wildness when millions of people live next door?
Or put the braids back into a straightened river? Or to free an imprisoned lake?
Or to reconstruct the gene pool of a vanishing predator? Or to guarantee a

toothy crocodile a home in the twenty-first century? Can we reverse a century of abuse and neglect?

To look for answers I covered much of the landscape by foot, by plane, and by boat, and engaged people of differing natures to learn about Florida's Everglades. With biologists in the high-tech pursuit of panthers along the edge of cypress swamps, into the coastal jungles in search of crocodiles, across a thousand square miles of marshland to band snail kites. With hydrologists who read the changes in the landscape and planned for its future. With an old man who adored tree snails. With another man, born in the glades, who speared frogs from a racing airboat and lived in an old yellow school bus. With agribusinessmen, who ruled an empire of sugar. With environmentalists, citizens, bureaucrats, all of whom were at odds about the extent and direction of restoration.

"The Everglades is a test," said environmental activist Joe Podgor. "If we pass, we get to keep the planet." After decades of abuse, the most ambitious ecological restoration ever attempted is under way, a more than eight billion dollars effort that involves approximately fifty-five federal, state, and county agencies as well as two Native American tribal councils. The world is watching, for the Everglades has become a model of ecological and political maneuvering.

A wilderness born of the sky and sustained by rain, the Everglades begins as a cloud above central Florida. It is desktop-flat and was once almost as large as New Jersey. It is the centerpiece of a watershed that extends from the suburbs of Orlando to the coral reefs off the Florida Keys. There are no mountains here that pour their waters toward the sea. The land itself spawns clouds. Before the Everglades was drained, the more it rained, the more it flowed, a shallow sheet of grassy water from the southern end of Lake Okeechobee to the coastal mangrove swamps, more than a hundred miles away. Most water from the northern glades (now under cultivation) or from Lake Okeechobee (now rimmed by a levee) never reached the sea. The sun and the plants called it back and returned it to the clouds, from which it fell again. Cumulus clouds still rise twenty thousand feet into the summer blue sky, transform into bruised thunderheads, then tear open. Passing clouds, mutable and spectacular, orchestrate lavish sunsets and supply South Florida with its lifeblood. Billed as the Sunshine State, Florida could more appropriately be called the Water State.

South Florida is ruled by tropical seasons, wet and dry, is hammered by big weather, and is cauterized by wildfires. The Everglades is the most distinctive feature in this landscape of variegated wetlands that once covered more than fourteen thousand square miles of shallow slowly flowing water, which included the Kissimmee River, Lake Okeechobee, Big Cypress Swamp, pine-lands, mangrove jungles, and Florida Bay. At the western edge of Big Cypress Swamp, in a maze of dark forests, royal palms tower above the sodden earth like green umbrellas. Below them, gardens of epiphytes—orchids, ferns, bro-meliads—crowd the branches of tropical hardwood trees. Crocodiles cruise the estuaries, and alligators, the marsh. Panthers roam within the shadow of four and a half million Florida residents and more than ten million tourists annually, many of whom don't even know that the wetlands are there.

The patterns of the Everglades are cued by the yearly cycle of rain and drought and shift with the vagaries of the season and of the year. At the onset of the dry season, for instance, legions of water snakes move westward to lower, wetter ground. Usually, the Everglades begins to dry in late November, and the snakes get impatient and move soon after. Some years the dry season never starts, and the snakes stay put.

One year, for three nights in late February, I watched hundreds, maybe thousands, of water snakes heading for a deeper marsh across a two- or three-mile stretch of park service road, seething across the macadam, thickly scaled and constantly moving. In stillness, the sound of snake bellies rose from the pavement, a light scratching noise like water over pebbles. I kept their company, flashlight in hand, stooping to identify serpents passing about my feet, ever mindful of chance encounters with water moccasins, which were also moving. Twice I nearly stepped on a moccasin. Once I nearly knelt on one. Each morning after the migration, the road was littered with more than a hundred casualties attended by scores of crows and vultures. On the fourth morning, I counted fewer than twenty roadkills. The migration had ended as suddenly as it had started.

Animals that have wandered the woodlands and marshes for thousands of years are now being forced into compromising habitats, where they run afoul of both traffic and senior citizens. Several years ago, my father returned home to find a terrified black bear stuck between a beauty salon and the entrance to the villas where he and my mother lived. The bear hugged the trunk of a slash pine less than a hundred yards from a busy four-lane road until a game warden shot it with a tranquilizing dart and took it to a nearby wildlife refuge, the drop-off spot for untoward wildlife.

The bear is not alone in its meandering. I find bobcat and gray fox tracks in the almond-colored sand behind the community clubhouse, alligators in the weedy ponds between the villas, and otters in the still-clear springs. When I visit the area in the summer, I almost always move a gopher tortoise away from traffic. As new developments spread into Florida's interior, wildlife either adapts or vanishes. A friend who lives north of Miami, hard by the eastern perimeter levee, told me that once, after a heavy thunderstorm, baby rat snakes appeared in his silverware drawer.

Since 1900 Florida has lost the monk seal, the red wolf, and the Carolina parakeet, which mined cypress seeds from tiny cones, adding both color and hope to otherwise gaunt winter swamps. In May 1917 a pair of ivory-billed woodpeckers and their young were observed in Royal Palm Hammock in the southern Everglades, the last reported ivorybill sightings in South Florida. Even Everglades National Park, comprising more than two million acres, has not been immune to local species extinctions. Pine islands outside the park either were developed, burned, or changed vegetation because of fire suppression. The park's islands also changed because of fire suppression. Without adequate numbers of islands of sufficient size, several species of birds gradually disappeared. Bluebirds, brown-headed nuthatches, and red-cockaded woodpeckers all vanished during the 1950s. (Bluebirds have subsequently been reintroduced.)

There are surprises, and that's what I love about Florida, the irrepressible presence of primeval nature on humanity's doorstep. Once I found a three-foot water moccasin, *Agkistrodon piscivorus,* in my parents' neighborhood, resting peaceably on the bank of a marsh less than a hundred feet from the home of the president of the community association, a man who had a reputation for bludgeoning wayward snakes. "Most people have a vague feeling that no reptiles except turtles are to be trusted," wrote Archie Carr, so I decided to relocate the moccasin. It heard my footfalls and condensed, taut like coiled cable. Its jaws gaped. I peeked down its cotton-white gullet, which Peter Matthiessen once described as the spreading petals of a flower, and saw the hypodermic fangs folded back against the roof of the snake's mouth. Its nervous tail twitched against the brittle leaves, sounding like castanets. A no-rattle-rattlesnake relative, a primitive pit viper, loaded with venom not meant for humans unless provoked beyond the threshold of security, its striking range about half its body length. Hence, the performance. I watched for a moment, then stepped a bit closer. Driven to further histrionics, the snake rose up a little higher, a little more determined, its mouth ratcheted like an open hand. I touched the moccasin with my camera tripod leg. Cold metal elicited no response. I slid the leg under the snake's body and picked it up, perfectly balanced, its tongue suspended in midflick, reading the air, and moved it deeper into the swamp.

Another time, I drove into Naples to see a bald eagle nest in the crown of a front-yard pine. The nest was beautiful. Trumpet creeper, a woody vine with bright, trumpet-shaped orange flowers, wrapped around the tree, climbing snakelike up the trunk and out across the upper limbs. The nest glowed in the morning sun. A month earlier, when the vine had supported thousands of bright flowers, the nest could be seen from across the bay, framed against the blue sky.

This was not a typical neighborhood for nesting bald eagles. BMWs and Mercedes-Benzes lined the street; the air was thick and sweet with lemons. Sanitation workers in golf-cart-like vehicles scooted up and down the driveways, collecting pails of garbage that they then delivered to a mother ship down the street. Cuban royal palms and Norfolk Island pines, tufts of saw palmetto, pampas grass, and tightly pruned sea grape decorated front yards. The bay lapped at backyard dikes. Down the block, hotels and condominiums rose in the morning light. All day the eagles towed their shadows across the suburbs.

Wild South Florida is predictably unpredictable and undeniably unique, an absorbent plain of limestone rife with tropical greenery. It is land on the verge of water, water on the verge of land. Cockroaches smell like Drambuie, and orchids grow in trees. There are no spectacular panoramas. No volcanoes. No crater lakes. In fact, Everglades National Park was the first park in the world protected for its biology rather than its scenery. The loftiest ridge in South Florida is twenty-two feet above sea level, and a road sign in Everglades National Park announces Rock Reef Pass, elevation three feet. So subtle and varied is the landscape that a lexicon of rich endemic nouns name its delicate features: an island of tropical hardwoods in sawgrass or pinelands is a *hammock*; an island of pine or mangrove, a *key*; an island of willow or bay, a *head*; an island of cypress, a *dome*. A marsh is called a *prairie*; a wide channel in a marsh or swamp is a *slough,* which may be only three or four inches deeper than the surrounding sawgrass and, from a racing airboat, is recognized only by the sudden shift from sedges to water lilies; a river is a *hatchee*; a long, narrow stand of cypress that grows in a slough is a *strand*; and limy mud is *marl*.

There is no spring here, not by northeastern standards, at least, my yardstick for seasons. In South Florida, bald eagles nest in November; wood storks, in January; white ibises, in March; eastern kingbirds, in June. Flickers and red-bellied woodpeckers often raise two broods in a year, more rarely three. Flowers bloom after fires. One December I stood beneath a Goliath of a red maple in Fakahatchee Strand as it unfurled its new leaves amid a thin, scarlet haze of the previous season's dying leaves. Plants and animals from two biomes, the Temperate Zone and the Tropics, entwine. Cuba, the nearest island in the Caribbean, dwells in Florida—white-crowned pigeon, roseate spoonbill, gray kingbird, gumbo-limbo, West Indian mahogany, lysiloma, and many other plants and animals. And Florida dwells in Cuba—mockingbird, mourning dove, northern flicker, mangrove water snake, gar, sawgrass, wax myrtle, Carolina willow, pop ash, and live oak are to be found there.

Nowhere else in North America can you find crocodiles, manatees, and rainbow-colored tree snails, great white herons and ghost orchids, or towering royal palms. Nowhere else did a wild, shallow marsh creep southward through a hundred-mile-long valley of sawgrass, and nowhere else does a wildness border a megalopolis the size of Miami. The only population of mountain lion east of the Mississippi roams the swamps and pines.

Where else on North America can you find an Everglades? And for how long will this one survive? In what condition? Can it be saved? For this lean inscrutable wetland, besieged by a roster of environmental problems, is on the threshold of the world's largest ecological restoration effort.

(((((

For Europeans and later Americans, the Everglades became synonymous with foreboding, a strange and otherworldly landscape immortalized in fiction, myth, and song. Three times the United States cavalry failed to round up the recalcitrant Seminole, who still live in the Everglades, having never signed a peace treaty with the federal government. Caucasians feared this land. In 1887 Daniel Hosea Ballou, writing for *Harper's Weekly*, described the region as "inhabited with all manners of worms and insect life with and without legs, bugs, ticks, and other animals, minute in size but terrible in action, which drop willfully and accidentally on the sleeper and promenade with great effect." Though the Everglades is now much diminished, it remains a beautiful and mysterious wetland, and we still stand at the edge of this inhospitable realm and timidly peek in.

On 8 January 1841, the *St. Augustine News* ran an anonymous account of wild South Florida, delivered by a member of Lieutenant Colonel William S. Harney's command, who had fought the Seminole in the Everglades: "one boundless expanse of sawgrass and water, occasionally interspersed with little islands, all of which are overflowed, but the trees are in a green and flourish-ing state. No country that I have ever heard of bears any resemblance to it; it seems like a vast sea filled with grass and green trees." To immerse yourself in a landscape, to penetrate a world so unique and so seemingly full of contradic-tions, is to face the wild and wondrous variation of life. The Everglades holds songs and secrets, the breath of another biological province, the pull of strange seasons surrounded by an immense and gorgeous sky. A line of white pelicans moving over Florida Bay suggests a world composed of light and water and earth inhabited by diverse forms of life, and that this diversity is essential.

Before the 1900s, the Everglades carried so much water that it rarely dried. Now, in the aftermath of drainage, it dries every second or third year. Between 1930 and 1960, eighty thousand to one hundred thousand white ibis roosted in the mangroves between Lostmans River and Everglades City, south of Big Cypress Swamp. Now the birds roost elsewhere, the ibis having moved away. What's an ibis worth? A hundred thousand ibis, blood-red bills probing puddles in the sawgrass? What's the Everglades itself worth? Imagining a life without goose music, Aldo Leopold wrote, "We may as well do away with stars, or sunsets."

Environment

My advice is to let every discontented man
make a trip through the Everglades; if it don't
kill, it will certainly cure him.

ALONZO CHURCH, 1892, who crossed the
Everglades between Fort Myers and Miami

1 The Ambiguities of South Florida

On a January night I stand wet to my waist in sawgrass, listening to an owl's lusty pronouncements and the riotous jamming of frogs. Four inches of muck oozing over my sandaled feet, I am part of the diversity of Everglades National Park. Yet that diversity now depends on an ironic reality—a fabricated water-delivery system. Bridled and balkanized by 1,074 miles of canals, 720 miles of levees, 18 major pumping stations, and 250 control or diversion structures, the "true" Everglades has become a computer-controlled watershed almost as artificial as Disney World, two hundred miles to the north. Ironically, the land is so flat and porous that it's hard to get water to move in the right direction even with pumps.

Most people who have never visited South Florida believe that the Everglades is a river with visible banks, or a dark, menacing swamp—an image perpetuated by B-grade movies like *Wind across the Everglades*. The Everglades is neither river nor swamp; it is a marsh, a shallow sheet of water flowing lazily toward the sea, and in its heyday it measured as much as sixty miles across. The word *Everglades* is often used to mean more than the vast freshwater marsh. "I'm going to the Everglades" may mean going anywhere wild and west of Miami or east of Naples—cypress swamp, pineland, mangrove jungle, even Florida Bay. Or it may mean going to the national park, less than one-fourth of which is actually Everglades. Subtle and flat like West Texas, the Everglades tilts imperceptibly south at less than two inches per mile. This makes it so level that I could stand here in the sawgrass all night and not notice a current. It is so flat that I could walk most of the entire three-hundred-mile-long watershed from Orlando to Florida Bay without wetting my hair.

Such sameness does not create botanical monotony. Minuscule elevation changes spur a stunning variety of plant communities, of which thirteen are listed for the Everglades region. To my left the oval leaves of water lilies float above a depression less than six inches deeper than the surrounding sawgrass. Wetlands (here and elsewhere) are measured in *hydroperiods,* the length of time each year that a piece of land has standing water. Some areas in South Florida are visibly soggy all or most of the year; others, like the pinelands, usually appear to be bone dry but may be inundated for a month or more each year. When the southern Everglades looks parched in February, beneath the surface, both water and animals move through a maze of tunnels and caverns in the porous limestone.

Not only are we unsure what the Everglades is, we're unsure about the word itself; is it a singular or plural noun; a proper noun or common noun? Everglades is often shortened to *glades,* which sometimes gets a capital *G.* No one knows what the Calusa, the native culture of the southwest coast of Florida, called it; after driving off the Spanish for forty years they died of smallpox or were assimilated into the island cultures of the western Caribbean. Pushed south by an expanding nation, the Seminole and Miccosukee arrived in the Everglades early in the nineteenth century, more than a hundred years after the Calusa disappeared, and fashioned a culture amid mosquitoes and egrets. They called their new home Pay-hay-okee, which means "grassy waters." The name Everglades was coined in 1823 from the Old English word *glyde* or *glaed,* which means "an opening in the forest." In 1947, Marjory Stoneman Douglas gave the world a lasting image of the region in *The Everglades: River of Grass.* What grows in lush profusion in the marsh, however, is not a grass but a sedge called sawgrass, a lean, sharp vegetative blade.

《 《 《

Nothing in South Florida is less certain than its weather. Today it is delicious, in the sixties, cloudless. Although the seasons are Caribbean—more or less six months wet, six months dry—they are not reliable. On average, a quarter of the yearly rainfall occurs during the winter dry season, and the seam between the seasons is periodically obliterated by longer multiyear cycles of flood or drought.

Anything that lives here must tolerate these swings; some life-forms rely on them. The seeds of cypress and sawgrass, for example, germinate only on dry ground, even though the plants themselves survive a year or more of inundation. Six species of frogs spawn only during the first rains of the rainy season, which in some years fail to appear. Drought favors the spread of wildfire, which rejuvenates marshes and pinelands and annihilates hardwoods. Hurricanes level jungles while casting seed.

The whims of South Florida's weather place the snail kite—a red-legged crow-sized hawk—and the wood stork at opposite ends of a meteorological seesaw. The annual wet season and the prolonged periods of flood are good for kites, which troll for snails above the flooded marshes. The annual dry season and the prolonged cycles of drought are good for storks, which gorge on fish concentrated in shrinking pools. Only a capricious wetlands, a wetlands enriched by yearly cycles of wet and dry, punctuated by violent drought and alarming flood—an Everglades—could accommodate two species of birds dependent on divergent meteorological swings.

Before the flow patterns and volume of water were disrupted, the breeding behavior of most wading birds began when marl prairies on the eastern rim of the Everglades—called the Atlantic Coastal Ridge, now mostly developed—dried to puddles in early winter. Only later in the season did the sawgrass and, eventually, the deeper sloughs of the interior Everglades begin to dry, thus attracting hungry birds. From 1931 to 1946, an average of 60,000 to 88,000 herons, egrets, ibises, and storks crammed the rookeries in the national park. In some years as many as 250,000 birds would nest; in other years none.

Early in the last century the skies of South Florida were filled with wading birds, and the inland waters, with alligators. Everglades National Park biologists Bill Robertson and Jim Kushlan estimated that at the beginning of the twentieth century one and a half million wading birds nested in the mangroves between Rodgers River and Shark River. In 1940 Audubon biologist Alexander Sprunt III was overwhelmed by the activity in Broad River rookery. "We pushed through the rookery, with both sides of the creek simply boiling and seething with young [birds] scrambling back into the deeper portions. We at last could go no further, so sat in the boat and watched. It was an incredible, unbelievable sight, even while looking at it! It seemed a sort of dream. There was an unreality about the whole place which seemed at any moment to be on the verge of being dissipated, yet which never did so! It was a sight which might have been imagined in past days, when the Everglades really had big rookeries, but it did not belong in the present. Yet there it was." The birds would fly north to the edge of the sawgrass to feed, squalls of birds so large and white you'd have to shield your eyes from the glare. No one knows for sure whether that many ibises and herons and egrets and storks really gathered in what is now Everglades National Park or if a hundred thousand alligators—the oft-quoted number—actually lived there. Yet birds and alligators must have once lived in the Everglades in extraordinary numbers to have generated those sorts of estimates. These animals must have been a visual feast, like this boundless, soaking plain of sawgrass.

The true Everglades alone was nearly six thousand square miles. When you add the tessellation of inland and coastal swamps, bays, coral reefs, lakes, ponds, rivers, wet meadows, tree islands, and pine flatwoods that are part of the watershed, this subtropical ecosystem occupies most of the lower third of the Florida peninsula. The Atlantic Coastal Ridge, broken by only a few transverse cuts, once funneled water southward down the vast marsh and supported a fire-prone slash pine forest.

Now buildings have replaced pines, canals bleed the watershed of more than two billion gallons of water each day, and the region has become a panorama of anemic wilderness, pasture, and farmland. Yet wildness still pokes through. In Big Cypress Swamp, along the western rim of the watershed, natural grooves in the limestone three or four feet deep and more than a mile wide are filled with organic material that supports linear cypress and pond apple swamps. Epidermal grooves (the sloughs), wide, long, and shallow—the native channels of the Everglades—support water lilies, pickerelweed, and bladderwort, and curve through fields of sawgrass. Sawgrass stretches as far as I can see and then some. Dense sawgrass. Sparse sawgrass. Tall sawgrass, higher than an elephant's eye. Short sawgrass. Sawgrass and water lilies. Sawgrass and spike rush. Sawgrass and sawgrass, and more sawgrass.

In the southern Everglades, shadowy hammocks, which rise above the sawgrass on limestone pedestals, support miniforests of tropical hardwood

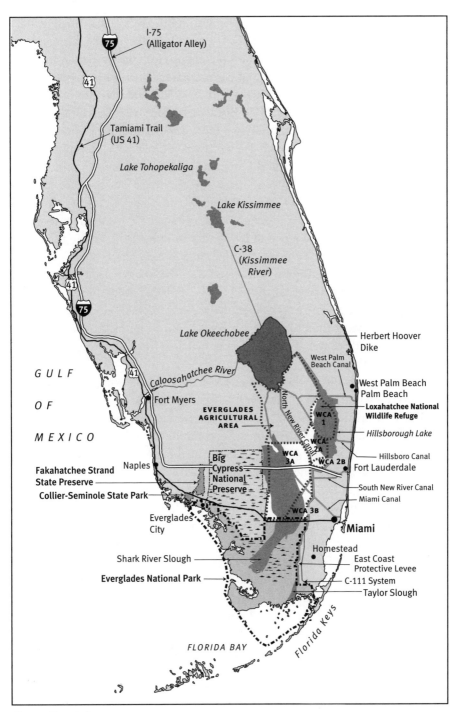

Current Everglades

trees—trees with exotic names like gumbo-limbo, West Indian mahogany, satin leaf, pigeon plum, lysiloma. To the north, in the central Everglades, where the peat is deeper, organic mats bubble up from the limestone and are colonized by red bay, cocoplum, and coastal plain willow.

Hydrologically speaking, everything in South Florida is connected: the Everglades, Big Cypress, Florida Bay, Biscayne Bay, the coral reefs off the Keys, Big Sugar, Miami. The Everglades' two most important drainages are Taylor and Shark sloughs. Taylor Slough, fed by rising groundwater, drains 150 square miles of upland marl prairie and flows almost due south into the northeast corner of Florida Bay; to its west, Shark Slough, driven by rainwater, drains 4,000 square miles of sawgrass and water lily and, like a gleaming scimitar, curves southwest, emptying its freight in Whitewater Bay, more than seventy miles away in the southern end of Everglades National Park, and in the Gulf of Mexico. Before the building of canals and levees, Shark Slough spilled over its eastern rim during the wet season into the Rocky Glades, where the short-hydroperiod marshes functioned as a floodplain. Except during very wet years, surface water from Shark Slough now rarely reaches Taylor Slough. For five thousand years the Everglades has been hemmed by rocky rims that rise a scant two or three feet above the deeper marshes. The only thing that purls down here is the wind.

When John Muir reached central Florida in 1867, having walked from Indiana, he wrote in his journal that he was in "the hot gardens of the sun" and that no stream he crossed "appeared to have the least idea of where it was going." He touched on three points that combine to set Florida, particularly South Florida, apart from the rest of the United States: a hot, humid climate that drives year-round photosynthesis, an unfathomable lushness, and a flatness that confuses even the water.

Unfortunately Muir's sensitivity to the way life works has not been universally appreciated. Humans have tried for most of the last century to make the Everglades less sodden. Since 1884, when William Harney proposed in *Harper's New Monthly Magazine* an elaborate system of canals and dikes to harness the flow of water out of Lake Okeechobee, the motto of most regional politicians and entrepreneurs has been: dam it, dike it, drain it, divert it. In 1905 Napoleon Bonaparte Broward was elected governor of Florida largely by promising to create an "Empire of the Everglades" by wringing the last drop out of that "pestilence-ridden swamp." To let all the water drain, Broward suggested blasting a hole in the bedrock limestone.

Since then the state and federal governments have spent most of the twentieth century trying to destroy the Everglades, and much of it trying to save the

Everglades, often at the same time. Since 1948 the United States Army Corps of Engineers, unable to grasp the subtle workings of an ecosystem shaped and dependent on the divergent meteorological swings of flood and drought, has constructed massive flood-control projects to "tame" a landscape and in the process has shut down the area's hydrological breathing. In 1947 torrential rains had dumped about ten feet of water on the Everglades, flooding most of southern Florida, including much of Miami. Millions of acres remained underwater for more than six months. Flooded-out dairy farmers evacuated Broward and Miami–Dade counties and moved north into the Kissimmee River valley; the residents who remained behind demanded relief. Their outcry prompted a call to arms. Congress established a public works project called the Central and Southern Florida Flood Control District and charged the Army Corps of Engineers with controlling the flow of the Everglades. During the next three decades the Corps constructed the elaborate network of more than sixteen hundred miles of canals, levees, and spillways that subdivided the Everglades into an agricultural district, three water conservation areas, and a national park. The Engineers straightened the Kissimmee River, Lake Okeechobee's principal tributary, transforming it from a gorgeous, curving 105-mile-long waterway into a dead-straight 56-mile-long, 30-foot-deep canal. They also guaranteed an overland water supply for southern Miami–Dade County and dredged and widened the Caloosahatchee River, which diverts Lake Okeechobee water to the Gulf of Mexico.

Ironically, in December 1947, two months after the rain stopped falling, Harry Truman dedicated 1.3 million acres for Everglades National Park, declaring, "Here is land, tranquil in its quiet beauty, serving not as the source of water but as the last receiver of it...a land of subtle charm and complexity, preserved forever for the inspiration and enjoyment of mankind," thus ending a forty-year struggle to create a national park in South Florida. (The $2 million the state was obligated to give to the federal government as a stipulation for the establishment of Everglades National Park was committed in a heated poker game between key legislators and John Pennekamp, the editorial director of the *Miami Herald* and a member of the Everglades National Park Commission.)

Although the Army Engineers built the levees, canals, and flood gates and write the operating permits, the South Florida Water Management District controls them, dictating the quantity, quality, distribution, and timing of water release. Only the rain is beyond their jurisdiction—but only until it hits the ground. To accomplish its goals of research, planning, and dominion, the water management district levies ad valorem (property) taxes, something the state legislature cannot do.

Today, at the onset of ecological restoration, an effort overwhelmingly blessed by both Washington and Tallahassee, some federal and county officials still want to build an international airport in Homestead, gateway to Everglades National Park. And bureaucrats in Miami–Dade County want to hem the entire eastern boundary of the park in plastic to make South Florida safer for winter tomatoes.

Half the original glades is already gone, replaced by farms, suburban lots, and a dense tangle of alien trees. Water (laden with agricultural runoff) must go through the underpasses of two east-west highways to flow through the remaining marshland. In the interest of flood control and agricultural and urban expansion, water destined for the Everglades is detained in diked "water conservation areas" or sent directly to the sea. Within a morning's drive of a roadless wilderness sixty miles across, four and a half million people brush their teeth in water originally meant for spoonbills and crocodiles.

Yosemite and Yellowstone, two other crown jewels in the national park system, lie at the headwaters of their respective watersheds. But the 2,350-square-mile Everglades National Park, which includes most of Florida Bay, lies at the bottom of its watershed. Although the park has been designated a World Heritage Site, an International Biosphere Reserve, and a Wilderness of International Significance by the United Nations, novelist Joy Williams calls it "the Park at the End of the Pipe," America's most imperiled national park. Williams believes that the Everglades is already an illusion, a wetland propped up by the Army Corps of Engineers' smoke and mirrors; writing in *Outside,* she asked whether the park should invite "each of the million visitors each year to bring a gallon of water and pour it on the ground."

《《《

Monumental problems require mammoth solutions. In 1994 Richard A. Pettigrew, former speaker of the Florida House, began a five-year stint as chair of the Governor's Commission for a Sustainable South Florida, a forty-nine-member group that included representatives from every area—local, regional, state, federal, and tribal governments and the national park; sportsmen, fishing guides, and environmental organizations; farmers, educators, developers, business owners, and tourist-related enterprises. By all accounts, Pettigrew ran tight, efficient meetings, where people of opposing views developed trust. He was masterful in gaining consensus for more than a dozen reports. "Everyone had to be on the bus when it left the station," remembers Mike Collins, chairman of the governing board of the South Florida Water Management District. The commission's first finding was that on its present course South

Florida was not sustainable, and a later report, "A Conceptual Plan for the Central and South Florida Project Restudy," evolved into the Army Corps of Engineers' Comprehensive Everglades Restoration Plan (CERP), endorsed by both Governor Bush and President Clinton. Several of the commission's benchmark recommendations are still being called upon.

Repairing the drainage of the Everglades is the cornerstone of the ecological restoration of South Florida. The goals of restoration are clear: to improve the quality of the water; to reestablish an overland connection between the state-owned central Everglades and the national park to the south; to restore what is left of the peripheral wetlands that border both sides of the Everglades; and to return more freshwater to Florida Bay. The process of restoration, however, is not so clear.

Restoration means different things for different species. For the Florida panther it means the acquisition of more upland habitat north of Big Cypress Swamp, an improved relationship between biologists and area ranchers, and an influx of new genes from West Texas cougars. For the American crocodile and the snail kite it means more clean water flowing from the Everglades into Florida Bay at the right time of year. Scientists are not sure how restoration will affect the itinerant white ibis, whose population has relocated itself in the southeast four times since the 1930s, after having decreased by more than 90 percent in the Everglades.

Regrettably, water management in South Florida is often driven by lawsuit, not by scientific plan. Although the Army Engineers now come down on the side of restoration, it is often blocked by parties that one would normally think of as being pro-environment—the Miccosukee, the National Park Service, and the Sierra Club for instance—and by the Endangered Species Act of 1973, which places the well-being of an individual species ahead of broad-scale efforts to restore the ecological function of a debased wetland.

"In time, and with water, everything changes," wrote Leonardo da Vinci. There are a multitude of biologists, hydrologists, and engineers in South Florida who hope that Leonardo was right and that when the restoration party is eventually thrown, everyone will come, and everyone will be healthy.

It may be that the mystery of the Everglades is
the saw grass, so simple, so enduring, so hostile.

MARJORY STONEMAN DOUGLAS, 1947

2 The Everglades Itself

To the uninitiated, the Everglades may appear monotonous, an endless run of
fierce-edged sawgrass. With a long look, however, one sees the Everglades as a
mosaic of marshes and sloughs, shallow, weed-choked lakes, marl prairies, and
cypress strands, all punctuated by tropical hardwood hammocks, bay heads,
and willow heads, and bordered by pine uplands. These drain into a maze
of bays, tidal rivers, and saltwater jungles. A protean wetland often at odds
with itself, the Everglades has spread and shrunk over several thousand years,
transforming not only in size but in abundance of species and biodiversity.
Its dimensions are determined by such gradual, long-term processes as the
rise of the sea and the accretion of peat. Species composition responds to
the short-term brutality of nature—droughts and floods and big weather—
and to alligators.

Geologically speaking, the Everglades is a recent landscape, only five thousand years old. By the time sawgrass peat defined what was to be the Everglades, humans had been in Florida for five thousand years; elsewhere in the world people were writing letters and numerals, growing grains and raising animals, smelting gold, baking bread, and brewing beer; the wheel was already in use.

Five thousand years ago, when the sea level was approximately fifteen feet lower than it is today, the Everglades stretched farther south, covering what is now Whitewater Bay, Florida Bay, and the mangrove jungles from Cape Sable north to the Harney River. Deposits of freshwater peat lie hidden beneath the region's more recent brackish sediments and mark the prehistoric boundary of the southern Everglades. The glades once extended farther north as well, into what is now Lake Okeechobee.

Each layer of peat is a sodden page in the history of a restless landscape. Layers of ash suggest that some sloughs may have been formed by fire. Striking after a severe drought, lightning ignites the dried sawgrass peat, which may have smoldered for months until drenched by rain. Other sloughs began as alligator trails, which the wandering reptiles etched into the peat. When the rainy season came, flowing water widened and deepened the channels. Which is to say, sloughs were born of disturbance and are maintained by water. Eventually, such deeper-water plants as water lily and spatterdock replaced the sawgrass and left their own layers of peat.

No one today remembers the predrainage Everglades of the 1870s. Our oldest memories date back to the 1930s, 1940s, and 1950s, when the glades was already a long-suffering wetland. To understand the nature of the predrainage landscape, hydrologists and soil scientists consult chronologies formed by peat deposits and the journals of early explorers, some distorted and some describing a gorgeous flowering wetland.

⟪ ⟪ ⟪

Although South Florida's coastline was known to Europeans early in the sixteenth century, much of the interior remained unmapped until the later half of the twentieth century. In 1750, a French cartographer drew Florida wedge-shaped with lofty peaks extending the length of the peninsula. Another eighteenth-century French map transformed Florida into an archipelago. Except for what was known to soldiers who had crossed the interior of Florida during the Seminole Wars, by the close of the nineteenth century, more was known about the heart of Africa than about the heart of the Everglades.

In 1943 John H. Davis Jr. wrote *The Natural Features of Southern Florida*. He divided the Everglades into thirteen plant communities. A few of Davis's plant communities were the by-products of the previous sixty years of drainage. More recently, plant scientists suggest that the predrainage Everglades had only five physiographic regions, two of which—pond apple swamp and peripheral cypress swamp—no longer exist.

A 150,000-acre pond apple swamp once rimmed the southern shore of Lake Okeechobee. According to the botanist John Kunkel Small, who visited in 1914, the swamp was the most beautiful corner of the Everglades, an eerie forest of misshapen trees and junglelike growth. Seasonally flooded, the three-mile-wide swamp buffered the sawgrass marshes to the south from the waters of Lake Okeechobee, which overflowed during the wet season. Eight short rivers carried lake water through the pond apple swamp into a narrow, one- or two-mile-wide white-water-lily marsh. The lily marsh was the transition zone between the pond apples and the dense sawgrass plains.

Pond apple (*Annona glabra*), often called custard apple, alligator apple, or corkwood, is a short swollen tree that grows from a buttressed trunk that flares in every direction. The trunk tapers abruptly, disappearing into a spray of contorted limbs. According to Small, a living net of vines tied the swamp into a vegetative conglomerate, and crowds of air plants and ferns grew on the tree limbs, which often broke under the added weight.

When Small traveled up the New River Canal to Lake Okeechobee in 1914, he found the large white flowers of moonvine everywhere and declared the flower-covered pond apple swamp "more beautiful than words can describe." By the 1920s almost all of the swamp had been cleared for agriculture, and the exposed muck began to decompose and blow away. Today, the elevation of the Everglades Agricultural Area—the seven hundred thousand acres of sugar cane and vegetables that occupies what was once the northern Everglades—is lower than Lake Okeechobee.

Though not a true apple, the fruit of pond apple is large—five inches by three inches—yellowish, sweet-smelling, and edible. The hard winged seeds remain viable in water for some time, which may explain why pond apple grows in west Africa, the Caribbean, and the Bahamas, as well as in South Florida. Although the tree still grows in the Everglades, scattered in the open marshes, along the edge of hammocks, and in the deep sloughs of Big Cypress, nowhere does it approach the size and expanse of the long-gone swamp. The few remaining *Annona glabra* stumps inside Herbert Hoover Dike, along the south shore of Lake Okeechobee, some as big as a kitchen sink, remain, waterlogged and rotten, mute testimony to a vanished corner of the Everglades.

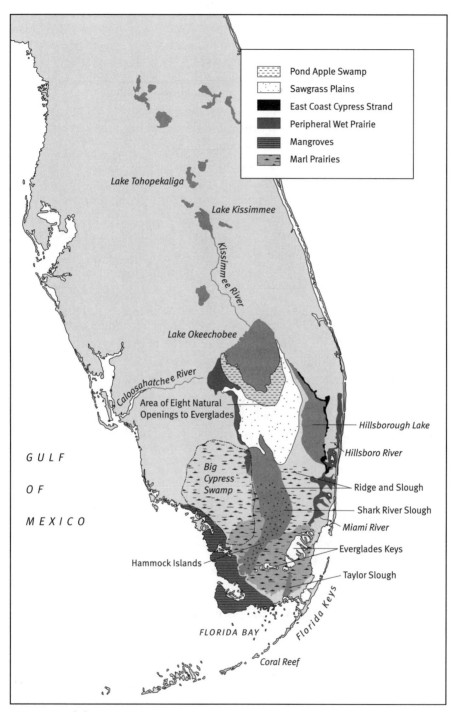

	Pond Apple Swamp
	Sawgrass Plains
	East Coast Cypress Strand
	Peripheral Wet Prairie
	Mangroves
	Marl Prairies

Lake Tohopekaliga

Lake Kissimmee

Kissimmee River

Lake Okeechobee

Caloosahatchee River

Area of Eight Natural
Openings to Everglades

GULF

OF

MEXICO

Big
Cypress
Swamp

Hammock Islands

Hillsborough Lake

Hillsboro River

Ridge and Slough

Shark River Slough

Miami River

Everglades Keys

Taylor Slough

FLORIDA BAY

Florida Keys

Coral Reef

Historic Everglades

《《《

A long, narrow thirty-thousand-acre cypress strand once bordered nearly the whole eastern periphery of sawgrass marshes from the east side of Lake Okeechobee to the New River in Fort Lauderdale, smallest of the original predrainage landscapes. Cypress separated the marshes from the pinelands to the east. Today agriculture and urban sprawl have replaced the cypress.

A four-hundred-acre remnant along the eastern edge of Loxahatchee National Wildlife Refuge is virtually all that's left of the cypress swamp. The patch was larger until the 1950s, when refuge managers logged most of the trees to create duck habitat for hunters. A quarter-mile-long boardwalk winds through what is left of the swamp.

I visited the boardwalk late one February. Water the color of weak coffee barely moved. Yellow-rumped warblers were everywhere and busy, flitting through bare branches. Without their coif of bright green needles, the trees looked dull and gaunt. Everything else, however, was an explosion of green. Ferns carpeted the ground; twelve-foot plumes of leather fern spouted from tussocks. Air plants vied for space on cypress limbs. According to biologists, these trees were about eighty-five years old. The original growth had been logged during the building of Florida's east coast railroad.

For cypress seeds to germinate, the ground must be dry. A swamp, however, does not have to be dry often for cypress to get started, once a century—or an even greater interval—is sufficient. Every five-hundred-year-old tree rooted in four feet of water during the wet season got started on dry ground, which is why swamps like the one at Loxahatchee often form even-aged stands.

The entire eastern cypress strand followed a southerly depression in the limestone, fingering east to west in Broward County along a series of ocean-bound streams. Driving north on Florida's Turnpike from Fort Lauderdale, I can catch another glimpse of the stand's tattered remains. Here and there patches of cypress gather along relic swales in sharp contrast to the suburban landscape. If I blinked, I'd miss them.

《《《

Sawgrass is the prominent wetland plant in two Everglades predrainage communities: the sawgrass plains and the ridge and slough. More than any other plant, sawgrass has contributed to the Everglades' reputation as one of the most inhospitable landscapes on Earth, a hellish, featureless wetland.

Sawgrass, *Cladium jamaicense,* is found in shallow-water wetlands of the coastal Piedmont from Virginia to Texas and into the West Indies. The edges of Zapata Swamp in Cuba and the Sian Ka'an Biosphere Reserve in the Yucatán supports hauntingly familiar sawgrass marshes. In the Everglades, sawgrass created and defined the landscape upon which it is rooted. The popularity of Marjory Stoneman Douglas's *The Everglades: River of Grass,* writes historian David McCally, "has indelibly imprinted the inaccurate metaphor 'river of grass' on the American psyche, with the result that a literary expression has been assigned a physical reality that never truly existed." McCally calls the Everglades "a river obscured by grass."

Sawgrass is stiff, thick, and razor-edged, a living band saw. Minute teeth run up the leaf margins and midrib. A blade of sawgrass can easily slice through skin. Twelve feet tall and dense in the northern glades, shorter in the south, sawgrass appeared in virtually every Everglades community from the transverse glades to puddles in the hammocks and pinelands.

Sawgrass rises from a horizontal rhizome, or underground stem. There is a crease in the middle of each semifolded leaf, which is about half an inch wide at the base, tapering to a thread at the tip. Like that of prairie grasses, much of sawgrass reproduction is vegetative; the rhizomes spread and send up shoots of genetically identical offspring. Deer eat the soft leaves emerging from the ground, which, according to Julia F. Morton, author of *Wild Plants for Survival in South Florida,* can also be eaten by humans. The "heart" of overlapping central leaves for the first three inches tastes like hearts of palm.

Flower stalks rise here and there above the marshes. For years residents of South Florida believed that when sawgrass flowered a hurricane was imminent. What makes for wide-scale periodic sawgrass blooms is still a mystery. Flowering may be induced by the stress of fire or prolonged flood. Or maybe the plant is hardwired for extensive flowering every so many years as a way to shuffle its genetic deck, hedging bets against an ever-changing landscape.

When Marjory Stoneman Douglas wrote, "The truth of the river is the grass," she described the plains of the northern Everglades, a vast monospecific stand of sawgrass that dominated 30 percent of the predrainage Everglades, a knife-sharp fortress that excluded all but the smallest creatures. Nowhere else did sawgrass grow to the horizon, its pale green blades rising out of the compressed remains of its own history. Before drainage, the plains covered approximately twelve hundred square miles, from the southern edge of the pond apple swamp south forty miles until it opened into sloughs and tree islands. Thick deposits of peat that once supported stands of sawgrass eight to ten feet tall now support sugarcane, rice, and assorted winter vegetables.

Christopher McVoy, a soil scientist with the South Florida Water Management District, revived "ridge and slough," an old name for the central

Everglades, to distinguish it from the sawgrass plains to the north. I examined photographs in McVoy's office taken in 1917 that showed the well-defined strands of sawgrass in open water channels of the central Everglades. Like pieces from a jigsaw puzzle, each ridge had wavy edges, worn smooth by flowing water, and long, thin, parallel strands of sawgrass, waterlogged and impenetrable. Between the strands were sloughs of roughly equal width, where scattered patches of water lilies bloomed, the scent of their white flowers perfuming the air for miles.

❨❨❨

According to William A. White, who wrote *The Geomorphology of the Florida Peninsula,* approximately four thousand years ago the northern half of the prehistoric Everglades was bordered by four lakes. These lakes, wrote White, appeared as the level of the sea rose, forcing the water table to rise along with it. Thick fibrous sawgrass peat dammed the lakes, which spread into the surrounding lowlands. Eventually sawgrass engulfed deeper-water plants, annexing all the lakes except Okeechobee, which was too big to be subjugated.

Hillsboro Lake, which includes Loxahatchee National Wildlife Refuge, evolved over several thousand years into a ridge and slough landscape between the sawgrass plains to the west and the Atlantic Coastal Ridge, a short drive from West Palm Beach. Some biologists consider the 220-square-mile refuge the most beautiful corner of the Everglades. A mosaic of sloughs, tree islands, and sawgrass marshes, the refuge supports thousands of migratory waterfowl and impressive colonies of wading birds.

Uncountable numbers of islands, mostly bay heads and dahoon holly heads that range in size from less than one acre to more than three hundred acres, eclipse visibility, challenging the most intrepid navigators to find their way across a shapeless maze of marsh and island. On a map, the islands curve south and southeast, shaped by flowing water, which at one time emptied into the Atlantic through breaks in the coastal ridge. This marks the northern portion of what Christopher McVoy calls "the east coast watershed," one of the Everglades' two major drainage basins, almost entirely separate from Shark Slough, the western drainage of the Everglades.

Now, however, Loxahatchee is cut off from the rest of the Everglades by an earthen corset, fifty-seven miles of peripheral levees, and has become a microcosm of the disturbing management issues that continue to dog Everglades restoration. The federal government leases the refuge from the state under a lease that is automatically renewed every fifteen years. Water levels in

Loxahatchee are managed through a cooperative agreement between the Army Corps of Engineers, the South Florida Water Management District, and the United States Fish and Wildlife Service.

In 1911, before the construction of the perimeter levee and its accompanying canal, water flowed through Hillsboro Lake. After the region was walled off, wax myrtle, a native shrub related to bayberry, began to invade the artificially drier sawgrass ridges. One labyrinth of myrtle, known to area froggers as Hell's Nest, became a navigational nightmare.

Because water no longer flows through Loxahatchee, the water management district sets levels to maintain water storage capacity during the hurricane season, for seasonal cropland irrigation, and to release into coastal canals to prevent saltwater intrusion into the Biscayne aquifer. Unfortunately, because its topography naturally slopes south, Loxahatchee is drier in the north and wetter in the south. To maintain a semblance of communities of healthy vegetation and to enhance feeding opportunities for ducks and wading birds, water levels must be constantly manipulated.

Today nearly three-fourths of the water that the South Florida Water Management District pumps into the refuge is runoff from fertilizer-laden sugar fields to the north and west. Consequently, a corner of the wildlife refuge suffers from a plague of nutrient-loving cattails, which grow at the expense of sawgrass. On a still day in April clouds of golden cattail pollen rain across the wetland.

Shark Slough cuts a great southeast to southwest arc between the sawgrass plains and the mangrove jungles inland from Whitewater Bay. Hydrologists believe that the slough dried every twenty to fifty years, with the water table not going far below the surface for very long. Although compartmentalized, most of Shark Slough still remains in the hands of either the state or the federal government. Returning the slough to free-flowing wholeness remains the only hope for Everglades restoration.

Taylor Slough, the other important drainage in the southern Everglades, is primarily a groundwater system. The slough is a breech in the coastal ridge, where softer limestone gave way to flowing water. When high water from Shark Slough spreads across the marl prairie, the two sloughs mingle, a phenomenon that was more common before drainage.

❨❨❨

The word *prairie* has multiple uses in the Everglades. It refers to three geographically separated and biologically distinct marshlands: predrainage marl prairies of the southern Everglades, peripheral wet prairies, and interior wet prairies. Recent research suggests that like the wax myrtle invasion of Loxahatchee, both the interior and peripheral wet prairies are postdrainage landscapes.

The peripheral wet prairies were originally sawgrass and a mix of sawgrass and slough that shifted toward prairie vegetation when the underlying peat oxidized. By the 1930s wet prairies had formed the western border of the Everglades from Fisheating Creek through the Caloosahatchee River Valley south to the northern rim of Big Cypress Swamp. On the eastern side, prairies traced the pineland border of the Everglades from south Miami to Fort Lauderdale. A narrow peninsula of sawgrass paralleled the east coast cypress swamp from Fort Lauderdale to Palm Beach and then shifted to wet prairies when its peat soils gave way to sand. Today the peripheral wet prairies, approximately 300,000 acres, are essentially gone, converted to shopping centers, pastureland, and citrus orchards.

Drainage has also promoted the spread of interior wet prairies, mostly at the expense of sloughs. Recently I drove west from Fort Lauderdale with Christopher McVoy. Across the northern end of Water Conservation Area 3A, instead of hosting disks of floating lily pads, sloughs were clogged with gray ribbons of spike rush that cut through fawn-colored sawgrass ridges, themselves invaded by cattail.

One of the vexing problems that confront the restoration effort is that no one knows from firsthand experience how the Everglades looked before drainage. "Somebody's opinion of what the Everglades ought to look like when it's finally restored depends on which version they first saw," says McVoy. Sportsmen who began hunting deer in the 1960s prefer the drier wax myrtle version of the Everglades. Naturalists who first visited the region in the 1930s remember a wetter Everglades, skies filled with ibis, prairies filled with gators. Does repairing the Everglades mean recreating the open, deeper-water lily sloughs of predrainage? Or the shallower sloughs of the 1940s? Or, perhaps, maintaining the hydrologic status quo by preserving an extensive set of interior wet prairies or the 1980s version, where water pools in the central Everglades and snail kites hover above a stagnant winter marsh, sparsely vegetated and as yellow as a lemon.

The sun shines full bore on the wet prairie floor, stimulating a woolly aggregation of algae called periphyton. Periphyton coats the round stems of spike rush and floats on the surface in large mats. During a drought brittle sheets of periphyton cake the ground. It is the base of the aquatic food chain and a protective carpet for small aquatic animals, particularly during the dry season, when aquatic insects and the eggs of marsh killifish overwinter.

A by-product of periphyton photosynthesis, large quantities of calcite collect on the marl floor of the Rocky Glades. To precipitate calcium, periphyton needs exposed limestone. No periphyton, no marl. And no marl, no marl prairies. Originally marl prairies, hammock-studded and seasonally dry, covered more than 620,000 acres along both sides of the lower end of Shark Slough. They extended northwest to Ochopee and northeast to the salt marshes and mangroves of Biscayne Bay. The Everglades Keys—the fractured southern end of the Atlantic Coastal Ridge—were actually islands of pinelands within the marl prairies. By the 1940s, after drainage had dried many of the transverse glades, the islands look more like a continuous ridge.

Approximately 150,000 acres of marl prairie have been lost to agriculture and development, mostly on the eastern side of Shark Slough. Many of the transverse glades that watered the marl prairies east of the ridge had dried out by 1940. Deprived of freshwater the marshes became more saline. Although different today, the prairies east of the ridge were part of the marl prairies and were once a functional part of the Everglades.

The Cape Sable seaside sparrow, *Ammodramus maritimus mirabilis,* is an ecologically and geographically distinct race of the common seaside sparrow, which nests in salt marshes from Massachusetts to the Gulf Coast of Texas. The tiny, greenish, spike-beaked sparrows are a metaphor for the complexities of the ecological restoration of the Everglades. Nesting in clumps of *Muhlenbergia* grass, eight or so inches off the ground, the sparrows live entirely on the floodplains of the southern Everglades, where the veneer of marl, as slick as grease, spreads over the surface limestone. Their marl prairie habitat is no more than two feet higher than the adjacent sawgrass.

Northeast Shark Slough, just south of the southernmost cross-state highway called the Tamiami Trail, was once one of the deeper parts of the Everglades. In the early 1970s the Army Engineers completed construction of the L-67 extension levee (in the lexicon of the Corps L is for levee, C for canal, S for structure; all are numbered), which runs south from the Trail. Here, within sight of tomato fields, Shark Slough curves southwest, and the last undeveloped marl prairies in south Miami–Dade County stand wild. Since the building of the L-31 levee, the northeast corner of the Shark Slough and the adjoining prairies began to dry. Then eight and a half square miles of agricultural fields and houses, built in violation of local zoning requirements while county officials looked the other way, sprang up in the midst of the ecologically sensitive marl prairie.

During recent flood years the water conservation areas north of the national park were brimful with water. Because of lawsuits from the Miccosukee, whose lands were flooded, and from the landowners in the developed area, who did not want their lands flooded, the water management district routed water to the western end of the slough each spring, inundating the Cape Sable seaside sparrows' nests. "The water rose sixty inches," recalls Stuart Pimm, a biologist at Columbia University, who has been monitoring the sparrow population since the summer of 1992. "And in that area, it's only twenty inches from the bottom to the top of the hill."

Although marl prairies flood from three to six months each year, fire also plays a crucial role in maintaining them. Without fire, grasses give way to shrubs. On the other hand, frequent fire destroys the sparrows' habitat. Lightning fires normally occur in the wet season, peaking in July, usually after the birds have finished fledging. "Unplanned human ignitions," the park service's term for arson or for careless fires, occur more often in the dry season, peaking in April and May while the sparrows are nesting. According to Pimm, "Grasses don't recover if fire frequencies approach every other year." Because of its proximity to people, northeast Shark Slough has become a tinderbox, and the sparrows that once nested along its fringe are virtually gone.

Four colonies of Cape Sable seaside sparrows remain, but only one colony—wholly within the national park—is stable. This worries Pimm, who places the sparrow population at approximately four thousand birds, down from sixty-five hundred in 1992. To restore the marl prairies, water must flow through northeast Shark Slough. Unfortunately, levees cannot be ruptured and canals plugged until something is done about the development.

Pimm wants to be there with his bottle of champagne when the Corps finally lets water back into northeast Shark Slough. "It'll be a small reward for the gallons of blood I've given to mosquitoes."

Pristine marl prairie is found south of Ingraham Highway, in Everglades National Park. Built in the 1920s, the highway connected Homestead to Flamingo for the first time, and according to Glen Simmons—whose autobiography, *Gladesmen,* is a memoir of life on the frontier Everglades—for the last five miles, the marl was so soft that if a car made it all the way "it wasn't worth it to the people pushing it." A nine-mile segment now crosses the marl prairie between East Bay Pond and Taylor Slough. The road is deeply rutted and off-limits to unauthorized vehicles.

From the window of the park service research van, a lush marl prairie, less disturbed and more densely vegetated than the Rocky Glades, stretches south. Although prairies usually burn every three or four years, this prairie hasn't burned since 1989, and the clumps of bunchgrasses and sedges are as thick as the hair on an otter's back, a situation ripe for a major fire. Scientists are uneasy, because this corner of marl prairie harbors the largest colony of Cape Sable seaside sparrow in the world, more than two thousand birds. With all the unburned fuel, if a fire started during the nesting season, the sparrow would be devastated. Today the vegetation is dry, and the marl cracks in the heat like oven-baked clay. "It's only a matter of time before the prairie goes up in flames," says David Okines, an itinerant British bird-bander, who runs the field portion of Columbia University biologist Stuart Pimm's sparrow project.

Okines is a zealous bander and has become indispensable to the sparrow program, freeing Pimm to tackle the contentious political issues of restoration. Okines is beginning his third year on the project. In his first year of fieldwork he banded more sparrows than Pimm had in the previous five years. When he was a child, a jar of peanut butter led Okines to birds. "The jar had a free booklet about garden birds. I was hooked," he says. When Okines graduated from high school, he skipped college to band birds full-time. He has little interest in much else; consequently his lackluster social skills often irritate coworkers, with whom he shares living quarters. But Okines, who can expertly read the contours of the prairie, knows how to catch birds.

I follow Okines while six other technicians mill outside the van, tugging at their canvas, snake-proof leggings. Much of the prairie is tufts of "muhly" grass and black-topped sedge, but strands of sawgrass grow in ten- to twenty-foot-long swales, streaking the land. Okines tells me that sparrows love the swales, where a nearby male perches on a six-foot flowering stalk of sawgrass, bill skyward, and sings his tiny heart out. His song is like a whispered red-winged blackbird's, except the last note rises instead of falls. In the background, the voices of blackbirds, meadowlarks, and yellow throats blend. A sedge wren flits past, followed by a sparrow flying low over the marl prairie, buzzing like an insect.

To lure a male close to a mist net, Okines turns on a tape recording of a singing sparrow. When the bird settles in a tuft of muhly and refuses to fly closer, we flush it into the net. Then Okines gently weighs, measures, and bands the bird, whose olive wings, darkly streaked belly, white throat, and yellow wing linings and lores mimic the light and shadows of the marl prairie.

Cape Sable seaside sparrows breed on both sides of the southern Everglades, wherever muhly grass grows out of the marl. The birds feed in the open spaces between the tussocks, dining on assorted invertebrates—spiders, grasshoppers, beetles, dragonflies. Classified as critically endangered, this sparrow has become a victim of an altered landscape: too wet on the western marl prairies and too dry on the eastern. At the same time, the healthiest population, the one Okines monitors, is a spark away from being roasted into extinction.

Behind Okines the marl prairie extends to the horizon, or until a wall of hammock trees blocks the view. Enriched by accumulating stem and leaf litter, the grasses appear to merge into a dense, impenetrable stand, but a maze of paths winds around the bunchgrasses, some clogged with toppled vegetation. Not far from the mist net a Florida water snake, waiting for rain, lies across an elevated mat of grass. Beyond the water snake, a small cottonmouth coils on another mat, two feet above the brittle earth. When water levels in the marl prairies are abnormally or unnaturally high, both snakes prey on nestling sparrows.

(((

It is early June. A southeast wind sends rain slantwise. Dragonflies and mosquitoes drop out of sight in the grass; a Cape Sable seaside sparrow hunkers in her nest, inches above the spongy ground, doggedly shielding her three chicks from the rain. This is the sparrow's second clutch of the breeding season. Her first hatched four weeks ago, when the sky had been blue and cloudless for weeks on end. Only one of those chicks survives somewhere in the vast expanse of marl prairie west of Shark Slough. Two were swallowed by a snake; a third was caught by a migrating merlin. The sparrow hasn't seen her surviving chick in two weeks. If she saw it again not a feather would ruffle in recognition.

When the rainy season starts, the Cape Sable seaside sparrow's nesting season winds down. Fewer and fewer juvenile birds fledge, until the last nest is lost to rising water. As a massive thunderhead builds above south-central Florida, northeast of the mother sparrow, the South Florida Water Management District, in an effort to ease severe flooding in the conservation areas, has opened four flood gates that hold water north of the Tamiami Trail. Although the sparrow is unaware, soon her corner of the marl prairies will be swiftly and unseasonably inundated.

The Everglades, its area reduced, its hydrologic and ecological functions compromised, is so far out of sync with the rhythms of the seasons and the lay of the land that even the sparrow cannot read its home ground. Too wet. Too dry. Spreading prairies. Shrinking sloughs. An invasion of sawgrass or wax myrtle.

How do you restore a rain-driven watershed when 100 percent of the rain collects on 50 percent of the original landscape? In less than a century we have eviscerated the Florida Everglades. Today, on the verge of the largest ecological restoration ever undertaken, our obsession with gathering more and more information, although fascinating and provocative, in many cases undermines the task of getting the process under way. Where we have sufficient information to make some tough choices, let us take restoration out of the forum and into the field.

The morning after the thunderstorm, three young sparrows leave their nest, then scurry mouselike through the muhly grass. When a parent lands on a tussock, its mouth crammed with a dragonfly or a fat spider, the closest chick begs incessantly, the universal cry of the hungry. Its crop filled, the chick cowers in grass shade, sharp-eyed and defenseless.

To understand the Everglades one must
understand the rock.

MARJORY STONEMAN DOUGLAS, 1947

3 A Geologic Primer

The southeastern floodplain of the Everglades is called the Rocky Glades, a region pitted by thousands of bedrock depressions and deep solution holes that plumb groundwater. It is a karst landscape, water-eroded limestone, thousands of pockmarked pinnacles, holes, and subterranean channels. The exposed limestone evokes an image of fossil Swiss cheese, and is so hard on an airboat—a shallow, rectangular aluminum vehicle that resembles an oversized paint pan—that models built for use south of the Tamiami Trail, called "rock boats," have heavier framing and a sheet of stainless-steel-reinforced bottoms. Hundreds of tropical hardwood hammocks grow on the largest pinnacles; sculpted by flowing water—wide upstream, narrow downstream—the orientation of these tree islands reveals the direction of water flow. Like much of the bedrock geology of the southern Everglades, the Rocky Glades is a relatively recent product of an Ice Age sea level that rose and fell like a yo-yo over the past one hundred thousand years. During episodes of global flooding, a warm lime-saturated lagoon and its colonial invertebrates built the rock grain by grain; eventually a wetland carpeted the porous limestone, and groundwater rose to the surface and flowed.

《《《

The odd-shaped pinnacles of the Rocky Glades and all the rest of Florida are the emergent portion of a sedimentary platform called the Florida Plateau, the southernmost extension of the continental shelf. The plateau stretches from the Florida panhandle to the Keys, and west 150 miles into the Gulf of Mexico, where it drops off into the abyss, more than two miles below the surface. The eastern edge of the Florida Plateau sticks close to shore and intersects the coast at Palm Beach.

When the glaciers buried much of the Northern Hemisphere, the ocean receded more than three hundred feet below its current level, exposing the entire plateau, doubling the size of prehistoric Florida. Then, during cycles of interglacial warmth, the ocean rose twenty-five to thirty feet higher than its current level, inundating most of the state. At least four times during the past two million years, the peninsula alternately dried and flooded; sometimes its western boundary reached more than a hundred miles into the Gulf; other times it shrunk back to the sand ridges north of Lake Okeechobee.

Whenever the Gulf of Mexico withdrew, Florida became a resort for Ice Age mammals, which sought refuge from the bone-chilling cold that engulfed much of the continent. Eventually the innumerable limestone sinkholes became mausoleums for wayfaring vertebrates. The fossil bones of alligator, capybara, catfish, garfish, and bowfin suggest that an Ice Age lake or river once existed in the midst of a wet grassland. The fossils of mammoth, mastodon, an extinct horse, a bison, and a camel, recovered from the edge of the Everglades, suggest that at times Florida was drier than today.

Whenever the level of the sea fell during the Ice Age, Florida was much closer to the Bahamas and Cuba and to the Yucatán peninsula, whose shallow, offshore beds also became dry land. Then, a broad zone of semiarid savanna connected Florida across the Gulf Coast to the Yucatán. During this cooler, drier time, plants and animals moved into Florida from Central America. Jaguar, jaguarundi, margay, spectacled bear, vampire bat, pronghorn, hog-nosed skunk, and antelope jackrabbit (to name a few) died out in Florida when conditions changed yet again. Other, more successful, western immigrants remain today, living links to the geologic past: cacti, yucca, coral bean, pocket gopher, burrowing owl, caracara, Florida scrub jay, gopher tortoise; several types of lizards and snakes, including the gorgeous coral snake and the rim-rock crowned snake—a secretive serpent that dwells where limestone pinnacles break the surface. A map drawn of prehistoric Florida at that time would have only a vague resemblance to the peninsula's lithe, modern look. Back then Florida was much wider, but not appreciably longer, a bloated caricature of its shape today.

《《《

The Everglades, hemmed by shallow ridges, evolved in a trough-shaped depression in the bedrock limestone. The trough fostered the wide, shallow flow of water, called sheet flow, a singular feature of the Everglades. Historically, the rims of the trough kept most of the water from leaking out. For much of its western flank, the Everglades is bordered by the level, slightly higher Big Cypress Swamp, which is still wild country. The Immokalee Ridge—now a mosaic of pineland, pastureland, vegetable farms, and citrus groves—forms the northwest rim. Along its eastern perimeter, the Everglades is bounded by the gentle slope of the Atlantic Coastal Ridge, a narrow wrinkle in the landscape that borders the ocean and runs from Georgia to Everglades National Park, southwest of Homestead.

South Florida's bedrock is mostly limestone, five different formations, none older than six million years. The Rocky Glades is the western perimeter of the coastal ridge, which, south of Miami, is nowhere higher than twenty feet. The ridge tapers south of Coconut Grove, turns west at Homestead, then breaks apart into the Everglades Keys, islands of pine surrounded by marsh. Eventually the ridge disappears underneath the marshland near Mahogany Hammock. From any vantage point, the Rocky Glades appears level. There is a consensus among scientists that the geologic processes that formed the southern Everglades are parallel to those taking place today on the Grand Bahama Bank.

The last interglacial warming period began about 128,000 years ago. South Florida was covered by a warm, tropical lagoon, in which the coastal ridge and much of the limestone bedrock of the southern Everglades were being formed. As the edge of the Gulf Stream flowed over South Florida, the incoming water heated and evaporated. The warm water was saturated with dissolved calcium carbonate, the building block of limestone. Calcium began to coat any speck suspended in the water. Eventually tiny calcareous grains of sand, called ooids, rained on the bottom, where the gentle wave action of the lagoon piled them up.

On the floor of the ancient lagoon, west of the ooid ridge, colonies of bryozoans, or moss animals, grew on sea grasses. Each bryozoan secreted a calcium shell, often multilayered. As colonies died, skeletons buried the floor of the lagoon. I've seen living bryozoans, *Schizoporella floridana*, the same species that made the fossil floor of the southern Everglades, encrusting sea grasses in Florida Bay. Because bryozoans always take the shape of their host, tubes of calcified shell laminated the grass, layer after layer until the blades disappeared under a patina of calcium.

Beginning about sixty-seven thousand years ago, Earth's temperatures fell; advancing glaciers began to convert water to ice. Worldwide, sea level dropped. South Florida's warm lagoon dried out, exposing first the ooid mound and then the lagoon floor. Rain trickled between the lime grains, melting and redepositing calcium carbonate, cementing the ooids and bryozoan fossils, eventually forming solid rock.

Today bryozoan limestone covers approximately two thousand square miles of the southern Everglades, extending as far north as Fort Lauderdale and as far south as the Gulf of Mexico. Oolitic limestone underlies the southeastern rim of the Everglades. The two rocks, soluble and permeable, are collectively called Miami limestone, bedrock of the southern Everglades.

Approximately eighteen thousand years ago, the world again began to thaw. Glacial meltwater poured down the Mississippi River, and the ocean again slowly rose over the interior of South Florida. Nine thousand years ago, as the last of Florida's giant tortoises, dire wolves, and ground sloths died (long after they had perished elsewhere in North America), South Florida lay submerged beneath warm tropical waters.

About five thousand years ago, when the ocean's rise dropped to approximately nine inches per year, the mangrove coast of South Florida and the recently deposited sand barriers like Cape Sable started to stabilize. The Everglades was born when the saltwater lagoon in the interior trough began to freshen. As the surrounding ocean water warmed, rain fell more frequently over the interior of South Florida. Rainwater followed the natural contours of the bedrock, eating away the softer limestone, which created flow-ways like Shark Slough.

Eventually, as the climate became subtropical, the roots and rhizomes of marsh plants built carpets of peat, dark, unoxygenated, decay resistant. Peat deposits become thinner as you move south from the impenetrable sawgrass plains of the northern Everglades. Buried under this burden of organic matter, the limestone was shielded from both flowing, slightly acid, water and from the corrosive effects of repeated drying and flooding that today erode the exposed bedrock of Rocky Glades. Most of the limestone's uneven water-pitted surface disappeared beneath a smooth covering of peat. Where ancient tides wore channels across the ooid mound, bare-bottom rivers and shallow weedy transverse glades leaked water to the sea: Hillsboro River, the twin forks of the New River, Snapper Creek, Arch Creek, Little River, and the Miami River, whose rapids were dynamited in 1909 and whose sensuous curves slicing through downtown Miami can still be seen from the air.

Collectively the transverse glades and the rivers of the coastal ridge, from the Miami River north, formed a significant natural drainage within the historic Everglades, says Christopher McVoy. "Tree islands don't lie," he once told me, pointing to a landscape map of the predrainage Everglades. He gestured toward two distinct groups of islands, which looked like fish schooled against the current. Like the hammocks in the Rocky Glades, each island bore the imprint of the current. One group curved toward the Atlantic Coastal Ridge in what are now Palm Beach, Broward, and northern Miami–Dade Counties. Another echoed the drainage of Shark Slough, turning toward the southwest. "The river of grass is a wonderful metaphor," McVoy told me, "but when it comes down to it, it's not accurate. There were two rivers of grass."

((((

Buried among the Florida Plateau's sedimentary layers lies an ancient bubble of freshwater, the Floridan Aquifer, the largest in the world. Like Florida, the aquifer is bounded on three sides by saltwater. Some hydrologists say the rocks hold more water than the five Great Lakes combined—approximately forty-five hundred cubic miles of potable water. The Floridan Aquifer lies more than a thousand feet below the Everglades, sealed away from the surface by a layer cake of rock. Not far below the Rocky Glades, however, lies a waterlogged honeycomb, a great rock sponge called the Biscayne Aquifer.

The Biscayne Aquifer, which today waters the farmlands east of Everglades National Park and provides drinking water for Miami and Fort Lauderdale, is recharged by rain and lies so close to the surface that for much of the year it flows through the Everglades. Because the Miami limestone lacks a mantle of peat, rainstorms etch pockets and groves and dissolve solution holes and subterranean channels into it. The acids from decaying leaves widen and deepen the holes.

When the first thunderstorms of summer drench the Rocky Glades, rain quickly disappears into the ground. Water travels downward in the porous limestone until it reaches the water table, the zone of saturation. As the rainy season progresses, the water table rises to the surface of the Rocky

Glades. "From a hydrologic perspective," says Tom Van Lent, a hydrologist at Everglades National Park, "there is very little difference between groundwater levels and surface water levels in the southern Everglades. They're a connected system, one and the same."

Once rainwater has trickled into the stone pores, it may course unseen toward the sea. National Park Service biologist Sue Perry believes that before drainage there may have been a true underwater subterranean fauna beneath the Rocky Glades, which included blind crayfish. One of her researchers may have discovered a new family of copepods.

So much freshwater once gushed from springs in both Florida Bay and Biscayne Bay that the native people and early explorers regularly filled their gourds and pots offshore. In 1838, during the Second Seminole War, Jacob Rhett Motte described a spring in Biscayne Bay: "We were fortunate in hitting upon this spot for there we found a remarkable spring of fresh water, of the coolest and most delicious flavour I ever drank." Nearly fifty years later, Ralph Middleton Munroe photographed a boatman dipping freshwater from the same spring.

Because of their slightly higher elevation, the marshes of the Rocky Glades are the last to flood and the first to dry. During the rainy season, the holes and depressions pool first. Eventually the pools overflow to become one slowly moving sheet of water that creeps westward toward the Everglades, which itself has risen and spread across its floodplains. Before the Army Corps of Engineers disrupted the natural drainage patterns in South Florida, when the rainy season ended, alligators dug muck out of the larger willow-lined cavities and then lounged in water holes of their own design.

Drainage ruined many of these well-honed ecological functions. In 1881 the first Everglades reclamation effort was launched by Hamilton Disston, a Philadelphia millionaire. Disston, who believed that South Florida could become an agricultural utopia, bought four million acres from the state of Florida. Within ten years he had drained fifty thousand acres. By the time the financial depression of 1893 ruined him, Disston had dredged a canal between Lake Okeechobee and the Caloosahatchee River, connected the chain of lakes that feed the Kissimmee River, opened the Kissimmee for navigation, and cut an eleven-mile-long canal from Lake Okeechobee into the northern Everglades. "In most cases," wrote historian Mark Derr, in *Some Kind of Paradise,* "the canals his company dug were little better than gashes in the limestone that collected stagnant water where mosquitoes and hyacinths flourish." In 1896, unable to regain financial footing, Disston committed suicide. Although his dream of lowering the surface water level throughout the Okeechobee-Kissimmee system failed, he showed that it could be done. By 1917 four canals cut across the Everglades from Lake Okeechobee to the Atlantic Ocean, through coastal ridge rivers that had been dynamited, dredged, and deepened. These canals would later become the backbone of the Central and Southern Florida Flood Control Project. Named for the rivers they replaced—the Miami, the North New, the Hillsboro, the West Palm Beach—the canals lowered the water table enough so that by the first decades of the twentieth century the offshore springs ran dry.

The Rocky Glades is now the last undeveloped short-hydroperiod marshland between the ridge and Everglades. It was part of an apron of seasonal marshes that ran north to Palm Beach. The rest of the marshes have been transformed into suburbs, shopping centers, and rock quarries, where limestone is mined and crushed for cement. Before a devastating fire in 1934 most of the limestone pinnacles in the Rocky Glades supported a stately crown of slash pine. Each tree grew out of a shallow, muck-filled solution hole. Although the pines are gone, the pinnacles still bear witness to the geologic forces that shaped the southern Everglades.

《《《

Driving a pickup off-road across the Rocky Glades, northwest of Homestead, I fishtail on greasy marl. Gray-white pinnacles of limestone rise out of the ground like the ridges on an alligator's back. There is little water here, no peat, and too much sun; the sun cooks the algae and bacteria into mats of periphyton that sticks to everything: blades of sawgrass, willow bark, limestone, bare ground. Periphyton secretes the limy marl, the shoe-sucking, tire-sliding marl, the slippery earth through which the limestone pokes.

It is mid-January, blue from one end of the horizon to the other. The Rocky Glades are drying out. Today I am the guest of Mark Cunningham, a second-year veterinary student at the University of Florida and a member of the Florida Panther Recovery Team. Cunningham has come to the Rocky Glades to check a report of a panther prowling in the shadow of rural Miami–Dade County. I'm here to see the limestone bedrock.

Cunningham, who is built like a fullback, sits on the hood of the moving truck, bouncing and sliding, scanning for tracks. Before drainage the Rocky Glades was vegetated by open clumps of sawgrass and patches of wax myrtle and willow, prime habitat for crayfish, but marginal for panther. The C-111 canal system completed in 1983 has drained so much water away from the Rocky Glades that Australian pines—which are not pines at all, but wispy-branched alien eucalyptus—have invaded the marsh.

Shrinking puddles fill with desperate aquatic activity. I stop at one puddle, where dozens of tiny fish burrow into the marl. I scoop one out, a bluefin killifish, its blue and yellow flanks in vivid contrast to the gray mud that oozes between my fingers. These inch-long fish are at home in the Rocky Glades, where their drought-resistant eggs wait like desert seeds for rain to come. Biologist Sue Perry once told me that in May at the start of the rainy season she would see small fish streaming across the marl prairies, many plump and about to give birth. Where and how they escaped the dry season, which often cracks the marl, remains a mystery.

Close to a small hammock, where humic acid from decaying vegetation gnaws at the outcropped bedrock, puddles have coalesced into a six-inch-deep moat that nearly circles the island. Fish and frogs panic at my approach, roiling the surface. I cross the moat and step up through a screen of cocoplums and red bays that circle the hammock. Just inside the south shore is a small ankle-breaking solution hole, half hidden in the weft of vegetation. I peer in. The hole is about two feet across and ringed by sparse tufts of wire grass, shaded by pigeon plum and velvet leaf. Lacy maidenhair ferns cling to the wall. To get a sense of the depth of the solution hole, I drop in a pebble. It makes a soft plopping sound. Larger, drier solution holes may sometimes shelter surprisingly large creatures. Several years ago, the panther recovery team tracked a male cat across several of the Everglades keys into a solution hole. Cunningham told me he heard the cat shifting position, footpads abrading soft, crumbling limestone.

Having tracked a peripatetic alligator over the marl, I take a small souvenir piece of limestone, put it my pocket, and return to the pickup, which has now settled to the base of its hubcaps. Using the jack and chunks of limestone for traction, we urge the truck out and then scale the slick flank of the coastal ridge, a wake of marl spraying from the back tires.

《《《

Several days later, I am back home in Vermont. To see how easily Miami limestone erodes, I perform a simple experiment. I break four roughly thumbnail-sized pieces off the limestone. I place one in a cup of orange juice, another in Coca-Cola, a third in balsamic vinegar, and the fourth in water. The vinegar and the Coke go wild bubbling, as acid dissolves calcium carbonate, weakening the limestone. The orange juice is quiescent.

The following morning, a thin trail of lime streaks the orange juice. The juice-soaked rock flakes more easily in my fingers than does a piece that sat in water all night. Although the Coca-Cola has lost its fizz, the limestone in that cup is easy to flake. Hands down, balsamic vinegar is the most corrosive. Some more than a millimeter deep, Lilliputian cavities dimple the rock, solution holes for copepods and sundry other microscopic creatures. Under a magnifying glass the rock looks like a piece of the moon, all pits and ridges. A week later, the vinegar has virtually dissolved the rock. Like the ancient ooids themselves, limy sand swirls on the bottom of the cup, clouding the water as the little piece of Miami limestone becomes undone.

The whole system was like a set of scales on which
the sun and the rains, the winds, the hurricanes,
and the dewfall, were balanced so that the life of
the vast grass and all its forms . . . kept secure.

MARJORY STONEMAN DOUGLAS, 1947

4 Tropical Seasons

When I was twelve years old my parents bought me the *Golden Guide to
Everglades National Park and the Nearby Florida Keys,* which I cherished for its
colorful illustrations and its numerous thumbnail descriptions of indigenous
plants and animals. On the very first page of text, the guide tells us that South
Florida's climate sets it apart from everywhere else in the continental United
States, that it has two seasons, wet and dry, and that its daily weather patterns are governed more by tropical factors than by temperate ones. The book
reports that the wet season lasts from May to November; the dry season, from
December through April. This apparently symmetrical arrangement appears
as another triumph for the balance of nature, a crisp relationship, a precise fit,

as though the world were a crossword puzzle. This youthful notion of short-term meteorological harmony distorts the truth, for the forces that drive South Florida's weather are capricious and sometimes volatile.

Because Miami is more than four hundred miles farther south than San Diego, California, and because no point in Florida is more than seventy-five miles from warm ocean waters, in a climatic sense (and in a biological one, too) the southern third of the peninsula is more closely aligned with the Caribbean than with continental North America. Many of the world's deserts—the Namib, parts of the Sahara, the Sonora, to mention a few—occupy the same latitude as Florida, just above or below the Tropics; however, these regions either are flanked by cold ocean water or sit in the rain shadow of mountains, which renders them arid, barren land.

South Florida's warm oceanic waters spawn almost daily summer thunderstorms and mild winter temperatures, which favor the growth of lush, cold-sensitive greenery. In fact, 69 percent of the native vascular plants in South Florida are of tropical origin. Many species of animals—snail kite, short-tailed hawk, and manatee, for instance—reach their northern limit of distribution in Florida; others, such as the American crocodile, tree snail, and white-crowned pigeon, range no farther north than extreme South Florida.

There are also a number of periodic, and often disruptive, climatic influents that make the Everglades temperamental, a kaleidoscopic landscape that continually redefines itself. Cyclonic storms born off the west coast of Africa and off the Gulf Coast of Mexico tear into South Florida, rearranging forests and estuaries while scattering seeds and propagules. Once a decade or so, an Arctic cold front redefines the northern limits of tropical growth, pruning sensitive plants to the ground; the shifting of the cold ocean currents off the coast of Peru brings cycles of flood and earth-cracking drought.

To begin to comprehend the Everglades you must focus on its weather, which shapes everything that lives there, including man. The glades and its weather are entwined and inseparable. In the Golden Guide description, South Florida's climate has a classic bilateral symmetry. As the dry season progresses, fish and turtles and frogs coalesce in shrinking pools in the company of the alligators, otters, and legions of wading birds that eat them. Some of the pools are made by the alligators themselves. Called gator holes, these reptilian digs are critical dry-season habitat for aquatic life, particularly on the marl prairies, where water levels are lower than in the sloughs. During the dry season, in the coastal forests of Florida Bay, the shallow mangrove-lined creeks degenerate into ribbons of mud as viscous as pudding.

In the so-called normal years, when the wet season returns in May or June, aquatic animals disperse into expanding habitats. The voices of spawning frogs fill the night. The voices of amorous male gators mimic thunder. When wetlands become saturated, rainwater flows. Water evaporates from the landscape, the sky swells, then rain falls again, a six-month spell of steam-bath humidity, punctuated in late summer by hurricanes. To dramatize the importance of evaporation in the production of rain, the late ecologist Art Marshall referred to South Florida as "the rain machine" and warned that drainage and development threaten the balance of the seasons. By November the sky dries out, and the marsh cures under the full press of a blistering sun.

But the symmetry of the seasons happens only about half the time. Drought, a prolonged dry season, may last for a year or more, parching the Everglades, setting the stage for raging fires. Like an exaggerated dry season, drought alters the menu for aquatic and terrestrial predators by forcing animals like otters into confined spaces, making them vulnerable. In the late 1960s, during a severe drought in Everglades National Park, alligators were seen eating otters cooped in a tiny pool. During a drought in the late 1980s, I watched a bobcat stalk wading birds along the edge of a bird-crammed pool.

《《《

The symmetry of the seasons can also be disrupted by a prolonged wet season. Autumn 1994 was unusually wet. A succession of thunderstorms, broad fronts, drizzles, showers, and cloudbursts watered South Florida well into the new year, confounding tourists, who clung to Florida's well-known winter image of clear skies and low humidity. On November 10 Hurricane Gordon dumped eight inches of rain into already-flooded wetlands. Because water levels in the Everglades had reached the highest point since record-keeping began in 1952, the national park closed Shark Valley, a main tourist attraction along its northern border, from November until late February, leaving egrets to spear fish on the parking lot, and moccasins and otters to swim across the tram road.

In Fakahatchee Strand, on the west side of the Big Cypress Swamp, I slogged through waist-deep water to reach East Lake, and thigh-deep water in Four Stakes Prairie, where the previous year it had been dry enough to pitch a tent. Everywhere terrestrial wildlife was forced to bunch together on higher and higher ground. For the moment, biological rhythms had been inverted; instead of fish and grass shrimp packed into water-filled depressions, rabbits and opossums convened on hammocks. Water levels were so high in the central Everglades that indigo snakes developed blisters and deer developed hoof rot.

Bobcats drowned; so did an otter. In an effort to stay dry, snakes appeared on paths, stumps, levees, and boardwalks. Without seeking them out, I encountered eight species of snake in a few days.

As the water kept rising, overflowing low hammocks and bay heads, mammals gathered on levees and on the shoulders of bermed roads. One night, driving west on the Tamiami Trail, I counted fifty-seven road-killed raccoons between Fortymile Bend and State Road 29, a distance of less than thirty miles. Deer forded westward, island to island across the Everglades, in search of high ground. A park service pilot flying low over Shark Slough told me she had watched an alligator drag under a hapless doe. By early January, alligators guarding bloated deer carcasses were a common sight in the central Everglades, much to the consternation of sportsmen.

For snail kites the prolonged wet season was a boon. Apple snails, the birds' principal food, remained active in marshes that had dried the year before. Kites responded by forming new communal roost sites and breeding colonies. One roost I visited in late December held at least 402 snail kites. By early February two new breeding colonies had formed in the southern Everglades in areas that were often dry during most winters. Both fledged young.

Although kites benefited from the rising, spreading water, wading birds took a double hit. First, fish became harder to catch. Second, the prolonged high water favored the growth of larger fish, as the population dynamics of the fish community slowly shifted from innumerable little fish to bigger predatory fish. Fattening on forage fish, large-mouth bass directly competed with wading birds. In marshes adjacent to Fort Lauderdale, fishermen were landing what seemed to be an endless supply of seven-pound, twenty-inch-long bass. For a moment the Everglades had become a bass bonanza.

My late-February morning begins in the dark in a tent behind the park's Key Largo Ranger Station, a short walk from Sunset Cove on the west side of Key Largo. It is not yet seven, and the temperature is a chilly fifty-three degrees. There are small-craft warnings from Lake Worth to the Dry Tortugas, four- to six-foot swells, and a steady twenty-mile-per-hour wind out of the northeast, gusts to thirty. Fortunately, there is no rain in the forecast.

Sunlight fingers through the branches of gumbo-limbo and seven-year apple, which has leaves like rhododendron and green fruit that looks more like small green eggs than apples. Behind me the park's research and dormitory trailers glow in the morning light. An orange and slate-blue kestrel sits flicking his tail on a guy wire of a shortwave antenna. A dozen cars and trucks are parked on the lawn—once a dense tropical hammock, whose peripheral trees separate the enclave of scientists and rangers from U.S. Route 1.

Frank Mazzotti, a University of Florida biologist, is brewing coffee. I crawl out of my tent and into a jet stream. My hair, now a weathervane, extends southwest toward the Yucatán. Seeing me, the kestrel rises from his perch, tucks in his wings, catches the wind, and disappears over the hammock, all in a nanosecond. Frank waves me over.

To see the effects of high water in the mangroves, I will accompany Frank into the heart of crocodile country, the wild, shallow, blue lagoons in the northeastern corner of Florida Bay, territory off limits to the public. This is his eighteenth year studying American crocodiles, this now waxing (although still-endangered) population of reptiles whose fortunes he monitors. I had spent ten days with him the previous August searching for crocodile nests, catching and marking hatchlings. Today I'll see record-high water and heron roosts, but I might not see crocodiles, for they are dispersed across miles of flooded swamps, tidal creeks, brackish ponds, lagoons, bays, and coves. We hold tight waiting for the wind to die down.

By midafternoon, although it is still a chilling sixty-four degrees, the winds have lessened enough so that we can travel across open water in Frank's Boston Whaler. Outside Sunset Cove, red-breasted mergansers peel off the bay. Brown pelicans, like pot-bellied airplanes, glide past. Seventeen white pelicans assemble on a marl spit, ambassadors from another world, lording it over a nearby flotilla of gulls and cormorants.

Inside Joe Bay the water level is a foot lower than it was in August. Frank tells me that the top eight inches of water in the bay was blown out to sea last night. As if to emphasize the point, he hits an oyster bar. "I'm scouting, now," he tells me, "so we don't hit bars at night, full throttle." He hits another. The sun's diaphanous rays glisten on recently exposed mangrove roots that at a distance look like ivory-colored snakes. Several weeks ago, when I traveled across the interior Everglades, the evidence of high water was obvious—sloughs five feet deep—but here in Joe Bay, evidence of the flood seems to be missing.

As the sun steals away, the wind gains prominence. Frank reads the salinity in Joe Bay, only three parts per thousand, down from twenty in August (seawater is thirty-six parts per thousand). A pulse of freshwater came through Taylor Slough, pushing the briny water of Joe Bay far out into Florida Bay. Although not as deep as in the summer, the water in Joe Bay is almost fresh. Garfish and alligators have moved from the sawgrass marshes of the Everglades into Davis

Creek, a wispy mangrove-choked tributary that connects Joe Bay to Florida Bay. It is a migration more often associated with September, the height of the wet season, than with February. As the sun disappears behind a curtain of mangroves, the sky becomes flamboyant.

On an island whose guano-stained leaves suggest bird roosts, great egrets, white ibises, and tricolored herons pitch into the mangroves, their business for the day apparently done. Frank says that although the wading birds must travel farther afield to find food, during drought or flood their numbers at this roost have remained consistent. As the birds quiet down, darkness descends into crocodile time.

(((

Historically, catastrophic events—flood, drought, wildfire, hurricane, and freeze—have had a resetting effect on the Everglades, releasing nutrients bound up in the muck, for example, or limiting the distribution of tropical plants, or favoring various suites of animals by making new habitat available to them. The floodwaters of 1994 were the result of El Niño—a shift in ocean temperatures and atmospheric conditions in the tropical Pacific that affects global weather patterns. El Niño usually occurs every three to seven years and may last up to fifteen months. It may, however, appear in two successive years or may vanish for twelve or more years. During El Niño conditions the jet stream is straightened and strengthened, sending more storms to Florida. When water levels in the Everglades rise, wildfires decrease, snail kites spread into new territory, wood storks skip breeding. In Florida a drought cycle called La Niña, caused by the realignment of the Pacific Ocean currents, often follows, confining fish and bringing a banner year for wading birds.

Because half the Everglades has been converted to farmland and housing, rain drains into a smaller area. This may exacerbate an already high water level. On October 17, 1999, for instance, Hurricane Irene dumped nearly fifteen inches of rain on parts of South Florida. The *Miami Herald* reported that more than seventy-five million dollars' worth of crops were destroyed in southern Miami–Dade County. Front yards became lakes; streets became rivers. Between Fort Pierce and Homestead, the South Florida Water Management District released billions of gallons to the Atlantic, killing fishes and sponges and causing a giant plume of dirty water, described as looking like wet cement, to spread across eastern Florida Bay.

During floods, Everglades deer formerly escaped east to the Atlantic Ridge as well as west to Big Cypress. Because of suburban sprawl, escaping east is now out of the question. In 1983, another flood year in the Everglades, concerned sportsmen known as Airboat Rangers took matters into their own hands, rounded up thirty-one starving deer, and ferried them to high ground. All but one deer died of stress during the rescue. Since the resilience of the system, buffered by its large spatial scale and diversity of habitats, has been compromised, deer drown, get eaten by alligators, or, because their feet are constantly in water, simply rot from the hooves up. The pine flatwoods of the Atlantic Coastal Ridge, once a seed bank for many species of terrestrial animals that might have been wiped out in the eastern Everglades by flood, are no longer a repository for depleted stocks.

《《《

Color has faded from the western sky. Stars appear, twinkling brush stokes across the night. Inside Davis Creek we see that crocodile claw marks have gouged the marl bank, a basking site, but we do not see an animal. Back in Joe Bay, Frank's spotlight runs the chop, scanning for the red glow of crocodile eyes. Twice we approach a set of widely spaced eyes, slowly, deliberately, expectantly. The animal sinks, rises again after we move off. As we cruise the coastline, I strain not to miss a thing. "Crocodile," Frank mutters, boat swerving toward a phalanx of young mangroves. A second pair of expressionless eyes, closer together than the first, shines back red orange, an echo from *Night of the Living Dead*. Frank cuts the engine, steps off the boat with alacrity, noose pole in hand, and wades toward the reptile as though he were about to cast a plug for a tarpon. My senses gush. He slips the wire noose over the crocodile's head. The beast sculls forward. "Shit, I lost it." He tries again, shuffling forward, and reaches the noose pole over the crocodile. Water explodes. The crocodile surges. It leaps, twists, turns, and crashes back into the bay. It leaps again. Frank handles the wild exuberance with aplomb and lets the reptile play itself out, as though he actually has a tarpon on the line. When the animal finally tires, Frank grabs it; he places one hand behind its head, the other at the base of the tail, then calmly walks to the boat. "Here take this." I hold the crocodile—an unmarked female, six or seven years old, thirty-six pounds, four and a half feet long, and kitten-calm—in my lap. Frank marks her, slicing off the appropriate tail scutes with a hefty knife, number 113. After several minutes, the raw ossified skin, the color and texture of marshmallow, oozes tiny drops of blood.

Frank's CB comes alive. Biologists from the water management district, who were inventorying fish in a tidal creek, have a seven-foot crocodile in their net. Frank releases his trophy, "Say good-bye, sweetheart." The crocodile flicks her tail and vanishes into black water.

We float over a net drawn across the mouth of the creek and motor slowly toward the boat, where two men lift an empty net, a gaping hole in its middle. The biologist says the net had felt unusually heavy for one fish, so he had reached in, thinking that the weave had snagged a clump of oysters. When he grabbed for a shiny mullet, he had seen a grim, toothy face. He shows me a line of V-shaped tooth marks on the fish, which he keeps as a memento, and points to his headlamp, dropped in the commotion, shining up from the murk.

(((

The hurricane started as a spout of hot air in the summer sky over West Africa. By the time the National Hurricane Center in Miami–Dade County began monitoring the storm, it was only a tropical depression. Three days later, it had a name, Andrew. And three days after that, in the early hours of August 24, 1992, the anemometer on top of the National Hurricane Center clocked a gust at 164 miles per hour. A moment later, the center's radar unit, a spinning dish antenna inside a protective dome, blew off the roof.

There is no storm on Earth more powerful than a hurricane, an enormous heat engine that feeds on the ocean's warmth. A hurricane may grow to be five hundred miles wide and forty thousand feet high, and may orchestrate more than a million cubic miles of atmosphere. It has a shearing edge of thunderstorms that swirl around a calm center, the so-called eye, which spawns tornadoes that spin from the hub like so many raging tops, and rearranges landscapes with the force of a nuclear explosion. For all that awesome power, a hurricane is still one of nature's necessary evils.

More energy from the sun is absorbed in the Tropics than is radiated back into space. If this excess energy were not released, equatorial regions would grow perpetually warmer, threatening the balance of life. The one constant release is northward-flowing ocean currents like the Gulf Stream that carry heated water away from the Tropics toward the middle latitudes, which is why southern England supports palm trees, and sea turtles swim off the coast of Cape Cod. In some years, however, generally between June and October, tropical waters heat up so much that even the great currents cannot sweep away the excess thermal energy. Then conditions are right for the sudden, and sometimes violent, transfer of energy from the Tropics to the middle latitudes, a phenomenon key to the maintenance of Earth's delicate energy balance. If converted to electricity, the heat energy released from a hurricane in a single day could power the entire United States for three years.

The word *hurricane* comes from the Carib word for "storm god," or "evil spirit." About 70 percent of the tropical cyclones that move into the North Atlantic form near the Cape Verde Islands, off the west coast of Africa; the rest originate either in the Gulf of Mexico or in the Caribbean Sea. If a tropical cyclone has sustained wind speeds between thirty-four and seventy-three miles per hour, it's called a tropical storm; if the winds exceed seventy-three, it's a hurricane.

When the path of each of the more than 860 tropical storms and hurricanes known to have entered the North Atlantic between 1886 and 2002 is plotted on a map, the outline of Florida is eclipsed by ink. Thus plotted, the track of Hurricane Andrew, the United States' most economically devastating natural disaster, would barely be noticed.

On August 31, seven days after Andrew passed across the southern tip of Florida, from my vantage point, flying in a small plane at vulture-cruising height, there was no mistaking the storm's westward course. After crossing Biscayne Bay, Andrew disembarked at Turkey Point, bulldozed Homestead and Florida City, ravaged exotic trees like melaleuca, which suffered greater damage than native vegetation, and then, like most visitors, entered Everglades National Park along the Flamingo Road.

Tropical hardwoods on Royal Palm Hammock, Long Pine Key, and Pa-hay-okee Overlook buckled under the power of the hurricane, which then pressed northwest above Shark Slough, weed-whacking green hammocks. Resilient sawgrass bowed before the wind, then sprang back. Most pines and cypress also withstood the onslaught.

Andrew next exited the mainland near Key McLaughlin and swirled north-west toward the Ten Thousand Islands, stripping leaves, pruning limbs, and toppling trees. From five hundred feet above Lostmans River, I saw miles of brown, leafless mangroves meeting the sea. The odor of mangrove-leaf-rot filled the plane. (The stench was so strong that several days after the flight, while driving along the Tamiami Trail, I could still smell it more than twenty-five miles from the coast.) A manta ray, a shark, a manatee, and four sea turtles foraged in the shallows, trailing plumes of coffee-colored sediment that spread on the surface to merge with clouds of white organic ooze, the aftermath of the storm-torn leaves and battered marine life that radiated from the leeward side of the mangrove keys.

Twenty miles from the eye, despite seventy-mile-per-hour gusts, Fakahatchee Strand State Preserve looked green and lush, as though the hurricane had taken a route along the shore of another continent. A few miles farther north, the old-growth cypress at the National Audubon Society's Corkscrew Swamp Sanctuary were also healthy, although a rain of needles had covered the length of the boardwalk with a green veneer.

Tight and narrow, Hurricane Andrew raced through South Florida at eighteen miles per hour on a jagged twenty-five-mile-wide course, flattening virtually every hardwood hammock along the way, as though a giant bowling ball had rolled from the state's east coast to its west. The Ten Thousand Islands stood brown and leafless.

Although devastating, Andrew was also "dry": the only significant storm surge—the rapid increase of sea level along the coast, usually the most deadly aspect of a hurricane—occurred on the outer rim of Key Biscayne. Only two feet of water ran through the streets of Everglades City. Less than four inches of rain fell in Homestead, less than two at Corkscrew Swamp. Sometimes as much as a third of the Everglades' total wet-season rainfall comes with a single hurricane. "A typical hurricane," writes meteorologist James A. Henry, "usually brings five to 12 inches of rain to much of the area affected, and in the process produces over 200 billion tons of rainwater each day, an amount equal to the average annual flow of the Colorado River." By contrast, Hurricane Donna, which struck Florida's southwest coast on September 10, 1960, packed steady winds of 140 mph and gusts as high as 180 mph, crept along at four or five miles per hour, unloaded twelve inches of rain, and drained most of Florida Bay; when her eye passed, winds shifted to the south, and a wall of water returned a twelve-foot storm surge that refilled the bay, poured through the mangroves, suffocating trees with root-choking sediment, and propelled sea turtles and a porpoise far inland, eventually to bake to death beneath the subtropical sun.

A dry hurricane does not recharge water-starved aquifers. A dry hurricane does not flood the Everglades, flushing nutrients into Florida Bay, freshening shallow estuarine waters. Andrew never rearranged Florida Bay's shallow submarine mud banks, changing the bay's pattern of circulation, reversing the stagnation that has plagued the bay for more than a decade.

I had come to Florida in 1992 to see if the Everglades had been cleansed. Instead I found a wake of busted hammocks, brown and broken hardwoods splayed in all directions. Surprisingly, on the outside of the hardwood hammocks, a ring of cypress had endured the wind, but inside, trees splintered. Some slash pines bent toward the ground or were snapped in two, but most, perhaps 80 percent of them, still stood their full fifty feet in height. I found a skeletal forest of mangroves as bare as Vermont in November, windrows of debris, a dead and twisted egret, and the eerie emptiness of a national park without tourists.

Eventually, after park scientists dug themselves out from under their own debris, they began to study the effects of Hurricane Andrew on the natural resources of Everglades National Park. All radio-collared panthers were accounted for; American crocodiles had also weathered the storm, although one was seen swimming through the mangroves west of Cape Sable, well out of its range. The colonies of Cape Sable seaside sparrows, each bird barely heavier than a wet leaf, survived the wind, presumably by hunkering down in the swales. Orchids and tree snails were stripped from trees. In Big Cypress National Preserve, two colonies of endangered red-cockaded woodpeckers lost their nest trees when the wind snapped the pines in two.

The Everglades gets hit by a severe hurricane every twenty or thirty years. Although a hurricane may reverse plant succession by destroying mature forests, biological communities recover. A healthy Everglades is resilient, bounces back from natural catastrophe; however, today's Everglades suffers from the ecological equivalent of AIDS—its recuperative powers are jeopardized.

Their airborne seeds spread by Andrew, exotic plants invaded the Everglades. Melaleuca sprouted across the water conservation areas, and Brazilian pepper appeared in the damaged mangrove forests. After Andrew passed, wetland marshes that had supported concentrations of apple snails, crayfish, and grass shrimp became thickets of melaleuca and Australian pine growth.

Vines began to close the damaged crowns of hammock trees, holding moisture and heat inside the woods. Pole-like trees sprouted branches and grew rakish canopies. Inside damaged hammocks, secretive pileated woodpeckers mated in full sunlight. Eighteen months after Andrew, a seemingly healthy stand of pine outside the park succumbed to an invasion of bark beetles and pine borers because the artificially lower water table outside the park prevented the trees from producing enough pitch to ward off the insects.

《《《

Shortly before dawn, several days after I left Frank Mazzotti, the smoke and ground fog merged into a gray conglomerate as thick as chowder. With visibility nearly zero, I drove slowly northeast on the Flamingo Road, door open and flashlight in hand to keep track of the pavement. Three times I veered off the road and onto the sloped shoulder, my car tilting toward the Everglades. Once, from less than twenty feet away, a pickup with a boat in tow emerged from the smoke like some bright-eyed beast. Inadvertently we faced off, the air thick between us.

By the time I reached Long Pine Key, the fire had run through more than a thousand acres of pines and hardwood hammocks. Poor visibility finally forced the park service to close the southbound lane to Flamingo; fishing guides, mostly from the Keys, were backed up for miles, their boat trailers at odd angles to the road. A ranger told me that the blaze had started the evening before when a misfiring off-road truck ignited some brittle grass. It was the dry season, and rain would not soon play a role in putting this fire out.

The fire crew at Everglades National Park closely monitored the blaze, which had spread across portions of Long Pine Key and its neighboring marshes, torching tufts of grasses, blackening the trunks of the tall pines whose fire-resistant bark and thick sap kept the heat from damaging living wood. The fire pruned to their roots many tropical hardwoods that had sprouted in the pine-lands, leaving fire-resistant slash pine and saw palmetto favored in the open and temporarily charred woods. In fact, fire is an integral part of Everglades ecology; without it the pinelands would cede to hardwoods, and much of the sawgrass Everglades would be replaced by thickets.

Each summer more than ninety thunderstorms hit South Florida, tattooing each square mile of land with an average of twenty-five lightning strikes, nearly three times the national average. When fire opens the pinelands, pine warblers and bluebirds are favored. Ground fires clean up needle and leaf deposits, and within a month, a skin of green rises from the ashes. Months later the pinelands and marshes bloom with a magical intensity.

Several years ago I helped Harry Slater, at the time a graduate student from Louisiana State University, measure and tag trees in a hardwood hammock on Long Pine Key. Slater was part of an LSU fire ecology research program in South Florida. The hammock was dense and thorny, and our work was sometimes torturous. Fire wreaks havoc in hammocks, I learned. They burn periodically, usually after a drought has sucked most of the moisture out of the soil or after a hurricane or a frost has broken or killed enough growth to supply ample kindling. Sometimes a crown fire in the pines spreads into an adjacent hammock. Although a fire may have a dire consequence for a tropical ham-mock, pruning the vegetation to the ground, the wild tamarind, a common hammock tree, depends on light ground fire to steam open its seed pods.

Slater, who cataloged the dates of hammock fires in the national park, discovered that the germination for crops of wild tamarind often coincided with fire dates. He assumed that heat had opened the pods, releasing the seeds, a phenomenon that occurs in several species of northern pine. To test his hypothesis, Slater placed the pods in his oven and turned up the heat to see which temperatures prompted the pods to crack open. No matter at what temperature he set the oven, the pods remained sealed. On a whim, he tried steam, which opened the pods, freeing the seeds. Slater concluded that heat

from a ground fire pulls moisture from the humus and that the proper combination of both temperature and humidity was essential for the germination
of wild tamarind.

In portions of Long Pine Key that have not burned in years, hammock trees
smother pine seedlings in shade. Driving past, you see tall pines rising out of a
crowded, tree-choked landscape. The developing thickets favor cardinals and
Carolina wrens, whose vivacious songs fill the wooded tangles with loud, clear
notes. A fire under these crowded conditions may burn up into the crowns
and down to the limestone, killing even the fire-tolerant pineland species. The
blaze whose smoke had swept across the Flamingo Road, making driving so
difficult, was such a fire. Accidental and out of season, it raged through Long
Pine Key for several days.

Human-ignited fires have been both a blessing and a curse in South Florida.
Seminole and Miccosukee intentionally burned marshes and pinelands to
increase deer food. Later, commercial hide hunters torched the sawgrass to
locate gator holes. More recently, Everglades National Park became the first
park in the United States to use prescribed fires to perpetuate fire-dependent
plant communities, and now Big Cypress National Preserve has the largest
burning regimen of any park in the nation. Long Pine Key, in fact, is cut by
one-lane fire roads that divide the pinelands into blocks of a couple of thousand acres each. Whenever there's a fire, intended or otherwise, the fire crew
patrols the lanes to make sure flames don't jump blocks.

On several occasions I've watched controlled fires set in marshes and
pinelands. Marsh fires burn hot and quick. Their roaring orange flames leap
and hiss, spitting showers of sparks into cloudless skies. Cabbage palms then
burst into flame, and in a moment, their charred fronds droop from blackened
trunks. The wind muscles a marsh fire, forcing it back on itself, then driving
it forward with frightening speed. A prescribed pineland burn is less impressive. The fire moves in lines across the ground like so many brightly colored
snakes. Shrubs and palmetto fronds may explode into flames, tufts of wire
grass may flare up, but the hungry flames only lap at the trunks of the mature
slash pine, then move on. The wind is a bit player in a pineland fire, relegated
to subservience by the trees themselves.

Throughout this past century, as water levels in the Everglades were lowered,
fires have gotten worse, burning hotter and longer than they did before drainage. In April 1916, after a yearlong drought, botanist John Kunkel Small saw
"miles of hammock rolling clouds of black smoke skyward." The February
freeze of 1917 glazed Flamingo with a quarter inch of ice, and two months
later, fueled by winter-killed vegetation, intense fires swept across Long Pine

Key. In April 1923 fire burned off four feet of humus in the swamplands on the east side of Lake Okeechobee. In the summer of 1931, muck fires smoldered for nearly a year until they were finally extinguished by the rain. After a severe drought and a killing frost, practically the entire glades went up in flames in March 1943. Then, a year and a half later, another severe drought began. Taylor Slough dried out, and the Everglades became a dust bowl that burned for months and led the *Miami Herald* to proclaim, "Only an Act of God can halt the flames." By May 1945 the lower east coast of Florida was so blackened by smoke that air traffic ground to a halt in Miami.

Draining the Everglades created an extensive drought, a condition that lengthens the effect of the dry season and exacerbates the natural cycles of drought. Across the Everglades, habitats have shifted toward drier associations of plants. In South Florida, perhaps more than anywhere else in the United States, the forces of nature ought to set the limits for human growth and development. "Our modern owned world is going deaf from listening to its own answers," writes the naturalist John Hay. "Listening to the wind is an exercise in the inner sense of a continent we have been leaving behind us in our haste."

Natural History

Mosquitoes were so thick you could swing
a cup and catch a quart.

ANONYMOUS

5 Mosquitoes

Late one April afternoon two surf casters wet their lines in the Gulf of Mexico, off Cape Sable. They fished for sharks and between them caught five black-tips, all over six feet long. As twilight descended, salt marsh mosquitoes arrived in force. Every few minutes their numbers seemed to increase exponentially. The fishermen retreated to their tent and stayed inside drinking beer and listening to sharks cut the surface. At two in the morning, in his haste to get outside before his bladder burst, one man broke the zipper on the tent, which allowed inside a biblical cloud of mosquitoes. Then, in a Florida rendition of the cliff scene in *Butch Cassidy and the Sundance Kid,* the two men ran yelling into the Gulf of Mexico and kept company with the accommodating sharks till sunrise, sandpapery fins brushing their bare skin. At that point, only their lips were showing above the surface of the water.

The two fishermen who told me this story at least had each other for commiseration. Everglades National Park rangers tell of a lone fisherman whose skiff broke down in nearby Whitewater Bay. He spent the night submerged, breathing through a straw.

The late George Craig, a Notre Dame biology professor who was considered a preeminent authority on mosquitoes, once estimated that it would require 1,120,000 bites from the pesky insects to drain all the blood from an American adult. (Only female mosquitoes, which need high-protein meals to produce eggs, suck blood; males sip plant juices.) Craig never said where to test his supposition nor which of the world's approximately thirty-five hundred species of mosquitoes would be up to the task of exsanguinating a human, but one of his former graduate students, George O'Meara, had an idea.

O'Meara, a professor of entomology at the University of Florida's Medical Entomology Laboratory in Vero Beach, is one of a team of scientists at the laboratory whose careers hover around mosquitoes. He chose Flamingo, on Cape Sable, in Everglades National Park to test Craig's hypothesis. At the height of the rainy season, shallow pools in the mangrove forest alternately flood and dry. If the cycles happen to be spaced five or six days apart, two species of salt marsh mosquitoes, *Aedes taeniorhynchus* and *A. sollicitans,* proliferate in astronomical numbers. Their eggs, laid singly on damp ground—those of *sollicitans,* in open coastal prairies; those of *taeniorhynchus,* mostly in shade—mature in five days. A colleague of O'Meara's once estimated that more than ten thousand eggs per square foot of soil carpeted one site near Flamingo. The mosquito embryos are fully developed one to three days after the eggs are laid, and the eggs of both species hatch within minutes of flooding, even after months of exposure.

I once saw a jar of larva-filled water that was as thick and dark as motor oil. Five days later, when the larvae completely metamorphosed, biologists found an average landing rate of three hundred mosquitoes per minute on a white-shirted human volunteer. When the landing rate approached two thousand per minute, the air was so saturated with bugs that the researcher had to wear a surgical mask to keep from inhaling mosquitoes.

In the predrainage Everglades, the high volume of flowing water would have held mosquitoes in check for much of the year, as most species lay eggs in stagnant pools. Infestations became worse after 1948, the year Congress approved funding for the Central and Southern Florida Flood Control Project. Then, after more than thirty years of manipulated delivery and flow patterns throughout the entire watershed, water tables had been lowered by four or five feet in the eastern periphery of the Everglades, and parts of the central Everglades had become so dry that they often burned to their limestone underpinnings. The volume of water reaching Everglades National Park was so low by the 1950s that depressions in the saline mangroves filled and refill with tides and rainwater and had become ephemeral pools, the ideal breeding grounds for salt marsh mosquitoes.

"You don't know what a good day is until you've seen a bad day," George O'Meara is fond of saying. He should know. For twenty-six years O'Meara has conducted research in Flamingo, and every year he must apply to the national park for a permit to collect mosquitoes. "You don't need a permit to slap them," he says. If the parking lot is empty of visitors when he arrives, and the ranger's white car is black with insects, O'Meara is thrilled, for he knows that the mosquito population is intense. Sometimes it's hard for George to find field assistants. Once, he brought a group of high school students to the Everglades. When it was time to leave, thousands of mosquitoes joined them in the van. For the entire four-hour trip back to Vero Beach, O'Meara kept the back doors open to flush mosquitoes, and still the sound of slapping filled the van.

Here is a story to place Flamingo's insect life in perspective. One summer in the early days of Everglades National Park, a pesticide-fogging truck had to spray five times a day to make Flamingo tolerable for the few summer staff members who lived there. Driven to distraction by biting insects—there are at least forty species in the park—rangers radioed park headquarters near Homestead, a comfortable thirty-eight miles away, and asked permission to pull back. Apparently, that summer, mosquitoes near Homestead were tolerable, and headquarters denied the request, suggesting that the rangers were sissies. To make a point, one Flamingo ranger followed the fogging truck and filled a large grocery bag with mosquito carcasses. He sent the bag back to headquarters. The next day a reply reached Flamingo: Pull back.

Fixed to the bulletin board in the Flamingo Ranger Station is THE FLA-MINGO MOSQUITO METER, which characterizes for park visitors the day's population of biting insects. The meter features a picture of a large, nasty-looking mosquito whose proboscis points to one of five categories: enjoyable, bearable, unpleasant, horrible, hysterical. Next door a gift shop sells a popular bumper sticker that looks like a cross between an ad for an exterminator and one for the Red Cross. It reads, I GAVE AT FLAMINGO.

Aedes taeniorhynchus ranges down both coasts of North America, from New England to Brazil and from California south to the Galapagos Islands. Florida females are facultative blood-feeders, which means that if they feast on algae, bacteria, protozoa, rotifers, and fungal spores during the larval stage, they can produce their first clutch of eggs on nectar alone, skipping a blood meal. Blood is required, however, for the production of all other clutches after the first. If a pool is overcrowded and begins to recede beneath the heat of the subtropical sun, *taeniorhynchus* may hurry metamorphosis and emerge small and wanting. Then the first clutch of eggs is made of blood. Although each female carries about 150 egg follicles in her ovaries, she lays only between twenty-five and seventy-five eggs on a blood-free diet. Blood more than triples the number of eggs produced.

For *sollicitans* there is no choice. It takes blood to make eggs. Males and females of both species derive energy for flight and other nonreproductive activities from sugars, mainly the nectar of black mangrove, white mangrove, and buttonwood, whose tiny flowers they pollinate in return.

Salt marsh mosquitoes avoid breeding in the red mangrove zone where tidal action would quickly wash away their eggs. They prefer the slightly higher swamps that are dominated by black and white mangroves and the adjacent marshes. Nature is a teeter-totter of checks and balances, and the narrow band of prime habitat that salt marsh mosquitoes seek has its own survival hurdle. When the moon is full or when a great wind pushes Florida Bay inland, small, hungry fish—marsh killifish, Gulf killifish, bluefin killifish, sheepshead minnow, gambusia, sailfin molly—surf into the mangroves and coastal prairie and feast on larvae. Several days later, when adult mosquitoes emerge, the mollies and minnows switch to a vegetarian diet. The other fish species continue to eat invertebrates. All wait for the tide to rescue them. As water evaporates, fish begin to coalesce, triggering one of America's grandest spectacles, the feeding frenzy of wading birds. A few appear at first—some egrets, perhaps some ibis, a spoonbill, a trio of green herons, a half dozen storks—arriving from parts unknown. Eventually flocks appear, whirling fragments of color, and the mangroves become snow white, the brown-water pools highlighted by living, moving blues and pinks and purples and russets, a fairy tale of birds whose presence is directly tied to the biorhythms of mosquitoes.

Salt marsh mosquitoes are not selective feeders; they're opportunists. Several years ago I watched scores of them engorge in the nostrils and around the eyes of an eight-foot-long crocodile, which basked in the sun, seemingly oblivious to the attack. When loggerhead sea turtles crawl out of the Gulf of Mexico to nest in the bone-colored sand of Cape Sable, each sports an entourage of mosquitoes. With surgical precision the insects work their stylus-mouths between the scales of diamondback rattlesnakes. Mosquitoes torment birds, particularly wading birds, whose long naked legs present inviting targets. Some biologists believe that the density of salt marsh mosquitoes on the mainland may have driven colonial wading birds to nest and roost on the isles of Florida Bay. Around Flamingo, mosquitoes thrive on the blood of marsh rabbits, whose crepuscular pattern of activity matches that of the mosquitoes. I've watched these poor creatures grazing along the edge of the park service road, their ears pin-cushioned by fat, blood-red mosquitoes. Raccoons, which are abundant in the mangroves and coastal prairies but active later at night than the rabbits, encounter far fewer mosquitoes and consequently shed less blood. O'Meara, who has vacuumed *A. taeniorhynchus* off black mangrove pneumatophores at rates in excess of ten thousand per minute, found that in Flamingo 8 percent of the females he captured had recently had a blood meal. Of those, nearly 3 percent carried human blood.

Outside George O'Meara's office is a mosquito flight cage in which he and other biologists have tested the responses of various bird species to hungry salt marsh mosquitoes. Birds that rely on stealth or camouflage to capture food—barred owls, green herons, black-crowned night herons, and great blue herons, for instance—stand stone still, rarely flinching while clouds of mosquitoes ply their trade. Active feeders, such as white ibises and snowy egrets, twitch and snip, often eating the bugs that try to bite them. Cattle egrets stomp their feet. Raccoons and marsh rabbits accommodate, but nibbly cotton rats and cotton mice do not. Mosquitoes avoid young opossums, but not their parents. Woodpeckers and songbirds, except for Carolina wrens, are too jittery to be good hosts.

In January 1996 I met with George O'Meara in Vero Beach. He showed me the walk-in flight cage, which is built like a large wood-framed screen porch. Some years earlier, O'Meara had enlarged his study population to include two officials of the Accutronics Corporation, which at the time marketed an antimosquito device called the Mosquito Hawk. The company claimed that the Mosquito Hawk mimicked the noise made by the beating wings of a dragonfly, a major mosquito predator, and thus kept the mosquitoes at bay. The inventor agreed to a test in the cage. To prepare for the event, O'Meara starved several thousand female salt marsh mosquitoes. The inventor of the Mosquito Hawk entered the flight cage, four buzzing black boxes fixed to his belt. The mosquitoes began to feed, undeterred by the high-pitched sound. Within seconds the man turned to flee, but the door had jammed. Panic reigned until O'Meara rescued him.

George O'Meara has been bitten by salt marsh mosquitoes so many times in the course of his research that he has become immune to their bites—no slapping, no itching, no swelling. Inhaled mosquitoes, however, can still cause discomfort. A hungry female mosquito is attracted to carbon dioxide and lactic acid, both of which are given off by the respiration and activity of birds and mammals. She also may key in on an animal's profile and on dark clothing, like the olive-green uniforms worn by rangers in Everglades National Park. Drinking ginseng tea or eating bananas, vitamin B, garlic, brewer's yeast, or Mrs. Paul's Fish Sticks—all suggested as can't-miss home repellents—will fail to keep mosquitoes away. Commercial bug repellents may keep mosquitoes from biting, but they contain DEET, the active ingredient in most repellents, which is absorbed by the skin and has been linked to seizures and deaths. It also dissolves plastic and vinyl, rendering binoculars and cameras permanently sticky. Although acquired immunity may be reliable and safe—the Zen approach to living with mosquitoes—who would want to get bitten the requisite several thousand times each year for many years to become desensitized?

Even though a small percentage of salt marsh mosquitoes survive to adulthood, the number is "still enough to get your attention," O'Meara assures me (not that I need assurance). To encourage coastal development in the 1930s and 1940s, Florida leveled and filled mangrove forests and ditched and drained salt marshes. The faint image of old mosquito ditches still crosshatches satellite photos of coastal Florida. The wetlands that did not drain were liberally doused with Paris Green, a larvicide made of copper arsenic. After World War II Florida switched to the magic bullet, DDT, in an effort to win the mosquito war. As DDT-resistant strains of mosquitoes began to evolve, Florida repeatedly upped the dosage until chemicals could no longer dissolve in solution. By 1959 DDT had damaged the ovaries of fish-eating brown pelicans and had turned palm fronds yellow, but it was no longer effective against *Aedes taeniorhynchus*. Throughout the 1960s, mosquito control once again relied on Paris Green.

Several years ago on Key Largo, I watched a plane pass up and down the island spewing the pesticide malathion from the armpit of each wing. At the sound of the plane I rushed outside to see a trio of fluffy gray kingbirds perched on an electric line. The mother kingbird, a dragonfly in her bill, flew in to feed one chick in a descending veil of pesticide. As the sun rose above the hardwoods, fingers of sunlight pierced the chemical mist like floodlights in a smoky arena. The air smelled like industrial cleaning fluid. For three days, I was not troubled by mosquitoes. How the kingbirds fared is another question.

Behind O'Meara's office is a web of canals sliced into a frost-stunted mangrove forest that feeds Indian River, a mile or so away. On this day it is sunny and warm, low 70s, and would have been good weather for salt marsh mosquitoes except that it hasn't rained in more than a month, and the temporary pools have dried out, leaving tableaus of opossum and raccoon tracks in the caked mud. Above the tide line, shaded by black mangroves, are the long, curved burrows of the great Atlantic land crab. The burrows, which extend to the waterline, are also the home of the crabhole mosquito, one of O'Meara's favorites. He pours water down a burrow, and a congregation of mosquitoes rises from the hole. The males' long antennae, which droop forward like an extra set of legs, are used to shepherd females still in their pupae stage. When an adult female sheds her pupa case, she is quickly bred by her tending male. Both sexes rest on the walls of the burrows by day and feed by night, the males on nectar or fruit juice, and the females on either blood or the sugar of fruits and flowers. Unlike the salt marsh mosquito, the newly emerged crabhole female always produces her first clutch of eggs on a blood-free diet. If she has stored enough food in her body from her youthful days as a filter-feeding larva in the bottom of the crabhole, she may stay with sugar for the second clutch and never suck blood. "They're nice mosquitoes," O'Meara chortles.

George O'Meara is pushing sixty. He is a round, jolly man with white hair and blue eyes who broadcasts exuberance for the world's most deadly group of insects. He rates national parks and cemeteries by the number and species of mosquitoes he has collected there. Along with Jack Kerouac and textiles, O'Meara is one of the better-known products of Lowell, Massachusetts. As a boy he never had a bug collection and never dreamed of biology, let alone a lifetime of mosquitoes. He once hoped to be a ballplayer, to patrol the outfield at Fenway Park, but he couldn't hit a curve ball. At Notre Dame, George Craig introduced him to the rewards of mosquito research. He stayed on to complete his doctorate before moving, more than thirty years ago, to Florida and its seventy or so mosquito species.

Except for a white *Aedes sollicitans* that his wife, Mary, embroidered on one of his ties, nothing in the O'Meara household suggests mosquitoes. None of his four grown children followed in their father's footsteps. "There's still hope for my fourteen-year-old daughter, Meg," he tells me. "But I wouldn't count on it."

Returning from the salt marsh, O'Meara walks me along a trail through a live oak hammock. The trees are tall and festooned with Spanish moss, and for the most part they block the sun. Here and there pines and cabbage palms accent the oak woods. Some of the rough-barked trees support tank bromeliads, air plants that look like the tops of pineapples and hold water between the tight weave of their long, tapered leaves. O'Meara pulls a turkey baster from his back pocket, squeezes the ball, and inserts it into a bromeliad, removing half a dozen mosquito larvae, which he squirts into a petri dish.

One larva is nearly a half-inch long and has an oversized head that is four times the size of the others. The big one is a predator of other species of mosquito larva. Its prolonged development puts it in contact with several hatches of prey, which it devours before maturing. Later, in a warm, humid cage in the center's laboratory, O'Meara pulls out the adult incarnation of the same species. These are huge and beautiful, more like tiny butterflies than large mosquitoes—blue-black bodies with phosphorescent stripes, iridescent purplish wings. The lower legs are white, as though the mosquitoes are wearing stockings, and the males' antennae are bushy. As adults the females drink only plant juices. O'Meara squirts the big one into a bromeliad and wishes it well. "Go, do your job," he says.

Mosquitoes are far more varied than the average halter-topped tourist in Everglades National Park realizes. Forty-five species occupy forty-five niches across the Everglades, some so subtly different from each other that it requires the patience and perseverance of George O'Meara to notice any difference at all. A few species bite only during the day, others at night, and still others—like the salt marsh duo—prefer twilight, except when a bright moon extends their hours of feeding.

Some lay eggs in permanent freshwater, some in floodwater. One mosquito prefers pools cradled in cypress knees; treehole species choose egg-laying sites by the height of the cavity or the pH of the water. Two species of *Wyeomyia* are bombardiers, dropping eggs like depth-charges while hovering over a bromeliad. Another lays eggs on the undersurface of floating plants. Members of the genus *Anopheles* place their eggs singly on water; the *Culex* mosquitoes glue theirs into iridescent floating rafts that curl up along the edge and drift about like Lilliputian dugouts. The eggs of *Aedes* wait for water—even those that breed in bromeliads depend on rain to wash their eggs into the tank. Too much rain, however, may wash them out again. (To avoid a similar fate, larvae settle to the bottom of the tank where there is less agitation.) The two species of *Wyeomyia* include powdery catopsis, a carnivorous bromeliad, in their list of nurseries; their larvae frolic amid the fermenting carcasses of less fortunate forms of insects. The larvae of three species of freshwater mosquito live in ooze and siphon oxygen from the interior of root hairs. Other types dwell at the water surface, suspended like inverted question marks. Still others rise from the depths, take a breath, and then sink again.

Some species of blood-hungry mosquitoes specialize on birds or mammals, either big or small, or turtles or frogs. O'Meara says he would not be surprised if the connoisseurs of amphibian blood tune in on the pulsating sound of frog operas. Other species, like the salt marsh mosquitoes, are catholic feeders, their diet reflecting whatever is available at the moment.

Culex nigripalpus, a mosquito associated with summer showers, is the main vector for St. Louis encephalitis, a disease sometimes fatal to humans. In 1990 there were 230 clinical cases and 20,000 subclinical cases in Florida. Although *nigripalpus* bites frogs, snakes, turtles, raccoons, armadillos, humans, owls, egrets, herons, and pelicans, the viral reservoir is predominantly dooryard birds—cardinals, mourning doves, blue jays, and boat-tailed and common grackles—all of which are widespread and abundant. The disease travels from mosquito to bird to mosquito to human. Fifty-eight percent of the black vultures in South Florida tested positive for St. Louis encephalitis, but their spotty distribution did not amplify the disease. Grackles had a banner year in 1990. A year later, when the population of both grackle species crashed, St. Louis encephalitis all but vanished from Florida.

Mammals, from black bears to rodents, are the reservoir for Venezuelan equine encephalitis. In the Everglades a hammock-loving *Culex* transmits the disease from cotton rats to cotton mice. Some viruses are indigenous to Everglades National Park and are named for the site of discovery, such as Mahogany Hammock virus and Gumbo-Limbo virus. Fifty percent of the Seminole tested had antibodies for Venezuelan equine encephalitis, a splendid adaptation for a culture intimate with the Everglades.

As I leave Vero Beach after seeing O'Meara, I remember a previous trip, in 1993, during which it rained a long, hard rain. When the storm finally blew out to sea, the sun reappeared, and the million raindrops on a million leaves made South Florida sparkle. The air smelled fertile. Four days later in Everglades National Park much of the Christian Point Trail, which winds through a storm-torn buttonwood forest, lay beneath six inches of stagnating rainwater seething with life. I dipped a mayonnaise jar into the opaque broth, held it to the light, and watched thousands of salt marsh mosquito larvae snap up and down like grains of rice in a rolling boil.

Six days after the rain, adult salt marsh mosquitoes began emerging from the flooded ground. Every hour their numbers swelled. I had a flat tire that morning and, unfortunately, changed the tire dressed in sandals, shorts, and a paper-thin shirt. By midafternoon, my ankles and arms looked like a relief map of the Appalachian Mountains, and I was scratching my back against a tree like a bear.

Candy-striped tree snails hung like grapes
from the trunks and branches.

E. O. WILSON, 1994

6 Tree Snails

Archie Jones, eighty-five years old, bushwhacks alone in the southern Everglades, often miles from the nearest road, on pilgrimages in search of lovely,
painted tree snails, "the essence of tropical Florida," according to herpetologist
Archie Carr. The national park lends Jones a two-way radio, the next best thing
to dialing 911, because the karst topography east of Rock Reef Pass is scarred
by solution holes, treacherous cavities in the limestone, often hidden by a
sweep of bracken fern or sawgrass. A man's weight can break the thin roof of
an embryonic hole, legs kicking creatures of dark water, newt and gambusia
and who knows what else.

   One day, as Jones knelt miles from the nearest road to look for hatchling tree
snails, he heard an ominous buzz. Every time he moved, he heard that nerve-

wrenching sound. No matter where he turned, the buzz was there. Although the bite of a pygmy rattlesnake is seldom fatal, the prospect of limping across the Everglades, leg swelling, heart racing, mind fumbling, was not pleasant. Slowly, Archie stood up, hoping not to provoke a strike. The sound was in his knapsack. Carefully he opened the top and found that his radio was buzzing.

On a January afternoon in 1993 I wait for Archie in front of the main visitor center in Everglades National Park. He will tutor me in the ways of the Florida tree snail, *Liguus fasciatus,* a visually and biologically stunning invertebrate whose rainbow colors once inspired a legion of collectors and whose varied patterns are echoed in the brilliant fabric stitched by Miccosukee women. The well-being of the species now depends on the generosity of former collectors turned preservationists. Archie has been a tree snail aficionado for more than sixty years, since the day he looked up while fishing and saw one inching along a branch in the green twilight of Big Cypress Swamp. "It remains the most beautiful thing I have ever seen," he recalls.

Archie drives a roomy station wagon. Lying in the back are telescoping aluminum poles crisscrossed over a couple of water bottles, a dog-eared copy of a 1965 *National Geographic* featuring "Tree Snails, Gems of the Everglades," and a change of clothes. "I always bring a change of clothes no matter how beautiful it is or what the weatherman says. If you get wet it's miserable driving home in an air-conditioned car, trying to keep the windshield clear." A retired pharmaceutical executive, Archie is elfin and energetic. He moved to Miami from the east coast of Maryland in 1920, when Miami's population was a mere twenty-seven thousand. He speaks slowly, gently, distinctly. So smooth is his southern lilt that I settle into the front seat and imagine I am in the presence of Red Barber.

Darwin would have loved *Liguus,* had he made its acquaintance, for Florida's snail comes in fifty-eight color patterns, or morphs, the Baskin-Robbins of gastropods. Cuba, the source of Florida's snails, has more than a hundred morphs. Hispaniola, even more. Biologists have found classifying the Florida tree snail a challenge. One authority recognized three distinct species collectively divided into thirty-five subspecies. Others recognized three or four subspecies of a single species. H. A. Pilsbry, who spent much of his adult life tinkering with *Liguus* taxonomy, believed that each subspecies reflects a separate landing of a Cuban tree snail somewhere in South Florida, each spawning its own related groups of morphs. Perhaps a hurricane sent *Liguus,* sealed to a tree limb, sailing or flying over the Straits of Florida. Or maybe small snails boarded the legs or feathers of hammock birds, perhaps white-crowned pigeons. (This was

Darwin's answer for how terrestrial snails originally reached islands from the mainland.) Whatever the vehicle for dispersal, current thinking holds that all morphs descended from a single beachhead and that the subspecies are all invalid. Controversy aside, all agree that the rapid development of fifty-eight variants (none of these found in Cuba) in the five thousand years since South Florida emerged from the sea—a blink of the geologic eye—is explosive microevolution.

Why should a species of tree snail develop such a bewildering and wondrous diversity of color? They cannot see themselves or each other, for their eye-tipped antennae are feeble organs of vision. Their beauty warns no potential predators, offers no camouflage, attracts no members of the opposite sex. In fact, tree snails have no opposite sex. They are hermaphrodites. When snails come together, they caress for hours, then either fertilize each other or lay viable but unfertilized eggs. Archie's own experimental crosses did not yield a hybrid in fifteen generations. Every Florida morph once occurred as a pure colony on hardwood hammocks, often isolated from other variants as though on oceanic islands. Hybrids, however, were common in zones of overlap. A 1991 study in the *Journal of Heredity* reported that although *Liguus* morphs have very low genetic diversity—a good indication of self-fertilization—the genes responsible for shell pattern have a high rate of mutation. Isolation and self-fertilization permit these slight differences to become expressed and then quickly fixed in a given population. A saturnalia of color and pattern has resulted: snails as white as ivory, others as intricate as tortoiseshell; some marked with combinations and shades of orange, pink, green, yellow, gold, copper, blue, and brown. When you look upon all fifty-eight morphs arranged geographically in a cabinet you can almost hear Darwin musing.

Originally the Florida tree snail ranged from Cape Sable up the Everglades to Pompano Beach, from Pine Crest in Big Cypress north to Immokalee, on the Calusa shell mounds of Marco Islands, all the way to Key West—wherever tropical hardwoods grew amid the sawgrass, pines, and buttonwoods. Nearly every snail hammock had its own morph or its own combination of morphs.

Since the 1930s development has shrunk the snail's range. Four or five morphs are gone, and many of the survivors' populations are reduced or transplanted. Early in the 1950s Archie and three other shell collectors turned conservationists decided to protect *Liguus* from this encroachment of civilization. They met with Daniel Beard, first superintendent of Everglades National Park, and drew up plans for relocating threatened morphs to safe havens within the park. The men volunteered their time and money for the project; the park provided occasional use of an airboat.

First Archie and a colleague searched the Flamingo Road for suitable hammocks. They circumscribed a narrow, horseshoe-shaped arc six miles long, two miles deep, and three hundred yards wide across the pockmarked southern glades, exploring, mapping, and marking every hammock in the loop on foot. They found more than four hundred hammocks that had plenty of food and no snails. Next they began collecting tree snails from the lower Keys. They temporarily transferred them to roadside drop hammocks along the route to Flamingo, then returned to these sites, segregated the snails into their respective morphs, and stocked them in the marked interior hammocks. Archie participated in four hundred introductions of more than thirty morphs and checked the stocked colonies twenty-five to thirty times a year. The rarest morphs were introduced into several hammocks separated by great distances. "An insurance policy," he tells me. If fire consumed a hammock, wiping out its snail colony, that morph might still survive in another hammock. Although snail eggs are laid three inches deep in the ground and are well insulated, hatchlings would be hard pressed to survive if fire burned their hammock down to rock. Archie is the only survivor of the transplanting team; the other three have passed on, he tells me grinning, "to the happy snail hunting grounds in the sky."

We drive down the Flamingo Road beneath a blue winter sky. The day is warm and dry, seventy-three degrees. A light wind blows out of the northwest. Three crows hop into the next lane, let us pass, then resume picking at some unfortunate snake. A red-shouldered hawk flushes from a cypress. We park alongside one of the original drop sites.

Archie wears a long-sleeved khaki shirt, long khaki pants, and boots. An orange baseball cap that reads *Liguus* covers his thin crop of hair. He carries his knapsack and an aluminum pole for balance. Exuberantly he strides toward a hammock. I work to keep up. Archie has done what Barry Lopez calls "marking the country." He taught himself to look, to listen, to find whatever the Everglades has to offer. *Liguus* is his window into Florida's real "magic kingdom," a diminutive totem whose beauty he still finds unfathomable. After years of studying alewives, John Hay wrote that their "lidless eyes . . . seem to offer messages from a depth I am unable to conceive of." What messages lie within the stalked and retractable eyes of *Liguus*?

We wander deeper into the Everglades, sawgrass tugging at our pants. Eventually Archie announces that a snail glued to the underside of a lysiloma limb is *dryas,* a white-banded, yellow morph so glossy that it appears lacquered. "To hunt snails, you've got to think like a snail. It helps not to have too high an IQ," he says, marveling at a morph he has seen a thousand times. A long, uneven scrape through a patch of gray-green lichen runs down the lysiloma trunk: the snail's feeding trail. No trail, no snail. A tree snail's *radula,* a band that protrudes from the mouth and bears numerous rows of microscopic teeth, rasps off dinner. Like a self-inking typewriter ribbon, worn radula teeth are continuously replaced. Every day *Liguus* wanders around grazing on slime mold, fungus, algae, or lichen along the limbs and trunks of smooth-barked hardwoods, leaving behind a squiggly track about twenty-five feet long where it had scraped its meal down to the bark.

Ligs, as they are commonly called, are prized among malacologists. Driven by beauty, and in some cases greed, shell collectors developed a meticulous knowledge of wild South Florida before the days of airboats, helicopters, and swamp buggies. They waded into or poled across the Everglades and combed hammocks from West Palm Beach to Homestead—a task I find truly daunting. Americans are not the only people who covet ligs. Several years ago, while I was attending a botanical conference in Havana, the host, La Academia de Ciencias de Cuba, sold *Liguus* shells, four for a dollar, neatly packaged in plastic zip-locked bags.

Early in the twentieth century, John Kunkel Small, the botanist and keen observer of South Florida natural history, wrote that some greedy malacologists would collect snails by the bucketful and then torch the hammock. The fire killed any snails that had not been captured and destroyed the habitat, dooming hatchlings that might emerge unscathed from the soil. The extinction of a morph would increase the value of the trader's own specimens; the price for rare shells rose accordingly. I ask Archie about this. That report is greatly exaggerated, he tells me, surprised that I would take such a story to heart. Although most tree snails in private collections were taken alive, sorted and stored or traded or sometimes sold in the quest for a complete set, only one morph was ever lost to greed, Archie claims, and fire had nothing to do with it. "Imagine trying to eliminate all the snails on a cluster of thirty or forty trees, each fifty feet tall and a foot and a half in diameter. Impossible. I couldn't even recapture all the snails in our drop hammocks." Most lost morphs have fallen to the bulldozer; one fell to the hurricane of 1935.

In the Everglades, where wildfire and big weather shape the evolution of biological communities, the canals and levees created by humans have gone beyond the forces of nature to threaten the foundations of Florida. When the very nature of the Everglades is in jeopardy, who has time to consider tree snails? Only a former collector who adores the candy-cane spirals can muster the energy, the time, and the resources to carry out his plan alone.

In May 1989, after a long and serious drought, five lightning fires converged into a single big blaze that wiped out 85 to 90 percent of the hammocks in which Archie had introduced snails. Within each charred hammock surviving snails were isolated from each other across a gulf of six-foot-tall bracken fern, which flourished in the sunlight. The animals could not communicate, could not find each others' slime trails. Even though tree snails self-fertilize, they need the company of another snail to reproduce.

Archie began to reunite members of each morph, bridging the bracken gaps in each hammock. Then, seven months later, on Christmas night, a cold front blanketed South Florida. Tropical leaves buckled and withered. When I visited Everglades National Park in February 1990, Flamingo looked as if it had been hit by napalm. Miles of cold-stressed mangroves held leaves brown and stiff. In the hardwood hammocks east of Rock Reef Pass, where the fires had left no overarching canopy to keep out frost, *Liguus* was devastated: the freeze turned most of the soft-bodied snails to stone.

The snails had less than three years to recover from the 1989 fires and 1990 Christmas freeze before Hurricane Andrew came in 1992. It was not enough time. For the stocked colonies of ligs, Andrew was the coup de grâce.

"Something happened in that Andrew," Archie says. "The numbers of snails are very low." His observations on the colony in his backyard in Coconut Grove have led Archie to believe that when the barometric pressure falls in advance of a big storm, tree snails descend three or four feet in the tree trunks to more secure perches. (During storms of less intensity, they ride out the inclement weather in the leafy branches or wherever else they happen to be.) But apparently these perches weren't secure enough to withstand Andrew's 150-mile-per-hour winds, for many of the snails seem to have been catapulted into oblivion—though perhaps a fortunate few were carried to distant hammocks.

Archie worries, for he believes *Liguus* should have recovered from its recent travails by now, and it has not. When hammock fires are suppressed for many years (the park's former policy), a dense leafy canopy shuts out the sun, and the snails die off. Brief periodic fires open hammocks and increase the amount of sunlight that reaches the limbs and trunks of hardwoods. Several years after a fire, snails usually prosper as their food supplies increase. When Andrew hit, the stocked colonies were still convalescing. As we stand in front of a storm-torn hammock a year and a half after the hurricane's passage, Archie's face sags. "See how open these hammocks are? We should be seeing hundreds of baby snails. This place looks like Hiroshima after the bomb."

Besides the fickle environment, raccoons and opossums claim many snails, particularly when the snails are on the ground laying eggs. Occasionally blue jays and crows pick them off limbs, break the shells, and devour the escargot. *Liguus*'s most fierce predators, however, are two invertebrates: the fire ant and *Euglandina rosea,* a carnivorous snail that forces its scythelike radula into the tree snail's aperture and literally eats it out of house and home.

I doggedly follow Archie across the Everglades. The shortest distance between two points out here is seldom a straight line. Any given line of travel reveals cryptic solution holes to fall into, marl to slip on, pygmy rattlesnakes to startle, and poisonwood to touch. On the edge of a small hammock, glued to a branch of poisonwood (whose glossy leaves raise blisters on sensitive skin), shining like porcelain, a dormant tree snail waits for rain to loosen its weather-tight mucus grip. When the weather dries, snails aestivate, sealing themselves to a limb to conserve internal moisture, which is essential because they have stopped feeding and cannot replenish water loss. To break a tree snail's seal is taboo. Although snails will often reseal themselves, the second mucus seal is not as thick or as tight as the first, and if the weather is dry, the snail may shrivel. During a winter rain ligs sometimes break their own bond to a tree and commence feeding, but if the weather turns, these animals may be in jeopardy.

This one-inch morph is *miamiensis,* a brown-banded, green-lined relict from a Miami pineland hammock razed in the 1960s. On the basis of its size, Archie thinks the snail is three or four years old and may lay only six to twelve eggs. Although ligs may live five or six years, possibly more, a well-fed snail in his backyard may reach its full three inches in one growing season and lay fifty eggs. Nearby a yearling *miamiensis,* which Archie calls a button, hangs from the limb of a Jamaican dogwood, a miniature replica of its parents.

Somehow, across a small gulf of limestone, Archie spots a *cingulatus* on the trunk of willow bustic. Through binoculars I admire the snail's spiraling white and yellow bands and thin brown lines. We walk over for a closer look, beating back poisonwood saplings. I spot another morph, a snail bearing green lines and a blush of pink, like a party favor. Once you develop the search image of brightly colored snails on smooth limbs, they become easier to find. Success feeds on itself. I find two more snails, both *cingulatus.*

To show me the contrast between the stocked colonies and a native colony, Archie takes me to a large, densely vegetated hammock in the midst of a pine forest on Long Pine Key, itself an island in the marshland near the eastern boundary of the national park. Driving on the Flamingo Road again, we cross Taylor Slough as Archie tells a story he believes unfit for print. When the settlers first waded across this belly-deep marshland one cold February morning, he said, their family jewels shriveled up. They christened the place Dead Pecker Slough. Everyone called it that. But in 1947, when the federal government became custodians of the southern Everglades, the name changed to Taylor Slough.

Once inside the pinelands, Archie opens a locked gate and drives down a fire lane. The pines are a tangle of logs and branches felled by Andrew. This is diamondback country, so I measure every step. A ground skink scoots by. The hammock is large compared with the ones we have just visited. It supports six or seven morphs, three of which we find on the same lysiloma limb within minutes of our arrival.

Part of the thrill of studying *Liguus* is the potential for finding a new color form. Archie has discovered and named six morphs himself. One he called *margareti,* for his wife. "I spent more time with the snails than I did with Margaret. To keep peace in the family, I named one for her," he tells me, an impish gleam in his eye. Then he disappears into the mosquito-plagued hammock.

For tree snails, rituals count. Although ligs are hermaphroditic, they still need each other to lay unfertilized eggs. So like the bee that meticulously visits one floral design at a time, Archie Jones will return here this next rainy season, the two-way radio in his knapsack and sporting his orange *Liguus* cap, to bring his morphs together.

Where do we draw the line helping endangered species when entire ecosystems recoil under the pressure of development? Micromanaging tree snails is a luxury. But just as the destruction of the Everglades has been both systematic and haphazard, so, ultimately, must be the efforts at restoration. While hydrologists and engineers work on the big picture—the timing, the quality, and the quantity of water flow down the Everglades—Archie Jones follows the fortunes of *Liguus.* Why shouldn't someone attempt to preserve these ambassadors for the inexplicable beauty of evolution, whose colors and patterns exploded in the hammocks of South Florida over the last several thousand years?

And is it possible that one man's effort could save those tree snail morphs that lost their original habitat? Or will they eventually succumb on their new hammocks, caged like canaries, to die in semicaptivity after the next fire or frost, or after the next big wind comes howling out of the Caribbean to reshuffle the landscape?

Known as "bullfrogs" throughout much of
the South, Pig Frogs are sought for their edible
legs. Where hunted regularly, they are wary of
humans and headlamps.

JOHN BEHLER AND F. WAYNE KING, 1979

7 Frogs and Frogger

"From the time ya left Dade Corners all the way across the glades, yer runnin'
on snakes," says Russell Yates. He lights a Chesterfield to stifle mosquitoes.
"High water comes up, ya hit strips of 'em for a hundred, maybe three hundred, yards, a strip of one here and there, and then here and there again.
Come down one year and ya won't see no snakes. Come back the next year
and everywhere ya look there's snakes. Frogs the same way. Every few years
they're everywhere."

Russell is a professional frogger, an affable man who supplies frog legs to the
gourmet-food market, one of a very few people who ekes out a living in the
midnight marshes. Although many individuals frog as a hobby or as a source
of second income, only three or four full-time froggers are left in Florida. After

alligator hunting was outlawed in the 1960s, frogging became a popular cover for gator poachers. At best, Russell makes $4.50 a pound for frog legs, a paltry sum when taken against the cost of equipment and upkeep, which includes maintaining an airboat. By the time his frog legs reach through the seafood market to a restaurant, they bring four or five times the price he was paid. Because no regulatory agency monitors the frogs, or licenses the froggers, the impact of frogging is anecdotal. For instance, a state biologist once told me that wherever pig frogs are hunted they are shy. Beyond that brief statement he had little else to say.

Russell hunts at night and sleeps during the day. His gray hair is cut military style. He wears a pink T-shirt, gray trousers, and high rubber boots. His smile frames three lonely teeth. Russell, fifty-seven years old, was born in Sebastian, Florida, and remembers the Everglades before the Army Engineers rearranged its southward flow. He lives with his ample wife, Eveleen, in a converted school bus set among several trailers in Frog City, an abandoned tourist trap, eight miles west of Dade Corners, the wild fringe of Miami. They have no running water in the bus, so they shower outside, clothes on. An assortment of itinerants—biologists, cane-pole fishermen, turtle-trappers—are the Yateses' temporary neighbors in the lot behind Frog City. One group studies the glades. The other eats out of it. A flock of free-range chickens and a pair of peacocks parade between the trailers. When frogs become scarce Russell and Eveleen park elsewhere. The Yateses are as nomadic as Navajo shepherds.

When Russell was ten he lived in a tent in East Everglades, where he learned to frog. "I done frogging all my life. All my ancestors done it—my daddy, my grandpas, all my uncles. They was into it back in the days of pole boats." Pole boats are short-hulled, boxy boats propelled by a pole pushed against the limestone floor of the Everglades. Russell, however, uses an airboat, the Everglades boat of choice. Powered by a small airplane engine, the wooden propeller mounted above the water and enclosed in wire mesh blows the boat forward. They skim over drying marshes and mats of floating vegetation, plow through walls of cattails, ride up boat ramps and onto trailers, cross parking lots and front lawns, and could, even if at great expense to the hull, go down a road. Where they are in continuous use, vegetation wears down. Short of wading or poling (or canoeing if the water is deep enough), however, there is no other way to travel through the Everglades.

We leave Frog City, April twilight closing in. There is a ring around the moon, half full and directly overhead. Headphones shield my ears against the screaming engine. Russell's ears are bare. This is one of Russell Yates's last frog hunts in East Everglades. The wetland we're coasting over has been purchased by the federal government as an addition to Everglades National Park. It is spring 1994; within a month all commercial use of the 107,000-acre East Everglades will cease. No more airboats. No more frogging. No more turtling. While preserving and restoring the Everglades, the federal government has created a new endangered species, the professional frogger. They have inadvertently destroyed the possibility of a relationship between a man and the night marshes.

Born into the culture of the Everglades, Yates knows these marshes the way few others do. His knowledge, honed on experience and dependence, is not easily passed on. Like a hardscrabble farmer, at the mercy of both the land and the seasons, Yates is bound to the Everglades.

The pig frog population is robust, off-limits in Everglades National Park, and hunted full-time in South Florida by one man. (Recreational frogging is still an enormous resource use in the water conservation areas, and its impact on the central Everglades has never been adequately measured.) Without the understanding and knowledge Russell Yates brings to the table, we are compelled to see the Everglades only through the eyes of science and art, helpful, fascinating, but not necessarily complete.

To spot frogs, Yates wears a headlamp and sweeps his head back and forth, light beam dashing like a rabbit. Russell steers the airboat with his left hand and holds a gig—an eight-foot aluminum version of Poseidon's trident—in his right. His powerful hands and steady hand-eye coordination belie his age. He works the gig, the way Wade Boggs worked a baseball bat. He rarely misses, but when he does, he stares the gig down in disbelief. Russell is a skilled mechanic, which can be lifesaving in the Everglades, and a self-taught naturalist.

The sky is a show of light, not all of it natural. The southern Everglades is glazed by moonlight. Lightning radiates far to the north. To the east, above Miami, the night is a blush of incandescence. The air is cool and filled with song: pig frogs, green tree frogs, cricket frogs, chorus frogs, oak toads. I sit below and in front of Russell, uncomfortable on an upturned grill footrest, an obstacle he has to maneuver his gig around, behind, and over.

"I just love to do this," Russell shouts as we move over the water. "I'm gonna do it till I die. Ya own boss. Nobody tell ya what to do and not to do—but yer ol' lady. But it's got its down side, too. A lot of hours put into it. When frogs runnin' decent, yer huntin' five, six nights a week. Ten hours a night. Thirty years ago, there weren't no levees, no canals. There weren't no Alligator Alley either. Used to leave three-thirty in the afternoon and never drop the throttle until ya passed that highway up yonder. Get there, make a pot of coffee, eat a snack. Sometimes you sit waiting two, three hours for the weather to straighten up. Hunt all night and get back here at eight o'clock the next mornin'. And two hundred, three hundred pounds of leg gotta be dressed and hauled to market. What I need to do is to figure out how to trap frogs. Just set traps out and come run 'em. Wouldn't have to come out here at night. But that would take all the fun out of it."

We aren't out thirty minutes when Russell spots an airboat in distress. "Can't leave nobody out here," he shouts to the frogs and me and then cuts directly for the boat, whose twinkling light looms above the sawgrass. Walking three miles across the East Everglades would take eight to ten hours, assuming you didn't break your ankle, so Russell carries an assortment of spare parts. The passengers, two men and a boy, praise our stopping and then confess their limited understanding of the boat's engine. First Russell replaces the fuel pump. Next, the fuel line. Then he rewires the electrical system. Bored, the boy, a twelve-year-old from nearby Miami, rings a friend on a cell phone. "I'm stuck in the Everglades, and there's no air-conditioning, and the frogs won't shut up," he says despairingly, his nasal voice cracking like a crow's. Coveting the lights of his hometown, which glow in the distance, the boy might as well be stuck on the moon. Bleats and oinks and grunts and clicks and chirps and snores, an amphibious cacophony, come from the edge of the largest freshwater marsh in North America. Everyone but Russell is driven to distraction by mosquitoes.

Once the boat is fixed, Russell heads for a pool of water surrounded by sawgrass—a remnant of northeast Shark Slough—and combs it like an otter trying to flush a bass, crisscrossing, circling, spiraling, a patternless pattern of unbending focus. Sliding across the Everglades in his airboat, Russell can discern the glint of a pig frog's eye from that of a dewdrop. This night he misses only four out of more than one hundred frogs.

"A lot of times ya see one sittin' on the edge of that grass with just his eye sticking out and ya reach in there and poke 'em," he told me. "Might bring out a jolly roaster, cause ya just seeing a piece of the eye. Next time, you reach in there and bring out a little fella."

Pig frogs, also called southern bullfrogs, are big, up to six inches long. They sit on lily pads, bolt upright, olive-green, wide-mouthed, and bug-eyed, or float at the surface, scheming for food. They prefer crayfish but take almost anything they can swallow as long as it moves, including small turtles, snakes, dragonflies, wayward mice, fish, grasshoppers, spiders, and even other pig frogs. Russell once caught one with a full-grown red-winged blackbird crammed in its stomach. "If he's big enough, I think he'd eat you."

Pig frogs prefer the deeper, more permanent sloughs of the Everglades. They mate throughout the rainy season. Males grunt like pigs (hence the name), chorus away from shore, often from lily pads. Tonight, in the auditory shadow of the airboat, I hear nothing but my own thoughts. Eggs are laid en masse on the surface of the water in emergent vegetation, up to eight thousand per frog. Tadpoles hatch in two to three days and take a year to grow four inches before transforming. Every step of the way, from tadpole to adult, a pig frog is fair game for an otter, a bass, a moccasin, or a heron—even for a barred owl. (Oddly, though, alligators avoid frogs of all kinds.)

Yates sticks frogs in the back, the head, the guts, the foot, pushing them below the surface with the barbed prongs of his gig. If one is stuck in the leg, he keeps it for himself, but through the years his appetite for frogs has waned. Four times he impales two hapless frogs in quick succession, frog on frog, contorted. The biggest of the night weighs nearly a pound, and Russell's arm sags as the frog kicks at the end of the eight-foot pole until the gig rests on my shoulder. The frog's fully webbed hind toes spread like a poker hand as Russell strips it into a metal funnel feeding into a net that sits in front of me. Inside the net, the newcomer sets the pile in motion. Frogs in death throes brush my bare feet.

I reach into the net and pull out a dying frog, still twitching. For an animal with such a wide mouth its head is surprisingly narrow. The webbing of the hind feet extend nearly to the tip of each toe. (On the "true" bullfrog, the fourth toe of each hind foot extends well beyond the webbing.) The frog's belly is bright yellow, heavily mottled, and its hind legs appear almost banded, a pattern that varies between individuals. The frog's eyes are gorgeous: iridescent green and gold flecks heavily pepper an iris that separates from the black, elliptical pupil by a narrow gold ring. Beauty, however, does not translate into visual acuity. Like most amphibians, pig frogs are nearsighted.

Several years ago I caught a pig frog in a canal and kept it in my motel room to photograph. The frog spent his idle time in the bathtub. When I returned to the motel the following afternoon, a note pinned to the door read, "Remove frog from bathroom." The manager told me that the housekeeper, a Miccosukee woman about twenty-five years old, slid open the shower curtain, spooking the frog, which jumped and splashed about the tub. The woman, equally spooked, fled the room screaming. My bed remained unmade for several days.

Clouds thicken and line up like a windrow. The moon gleams from the center of the mottled sky. As we cut through a narrow channel in the sawgrass, Russell raises the gig in front of the boat and severs strands of spider webs that stretch above the water. Globular orb weavers swing to the side, away from our faces.

Nothing distracts him. While I spot seven alligators, two of which are five feet long, several night herons, and a bittern, Russell never flinches. "When I'm settled down to huntin'," he says, "I've been where there's four, five gators in the slough with me, and a wave hits me where Ol' John run off. But I ain't lookin' for nothin' but a frog's eye." He's seen everything the Everglades has to offer, including black bears and panthers wading in the sawgrass beneath the southern moon.

The winter of 1991, the heel of Florida's worst drought this century, was a super frog year for Russell, for aquatic animals stacked in the shrinking pools. He dressed 80 to 130 pounds of legs a night. Winter's always best for frogging, he says, for frogs convene in the warmer sloughs, and the brittle sawgrass stays down when you run over it. Summer, by contrast, is wetter, greener, dewier. Frogs disperse then. One night, many years ago, he and Eveleen took 360 pounds of pig frogs by hand from the Lake Okeechobee shallows. Yet sometimes he returns at dawn dog tired with only 10 pounds, the legs barely paying for the airboat's high-octane fuel.

Tonight he brings in more than 30 pounds, finishing his run on the morning side of midnight. When Russell cuts the engine, silence finally comes to the East Everglades. He grabs his catch, shrugs his shoulders, a smoke teetering on his lips, turns to me, and says, "Nobody never figured a frog out."

The snails that hatch from these eggs are hunted
by the shy limpkin and the Everglades kite, that
rare bird known here as the snail-kite. Later we
found some of the shells discarded by birds,
roundish, dark, almost filling the hollow of a
hand and with a bell-like, metallic ring when
dropped in the bottom of the boat.

EDWIN WAY TEALE, 1951

8 Snail Kites

On May 28, 1844, the first snail kite collected in the Everglades for scientific
purposes was shot near the headwaters of the Miami River, the current site
of Miami International Airport. If the marksman could have seen the living
bird's eyes, he might not have pulled the trigger. An adult snail kite's eyes are
metallic, a two-toned red, the color of blood in the center, radiating outward
in points and spears into a pink base. They are eyes irrevocably tied to the
fortunes of Everglades restoration.

Roaming South Florida in an airboat fifteen miles from the nearest road, I
feel like I'm riding behind a combine on a Kansas wheat field. Broken cattails
and sawgrass spray in my face. Spiders, dragonflies, and beetles pummel me.
The boat looks like a mobile muskrat house, piled high with the chaff of the

Everglades. We stop, wedged in tall, spiky sawgrass, and the world becomes quiet. Wild Florida appears untroubled, unhurried, in a state of seamless grace. Time and thoughts lapse. A limpkin wails, wild, weird, eternally sad. I am in the central Everglades to see snail kites, which have been on the federal endangered species list since its creation on March 11, 1967.

I am not disappointed. A steel gray male labors into the wind, head down, searching for apple snails. His bill and legs glow orange in the afternoon light. His rump and undertail coverts are as white as cream. Spotting a snail, the kite hovers, his banded tail teases the wind, feathers flaring. He stoops, a tentative dip, rises, stoops again, and then delicately plucks a snail from just below the surface, barely wetting his toes. Nothing pugnacious here, none of the bluster of the osprey that hit the water's surface a few minutes before, just a handsome hawk, almost tame, a guttural troubadour, whose survival in the United States has been in jeopardy for decades. Rising, the kite transfers his prize from foot to bill, turns into the wind, and disappears into a willow head, rife with anhingas, ibises, and sundry herons.

I am the guest of Rob Bennetts, forty-five, a biologist who has been studying snail kites for eight years, since 1986. I sit in the front of his airboat. An American bittern flushes at the last moment, and the boat, inadvertently and unavoidably, bumps it. I wade into the marsh, momentarily drained of enthusiasm, and retrieve the bittern. Stunned, the bird rallies in my lap and, when released, resumes its stake-straight posture in the sawgrass. Rob silences the boat's screaming engine a hundred yards from a roost of fourteen snail kites.

Kites are loosely communal, which accounts in part for their Latin name, *Rostrhamus sociabilis,* "hook-beaked, gregarious." In November 1993 Rob counted 332 in one willow head not far from where we now sit, and he has recorded nests as close to each other as six feet, though most are aggregated within four hundred feet. A month and a half later, I would see five active nests in one small willow head, and the following December, 402 kites in the largest winter roost ever recorded.

A second dark kite passes, a snail in his bill. He gives a couple of frog-sounding calls, *ker-wak, ker-wak,* a half-hearted attempt to entice a female off her perch. Then he tucks his wings, drops five or six feet, rises stiffly, flapping down from the horizontal like an upside down limpkin. She is oblivious. So he stops showing off, settles on a willow snag, and eats the snail himself. When the breeding season is in full swing, usually in February, but sometimes later if cold fronts have rendered snails less active, no male is ignored. Then females crave attention, begging for snails in a soft, whining cackle. Dutifully the male provides most of his mate's food, defends her against interlopers, chooses the nest site, and builds most of the nest himself. This novel arrangement, where the male invests so much energy in courtship and nesting, is believed to be a by-product of the vagaries of the Everglades. If a nest fails, which happens frequently—more than half the seventy-three nests Bennetts monitored in the Everglades last year failed—the female quickly renests. And why not? She just hangs out eating her admirer's tributes and converts snails to eggs while the hot sun wanders across the Florida sky.

Rob Bennetts's mahogany-tanned face emerges from a wrap of curly salt-and-pepper-colored hair and beard and presides over an ursine body. For a large man, he possesses uncommon stamina. His breath is perpetually labored, and his forehead is usually bathed in sweat. He often toils from before sunrise to well after dark—on the computer, in the field, and on the telephone. Engineers, water managers, biologists, administrators, newspaper reporters, and park service naturalists leave messages on his answering machine, seeking his advice, his opinion, and his time. He answers the most critical messages, those that concern aspects of Everglades restoration—spraying alien trees or the breaching of a levee, for instance—and their possible effect on nesting kites, from a cell phone while deep in the Everglades. His thick, steady hands band, draw blood samples from, and radio-tag kites—a procedure he calls "processing." Rob Bennetts is witty, focused, and thoughtful, an eloquent advocate for the Everglades and snail kites.

He grew up in the Bay Area of California, far removed from Florida water politics. His grandmother, who was ambivalent about nature, gave him a field guide to birds. The gift proved fortuitous. A reluctant student who prefers the field, Rob has completed a doctoral program at the University of Florida. He radiates information and thrives on the tie between research and interpretation, particularly in the Everglades, where restoration depends on the sympathy of an educated public. When I told him how a park service naturalist had incorporated his fieldwork into her Shark Valley tram tour, he beamed. Another Everglades ranger, who had just returned from a stint in the field with Bennetts, declared, "If everyone in the park service had his work ethic, this would be one efficient operation."

Rob is here to catch and radio-tag a kite, a difficult proposition without an active nest to lure an adult within range of his net gun. Like the man, the gun is big—in his hands it looks like a space-age blunderbuss—and fires a ten-foot triangular nylon net fixed to three padded projectiles. Because he attempts to net the kite on the wing, Rob calls this strategy "L.A. drive-by shooting." It is more sport than science, a rodeo. We swerve around a lone pond apple and flush a snail kite; the airboat races and skids like a disc on ice. Rob relinquishes control of the boat and puts the gun to his shoulder. To steady the boat, I twist in my seat and grab the steering rod, my principal assignment. As Rob fires, I peek under my arm to see the kite, aided by a brisk Caribbean breeze, flick his tail and fly on. The net floats down like a child's toy. Eight times during the afternoon, Rob fires and misses.

Around us is a cacophony of giggling moorhens. Rob and I have become the laughingstock of Water Conservation Area 3, the largest remaining tract of Everglades, an impounded wetland managed by the South Florida Water Management District. At 950 square miles, Water Conservation Area 3 is three-fourths the size of Rhode Island, a roughly rectangular mosaic of marsh plants. Like foam insulation jackets, thick, tan-colored mats of periphyton litter the open water and cling to submerged stems of spike rush. Tree islands pepper the marshland. Alligators live in black pools dug in the midst of the largest heads. The elevation at the western end of Water Conservation Area 3 rises slightly, grading into Big Cypress Swamp, and forms one of the rims of the Everglades. Here a dwarf cypress forest supports half a dozen snail kite nests.

When Rob fires up the airboat, I adjust my headphones, and my attention drifts back and forth between the vastness of the Everglades and our expand-ing, contracting shadows on the watery land. Open water mirrors the sky, reflects herons and egrets lifting off the surface—tranquillity framed in high-octane noise. At this stage in my tutorial, to recognize the watery reflection of a snail kite is beyond my capabilities.

Snail kites are nomadic. Unlike many species of hawks, which may use the same nest site for years, kites do not have a strong attachment to a particular breeding area. Florida's entire population of snail kites, which once extended throughout the state, is one large unit that now depends on a much reduced network of habitats in Central and South Florida. The number of birds in each subpopulation fluctuates according to the availability of snails. When an individual habitat within the network fails to provide food, kites drift to whichever area offers the most snails. In 1994 Water Conservation Area 2B catered to the largest concentration of kites. When apple snails become scarce, a few kites may continue to eke out a living, perhaps skipping a breeding season; the rest either disperse or perish. Hence, the distribution of snail kites is dynamic, booming and busting like the Everglades itself.

Drought is both common and crucial in the Everglades, so the issue is not whether an area will be dry, but when and for how long. Because snail kites depend on apple snails, which in turn depend on long wet periods, the birds have adopted a strategy: they maintain one unbroken population that shifts constantly to areas of deep water. Everywhere else in the range of this species—in Central and South America—the wet and dry cycles are more predictable and so, presumably, is the kites' whereabouts. But here at the northern edge of their distribution, they respond to a fickle habitat.

Rob's banding and radio-tagging records bear this out. In mid-March, as a living cloud of dragonflies rises from a knot of the sawgrass, we slide up to a kite nest in a lonely pond apple. A male flies in, a stick in his mouth. Perched above the nest, his brown and white mate sports a white-numbered green leg band, which means she hatched on the shore of Lake Kissimmee, more than 150 miles north. Later in the afternoon, Rob spots a red-over-yellow banded female, a kite from Lake Tohopekaliga, almost 200 miles away. Several days later we find a nest in a gnarled willow. The resident female wears a black band, number 69. Rob is delighted, for this bird was banded shortly after the inauguration of Jimmy Carter. She's eighteen years old, still breeding, and still peripatetic. He radio-tagged her 50 miles northeast of here two years ago, then tracked her to Lake Okeechobee. When he lost her signal last year, he assumed she had died. A vagabond exquisitely tuned to the fortunes of the Everglades, Black 69 is also a Methuselah among snail kites, the oldest ever recorded in the wild.

An alternative demographic view held by several biologists is that Florida snail kites live in a series of primary habitats. During severe drought the birds move to secondary habitats called refugia, where snails are available but limited. Once the drought ends, surviving kites will return to their primary habitats. Taking this notion one step further, federal wildlife managers assumed that if the primary habitat were permanently inundated, kites would be favored. But subsequent research has shown that prolonged inundation alters the aquatic communities; bay heads give way to willow heads, and eventually, willow heads phase out. *Sagittaria* and sawgrass, the emergent marshland plants upon which snails attach their clusters of round, white, BB-sized eggs, yield to floating plants. And whatever affects snails directly affects snail kites.

When the Army Engineers developed four alternative models to help restore historic water distribution patterns to Everglades National Park, a small war between government agencies began. Snail kites lay at the heart of the controversy. The four proposals ranged from doing nothing, which would allow the Everglades to die, to removing the parallel levees in Water Conservation Area 3A and pumping water from 3A to 3B south through Shark Slough, which would echo the original sheet flow.

Fish and Wildlife Service—the government agency legally mandated to protect critical habitat for endangered species—favored the plan that would always maintain a small but appropriate kite habitat during drought. After a series of meetings with biologists and hydrologists from the South Florida Water Management District, the Fish and Wildlife Service, and the National Park Service, however, the Corps settled on the plan that attempted to replicate the sheet flow.

In response the Fish and Wildlife Service issued a jeopardy opinion against the plan. According to the agency, restoring sheet flow to Shark Slough would adversely affect the southern part of Water Conservation Area 3A as a kite refugia. They *had* to manage the impoundment for a single species, a compartmentalized approach that threw a wrench into the gears of Everglades restoration. For a brief, ugly moment, the Fish and Wildlife Service squared off against the park service, its sister agency in the Department of the Interior. The park service—a tenet of which is to preserve the integrity of whole eco-systems—lobbied for a natural hydrologic regime, a system driven by rain.

In an effort to sidestep the jeopardy opinion, the park service unsuccessfully attempted to draft legislation that would have exempted Everglades restoration from the Endangered Species Act. "People are always afraid of extremes; they always look for an annual mean," says John Ogden, of the South Florida Water Management District. "But in nature that mean can only be found over a number of years. I say let things run amok." Rob Bennetts, who was funded by the park service and the Fish and Wildlife Service to settle the speculative ideas about what influences snail kite dispersal and mortality, agrees. The so-called primary areas are not permanent; they rotate throughout several thousand square miles of marshlands as the availability of snails changes. Surprisingly erratic and simultaneously predictable, snail kite dispersal is mutable. "The more I study the bird," says Rob, "the more I revise my opinion." Thanks to Bennetts's work, which showed that distribution of snail kites is fluid, the disagreement between the agencies has been resolved, and kites are no longer a major factor in determining which water distribution plan to follow.

Today we reach Lake Okeechobee before sunrise and launch the airboat from Moore Haven's public ramp. A forest of melaleuca flanks the canal that leads into the lake. Rounded melaleuca heads extend into the littoral zone. A snail kite lifts from a gray melaleuca limb. By my standards Okeechobee is too weedy to be a lake and too big to be a pond. We lose our way momentarily in some dense stands of phragmites and cattails that have proliferated since Rob's last visit, crowding out native rushes and arrowhead and filling open water. Using a Global Positioning System unit, Rob determines that we are west of our destination. As we head due east through a wall of invasive cattails, the airboat becomes embedded in mounds of last year's growth. Rocking the boat, we hack at brittle stalks. Families of moorhens skitter out of our way.

We mark four kite nests, three in willow, one in buttonbush. An unbanded female, a bird of unknown age and origin, sits on a willow snag, calling, *ka, ka, ka, ka, ka, ka*. Rob fires the net gun. Just as the bird takes off, the net hangs her in the willow, upside down and angry. Deftly Rob untangles the kite and hands her to me. To hold a bird I have rarely seen, a feathered expression of the climatic whims of the Everglades, is an honor. I place the kite headfirst in a specially adapted two-liter plastic Pepsi container, a gentle and secure bivouac that nevertheless seems sacrilegious. Rob weighs her: 428 grams, slightly less than a pound. I work the back of my hand against the belly, grasping her legs between my thumb and forefinger. Her heart pulsates against my knuckles. Her brood patch warms my wrist. Somewhere in the twisted willows her breast down decorates a nest. The nape of the kite's neck is slate gray, grading to brown. Her chin, rump, undertail coverts, and the base and tip of her tail are cream-white. A white line extends above both eyes. The belly and chest are streaked brown. Her talons are long, sharp, and weak for a raptor; her bill is slender and deeply curved. The kite submits as Rob first rings one leg with an aluminum United States Fish and Wildlife Service band and then the other with a black plastic band.

Rob carefully dresses the kite with a tiny radio transmitter attached to a harness, slipping a loop of thin Teflon ribbon—expensive, at more than two dollars per foot—over her head and under her wings. He ties it off, checks the fit, then epoxies the knot, placing tiny cardboard wedges between her feathers and the knots. I hold the bird, still hooded, upright in my lap while the epoxy dries. When we release her, ten minutes later, the radio transmitter and antenna lie flat on her back. Rob assures me that although saddled by technology, the kite will live a normal life. Within a few hours, he says, she'll preen the ribbon under her feathers.

On the way to Moonshine Bay we flush hundreds of moorhens and a least bittern. The bay's littoral zone seems to stretch forever. Open water lies somewhere out there, beyond sight. Rob hopes to radio-tag a hundred birds this year, sixty adults and forty juveniles. He needs a sample large enough to help unravel the mysteries of kite dispersal and mortality. No one has radio-tagged more snail kites than Rob Bennetts. Adult birds, though harder to catch, are the most important parameter in a survival study.

Seven kites forage for snails above the rushes and white water lilies, whose leaves flash red whenever a gust of wind lifts a corner. Goaded by the wind, the birds drift slowly toward us. Near the cattails, two males dive, then slowly rise, almost in unison, then fall, rise, fall, like yo-yos. Two females, the object of their affections, sit on exposed willow limbs, begging with a compressed cry that excites Rob as much as the kites. One gray bird plucks a snail from the water, transfers it to his bill, then gives it away to a female, who, sensing an impending gift, flies to him, croaking softly like a frog.

A third female kite hunts for herself, methodically combing the flats. She spots a snail, stoops, captures, switches, all the while flying smoothly toward a buttonbush snag. Landing, she holds the snail against the perch, spire down, aperture up. First she twists off the operculum, the hard disc that seals the snail in its shell, flipping it aside; then she works the tip of her long, slender, deeply hooked upper bill into the shell, severing the columellar muscle, which attaches the snail to the shell. The shell falls. The arc of a kite's upper bill mirrors the spire of the snail's shell—it always twists to the left—a perfectly honed lock and key arrangement.

Rob has watched a snail kite attempt to remove the shell of a musk turtle, a small chelonian not much bigger than a large apple snail. Pressing the turtle to the branch, the kite entered the shell through the right rear leg, which vaguely resembles a snail's aperture, and pruned meat for nearly an hour. When apple snails are scarce kites have been reported dining on three other species of turtles, a cotton rat, a dead American coot, a white perch, and a ring-necked snake.

On the way home from the Lake, Rob checks his answering machine. The South Florida Water Management District wants to know the location of nests in Water Conservation Area 2B so that its melaleuca removal crew doesn't bother the birds. Rob responds immediately.

Holey Lands Wildlife Management Area, 35,350 acres of abused wetlands sandwiched between Water Conservation Area 3A and the Everglades Agricultural Area, served as a bombing range during World War II. Literally the land is "holey," pocked by repeated detonations. Towering sawgrass grew here, whose lacerating edges once held men at bay. Broken by few sloughs, spotted by few islands, this was part of the fabled sea of grass, dense beyond belief. Then came flood control. Water destined for Holey Lands ran down canals. The sun seared the marshland. Sawgrass yielded to willows and wax myrtle; white-tailed deer, a marginal species at best before diversion, began to prosper. Hunters rejoiced. In an attempt to restore Holey Lands to more natural hydrologic conditions, the Florida Fish and Wildlife Conservation Commission installed two pump stations in 1990 to move water south from the Everglades Agricultural Area. At first the deeper, nutrient-rich water favored *Sagittaria,* which was quickly followed by a mushrooming population of apple snails. In 1991 Holey Lands hosted between twenty-five and fifty nesting pairs of snail kites, an enchanted and ephemeral hot spot that was abandoned the following year.

Cattails followed. Since 1990 Holey Lands' meager one hundred acres of cattails have expanded to more than six thousand acres. Although cattails are native to the glades, enhanced by the nutrient loads in a gator hole or beneath a heron rookery, the primeval Everglades was oligotrophic, as nutrient poor as a glacial lake. Rob has noticed a lag phase that aids apple snails at the onset of a nutrient overload. "*Sagittaria* is very good habitat for snails," he says. There is an early phase in the nutrient overload that favors blooms of *Sagittaria*, which in turn favors apple snails. Eventually cattails spread at the expense of everything else. Like aging athletes, sawgrass and *Sagittaria* lose their competitive edge when phosphorous is pumped into the system. Ultimately kites loose their foraging grounds, an inverse relationship between the bird and the presence of high nutrients that plays itself out wherever fertilized water enters the Everglades. In 1993 only two pairs of snail kites nested in Holey Lands.

《《《

For hawks, snail kites have an unusually high reproductive potential. Some birds breed as yearlings; some produce two broods in a bountiful snail year. It is to their advantage to be fruitful, because the periodic droughts are devastating—on average more than 80 percent of all kite nests fail to produce young during droughts. During wet years, three to five weeks after hatching, when the young are nearly full-grown, one parent may desert the family, choose another mate, and nest again: An odd behavior known to ornithologists as ambisexual mate desertion. The forsaken parent then raises the young alone. Snail kites are the only polygamous bird species in which either sex will abandon one family and start another. According to kite biologist Steve Beissinger, who first reported this behavior, the single-parent families usually succeed. From an evolutionary standpoint, ambisexual mate desertion maximizes the birds' opportunity to produce young during a wet year, for sooner or later a drought will visit.

It is mid-April, peak of the nesting season. Kite chicks have begun to hatch. Everything is greener than in March. Rob puts in at Sawgrass Fishing Camp on Water Conservation Area 2B, then threads the airboat between islands of melaleuca, searching for marked nests in a superficially monotonous landscape. Outdoor writer Charles Richard Dodge said, a century ago, "It is not safe to enter the glades without a guide, on account of danger of bewilderment. . . ."

Fortunately I have a guide whose sense of direction is uncanny—he moves day or night across trackless marshland to isolated islands and lonely shrubs. Rob skids directly to a nest in a stunted pond apple.

What besides drought kills kites? A week before Rob had found the head and feathers of an adult female in a nest, probably the work of a great horned owl. A chick huddled alongside its mother's head. Last year a bass fisherman interrupted a water moccasin while it swallowed a nearly full-grown chick. Yellow rat snakes eat eggs and chicks, as do boat-tailed grackles, which often nest in the midst of kite colonies. Black-crowned night herons, marsh hawks, and red-shouldered hawks are all potential predators.

Although he does everything in his power not to injure kites, Rob himself once contributed to kite mortality. He lost his first kite when a net projectile broke a male's wing, and it died of shock the following morning. The death of one snail kite, though regrettable, is an admirable record, considering that Bennetts has handled more than a thousand birds.

Still, the bird's death constricts Rob. He is tense whenever we process birds, which today number fifteen, twelve juveniles and three adults. He cannot wait until nesting is over, when he has a chance to mellow, admonishing me to "please don't take anything personal, I'm thinking only of the bird." Over the next ten days I adjust to ornithological boot camp.

Like Holey Lands, Water Conservation Area 2B is a zone of abused sawgrass. I wade to a nest set in the midst of a willow head, tightrope walking along submerged limbs, mindful of alligators and moccasins—which I never see—and carrying a telescoping aluminum pole fixed with a mirror. I probe the nest like a dentist. Two chicks. Then replace the mirror with a net and press the net against the belly of the closest chick forcing it to step in. Once the bird is aboard, I sweep the net over my head and pass it to Rob.

The juvenile snail kites look like adult females except that their facial markings, tail bands, and mottled undersides are rusty yellow, not white. Tail feathers are three-quarters of their full length, and wing feathers still erupt from their sheaths. Blooms of russet decorate the ends of each contour feather, spangling the kites in warm earthy tones. Their eyes are dark, their legs yellow.

After both chicks are banded, I airlift the smallest to the nest. The other, a squawker, I hold overhead in the net to draw the adult male inside the range of the net gun. The ruse fails. I jiggle the second chick off the net, back into the nest. The male settles on a willow limb, waiting, molten eyes defiant. He stays as the airboat slowly approaches. Rob fires the net gun, and the gray bird hangs from a limb, tangled in nylon mesh. Diligently Rob works the net and the kite out of the willows. A talon slices his face below the eye. Blood trickles down his cheek. The snail kite becomes Black 9, a bird of unknown origin. He weighs 410 grams, less than some juvenile females we radio-tagged. I place the bird face up on my thighs. Rob opens the kite's left wing, finds a vein, and takes a blood sample that will be sent to the University of Florida to be checked for internal parasites. Rob then weaves the radio transmitter over the bird's head, around his wings.

The next day on the way to Loxahatchee National Wildlife Refuge I ask Rob about the counts that placed the United States population of snail kites at fewer than twenty-five birds in the 1950s, a figure that still haunts publications four decades later and suggests that kites could disappear from Florida in a nanosecond. "I have a very hard time trusting those old counts. Back then there was no radio-tracking. Biologists would estimate the population after a one-day plane flight. Now it takes us three weeks, and we always miss a few radio-tagged birds."

Loxahatchee is 220 square miles of tall sawgrass and innumerable tree islands between Lake Okeechobee and Palm Beach, the last remnant of Hillsboro Lake. Fred Broerman, one of Loxahatchee's three biologists, joins us. A willowy, bearded man, Fred sits in front of Rob to help navigate. I sit on the port side, legs draped over the gunwale. Sawgrass snaps back in my face. Green tree frogs, anoles, countless jumping spiders, orb weavers, ants, beetles, and weevils land in my lap. Dragonflies cling to my hair. I hide my face from the slapping, stinging wall of greenery that passes before me. Scraps of sawgrass and cattail collect on me. Eventually I'm buried to my chest in debris.

Because this backcountry is closed to the public, we see no one. Peat twelve feet deep produces sawgrass ten feet tall; thousands of small red bay and dahoon holly heads, clusters of small, gnarled shrubs, float on mats of peat. Rob carefully picks our route, threading between islands, selecting two or three alternatives to reach our destination. Often he backtracks, consults Fred, a map, and the heavens. I spend my time tossing armfuls of stems and leaves out of the airboat, a fruitless task.

Pairs of mottled ducks rise from the sloughs, turquoise wing-patches gleaming. A green tree frog lands on my foot. Spiders cover the hull and fasten webs down from the gunwale; blades of snapping sawgrass quickly destroy the webs, and blindly obedient, the spiders rebuild, again and again, all day. A second tree frog, brown as the airboat, turns green on my foot. So does an anole. When I grab the lizard, it turns mostly brown; where my fingers touch it, it stays green. A doe in waist-deep water wades into a slough. An unseen alligator bellows.

Rob spots a kite nest in a buttonbush and abruptly shifts direction. Both chicks flush. The larger one labors over the water and crash-lands at the base of a red bay. The bird weighs 420 grams, the largest juvenile we've caught so far, probably a female, and the first kite ever radio-tagged in Loxahatchee. Fred is ecstatic, but the kite remains stoic, brown eyes glaring. We capture and band the smaller, less active chick and return both birds to the nest. Several miles to the west Rob spots a banded adult female. For more than hour he stalks the kite, trying to read the number on her band in a spotting scope. Using a bay head for cover, the airboat finally creeps into range: Red, OD, a Lake Okeechobee bird. As the kite flushes, she lowers and draws her legs stiffly back. A stream of guano squirts across the marsh.

A mixed flock of a thousand wading birds lifts into the afternoon. We pause; the airboat is silent. Conditioned to the noise of the engine we continue to shout. Cattail down sticks to the hairs on my arms and face like laundry lint.

I prefer the openness of the central Everglades, the broad plains of brown and green sawgrass cut by sloughs, to the tight, island-framed views of Loxahatchee. I like the water lilies and the purple-flowering bladderwort. They promise subtle treasures, string lilies or spider lilies or skeins of orange and black dragonflies flitting in the sun. The overarching sky, so wide and round, gives the vast marshes a hint of the primeval. I struggle to define the Everglades by what I see, not by what is missing. I hear tourists in the national park wonder, "What's so special about this park? Where're all the birds?"

Rob had spent much of the morning carefully shaping, stitching, and gluing Teflon ribbon into harnesses for new radio transmitters in hope of netting birds today. It is an activity that requires such deep concentration that he asked me to eat breakfast outside the trailer while he worked. At our first nest, a large, flightless chick leaps out. While Rob gathers the banding gear, I go after the kite, a task I have performed several dozen times. Chicks always freeze close to the nest. I search in vain. Ten minutes elapse. Frustrated, Rob asks me if I stepped on the bird. The image of a kite pressed into Everglades peat is unsettling. Visibly distressed, he silently begins his own reconnaissance. Where is the bird? Rob's dedication is legendary—there is no way we are leaving without accounting for this chick. Stress mounts by the minute. He squats in my tracks and like a disgruntled dowitcher plumbs the peat with his arm. I didn't step on the kite; I know I didn't. When Rob's hand emerges empty, I inwardly rejoice. Ten minutes later he finds the chick cowering below the nest, precisely where we thought it had been, perfectly camouflaged, a fearful bundle of down. Too small for a radio, the chick is banded and returned to its nest.

Five o'clock, Thursday evening, April 21. I am flying with pilot Karen Dunne, of Wyatt Aviation, on the weekly survey for fourteen radioed snail kites that Rob believes are somewhere in either Water Conservation Area 3A or Everglades National Park. Karen is delighted to have me in the plane. Rob takes up too much room, she jokes.

From the air the central Everglades appears much wetter than the national park, just across the Tamiami Trail, whose water it hordes. Airboat trails of flattened vegetation, which will endure as long as recreational boats are permitted in the conservation areas, lace through the mats of periphyton and the stands of sawgrass and spike rush. Willow heads glow in the afternoon light. South of the Tamiami Trail, the land adjacent to the Shark Slough is drier and punctuated by outcrops of oolitic limestone. Although rock lurks just below the surface in the East Everglades portion of the Shark Slough, the slough itself stands out as a string of giant puddles studded by hardwood hammocks interspersed with patches of sawgrass and spike rush. Below me is a variegation of green: gray-green, light green, yellow-green, brown-green, deep green. One by one we catch the radio frequencies of the kites, eleven of fourteen and one "lost" bird, a female from Water Conservation Area 2B that beeps back to us south of the Shark Valley observation tower. Karen buzzes a hammock where the day before she had picked up the frequency of a radio-collared Florida panther, number 16, a male that circulates between Big Cypress and Shark Valley. For a dreamy moment, she thinks she sees a tawny cat, motionless in a fringe of sawgrass. When the plane dips for a closer look, a doe splashes away.

Rob knows that kites will be monitored long after he leaves South Florida. Although the Everglades would certainly survive the absence of snail kites— other, more numerous, birds, notably limpkins and boat-tailed grackles, eat apple snails—the kite population is a barometer of the region's health. Because wood storks breed in northern Florida and Georgia, and white ibises, in South Carolina and Louisiana, their survival is influenced by factors outside of South Florida's suite of ecosystems. But the North American population of snail kites is Everglades dependent. Like pulling a thread from a tapestry, their loss would be tragic, but not catastrophic. Pull enough threads, however, and the tapestry unravels.

The alligator dominated the freshwater marshes
of South Florida much as did the buffalo on the
Great Plains before white man appeared.

FRANK C. CRAIGHEAD, 1968

9 Alligators

Using their faces as shovels and their tails as plows, industrious alligators once kept hundreds of thousands of depressions in the bedrock limestone open by uprooting vegetation and reaming out muck. Their collective busyness created life-giving pools in an otherwise dry winter landscape. Called gator holes, these havens once pitted the peripheral marshes of the southern Everglades and were used for centuries, perhaps millennia, by countless generations of alligators.

Although many holes appeared large during the wet season, more than twenty feet across and three or four feet deeper than the adjacent marsh, during the dry season they shrank and became a bower for Everglades wildlife, where a few of each species survived to the wet season. A writer for *Life* once described a gator hole as "a sort of Noah's arc in reverse," and a "killing field," where predators feasted on trapped prey. During the winter, gator holes supported a jubilee of fish, turtles, frogs, grass shrimp, crayfish, snails, aquatic insect larva, water snakes, mink, otter, and round-tailed muskrats. Raccoons, opossums, gray foxes, and bobcats stalked the edges. Panthers stopped by on their endless quest for deer. Birds—herons, ibises, storks, anhingas, rails, hawks, owls, crows, grackles, grebes, ducks, gallinules, moorhens, rails, vireos, warblers, wrens—fed in or around the water. When the May rains revived the surrounding marshes, the animals left the gator holes and repopulated the Everglades. And what price did the reptilian landlord exact for providing a drought-free refuge? Just a meal or two each week.

Because Florida's colossal drainage schemes severely dried the peripheral wetlands, alligator populations have shifted from the edges of the Everglades toward its center. Today the reptiles and their holes are common in the sloughs and sawgrass and rare in the marl prairies. From the air most gator holes are easy to spot: brown pools circumscribed by small green trees. Trails in the marsh, cut by the alligator's low-slung body, radiate from each hole. From the inside, these biological microcosms are another world.

Late one evening several years ago, while Rob Bennetts and I were tracking snail kites, Rob slammed his airboat into a bay head in the central Everglades. We never found a kite, but inside the weft of trees a six-foot alligator and at least half a dozen black-and-yellow-striped yearlings loitered in opaque water, eyes barely above the water. A pied-billed grebe bobbed on the surface like a tub toy. A white-eyed vireo crooned from a tree. A small plane passed overhead, and the mother alligator roared. As darkness gathered, dozens of birds came to roost in the willows and bays. Even these trees, rooted along the rim of the hole in debris pushed up by the gator, owed a debt of gratitude to the reptile. By nightfall the birds fell silent, and the mother gator circled her hole, her eyes shining an otherworldly red in the beam of my flashlight.

Walking into a gator hole is a primal experience. The water is dark and cool; the muck is soft and squishy. In February the red flowers of bromeliads decorate the gaunt gray cypress trees. Cricket frogs call from the shallows and pop up whenever you take a step. There might be a snake coiled on a cypress knee, or a dozen egrets in the canopy. I have found red-shouldered hawks nesting above the open water, a barred owl hooting, and green lizards fixed to Spanish moss. Sometimes an alligator basks on the edge of the hole in leaf-filtered light, or floats in the water, but most of the time when I visit it is hidden in a cave dug under the bank.

During the first half of the last century, when water levels were low, men who lived along the margins of the Everglades hunted alligators in their caves.

The reptile's hide was prized for leather belts and shoes. To find an alligator, hunters would prod the ground with an iron rod, searching for the hollowed-out cave. Once the cave was located, one man would poke the gator in an attempt to persuade it to leave the cave. If the animal stuck its head out, a second man gaffed the jaw with a metal hook; then a third man split the base of the gator's neck with an ax, what Glen Simmons calls "stickering." If a cantankerous alligator refused to leave its den, a man waded into the water and thrust into the cave a hook attached to a long cypress pole. When the gator bit the hook, the unfortunate man grappled the beast out of its cave—never an easy task—and then dispatched him with the ax.

I do not have the patience to wait for gators to emerge from their caves. They can stay hidden for days or weeks at a time, their sophisticated almost four-chambered hearts (a flap of skin covers the hole in the ventricle) and walnut-sized brains keeping pace to Cretaceous rhythms. Once I found a seven-foot gator at home, hauled up on the rim of his world, battle-weary and grim, like a tree dying a branch at a time. The alligator was missing most of his lower jaw, torn off by a bigger, meaner, more dominant bull. He was so emaciated that every rib pushed against his leathery sides, and his tail, the prime region for storing fat, was more bone than muscle. A cloud of flies swirled around the rotted meat of his lower jaw. His breaths were so few and shallow—a couple per minute at most—that I half expected him to die while I watched. When I approached within ten feet, the alligator summoned a series of steam-pipe-hisses—psss, psss, psss—but could not muster the strength to leave the bank. Letting him perish in peace, I backed away. A week later the alligator was gone, and in his absence a robust five-footer ruled the hole. Reptilian inheritance follows ancient lines.

Alligators also kept open the upper reaches of the tidal creeks that drain the Everglades, clearing the creeks of mangrove seedlings and etching trails into the freshwater marshes, thus enabling aquatic creatures to move between the Everglades and the mangrove jungles. During the winter these ribbons of deeper water functioned as long gator holes and attracted wading birds that gorged on fish. Some biologists believe that the abundance of fish in the creeks may have been the reason wading bird rookeries were set in the upper reaches of the mangroves, where Shark Slough splinters into a maze of tributaries. From the air, there is no mistaking this alligator-enhanced landscape: creeks flanked by mangroves radiating into the lower Everglades like so many crooked fingers. Even at the height of the dry season, from a canoe you can still find dozens of birds along Rookery Branch working the schools of fish half hidden in the labyrinthine prop roots. Though a few gators still muddy the creeks, the artificially reduced flow of freshwater from the north has turned the mangrove jungles more saline, an anathema to alligators, which do not have salt removal glands. Without an adequate flow of freshwater from the Everglades, most of the alligators have disappeared, the creeks have clogged, the biomass of fish has dwindled, the rookeries have disbanded, and the downstream estuaries have disconnected from the freshwater marshes.

When most people think of the Everglades, they think of alligators. And when most people think of alligators, they think of leathery, roguish beasts that feed indiscriminately on anything that blunders into the water: poodles, deer, cows, and, sometimes, people. Although on rare occasions a panhandling gator that has lost its fear of humans grabs a child—in 1993, one killed a ten-year-old boy on the Loxahatchee River—the ferocity of alligators is more myth than fact. And many of the myths go back more than four centuries.

The Spanish called the beast "*el lagarto*," meaning "the lizard," which eventually became corrupted to "alligator." In 1591 Jacques LeMoyne de Morgues, living in French Florida, called the alligator a "monster" and published a picture that showed the indigenous people battling a titanic beast. His caption suggested that much of the aborigines' time was spent battling alligators. The morbid tales of laundrywomen snatched from the banks of the rivers that flowed through the colonial south portrayed the alligator more like the Nile crocodile, with its appetite for human flesh, than the unique American reptile.

In 1791 naturalist-author William Bartram set the standard for alligator fear when he wrote *Travels,* his classic memoir of his exploration of the southeastern wilderness. Describing a feeding orgy on the St. Johns River, Bartram wrote, "The horrid noise of their closing jaws, their plunging amidst the broken banks of fish, and rising with their prey some feet upright above the water, the floods of water and blood rushing out of their mouths, and the clouds of vapor issuing from their wide nostrils, were truly frightful." Alligators scared the hell out of Bartram. After witnessing bull gators settle a territorial dispute, he confessed, "I expected every moment to be dragged out of the boat and instantly devoured."

Fear and loathing aside, alligator natural history is fascinating. They are temperate-climate crocodilians, which sets them apart from their decidedly tropical cousins, caimans and crocodiles. Alligators first appeared in the fossil record during the twilight of the dinosaurs, seventy million years ago, and have changed very little in the interim, though presumably there were more of them back then, since swamps covered much of the Earth. There are two surviving species: *Alligator mississippiensis* and the shorter, stockier *A. sinensis,* which is confined to freshwater marshes of China's Yangtze delta. The American alligator appeared in the southeast two million years ago, evolving from, and later replacing, *A. olseni,* which had enjoyed a twenty-million-year tenure. Today alligators live along an arc of coastal plain that runs from the mouth of the Rio Grande to nearly the Virginia line and northward in the Mississippi River Valley to southern Arkansas and west to southeast Oklahoma.

Adult alligators are as dark as the mud from which they rise. Their throats are white to creamy-yellow, and their sides and tails are faintly banded white. They have broad shovelish snouts, and their teeth are set in jawbone sockets. Though the largest alligator ever measured was a nineteen-foot monster killed in Louisiana, today fourteen feet is considered big. Even though the growing season is virtually twelve months long in South Florida, in the nutrient-poor Everglades large alligators rarely exceed ten feet.

The alligator is the quintessential aquatic reptile. Each eye is retractable and covered by a moveable, gogglelike transparent membrane; its eyelid is tough as steel and virtually impenetrable when closed. When underwater, the alligator can close its nostrils and its moveable earlid, and a wide flap of flesh seals off its throat so that it won't drown when wrestling prey underwater. An alligator can control its blood flow, stopping circulation to its lungs when it is submerged. Like mammals and birds, each alligator has a diaphragm, ten cranial nerves, and a complete palate that allows it to breath through its nostrils and eat at the same time. Its eighty hollow teeth are continuously replaced throughout its life, and its powerful jaws deliver a bite pressure of more than three thousand pounds per square inch, both advantages for an animal that often eats turtles. Archie Carr reported that alligators "goaded into biting steel pipes have been know to crush their own teeth or to drive them up through the top of their skull." Yet every Miccosukee alligator wrestler knows this essential truth: the muscles that open the animal's mouth are not very strong; you can easily hold an alligator's mouth closed with your hands.

To swim, an alligator sculls its tail and undulates its body, legs held against its sides. To walk, it either lumbers along, dragging its tail, or rises on its toes. The heels of its hind feet and most of its tail are held off the ground, and it can rush forward at thirty miles per hour for a short distance.

Several years ago a nine-foot alligator regularly left Eco Pond, the sewage lagoon in Flamingo, walked across the park service campground, and crawled into the gray lap of Florida Bay. The animal moved eastward up the coast for a mile or so, entered the Buttonwood Canal, and swam to the marina. There it hung around the fish-cleaning station for a few days, fattening on the heads and guts of snappers and redfish before retracing its route. One afternoon I shadowed the plump alligator out of the bay and across the campground. It walked high on its toes, and except for the tip, the tail arced off the ground. Every so often the alligator collapsed on the grass for a few minutes, seemingly to regain its strength or to catch its breath—or both. Like the Pied Piper, the animal attracted such a crowd of children that a ranger was dispatched to the scene to prevent trouble. The alligator cut a straight course to the pond, across the campground lawn, through a thicket of Brazilian pepper, over the road (where another ranger stopped traffic), under the boardwalk, and into the water. It rested so often that I have questioned the stamina of alligators ever since.

That the alligator is a musical reptile did not escape William Bartram, who, after hearing them emote, wrote, "You can scarcely be persuaded but that the whole globe is violently and dangerous agitated." Then Bartram left his readers this memorable line: "The earth trembles with his thunder." What so moved William Bartram was the alligator's bellow, the closed-mouthed roar that can be heard more than a mile away. Both the male and the female bellow (the voice of the female is higher), either on land or in water. Although alligators call at any month of the year, they more frequently bellow in April and May, during the peak of courtship.

One morning several years ago I watched a male gator bellow. He arched his head and tail, let his belly sink below the water, sucked in some air, and then vibrated his throat. The sound that rolled out of his clenched teeth was an antediluvian message rife with meaning: I'm looking for a mate; or, males beware, I am lord and master of this swamp. Although I have seen many maimed alligators, bellowing generally reduces the incidence of territorial fights. A female that is ready to breed may answer a prospective male. Out of that morning mist years ago I heard another alligator reply, a slightly higher-pitched bellow, presumably that of a female. Another alligator, whose head rested just above the surface in full view of the first, sank out of sight. Then, off and on, the two gators called back and forth for almost an hour. When the sun rose and the mist dissipated, the world fell silent.

In addition to bellowing, the adult alligator communicates by hissing and by head-slapping the water. Slapping often accompanies bellowing and can be a visual, as well as auditory, signal. Male alligators also broadcast subsonic sounds. Whenever an alligator issues a subsonic call, the water on its back dances as if touched by a giant tuning fork. The water dance may accompany a bellow or a head slap or occur by itself, the gator arched and the water sizzling above his back. These low-frequency sounds carry over miles of marshland. (American crocodiles, which do not bellow, also give subsonic sounds.)

Infant alligators grunt or croak, sometimes from inside the egg. When a mother gator hears this, she tears open the nest to free the hatchlings. When juvenile alligators grunt, mother comes to protect them. Under crowded conditions or during periods of food shortages, cannibalism is the way of the tribe. Alligators are so attuned to the juveniles' distress calls that squeaking is an easy way to lure them; for alligators of all sizes come, some for the promise of a quick meal. At night I visit the dock of West Lake, where I will purse my lips and squeak from deep in my throat—*urgha, urgha*—sweeping a light beam across the water, looking for the eerie red shine of the alligator's eyes. Those luminescent eyes, drifting in from all angles of the lake as though floating over the water, are all I'll ever see. When the alligators sense the fraud, they turn away.

In South Florida, courtship begins in late February, when earthy voices and head slapping punctuate the stillness and may serve to synchronize ovulation and spermatogenesis. Alligators have two pairs of musk glands, one on each side of the jawbone and the other, just inside the cloaca. Frequently after an animal bellows, an oily sheen paints the water around it. Scientists believe that the musk has both airborne and waterborne properties and may carry far beyond the alligator. Once they've found each other, the male and female move to deep water and begin a series of elaborate and sensual snout touching, back rubbing, nudging and pushing, circling, bubbling, and swimming that helps the female determine the fitness of her suitor. Because you would have to probe an alligator's cloaca to determine its gender, the identity of members of an amorous pair often remains a mystery. Mating takes place underwater, is short, about twenty or thirty seconds, and repetitive.

After copulation the female returns to her hole and clears out a circle on the bank, fifteen to twenty feet in diameter, her jaws yanking away vegetation. Then she builds a mound of clipped sawgrass, cattails, and flag, which looks like an oversized muskrat lodge and is as much as six feet wide and three feet high. She climbs on top, scoops out a small cavity, and gently lays approximately thirty eggs inside. After the last egg is out, she covers the cavity and returns to the water, often guarding the nest against potential nest robbers: black bear, raccoon, otter, wild hog, striped skunk, or gray fox. Red-bellied turtles sometimes lay their eggs in gator nests; the eggs then receive the unwitting protection of the mother alligator.

Within engineering limits, an alligator can adjust the height of her nest to reflect the height of the water at the time of nesting, and she chooses a nest site that avoids both flooding and desiccation. Historically water levels in the Everglades peaked during the late summer hurricane season, just after alligators hatched. Adjusted to the region's whim and fancy, Everglades alligators once enjoyed one of the highest hatching rates in America. Today, however, regulatory releases of water by the Water Management District have turned the national park's hydrologic cycles on end. For alligators, the Everglades has become an unpredictable landscape, and their nest mortality has increased fivefold.

In the Everglades, incubation lasts about sixty-five days, and hatching occurs between late July and late September. The gender of a baby alligator is determined by the temperature of the egg between the seventh and twenty-first day of incubation. Eggs warmed to ninety-one degrees or higher develop into males. Eggs at eighty-five degrees or lower develop into females. In between, either gender develops. Although the composting nest produces some heat, its moisture content and the position of the nest in relation to the sun has a greater effect on the male-female ratio of the hatchlings. A nest in the shade or a moist nest produces a predominance of females; one that is dry or in the sun produces mostly males.

Although dry as hurricanes go, Andrew, a powerful early-season storm, struck the Everglades in 1992, flooding nests and washing hatchlings away. Biologists in Everglades National Park believe that Andrew destroyed 27 percent of the eggs in the park and killed numerous infant gators, some in the process of hatching. Conversely, during a severe drought in 1971, the Everglades north of Alligator Alley was dry in early May, and alligators never nested.

Baby alligators, which are the color of winter sawgrass—bright yellow stripes against a background of black-green—stay nearby their mother for up to two years. This, of course, is a good thing, for baby alligators are "feeble and succulent," wrote Archie Carr, and "were it not for the asylum of the den pool, . . . it is hard to see how little alligators could survive in numbers great enough to keep their race alive." One morning in Shark Valley I watched a great blue heron wading along the edge of a densely vegetated canal as it snagged a baby alligator. To avoid retribution, the bird immediately took its prize to a paved walkway, well away from the water. Baby alligators are also eaten by bass, gar, pig frogs, water moccasins, three species of water snakes, snapping turtles, juvenile alligators, otters, mink, raccoons, red-shouldered hawks, barred owls, great horned owls, storks, egrets, and cranes. John James

Audubon's *Birds of America* contained a painting of a whooping crane dining on baby gators.

Alligators five or six feet long are killed and eaten by larger alligators and occasionally by panthers. Larger alligators live more or less free from predators but have been subjected to the whims of both human fashion and regional water use. In 1938 the Department of the Interior sent biologist Daniel Beard on a wildlife reconnaissance that would determine the importance of establishing a national park in South Florida. Beard reported that alligators suffered from overhunting and that drainage had already reduced the number of animals in the peripheral marshes. Buoyed both by protection in Miami-Dade and Monroe Counties and by the creation of Everglades National Park, the alligator population began to rebound in the 1940s. Although park service biologist Frank Craighead considered them abundant in the 1950s, I recall gift shops displaying rows of stuffed baby alligators, shiny and glass-eyed, dressed as baseball players and cowboys and ballerinas. Wide-mouthed alligators clenched cigars, waved pennants, or proclaimed Florida the tourist capital of the world. Alligator shoes, some with an animal's head on the tip, and alligator handbags and wallets had become chic.

During the 1960s the Everglades alligator population declined by more than 90 percent, the victim of hurricanes, natural drought, and water management. The soaring price of alligator hides, particularly the belly skin, rekindled an interest in poaching. Wardens, many of whom had been poachers themselves, often looked the other way or became silent partners in poaching rings. For a fee some wardens actually provided information on the location and density of alligators in the regions they were assigned to protect. So common was the practice of poaching alligators in the national park that two elderly retired practitioners had their memoirs published in the 1990s: *Totch: A Life in the Everglades,* by Loren G. Brown, and *Gladesmen: Gator Hunters, Moonshiners, and Skiffers,* by Glen Simmons. Although alligators began a modest comeback in the 1970s as a result of the Endangered Species Act and more seasonal water releases, their population had shifted from the peripheral marshes and the freshwater mangroves on the fringe of the Everglades to its liquid heart, the canals and central slough.

According to Brady Barr, who received a doctorate from the University of Miami and is currently the host of the National Geographic television series *Explorer's Journal,* alligators in the southern Everglades are not doing well. "In the national park," says Barr, "alligators begin nesting at an older age, nest less frequently, lay fewer eggs, are smaller, and grow incredibly more slowly than alligators elsewhere." While studying the food habitats of alligators in Shark Slough, Barr routinely caught emaciated, ten-foot gators that weighed only 250 pounds and three-foot gators that were up to ten years old. Farther north, in Lake Okeechobee, for instance, a ten-foot alligator could weigh 1,000 pounds, and a nearly three-foot alligator might be a yearling.

Barr, who has pumped the stomachs of more than one thousand Everglades alligators, discovered that 65 percent of the animals' diet in Shark Slough is aquatic salamanders—sirens and amphiumas—apple snails, and water snakes. Although the alligators also eat rice rats and cotton rats, marsh rabbits, mink, and otters, even the occasional bobcat or deer, they no longer have a moveable feast of wading birds from which to choose. In the 1930s, when the rookeries in the southern end of Shark Slough supported hundreds of thousands of ibis and herons and egrets, alligators gorged on the adults and chicks, sometimes climbing into trees to rob nests, or leaping out of the water to pick careless fledglings from low branches. They also scavenged birds whose lifeless bodies littered the water around the rookery, and ate food that spilled out of nests. When water levels in the Everglades were artificially and drastically altered, both breeding and wintering wading birds either moved away or died, and alligators that lived near those roosts, Barr speculates, have been forced to rely on secondary prey.

Barr also suggests that the water fluctuations of the Everglades' massive flood control system may have left alligators struggling to thermoregulate. Being cold-blooded, alligators regulate their internal temperature by moving either into or out of the water, basking or submerging. Because water levels are artificially low in the central slough, alligators are unable to escape weather extremes, and they use much of their energy trying to attract heat or to get rid of heat. "Maybe," says Barr, "the Everglades has become too harsh an environment for them."

During the winter dry season, many alligators living in Shark Slough struggle to stay both wet and warm. Some are lucky to reach deep-water, food-rich canals, which, although encouraging competition and cannibalism among alligators, have become critical regional habitats for the species. One February afternoon I counted more than forty in the canal at the south end of the Shark Valley tram road, basking, swimming, floating, their pleated backs glistening above the surface. Every one looked well fed. Potential food was everywhere: birds, fish, turtles, crayfish. (A friend watched a gator catch a swimming diamondback. The gator grabbed the rattler around its middle, rigorously slapped the snake against the water, chomped on it several times, then swallowed it in one gulp.) Elsewhere in the Everglades alligators live in canals year-round because the water levels are stable. Several years ago I accompanied a graduate student from the University of Florida that radio-tracked alligators north of the Tamiami Trail. All fourteen of his animals lived in canals that crossed the water conservation areas. He told me that the Miami Canal is choked with alligators that sink out of sight in twenty feet of water whenever his airboat passes. Considering the fate of these canals during the restoration of the Everglades, Brady Barr says, "In the long term, filling in the canals is supposed to help the whole ecosystem, but in the short term it will cause havoc among these alligators." Eventually, however, alligators may move back to their historic territory, where the increasing occupancy of gator holes would rejuvenate the southern Everglades.

((((

As far as freshwater turtles go, the Florida softshell is large; a robust female may reach a length of twenty inches and weigh more than fifteen pounds. It is streamlined and fast and appears to have been constructed of spare parts: a snorkel nose at the end of a snaky neck, which uncoils from a flatish, pancake-shaped shell. Four clawed flippers propel the softshell through the holes and gullies of the Everglades. Although it hides in the sediment and ambushes fish and crayfish, the Florida softshell is often seen basking at the surface, motionless like a gob of muck bubbled up from the bottom. Except to lay eggs or when carried off in the mouth of an alligator, the turtle rarely leaves the water.

Early one morning several years ago, as I strolled around Eco Pond, I came upon an eleven-foot alligator in the middle of the trail, more than fifteen feet from the water. The gator's upturned jaws held a full-grown female Florida softshell turtle, very much alive. The turtle arched its neck over the alligator's head and strummed the air with all four feet as if she were swimming. Sprawled on its belly, the gator appeared exhausted. There was no blood, no guts, just a few tooth marks and scratches on the turtle's shell, the sort of marks I had seen a hundred other times on a number of turtles.

After several minutes, the gator rose to his full height—about eighteen inches—and tossed the softshell in the air three times. Each time the alligator caught the turtle, its jaws slammed across the shell. Then the alligator sagged on the ground, collapsed like a prize-fighter on a stool. Fifteen minutes later, the alligator's clapping jaws again punctuated the morning stillness. The gator rested and bit for more than two and a half hours. Three times the turtle escaped. Three times the alligator hauled her back, away from the water. Progressively the turtle's shell became a latticework of cracks and perforations.

Eventually the alligator caught the turtle edge to edge, crosswise, and bit down. The softshell burst apart, caving in on herself.

Then the alligator swam across Eco Pond, crawled onto the far shore, and spent the next nine hours pulverizing and swallowing his prize, bones, shell, and all. Nutrient-rich Eco Pond has become a smorgasbord for hungry alligators, little more than a self-sufficient gator farm crammed with well-fed gators.

In the 1990s Jim Kushlan, a prolific author of scientific papers and a former national park biologist, wrote that restoration goals ought to be geared toward perpetuating alligator abundance in the central slough. Unfortunately that meant maintaining low water levels during the nesting season, followed by a gradual dry-down in the winter. But the central slough was historically the deepest part of the Everglades, and managing for alligators might place the entire wetland at risk by reducing the density and the diversity of other aquatic animals. A decade later, researchers are in agreement: a more realistic approach to restoration would mimic the suite of habitats in the original Everglades. Return alligators to the peripheral marshes and the freshwater mangroves where their benevolence can once again create the wellsprings of the Everglades.

Six months after the passage of Hurrican Andrew, injured slash pine trees growing outside Everglades National Park, where the water table has been lowered to support farming and suburban development, were unable to produce an adequate amount of resins ward off an infestation of bark beetles. Mortality of almost 100 percent resulted.

A cottonmouth (*Agkistrodon piscivorus*) in threat pose.

Cape Sable seaside sparrow in the hand of bird-bander David Okines.

Tree snail (*Liguus fasciatus*).

Pig frog (*Rana grylio*).

Rob Bennetts banding a snail kite in Water Conservation Area 2B

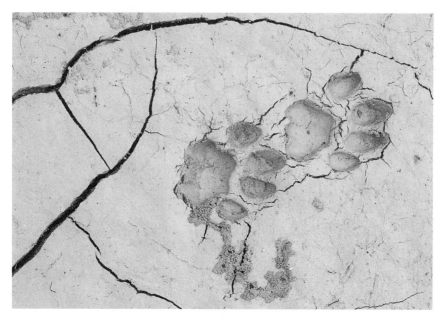

Panther (*Puma concolor*) tracks in the mud at the Florida Panther National Wildlife Refuge.

Florida panther (*Puma concolor*), part of the late Frank Weeds's captive collection. Immokalee, Florida.

White mangrove growing on the edge of Sandy Key in Florida Bay.

Frank Mazzotti and Laura Brandt processing hatchling American crocodiles in the northeast corner of Florida Bay.

White ibis feeding on a dry season concentration of small fish in Big Cypress National Preserve. Notice water depth in relation to the height of the birds' legs.

The wood stork (*Mycteria americana*) depends on touch to find its prey.

Matching the color of a white ibis's bill with a Pittsburg paint chip.

Brian Mealy taking a blood sample from a bald eagle chick caught on Sandy Key in Florida Bay.

Osprey (*Pandion haliaetus*) chick on a ground nest on an island in Florida Bay.

Harvesting cane by hand on small farm in the Kissimmee Valley.

[The Florida panther is] an incredibly adaptable
animal that has weathered a century's worth of
attempts to eradicate it as well as two decades
of misdirected efforts to save it.

DAVID S. MAEHR, 1997

10 Swamp Lions

Big Cypress Swamp, which includes Fakahatchee Strand, looks so inhospitable
that most visitors who cross the region rarely venture from their cars. For one
thing there is the possibility of a close encounter with an alligator or with a
water moccasin, ink-black and as thick as the sweet spot on a baseball bat.
When the swamp dries, large rattlesnakes cross open ground in search of
marsh rabbits and cotton rats. And then there are insects—mosquitoes, no-
see-ums, deerflies, and horseflies—that can turn a swamp outing into hell.
There are also at least twenty-eight Florida panthers, *Puma concolor coryi,* in
Big Cypress National Preserve, adding mystique and grandeur to an already
gorgeous landscape.

To get a closer look at panther habitat, I planned to walk across a section of the national preserve, a 730,000-acre tract that encompasses 40 percent of the swamp's drainage, still relatively intact, unlike the Everglades to the east. A third of the preserve is covered by the smooth, leafless, gray crowns of cypress that appear in the distance like the undulating crest of a roller coaster. Wet prairies, marl prairies, part of the sawgrass Everglades, sandy pine islands and hardwood hammocks, which panthers prefer, and mangrove swamps, which they don't, fill the remaining two-thirds of the preserve.

To prepare for the walk I bought the United States Geological Survey topographic map that covers the Loop Road section of the preserve, where the Florida Trail, a semicomplete footpath across the state, ends in obscurity. Unfortunately the map was drawn in 1972, twenty years before the Florida Trail was laid and two years before the national preserve was purchased by the federal government. The Oasis Visitor Center on the Tamiami Trail, the preserve's most notable manmade feature, is missing.

Because the swamp had been too wet to survey, the map itself was cobbled from aerial photographs and provided a vague likeness to the actual terrain. Tan for spike rush marshes; dark green for cypress swamp; light green for pinelands and hardwood islands. There is not one five-foot contour line on the map; consequently the light green portion is as rare as a panther. Tides merge into creeks; sprawling water, both confused and directionless, caters to the whims of wind.

The "Big" in Big Cypress refers to the extent of the swamp, twenty-four hundred square miles, not to the size of the trees themselves, although Gator Hook Strand once supported large trees, long since cut. Big Cypress is a vision of original southwest Florida: dark sloughs crowded with buttressed, moss-draped swamp trees, pinelands, and airy glades. When Everglades National Park was dedicated, acting on the recommendation of Daniel Beard, the national park included much of Big Cypress as its major upland component. At the urging of Florida's United States senator, Spessard Holland, within ten years the park service changed the boundaries, cutting the swamp out of Everglades National Park.

There was another view of the swamp, one framed by shiftless entrepreneurs. In the 1930s and 1940s, men looked at the cypress and saw only rot-resistant wood: wood for pickle barrels, fences, gutters, hulls of PT boats, coffins, and stadium seats. Others looked at the hammocks and strands and saw only orchids and tree snails; still others looked at the prairies and saw only pastures; others saw only fish in the tidal creeks. Loggers, plant collectors, cattlemen, fishermen, and guides settled in the tiny outposts of Ochopee, Monroe

Station, and Pinecrest. In 1943 Florida's first oil-producing well was drilled in Sunniland, close to what would become the preserve's northwest corner. By the 1960s, real estate agents arrived. Thousands of parcels were sold Florida-style, sight unseen, to investors all over North America. Canals were dug, and levees built. These were the interests Senator Holland served.

In 1968 the Federal Aviation Administration and Miami–Dade County planned to build a huge jetport and satellite community on the eastern edge of the swamp, close to Everglades National Park. The jetport would have degraded the water quality of lower Shark Slough. In that same year, Joe Browder, the southeast field representative for the National Audubon Society, organized environmentalists, hunters, Native Americans, and Miami businessmen likely to be hurt by a jetport outside Miami. The nationwide nightly news covered the debate for so long that the words *ecology* and *ecosystem* became common-place. Two independent environmental impact statements, one financed by the federal government, the other by jetport proponents and their real estate colleagues, slammed the proposed jetport.

"Environmental Impact of the Big Cypress Jetport," written in 1969 by ecologist Arthur R. Marshall, concluded that "development of the proposed jetport and its attendant facilities will lead to drainage and development for agriculture, industry, housing, transportation, and services in the Big Cypress Swamp which will inexorably destroy the south Florida ecosystem and thus the Everglades National Park."

In 1974 Congress authorized the purchase of Big Cypress National Preserve to protect the watershed of Everglades National Park. The federal government added land to the preserve in 1988. Although the jetport had been defeated, several miles of runway that had been built in 1970 close to Corn Dance Hammock, a sacred site for Miccosukee, still serve as a training airport for commercial pilots. The Port Authority of Miami–Dade County manages thirty thousand acres of land around the runway.

Because the preserve's southeastern tier is part of Shark Slough, "planning beyond the boundaries" has become a slogan for the National Park Service in recent years. Unfortunately, however, Big Cypress National Preserve quickly became a park service stepchild. Resource managers were obligated to abide by congressional concessions, unusual by National Park Service standards. Besides the scaled-down pilot-training airport, the federal government allows private interests to retain 98 percent of the area's mineral rights: thirty oil wells operate on ten pads that require thirty miles of roads. It also permits hunting, which the state regulates, and off-road vehicles. The Miccosukee and Seminole pursue traditional activities on Big Cypress National Preserve, and one hundred private properties within the boundaries are exempt from purchase—one hunting camp operates a thirty-person dorm with a front yard landing strip.

The Loop Road, known as State Road 94 on highway maps, cuts a narrow, twenty-four-mile-long path across prairie, cypress, and pine between Monroe Station and Fortymile Bend, off the Tamiami Trail. East of Pinecrest the road is paved; west, it is potholed and puddled, sometimes knee-deep in floodwater, more suitable for a swamp buggy than for a Buick. The southern end of the Florida Trail, marked by orange blazing, is eight miles out the Loop Road from Monroe Station, usually an uneventful drive. But in those years when water rises out of Gator Hook Strand and flows over the road, I'm forced to wade, ever mindful of the gators and moccasins that scull across my path. Today the road is reasonably dry. I pull onto the shoulder (what little there is) and begin a daylong search for panther signs—a track, a scrape, anything that might signal that a cat has passed. I find only the delicate tracks of bobcat along the road.

The Loop Unit, the land enclosed by the Loop Road and the Tamiami Trail, is a portion of the home range of a female Texas cougar. The cougar, known as TX 103, is one of eight females captured in the Big Bend region of West Texas and released in South Florida in 1995 to bolster the Florida panther's dwindling gene pool. Panthers are a charismatic but anemic race of mountain lion, perhaps the most loved, and certainly the most endangered, mammal in South Florida. Until recently no male panthers were known to regularly use the Loop Unit, a situation that Big Cypress biologist Deborah Jansen spent three years trying to change.

Finally, in 1996, two males taken from the wild and reared in captivity in northern Florida—part of a stalled captive-breeding program—were released into southern Big Cypress; one near the Loop Road range of TX 103, the other just north of the Tamiami Trail, near the Raccoon Point range of TX 107. Within weeks of their release, both males died with deteriorated lungs, possibly the result of chemical poisoning, leaving TX 103 alone in southern Big Cypress for the time being.

The mountain lion—also known as swamp screamer, panther, puma, painter, catamount, and cougar—once had the run of the Western Hemisphere, from the Yukon to Patagonia, coast to coast. The Florida panther roamed most of the coastal plain from Arkansas to South Carolina and south to Florida. They were first reported in Florida by Hernando de Soto in 1539, when he wrote that the indigenous people guarded their burial grounds at night to keep lions away from the dead. Biologists believe that Florida supported approximately fourteen hundred panthers at the time of de Soto. In 1882, when the

Caloosahatchee River was extended by canal twelve miles across pine flatwoods to Lake Okeechobee, connecting the lake to the Gulf of Mexico, panthers in southwest Florida lost their most important link to the central part of the state. When twentieth-century development closed the Atlantic Coastal Ridge as an avenue of migration, panthers were effectively isolated in South Florida, stranded in the most waterlogged habitat in North America.

Panthers are essentially confined to a five-thousand-square-mile wedge of private ranch land and public land that contains South Florida's last vestige of upland hardwood hammocks and pinelands. (Except for two young males that recently forded the Caloosahatchee and took up residence on the Lake Wales Ridge, fifteen miles south of Orlando.) No one knows exactly how many cats there are, because some of the best habitat is private land north of Interstate 75, and most ranchers are loath to let government officials inventory their properties. Current estimates place the population between forty and fifty adults and half again as many juveniles. Whatever the actual number, many biologists believe it is not nearly enough to sustain their population. Thirty-one panthers wear radio collars and are identified by a number that indicates the sequence of capture. Biologists use batteries that last approximately three years and prefer to change them every third year to minimize handling the cats. The genealogy of these particular cats is well documented; DNA testing has revealed that panthers have limited genetic diversity, the result of decades of inbreeding.

Virtually any panther in South Florida is a close relative of any other. Inbreeding is both common and unavoidable. Fathers mate with daughters, mothers with sons. The population is so severely inbred—an evolutionist's prescription for extinction—that the Florida Fish and Wildlife Conservation Commission has said that without the additional genes supplied by the eight Texas cougars, panthers might not last twenty-five years.

Of the eight, three are still alive (one was hit by a car, one was shot, one succumbed to metabolic complications a week before giving birth, and the other two died of unknown causes). Five of the eight Texas cougars bred with panthers, one of them four times, three of them twice. Since their introduction, the cougars have produced seventeen kittens, twelve females and five males. Of the seventeen, seven—five females and two males—have already bred.

The sun, rising behind a mound of brooding clouds, casts light haphazardly across the marsh. Tiny blue-banded killifish flash ahead of me as I splash down the trail, following the orange blazes that appear every so often on trail-side trees. Whenever I pause to marvel at the waterlogged haunts of TX 103, fish nibble the hairs on my toes.

TX 103 ranges over approximately 110 square miles of Big Cypress Swamp, from Lostmans Pines, where she was originally released, to the Loop Unit. When she passes through, mostly by night, there is not another female cat within her range to leave olfactory messages in the pines, adding a profound yet ordinary dimension to a viable panther landscape. According to biologist David Maehr, the former head of the Florida Panther Recovery Team, most female panthers patrol home ranges that average seventy-five square miles and extensively overlap those of other females. A cat with young kittens hunts a smaller range, which expands when the kittens begin to eat solid food and are capable of following their mother. In the Big Cypress, Jansen has found that unmated females expand their range while looking for a male; as soon as they mate, their home range shrinks.

Male home ranges average 200 square miles and overlap those of several females with whom they presumably mate. The ranges of males overlap very little with those of other males. When a resident becomes old and less active, say at nine or ten years old, his home range shrivels. Sometimes a transient or neighboring male moves in, kills the owner, and annexes the range. Transient males wander through the population, ever on the lookout for unoccupied territory, and in the process often fall victim to resident males. Their ranges average 240 square miles and are pinched between the home ranges of adjacent established males.

The two young males that crossed the Caloosahatchee River and took up residence on the panther-free Lake Wales Ridge wait for the equivalent of a feline miracle, a transient female to cross the river. Young females peaceably share portions of their mother's range and rarely move far from home. According to Maehr, female home ranges are so stable that "only death seemed capable of wresting a resident female from her home." Maehr claims that the big picture of panther population dynamics, called the land tenure system, evolved to encourage the occasional shuffling of individuals while maintaining an overall pattern of order.

I follow the orange tree blazes across six wet prairies separated by dense bands of cypress, where interior waters run belly deep. Because El Niño brought heavy and prolonged winter rains to South Florida, water levels across Big Cypress are unusually high in 1998. There are no gatherings of wading birds. Like the water, the birds spread across the landscape. Only a couple of ibis and herons scatter at my approach. On the edge of Roberts Lakes Strand lies a dead great egret, its orange bill circled by white feathers. This looks like the work of a bird of prey, perhaps a great horned owl that neatly plucked its victim where it was caught. A panther, on the other hand, which may on rare occasion take a wading bird, is messier, strewing feathers everywhere and burying what's left of the carcass.

After several miles of walking I have stepped on dry ground less than a dozen times. Standing in two inches of water, I eat lunch in the pines, my pack slung in a tree. A dark cloud of common grackles wheels through the pines, a thousand pairs of stiff wings rip the air as the birds gather momentum for the journey north. In contrast, TX 103 doesn't leave; she's tethered to her territory by behavior as old as her species.

The orange blazes grow fainter after lunch. A leopard frog splashes in front of me. By the sixth mile the blazes disappear, and I take out my compass. The only vertical relief to site from are tufts of air plants in the cypresses. Thirty feet to this one. A hundred feet to that. Nagged by the thought that I may be lost, I begin to pay more attention to my compass and less attention to the possibility of seeing a sign of TX 103. After several hours of bushwhacking, I hear the distant drone of cars along the Tamiami Trail. Shortly before sunset, the roof of the Oasis Visitor Center emerges through the cypress limbs.

I reach the center's parking lot, not at all sure how a panther living in the lowlands can keep its toes from rotting. A ranger pulls up in a shiny white car. He looks at me as though I had escaped from the nearby Copeland prison and inquires about my itinerary. I tell him, and bug-eyed he says, "You walked there! There's nothing out there but cypress and snakes."

(((

Perched in the back seat of a Cessna 172, cruising at turkey-vulture height, about seven hundred feet above southwest Florida, I stare at a quilt of pine and cypress, of red-tinted maples and towering royal palms. The sky is an early-morning blue, and the white birds above the green trees look immaculate. Glass office buildings in Naples, reflecting the orange of the rising sun, blink on and off, while the plane cuts tight circles, searching, as it does every Monday, Wednesday, and Friday for signals from radio-collared Florida panthers. To the west, beyond the birds, a grillwork of sand roads cuts the forest into wooded rectangles known locally as the South Blocks.

The roads mark the beginning of Golden Gate Estates, the world's largest subdivision. A projected community of four hundred thousand, Golden Gate Estates became one of Florida's most nefarious real estate scams. Spurious salespeople sold twenty-nine thousand lots over the telephone to out-of-state buyers who had no idea that by late June, despite 180 miles of recently dug drainage canals, they would need boats to reach their land. After several hundred homes sprang up on high ground, the enterprise went belly-up, and piece by piece the state began buying up parcels, nearly forty thousand acres, which has become Picayune State Forest. While the state was tracking down the legal property owners, squatters moved in. They live in wood and tar paper shacks, converted mobile homes, and rusted-out tractor trailers. They drink rainwater, bathe in drainage canals, poach game, and violate the night with their automatic weapons.

The introduction of canals has ironically improved the South Block's upland forests, creating more habitat for panthers as well as for members of Cuban-American paramilitary groups, drug runners, and assorted other criminals, and drifters. Hidden beneath a starburst of saw palmetto, TX 106 tends her kitten.

I became aware of the cougar's general location because Mark Lotz, a biologist with the Florida Fish and Wildlife Conservation Commission, who sits in front of me, had picked up the frequency of the animal's radio collar in his headset and then motioned the pilot to circle so that he could mark a precise location on a topographic map. Eventually the site will be entered into a computer, along with thousands of other points, to become part of an ongoing study, an eleventh-hour effort to restore the genetic diversity of the Florida panther.

Southeast of Immokalee, on private land, we pick up the signal of 46, an eight-year-old male that roams a 225-square-mile mosaic of deer-productive pines and oak, rangeland, fallow fields choked with dull green wax myrtle, and orderly rows of citrus. When heavy freezes in the late 1980s forced the citrus industry off the sand ridge in central Florida, landowners near Immokalee, in Hendry and Collier counties, increasingly converted their forests and pastures to orchards, eliminating critical panther habitat. Now when 46 pounces on a deer, biting through its first two neck vertebrae and severing its spinal cord, the scent of blood mingles with scent of orange blossoms.

During most of the twentieth century South Florida's wetlands were the focus of most of the region's conservation efforts, but the uplands, the habitat critical to the survival of Florida panthers and numerous other species, was all but ignored. Growth in nearby Naples and Fort Myers is exponential. Eight thousand people a week push eastward into panther habitat. According to David Maehr, technology and animal husbandry have been the principal tools of panther recovery, because the government cannot supply what the panther really needs, lots of land. Much of the private land, high-quality cat country, is owned by corporations and agribusinesses. To buy it all would cost the state nine hundred million dollars, about the price of a BI bomber. In 1997 David Maehr summed up the situation: "There are all kinds of things you can do to increase the population and make it healthier, but if you've got nowhere to put them, then what's the point? Without these private lands, all well-intended but misplaced efforts of ill-equipped agencies will work like aspirin on a terminal illness. Before real progress can be made, the malaise of government-only panther recovery must be cured."

The radio frequency of Florida panther 56, mother of three kittens, beeps into Lotz's headset. Over the north end of Big Cypress Lotz records panthers 36, 11, and 48, all adult females, and 45, an adult male, members of one extended incestuous family.

Because Florida panthers lack a fat layer to retain warmth in winter, they are among the smallest of mountain lions in North America. Most adult males weigh between 104 and 148 pounds, averaging about 120 pounds. Adult females are smaller, between 65 and 100 pounds, averaging about 80 pounds. The largest male inventoried weighed 154 pounds, the smallest adult female, only 50 pounds, scarcely bigger than a large New England bobcat. From the tip of its nose to the tip of its tail, a male averages just under seven feet long; a female, just over six feet. Both sexes stand about two feet high at the shoulders, have barrel chests, short, rounded skulls, and switchblade claws.

A panther's skull is dense and powerful. It is oblong-shaped and short-jawed, with a broad flat forehead, wide nostrils, and high arched nasal bones that give the animal a Romanesque appearance. There are thirty teeth in its powerful jaw, sixteen in the upper jaw, fourteen in the lower. The four daggerlike canine teeth—one on each side of the upper and lower jaws—are about an inch long and blunt. Cheek teeth, called the carnassials, form a shearing plane, like a pair of scissors, and slice red meat away from white bone.

White-tailed deer, wild hog, raccoon, and armadillo are the most important panther food. At night, when deer are feeding in the glades, panthers wait for them to return to the trees. They are an equal opportunity predator; they take bucks, does, and fawns. The average adult lion kills and eats about thirty-five to fifty deer-sized animals a year. Females with young require twice that amount. In others words, an adult panther kills a deer about every six to ten days, a female with kittens, every three to five days. Evidence of marsh rabbits, cotton rats, alligators, wild turkey, otters, bobcats, even the remains of a bear cub have been found in panther scat.

Physical characteristics once thought peculiar to Florida panther—the kinked tip of its tail, the cowlick on its back, the high-arched nose, the flattened frontal bones—may be the outward signs of inbreeding. But hidden beneath the panther's muscular and supple frame lies the debilitating side of inbreeding: holes in their hearts, leaky heart valves, disarmed immune systems, undescended testicles, crippled sperm, skewed levels of sex hormones, vaginal tumors, recessive traits rarely manifested in other subspecies of mountain lions. As a group Florida panthers have 85 percent less genetic variability than western mountain lions and a higher frequency of malformed sperm than any other subspecies of mountain lion examined. One biologist claims that if a Florida panther were a human sperm donor, he would be told he was sterile.

Since the end of the last Ice Age, as the level of the sea rose during the past ten thousand years, the Florida Plateau has shrunk, forcing the cats to inhabit a progressively narrower peninsula. The jaguar disappeared from Florida five hundred or more years ago. The smaller, slightly more adaptable panther is headed down the same path.

Outbreeding, the genetic blending of Texas cougars into the population of the Florida panther, is believed to be the best and last hope for the survival of panthers in Florida. Unfortunately, without additional land into which the population can expand, the wilds of South Florida will remain, as far as swamp lions are concerned, much like a stocked trout stream that periodically needs a fresh supply of hatchery fish.

Not everyone agrees that the introduction of Texas cougars is the solution to the panther's problems. David Maehr, for one, is not convinced that the panther is genetically bankrupt. In his book *The Florida Panther: Life and Death of a Vanishing Carnivore*, Maehr states that panthers in Florida have been confined to a peninsula for thousands of years, predisposing them to limited gene flow. Maehr contends that despite their low genetic diversity and low sperm counts the population is generally holding its own and exhibits normal demographics—that is, females still give birth.

The Texas cougar subspecies *Puma concolor stanleyana* was selected because its seamless boundary once flowed into that of *coryi* in the thickets and swamps of East Texas, where the mingling of gene pools no doubt occurred. It was further reasoned that female cougars would blend into the panther's social fabric without incidence. Everywhere, female mountain lions have overlapping home ranges that are superimposed on that of a dominant male. Males are intolerant of each other and often fight, sometimes to the death, which is a leading cause of panther mortality.

When they were caught in 1995 the eight Texas cougars were healthy, four or five years old, not pregnant, and showed none of deleterious abnormalities that plague the Florida panther. How would a mountain lion from arid West Texas fare in steamy South Florida? "A cat is a cat is a cat," claimed houndsman Roy McBride, who caught the animals and whose specially trained dogs have been treeing panthers for more than twenty years.

Again Maehr is not convinced. Calculating the dispersal and survival rate for male mountain lions, Maehr believes that at least seven hundred years would be required to deliver a gene from East Texas to Big Cypress Swamp. By virtue of their longer dispersal distances, males are the primary range extenders of the population. At least twelve panthers, each taking an eighty-mile one-way trip, would be required to transport one unique gene from East Texas to Florida. Barriers like the Mississippi River and the lions' own mortality factors would exponentially compound the delivery time of the unique gene. By 1900 the fluid distribution of mountain lions in the southeast had been segmented, much like in the modern Everglades. Cities, farms, and orchards effectively separated populations of panthers. Maehr feels that the spread of genes would have historically followed a path more circular than the linear model used to aid the Florida panther.

"What underlies the discussion of large carnivore taxonomy," writes Maehr, "is not simply that it takes centuries to move genes across space, but that a cougar from Texas has never, in all probability, interacted directly with a panther from Florida, let alone from South Florida. Further, by the time genetic material from Texas could find its way to the Big Cypress Swamp, the package would have changed so dramatically as to be indistinguishable from the standing residents."

If panthers function in a normal demographic manner after the introduction of Texas cougars into Florida, "does this mean the experiment has succeeded?" asks Maehr. "Or might this suggest that nothing was broken in the first place? The unspoken message—the real meaning in this recovery decision—is that for the Florida panther to be saved, it must first be destroyed."

From my lofty perch in the Cessna, high above the Big Cypress Seminole reservation, I see sunlight flickering in the windows of buildings in Fort Lauderdale, sixty miles away, and below on the surface of the watery woods. Again the pilot circles. It's TX 101 in the pinewoods, close to a large stand of melaleuca. Her first set of kittens was born in October 1995. Lotz examined them when they were two weeks old and helped insert a rice-grain-sized transponder under the skin between the shoulder blades of each of them. Thus far no hybrid kitten has a kinked tail or a cowlick; each has a sound heart and energetic sperm. By early November they had left the den and were accompanying their mother on hunting forays. If they're caught again, Lotz will simply scan them like a cashier ringing up bar-coded groceries and will immediately know who they are.

Kittens are born with their eyes closed, from one to four in a litter, and weigh about fourteen to eighteen ounces. Their fur is a soft, spotted gray, which becomes brown as they age. Male and female kittens are about the same weight until six months of age. After that males grow faster and for a longer period of time, although females reach maturity first. Generally females begin breeding at age two, some as early as fourteen months, which sets panthers apart from other mountain lions.

In December 1996, fourteen months after her first litter was born, TX 101 gave birth to two more kittens beneath a screen of saw palmetto. All four offspring are alive and well. In November 1997, after the cat's second litter dispersed, Lotz and his colleagues fitted her with a long-term contraceptive to prevent her from becoming overrepresented in the panther's genetic restoration. She still roams the Seminole reservation, hunting deer and hogs, twitching flies off her well-muscled frame, a sterile cougar caught in the fist of panther restoration.

Once Lotz tallies the last of the fourteen collared panthers and three cougars that are within his jurisdiction, the plane loops west toward Naples. Sunlight plays upon the water, interrupted only by the filigree shadows of cypress. We fly back over Big Cypress—the beachfront condos of Naples burn white-hot in the sun—then in succession over State Road 29, the Florida Panther National Wildlife Refuge, and its next-door neighbor the Ford Motor Company test track, where the only lions are the steel and plastic four-wheelers roaring around the track.

⟪⟪⟪

In the early 1980s the tabloid *Sun* reported, "Girl, 10, Raised by Wildcats . . . She roams the Everglades with panthers." A latter-day wild child, she had vestigial language skills: she could only growl, the story said. An illustration accompanied the headline in which the surrogate parents appeared huge and boxy, more like fangless saber-tooth tigers than lithe and supple Florida panthers. Nearly a decade later the front page of another tabloid, the *Weekly World News*, announced, "Half-Alligator, Half-Human Found in Florida Swamp!" Calling the creature "the missing link"—to what, we're not told—the story, accompanied by a photograph of a wizened human head spliced onto an alligator torso, said the beast had been taken alive a few miles east of Naples while sunbathing in Big Cypress Swamp.

I know of only one swamp in Florida singular enough to provoke such outlandish stories: Fakahatchee Strand, the largest, wettest, densest cypress strand in the Big Cypress Swamp. The state preserve there covers more than seventy thousand acres and is the least visited state-owned land in Florida. There is no lodging. No visitors' center. No stores. No bathrooms. Just swampland and pines and wet prairies broken by a gravel road that ends in the South Blocks. Fakahatchee is a primeval overarching forest that blocks the sun and chills the water.

At least six panthers and a Texas cougar use Fakahatchee Strand as a portion of their territories, and it remains one of the few places one has some probability of finding panther signs: tracks, or scrapes, maybe a kill. One February morning several years ago I found perfect tracks deep in the interior of Fakahatchee. A cat had apparently crossed a recently flooded prairie and left a line of prints in the silt. The sun had hardened the tracks. Each imprint—four oblong toe pads (all cats walk on their toes), no claws showing, and a three-lobed heel pad, creased at the upper end like a cleft chin—was the mark of an animal rarely seen but frequently discussed. A panther's front feet are larger than its hind feet, easily seen in the tracks. The front footprint was nearly three inches wide and slightly more than three inches long. Except for the track of a black bear, it is the largest in South Florida.

Fakahatchee is not inviolate wilderness. From 1944 to 1952 robber barons logged approximately five million board feet of cypress and pine there. Trains running along twenty engineer-straight narrow-gauge railroad tracks called trams, precisely 1,650 feet apart, removed the timber. Bob Globe worked on the logging crew in Fakahatchee. Today Globe is sixty-something, his gray hair putting-green short. A red scorpion and the word "Florida" are printed across the front of his blue golf shirt. His camouflage hat supports a fishhook and the brass caricature of a wild hog, a beast both reviled as a pest and managed as a game animal, a favorite panther food. In fact many biologists believe that panthers survive at the behest of wild hogs, which are both abundant and vulnerable. Between 1939 and 1941, when ranchers mistakenly identified the white-tailed deer, the cat's preferred native prey, as the carrier of tick fever, a disease lethal to cattle, a government-sponsored eradication program slaughtered an estimated ten thousand deer in South Florida. With the deer herd greatly diminished, wild hogs were all that stood between panthers and starvation.

Globe's dainty blue Velcro-strap sneakers are a counterpoint to the faded tattoos that run the length of both his arms and beneath the tufts of gray hairs that dot his chest. On his right biceps are a hammerhead shark and the words "catch and release." He tells me that his son has the same tattoo, but it reads "catch and fillet." Like a cypress knee, Globe is short, thick, and deeply weathered. Under the full press of the Florida sun, Globe asserts, logging was both monotonous and dangerous. Days were long and humid, and you toiled in the company of lightning, moccasins, and biting insects.

When Florida began acquiring the Fakahatchee Strand in 1972 to protect the unusual association of rare plants and animals, Globe became the state preserve's lone employee, part superintendent, part warden, part biologist, part custodian. In February 1981 Globe was present when the first Florida panther was radio-collared. By the end of 1982 seven more panthers had been collared in and around Fakahatchee Strand. Globe kept six trams open as routes into the swamp.

The morning after my aerial survey, I join Mark Lotz on a swamp buggy—a truck chassis on balloon tires—in Fakahatchee Strand State Preserve. As the buggy churns along one tram, dew-soaked branches whack our sides. Our destination is one of the twenty-three wildlife underpasses along Alligator Alley, a four-lane interstate that cuts across panther habitat. In the late 1980s Route 84 between Naples and Fort Lauderdale was converted into an extension of Interstate 75. The highway had been notorious for panther deaths. Because the proposed interstate would be more than twice as wide as the original highway, the state became concerned. Radio telemetry data suggested that panthers did not cross the highway at random locations; instead, they used narrow corridors of dense forest cover immediately adjacent to the highway, regularly crossing at the same sites. Roadkill locations confirmed what telemetry had shown; most cats crossed the highway through Fakahatchee Strand. In the face of mounting criticism, the state and federal governments invested ten million dollars to build the underpasses, twelve in prime panther habitat between Naples and State Road 29. For reasons known only to bureaucrats, eleven other underpasses were built east of State Road 29, across land not used by panthers. (Five other underpasses have been built on State Road 29, where three panthers were killed by cars during the first six months of 2001.) The tall fences that parallel both sides of the interstate keep animals off the road and funnel them into the underpasses.

Lotz pulls in front of an underpass. Panther tracks lace the muddy ground in both directions. An infrared beam set about eighteen inches off the ground controls a nearby camera. When the beam is broken, the camera fires a picture. Later that afternoon, back at the Florida Fish and Wildlife Conservation Commission office, Lotz showed me files of self-portraits taken by animals that broke infrared beams; besides panthers, there were bobcats, deer, hogs, raccoons, house cats, alligators, egrets, wild turkeys, and a person, knobby-kneed and muddy.

The Florida Panther National Wildlife Refuge covers more than twenty-six thousand acres of pine forest, cypress stands, prairies, and ponds. Purchased in 1989, the refuge was set aside to protect critical habitat for the Florida panther and to give the United States Fish and Wildlife Service a physical presence in South Florida. The panther refuge is a northern extension of the Fakahatchee Strand. To the east is Big Cypress National Preserve; to the west and north, private lands.

The morning after I visited the underpass, I joined Mark Lotz on the swamp buggy at the Florida Panther National Wildlife Refuge. Three cats are out there, two males and a female, 32, 54, and 57, the panther whose tracks we found the day before in the underpass. It's cool today, low 60s. The sky is overcast, a soft pewter light without direction or highlight. We travel through the pines, pausing here and there, antenna in hand, combing the air waves for panthers. The refuge is reasonably dry; that is, the eighteen inches of water that covered the pinelands last August has receded to puddles and ruts this January day, a thickening brew of gray silt roiling with life. Killdeer attend every depression, sampling a smorgasbord of tiny, ill-fated fish. The shallowest pools have already dried, leaving a halo of shriveled fish. The tracks of opossum and raccoon are everywhere, circumscribing the pools, monitoring the increasingly vulnerable fish. There are panther tracks, too, and those of a pair of black bear—a mother and her cub—but these animals are just splashing through.

In the middle of a blue-spotted prairie, lobelias blooming everywhere, Lotz gets a reading on 57, whose radio collar needs a battery change. To the west, the cypress, red maples, and willows signal wet terrain, a reminder that the refuge is not as dry as it appears. Lotz starts the engine. The buggy won't budge. Its huge wheels have settled into the slippery ground, and every time the engine revs, they spin, spraying gray mud and cutting deeper ruts. Lotz hooks the buggy's winch around a stout slash pine, and the vehicle pulls itself out.

We drive to another site in the pines and palmettos, and Lotz wires the antenna to his receiver. The signals of 57 and 54 are coming from the palmetto understory directly in front of us. There are three possible reasons that cats might be together: a mother with kittens, two males fighting, or a couple. Because 54 is a female, we assume that the panthers are courting. Lotz radios Naples to call off the capture crew —the cat dogs, the houndsman, the vets, and the biologists—as there will not be a collar change until 57 has moved off. Panthers mate for up to ten days, which leads Maehr to believe that a sufficient quantity of healthy sperm has a chance to impregnate the female.

Although panthers can mate in every month of the year, the peak breeding season occurs in the late fall and early winter. After an average gestation of ninety-four days, three or four kittens are born in the palmettos, usually between March and July, blind, deaf, totally dependent. As one might expect, the pattern of kitten births is not random. Inasmuch as water levels are lower, temperatures are cooler, and most deer fawns are produced in late winter and early spring, panther kittens born at this time of year would seem to have a higher probability of survival.

Lotz removes the antenna from its wire lead, and the receiver still buzzes loudly, even without the amplifying effect of the antenna. The cats are right here. I stare into the palmettos and imagine the panthers alert beyond my understanding, looking, listening, smelling, taut and tense, like coiled springs, screened by palmettos, invisible to me except for the images that run through my head. A woodpecker flits by, lands on a pine, walks up the trunk, and enters a hole above the cats. The sky brightens to ivory. The lions stay frozen in place, as I ache for something more, a blood-curdling screech or palmetto leaves set in motion by the twitch of a muscle.

《《《

When Stanley P. Young and Edward A. Goldman wrote *The Puma: Mysterious American Cat* in 1946, they listed thirty-two subspecies of mountain lion whose genus was then known as *Felis,* including *coryi,* named for Charles Cory, the late curator of the Department of Ornithology at Chicago's Field Museum of Natural History. Cory shot four panthers in the Everglades in 1895, the first scientific specimens of the Florida panther. Relying on seventeen skulls and skins, including Cory's animals, Goldman described the subspecies *F. c. coryi* as a "medium-sized, dark subspecies, with pelage [hair] short and rather stiff; skull with broad, flat frontal region; nasals remarkably broad and high-arched or expanded upward." He never mentioned either the kinked tail or the cowlick, which disappear in museum skins.

More recently, taxonomists have condensed the number of subspecies from thirty-two to twenty-seven, leaving *P. c. coryi* intact. Using genetic evidence, the recent trend among taxonomists is to reduce the number of subspecies within a given species. Stephen J. O'Brien, chief of the Laboratory of Viral Carcinogenesis, National Cancer Institute, and a longtime investigator of Florida panther genetics, reported in 1999 that the number of subspecies of *P. concolor* may be as few as five or six and that all North American subspecies belong to the same race; which is to say that *P. c. coryi* is genetically indistinguishable from neighboring subspecies of mountain lions.

Members of different populations within a given species may successfully reproduce with each other but not with members of another species. Reproductive isolation is often accomplished by behavioral differences between species or by geographic barriers. Mountain lions divide into one or more geographic races, each differing slightly from other races of mountain lion, a condition brought about by environmental differences, such as climate, topography, or plant communities. When I studied mammalian taxonomy, the guideline for recognizing a legitimate subspecies was, "If it doesn't look the same, give it a new name." Now it is understood that the line of demarcation between neighboring subspecies is seamless and that the subspecies concept is an arbitrary and vague reference, which, like appreciation for a piece of art, exists in the eye of the beholder.

The first panther was radio-collared in Everglades National Park in 1986. From the moment biologists saw her, they knew she was different. She had a straight tail. Her nose was not high-arched. Over the next few years biologists continued to note that panthers from the Everglades were smaller than cats from Big Cypress and that few had a kinked tail or the distinctive cowlick between their shoulders.

Then, in 1990, Stephen O'Brien, after a comprehensive molecular genetic analysis using mitochondrial DNA and nuclear markers, verified what field-workers suspected: panthers in Everglades National Park were genetically and morphologically different from panthers found elsewhere in South Florida. O'Brien found that "one stock confined to Big Cypress is derived from ancestors of *F. c. coryi*. A second stock, found largely in the Everglades, is descended primarily from pumas that evolved in South or Central America, but were introduced (probably by man) in the Florida habitat very recently."

O'Brien's hunch was correct. Between 1957 and 1965, Lester and Bill Piper, brothers who owned the Everglades Wonder Garden, a roadside attraction in Bonita Springs, had released seven cats in Everglades National Park, close to Florida City. The Pipers had bred panthers in captivity since the 1940s. Although their original stock came from the pinelands of Hendry County, Florida, at least one female of unknown geographic origin joined the menagerie and perpetuated her genes, which now course through panthers in the national park. Although the Pipers hotly deny it, genetic markers tell O'Brien that the cat in question was not a Florida panther.

According to a scientific paper O'Brien and his colleagues published in *Current Biology* in 1993, of the panthers examined in Everglades National Park 9 percent had kinked tails and 27 percent had cowlicks, compared with 94 percent and 88 percent, respectively, in Big Cypress. The introgression of a foreign cat had inadvertently bolstered that panther's gene pool in the national park, and five or six generations later, the contributions of a South American puma can still be detected. Everglades panthers not only looked different from their Big Cypress counterparts, they tested healthier. Males, for instance, had two testicles instead of one, and more viable sperm, obtained from the electronic ejaculation from anesthetized lions.

The southern end of Shark Slough separates Everglades National Park from Big Cypress Swamp. When water levels are low, male panthers wade the slough, which may explain why O'Brien has found trace amounts of a South American genetic marker in Big Cypress. Before TX 105 and TX 108 were released on Long Pine Key, the lone resident male in Everglades National Park, 16, regularly crossed Shark Slough, presumably looking for a mate or for something to eat.

When deer are unavailable, 16 ambushes five- or six-foot alligators while they sunbathe on the marsh edge of hammocks. He grabs them by their throats, feeds on them, then buries them, skin on, under a screen of leaves to keep the meat from rotting, which is typical of mountain lions throughout the hemisphere. Panther 16 has been known to eat bobcats, raccoons, and otters, which says something about the quality of his home range: limited uplands and limited deer.

During periods of drought, white-tailed deer living around the Everglades prospered. What is good for the deer is usually good for the panther. But drought, writes Maehr and park biologist Oron "Sonny" Bass may have a downside for panthers. It has been suggested that organic mercury, harmlessly bound in waterlogged peat, enters the food chain during extreme droughts. Two females that had fed heavily on raccoons died from mercury poisoning. Today any drought is an extreme drought. By 1991 the panther population in Everglades National Park had dwindled to one. In his book, Maehr called the park a "toxic panther cul de sac," the most marginal of habitats that periodically undergo population booms and busts. Without help the Everglades panthers would almost certainly disappear.

In 1995, when 16 met the two Texas cougars, he stopped crossing the slough. Thus far he has sired three litters, fathering a total of four kittens: three females and a male.

I join Sonny Bass and members of the recovery team in Everglades National Park, my last chance to see the team capture a panther, for I return home in several days. They are here to change 16's collar. He has been holed up on a hammock for three days feeding off a kill. The houndsman, Roy McBride, tells me he once tracked 16 to three gator kills on the same hammock.

When water levels are high, as they are this winter, panthers stay in the pines feeding on deer. Once, Bass radio-tracked a panther to a deer kill, only to find a park service colleague who had radio-tracked the deer, a subject of his own study, to the panther, which fled when the scientists arrived. Unfortunately the capture is called off today; a fire ravages the pinelands.

Instead I look for panther signs in the pinelands on the north side of the Flamingo Road, well away from the fire. I walk four miles along the edge of a hammock set between the pines and marl prairie. It's already hot and dry, and a long plume of smoke drifts to the northeast, thick and yellow-gray in the harsh mid-morning light. The trail is dusty, but where it dips an inch or two, there's mud. The woods are crisp. Crusted periphyton covers exposed limestone and portions of the road, cracking in the intense heat. Apple snail shells scattered along the trail are a reminder that there was water here recently.

My path is laced with faint tracks, mostly deer and bobcat. A set of panther tracks appears in the dust, disappears on the hard-packed marl, then reappears. Two more footprints, and they're gone again, cryptic and hard to follow. Several miles farther, on the far side of the pine island, the panther left the pitted, broken landscape of the open prairie and joined the trail. Even for a cat, walking the marl prairie is little better than stepping out of one hole and into another.

I train my binoculars to the north, looking for something other than heat waves moving across the landscape. Dozens of hammocks merge into a wall of shimmering green, closing off the view. The panther doesn't have to be seen to make this landscape wild. The wild comes with knowing it's out there, somewhere.

From the air, early the next morning, the fire appears half a mile wide and more than twenty miles long. Broken here and there by the wetness of the marsh, jagged lines of fire creep over the ground. Isolated trees burn; tongues of flames lick the sky. Behind them are blackened pines, some with green branches, others little more than vertical charcoal. Tendrils of smoke spiral into the morning sky, then coalesce into a single, massive wind-driven front. A blanketing ground fog hugs the marshes and circles the hammocks, which emerge from the vaporous coif looking even more like islands.

The antenna on the plane's wing tells us that 16 has moved back into the pines, east of the fire. After inscribing widening circles for ten minutes, the plane picks up a signal from TX 105 in a hammock just off a corridor of pines. Except for the connection to the pines, the hammock is surrounded by sawgrass. TX 105 is walking through the hammock, whose open grassy center looks like an unmowed meadow. We circle, hoping for a glimpse of the cat. As a deer bolts from the marsh directly into the hammock, the lion stops moving.

The weight of a man's body is enough to
impart a swaying motion to three or four
acres of floating forest.

JOHN W. MACGONIGLE, 1896

11 The Mangrove Coast

The mangrove swamp that buffers the coast of Florida from Vero Beach to
Tampa Bay reaches its greatest density and complexity in Everglades National
Park. Covering more than five hundred square miles, this is one of the grandest mangrove forests on Earth. In a few storm-protected spots trees reach a
hundred feet tall, and below them the peat is fifteen feet thick. At its northern
fringe, the swamp penetrates the Everglades along predominantly freshwater
creeks, which is the first hint that the boundless, airy marsh will soon cede
to dark forest. At its northwestern border, the mangroves fracture into keys
called the Ten Thousand Islands, which eventually peter out in the Gulf of
Mexico. Between these two boundaries lies the largest roadless area in the
lower forty-eight states, a green wilderness carved and drained by tidal creeks

and opaque rivers that flow into and out of bays, lagoons, and brackish lakes. When viewed from a small plane the region looks like a jigsaw puzzle; the brown and green pieces constantly destroyed, renovated, or modified by the passage of tropical storms. Egrets and ibis, white as fresh linen, illuminate the swamp's somber hues.

Here in the dank woods where Florida fades into the sea is one of the richest biological systems in the world. To experience it one must brave relentless wind, fierce sun, unforgiving tides, stinking gases, and mosquitoes, whose overwhelming presence cannot adequately be expressed. One must also traverse tidal rivers called Lostmans, Lostmans Five, Graveyard Creek, and the Nightmare, and pass through a bay, up two rivers and a creek, and around points called either shark or alligator. This is country so far beyond the end of the road that E. O. Wilson is sure that none "but a naturalist or escaped convict" would choose to enter.

The Wilderness Waterway, a one-hundred-mile canoe trail across the tip of Florida, runs through Everglades National Park from Everglades City to Flamingo. Although the trail curls through a labyrinth of mangroves, there are spur routes down to the Gulf, where you can follow the line of the jagged shore. To navigate the waterway, charts—the nautical equivalent of United States Geological Survey topographic maps—are essential.

My partner on the canoe trip is fifty-two-year-old Frank Asch, tall, round-faced, and thin, a gifted children's book author who schedules time each week to play with second-graders. "It's research," he says. He draws his own postcards, whimsical illustrations of stilt-legged birds and personable trees, and sends them home to young friends. "Alligators smile a lot," or, "I love you, manatee," they may say. Children adore him (my boys included).

Everglades City is a community of trailer parks and restaurants, hotels, B&Bs, convenience stores, a ranger station, and canoe rentals, the west gate of Everglades National Park. About a thousand people live here year-round, half of whom, according to a *Boston Globe* report some years ago, were likely to be in jail for drug smuggling. Outside of town myriad unnamed keys do in fact provide cover for drug runners. And an airstrip, known locally as Everglades International Airport, hosts clandestine flights from Central and South America. Only the regional school and the limestone courthouse remind me that people other than those who cater to tourists live here, though they are mostly hidden from view. Down the road on a cement dock by the ranger station, flocks of laughing gulls, royal terns, and black skimmers huddle together, facing the wind like fish in a current. The entire community is built in the mangroves, dredged and filled to rise out of Chokoloskee Bay.

Everglades City was once the county seat of Collier County. In 1960 it had a population of ten thousand (then twice that of Naples), most of them commercial fisherman, and was the largest city on the west coast of Florida between Fort Myers and Key West. On September 10, 1960, when Hurricane Donna passed northwest up the mangrove coast, everything changed. It blew without mercy; winds steady at 140 miles per hour, gusts to 180. Twelve inches of rain sliced sideways out of the sky. The Gulf surged five feet high through the streets. Houses were torn and scattered. Afterward the county seat was moved to Naples, and most of Everglades City's residents never came back. Those who did return continued to fish Chokoloskee Bay and the waters around the Ten Thousand Islands until commercial fishing was banned in Everglades National Park. Others attended tourists, poached gators, or hauled pot, which was more lucrative than fishing.

((((

The Turner River begins in waterlogged Big Cypress north of the Tamiami Trail, a sweet-water tributary destined for the tide. Before emptying into Chokoloskee Bay, the Turner River passes through cypress and sawgrass, brackish ponds, open coastal prairies, and dense mangroves—what locals call "the Hollywood Everglades," the Everglades of cinema, claustrophobic, rich, dark, wild. For the Calusa the river was an avenue into the interior, and they left behind scraps of pre-Columbian Florida, shell mounds and pottery shards.

Access to the Turner River is a weedy cement dam on a canoeable drainage canal that crosses the Tamiami Trail roughly ten miles northeast of Everglades City. The canal was built circa 1956, part of another unfulfilled real estate scheme. (In 1996, two years after I paddled the Turner River, Big Cypress National Preserve filled the canal and allowed the forest to return, a small project within the parameters of greater Everglades restoration.) The canal is straight, deep, and wide. A congestion of trees and shrubs and vines rises from both its banks. Strangler figs, sprouting in the crown of many of the palms, send their roots earthward, entwining trunks. In a weak parody of Vermont autumn, a few red maple leaves turn color in the midst of green. Overhead, vultures soar stiff-winged into the morning. An immature yellow-crowned night heron flushes a dozen times as we paddle toward the Turner River.

The river appears in the distance as a dogleg. A red-shouldered hawk on a bare cypress limb screams, fixed on something beyond my comprehension, its yellow eyes resolute. Past the hawk we drift, our eyes on his. Beyond, the river narrows and coils back on itself. The forest opens to a marsh cut by a pair of airboat trails, paths of flattened sawgrass. At first a few red mangroves join the freshwater trees. Eventually they dominate.

The word *mangrove* has two meanings: it is a catchall for unrelated tropical maritime trees or shrubs that evolved common characteristics for life in salty environments, including aerial roots and a fruit that germinates while still on the tree; it is also a synonym for the entire community of plants and animals that dwell along these muddy saltwater shorelines. In Florida there are three mangrove species that represent three plant families—black, white, and red; worldwide there are thirty-four species that belong to five families.

On a limb near the center of a tree sits a mangrove cuckoo, buff-breasted and brighter than the surrounding gloom. The river tapers to a slit and enters a fortress of trees. With a heightened sense of futility, we insert the canoe into the mangroves and, for the next half-mile, paddle through a silent swamp tunnel. Squeezed by the encroaching shoreline, which is really no shoreline at all, we duck overarching limbs and ricochet off prop roots and aerial roots. The windless shadows encourage mosquitoes. Peeling ropy spider lines off our faces and swatting mosquitoes, we bank off trees. When we finally emerge into light, our arms and legs reveal a range of welts; our hair carries a veil of webs. A bevy of ibises probe for fiddler crabs, their long, curved bills deep in the muddy banks of the river.

The Turner River is shown by a United States Geological Survey topographic map called the Chokoloskee Quadrangle. Everything on it is a variation of blue and green. There's yellow-green for freshwater swamp; light green, the saltwater marsh; dark green, the mangroves; and water-blue, deep or light or wispy white, for the bay. The invisible tug of the full moon rules the quadrangle, causing water to rise, ooze, and spread through lacy tributaries into and out of bays. Southwest of Hell's Half Acre—a labeled stand of mangroves on the map—Hurddles Creek connects the Turner River to Mud Bay, the Cross Bays, and the Lopez River, which is our destination the following day. Looking at the map and at the creek itself, one cannot tell how the water flows. The current is fickle. The direction of the creek is constantly revised by the tides, the storms, and the freshwater drainage from the north. It is an obscure line in the poem that is the mangroves and is directly and indirectly edited by the weather.

❲❲❲

When Columbus reached the New World it is safe to say that the Calusa knew it. Their dugouts roamed far out to sea and probably reached the Arawaks that lived on the islands on the far side of the Gulf Stream and those on

Cuba, across the treacherous Straits of Florida. To sixteenth-century Spanish explorers who followed Columbus, the Calusa were the Fierce People, the ones who killed Ponce de León; their home ground, the coastal jungles from Cape Sable to the mouth of the Caloosahatchee River, was the Lagoon of the Holy Spirit, a place that stirred Spanish imaginations. The beautiful and delicate estuaries along Florida's southwest coast teemed with food—conchs, oysters, clams, shrimp, lobster, mullet, snook, red fish, snapper, weakfish, bull sharks, hammerheads, alligators, sea turtles, manatees, marsh rabbits, raccoon, deer, bear, panther, and, in season, tasty birds from the four corners of North America—and the Calusa flourished. They fashioned a sophisticated economic base without the use of agriculture.

In 1545, thirteen-year-old Hernando d'Escalante Fontaneda, shipwrecked en route to Spain from Colombia, began seventeen years as a Calusa captive. Although the Calusa had "no gold, less silver and less clothing," Fontaneda wrote, they nevertheless fashioned a high prehistoric culture along the edge of the Everglades, building oyster shell islands and digging transportation canals up to thirty feet wide and eight feet deep. The Calusa had leisure time to carve wooden masks, to shape bone and shell tools, and to make canoes that held forty people. The oyster-eating Calusa, writes Peter Matthiessen, must have "sat there shucking a good while to fling a forty-acre shell pile over their shoulders." A few miles south of Everglades City, near the southeast corner of the bay, the road ends on a shell pile twenty feet tall that covers 135 acres called Chokoloskee Island. This is our launch site for the Wilderness Waterway, due south of marker 129 off the mouth of the Turner River.

It is early morning, warm, seventy degrees. The wind is out of the northeast at fifteen to twenty-five miles per hour. We've been paddling for more than an hour. Held by the wind, a brown pelican stalls in front of us, then sails eastward toward the Lopez River. Gulls are up, drifting and crying, gray birds against azure. Instead of receding, Chokoloskee Island appears to be getting closer. The tide begins to drop, and we struggle against the bay and the wind.

Southeast of Chokoloskee Island the bay is almost nowhere deeper than two feet. It is imperative that we follow the channel markers, particularly on a falling tide; however, we lose the channel and strand the canoe on an oyster bar. Shoals spread outward from the shore and appear to crystallize spontaneously at midbay. Sinking to our ankles, we tow the canoe toward deeper water, which rapidly moves away from us, as though the bay were evaporating on a hot skillet. Near the mouth of the Lopez River an osprey hovers over water deep enough for fish. The bird knows the channel, the lay of the land.

The Lopez River runs east four miles to the west end of Sunday Bay. The river is deep by Everglades standards, four to eleven feet, and changes direction on the tide. As we paddle against the flow, it seems as though all the Everglades pours down the river. The wind whacks us head-on. Five white ibises mine fiddler crabs feeding on decaying mangrove leaves along the far shore, their sickle bills deep in muck. Their eyes, which sit high on their heads, scan the sky for predators, bald eagles and peregrines.

Red mangroves, *Rhizophora mangle,* line both banks and extend back into darkness. The lower part of each trunk sends out prop roots that arch two or three feet into the muck like a jumble of croquet wickets. As the tide recedes, aerial roots, which grow down from branches, sway in the wind. The Seminole call the red mangrove "walking trees," a reference to their bizarre appearance and the belief that they spread seaward, as though by walking. The generic name, *Rhizophora,* is from the Latin meaning "to bear roots"; *mangle* is the Arawak word for mangrove, a common feature of their Caribbean home ground. To amuse themselves, some Australian scientists studying red mangroves hold foot races through the tangled jungle; the world record for the one-hundred-meter Mangrove Dash is twenty-two minutes and thirty seconds. Tiny pores called lenticles stipple aerial and prop roots. They diffuse oxygen down to subsurface roots at low tide and close during high tide to keep water out. Both the prop and longer aerial roots also anchor the tree against the relentless wind and tide. Patches of small oysters, called coon oysters, cover some of the prop roots, and tiny, stalk-eyed crabs play out their obscure lives among the oysters.

A huge cistern on the eastern shore, halfway up the Lopez River, is all that remains of someone's hard and lonely life. At marker 126 we enter Crooked Creek, a sinuous shortcut that loops three times before joining Sunday Bay, one of eighteen brackish bays between Everglades City and Flamingo. Sunday erupts with whitecaps. Taking advantage of the wind, vultures fleck the sky. A mullet shoots from the water like a bar of soap, splashes, and leaps again. Mullet are important food fish for snook, tarpon, osprey, eagle, crocodile, alligator, and dolphin as well as for humans. Grazing on algae-laminated detritus, they school through the flooded forest and pepper the surface whenever the mood strikes. Once, when I was kayaking in the moonlight, a mullet leapt onto my lap.

East across Sunday Bay and Oyster Bay, into Huston Bay. There is nothing beyond the water save mangroves, and nothing beyond that save water and more mangroves, a horizontal world walled by trees. I steer for distant eye-level shapes: a peninsula, an archipelago, a pocket in the shoreline where dead branches point nowhere in particular.

The southeast corner of Huston Bay narrows to a river's width and becomes a fork of the Chatham River. On the chart the Chatham appears as a blue y. On the water it is coffee-brown, a twisted, tannin-stained umbilicus that feeds the Gulf of Mexico a diet of fermenting mangrove leaves, the foundation of the estuarine and inshore food chains. On the Bend in the Chatham River, half a mile south of the fork, is Watson's Place, where the notorious murderer Edgar Watson lived until he was gunned down by the men of Chokoloskee Island in 1910. Six men and a boy camp here.

This is the boy's initiation into the Everglades. He is nine years old. A lacquered alligator toe hangs from a leather necklace around his neck. He shows me Calusa pottery shards, black and red chips he had plucked from muck. Reverently he fingers his shards as old Florida rises behind his eyes, five hundred years and more bridged.

I awake during the night to the hoots of a barred owl from somewhere in the forest and to the deep breathing of the bottle-nosed dolphins, which drive fish up the Chatham River. When the tide lowers, dolphins move upriver feasting on mullet and sea trout, which head for open water. Dark water is no obstacle for dolphins. So sensitive are their echolocation abilities that trained dolphins can distinguish between similar-sized aluminum and copper plates. Hot dolphin mist spews in the cool night, and all their riotous splashes, surges, and rushes send waves to shore that keep coming long after the dolphins are gone.

The following morning we paddle up the Chatham River, past the Huston Bay fork, into Chevalier Bay, named for a French milliner who collected bird skins for museums and was a contemporary of Edgar Watson. Then on into Cannon Bay. It is cool, sixty degrees and almost windless. The sky is wide and gray and dull. Chevalier Bay is riveted to Cannon Bay by a jumble of islands that restrict our view and fracture the narrows into four channels. From Cannon Bay to Tarpon Bay up Alligator Creek, a narrow, curving tributary. Inside Alligator Creek a canopy of low sun-blocking branches supports the elaborate webs of prickly crab spiders.

A red mangrove leaf floats down and lands on my lap. Older slime-coated, waterlogged, partially digested leaves sit on the river bottom. These are chunks in the rich mangrove soup, one of the most productive ecosystems in the world. In one year, each acre receives, on average, seven thousand pounds of leaves, twigs, branches, and flowers, a constant rain of debris day after day without regard to season. (Minor peaks occur at the beginning of the wet season after tropical storms.) A freshly fallen leaf is about 3 percent protein. A month later, after the leaf has been colonized by a potpourri of bacteria, fungi, nematodes, protozoa, and algae, its protein content has risen to more than 20 percent—the average can of dog food contains about 8 percent protein—and becomes a tasty snack for crabs, small fish, and segmented worms that are in turn eaten by predatory fish, blue crabs, terrapins, water snakes, wading birds, dolphins, ospreys, bald eagles, alligators, and crocodiles. Clams and oysters filter the soup. Snails scrape it. Crabs grind it. For pink shrimp, spiny lobsters, and many species of deep-water fish, the mangroves are a nursery; their estuarine migrations are as predictable as those of birds. I once saw a devil ray, and, on another occasion, a bull shark almost as long as my canoe, back in the mangroves; both beasts of deeper water were floundering in brown ooze, out of place and nearly out of oxygen.

Above us a yellow warbler gleans something from the undersurface of a leaf, then flits around like animated sunlight. Our paddle stirs deep, rich muck, thousands of years of accumulated roots, rootlets, and root hairs locked in an oxygenless void. Eaten by crabs, segmented worms, and small fish, leaves never last long enough to become muck. In this zone of constant flux, red mangroves thrive. Although they can grow in freshwater they are not competitive and are easily muscled aside by a score of freshwater vascular plants. The salty, anaerobic conditions exclude other trees, and the shifting tides exclude other species of mangroves. A living desalinization unit, the red mangrove separates freshwater from saltwater at the root. Root hairs also exclude hydrogen sulfide, the toxic by-product of anaerobic respiration.

Freshwater runoff from the Everglades and Big Cypress brings nutrients to the mangroves and flushes hydrogen sulfide, which smells like rotten eggs. We emerge from the tunnel into Alligator Bay. On the chart the bay is shaped like a rubber ducky, head tilted northwest. We cross it. Along the edge of a small creek on the north side of the bay cabbage palms, blades of sawgrass, and tufts of leatherleaf fern hint of freshwater. Because of the influx of fresh-water, Alligator Bay is clear, and its clarity reveals nervous mullet that agitate the surface like rain. I swish Alligator Bay in my mouth and spit it back. No salt.

Across Dad's Bay, an almost perfect oval; then due south down Plate Creek to Plate Creek Bay. On the far end of Plate Creek Bay, adjacent to a small island, is a chickee fashioned by the park service after the Seminole dwelling and used by boaters. It is an open-sided ten-by-twelve-foot platform five feet off the water; its roof is supported by four posts. It has been a short day, ten miles.

Carpets of thin, foot-long, gray pneumatophores rise like a thousand twisted fingers from the muck. They are the lenticle-rich breathing tubes of black mangrove, snorkels that send oxygen underwater. Black mangrove grows on ground higher than red mangrove habitat. It cannot survive in the lower tidal zone, where twice each day the sea would rise above the pneumatophores and drown the tree. It rims ephemeral salt ponds, thriving anywhere the tide is slight, clutching saturated soil often saltier than the sea itself. Red mangrove dies when salt concentrations reach sixty-five parts per thousand; black mangrove may grow in salinity of more than ninety parts per thousand. To survive, black mangrove drinks saltwater and excretes salt crystals over the belly of its dark, succulent leaves. Because of salinity stress, black mangrove has a higher respiration rate and less net production of leaves than red; it grows thicker, chewier leaves and contributes less energy to the detritus food chain. I run a salt-crusted leaf through my lips and taste the salt.

The tiny flowers of black mangrove, *Avicennia germinans,* produce abundant nectar that lures honeybees into the saltwater jungles. Honey fashioned from its blossoms, a favorite in South Florida, is as clear as the forest is dark. Although frost is deadly to red and white mangroves, black mangrove resprouts and persists as a tangled shrub on the Gulf Coast all the way to Louisiana and Texas. The genus is named for Avicenna, an eleventh-century Arab physician and philosopher whose musings on the mind of man and God were popular in the Middle Ages; *germinans* refers to the characteristic mangrove fruits that germinate on the tree.

The word *mangrove* itself is a construction of a Portuguese word for tree, *mangue* (probably derived from the Arawak *mangle*), and the English word for a stand of trees, *grove.* The tree dwells in heat, humidity, and salt, rooted in airless earth at the threshold of terrestrial life. It lives like a tree described by Wendell Berry, "a tree that does not grow beyond the power of its place," one that "stands in its place and rises by the strength of local soil and light, aspiring to no height that it has not attained. More time, more light, more rain will make it grow again till it has realized all that it can become, and then it dies into more life, deserving more by not desiring more."

All afternoon I stare at gnarled, wind-beaten trees. Birds peel off in the pewter sky and disappear below the green horizon. A friend of poet Gary Snyder once asked him what the rocks thought of the trees. "What do you mean?" Snyder replied. "Aren't the trees just passing through?" answered his friend. Who will pass through after the mangroves? They live in an uncompromising world, masters of one of the last places in North America to be explored.

《《《

The trees and the shadows of the trees merge and become a fortress of shapeless darkness. The voice on my weather-band radio alerts me to small craft warnings. Pale blue light steals in from the east. As the world awakens, a flock of white pelicans, perhaps as many two hundred, appears above the forest, the red sun behind them. The sky is a dilute orange, a theater for improvisational pelicans: each one rises and sinks in synchronous flight, an aerial pulsation called drafting in which a lead bird deflects wind and makes flying easier for those behind it. They bunch, separate, back and forth, black and white, then split into four soundless concertinas. One flock changes direction and then changes again. The core of the original flock arches, each bird equidistant from its neighbors. The last fifteen or twenty pelicans condense, unfurl, then snap up like a slow-motion whip. Below them flap a pair of stiff-winged wood storks.

In 1994 Alan Mairson, a *National Geographic* editor, wrote that there were "far too few magic moments" for him to be romanced by the Everglades. "Some days," he continued, "I felt as though I were wandering through a museum stripped of its artifacts." Unfortunately he missed the magic that blossoms at dawn and dusk in secret crannies of the backcountry. To fully appreciate the Everglades requires repeated trips, or possibly one long trip, where you go beyond the seemingly monotonous landscape. Idle time and idle landscapes can reward a patient observer with spectacular bursts of life. Nowhere will the effects of restoration be more important than here in the coastal jungles, where two worlds come together. Yet magic moments will still reward the patient observer.

The following morning we paddle toward South Lostmans, a spit of white sand jutting into the Gulf of Mexico. We push off at nine o'clock, tethered to a hefty northwest wind and a rapidly falling tide. A creek across from the chickee brings us to Lostmans Five Bay, a small arrow-shaped body of water named either for an army surgeon during the Seminole Wars or for five stranded soldiers. An unnamed, mile-long creek leads to Two Island Bay—which as far as I can tell has only one island—and on southeast into Onion Key Bay, a large, twisted body of water.

Onion Key, on the west side of the bay, was the one-acre field headquarters for *Poinciana Mainland,* another ludicrous real estate development, perhaps the prototype of all Florida scams. In the 1920s prospective buyers would drive to the Loop Road, park their vehicles, and trudge six long miles over slippery, sodden limestone to a canoe landing. From there they would boat a mile to Onion Key, to a congestion of portable houses. Most buyers never made the trip. If they had they would have found a Shangri-la for crustaceans and mosquitoes. Amazingly, the company sold nearly nine thousand lots in the mangroves along Lostmans River using a steady stream of factless newspaper advertising.

> History tells us that the first bananas were brought to Poinciana over a hundred years ago when the original Spanish settlement was formed here. Today the groves the Spanish planted, the bananas, oranges, limes, and coconuts are still flourishing and producing fruit of excellent size and flavor—proof of the wonderful fertility of the soil. (Miami, January 5, 1926, *Illustrated Daily Tab*)

Onion Key had been a Calusa settlement for more than a thousand years. A trash heap of shells, now covered by earth, lifts the island five feet above the water. The daily thrashing of the tides doesn't reach the buttonwoods that dominate the higher, dryer artificial habitat. Buttonwood, an associate of the mangroves, is not as salt tolerant as the other species and is restricted to the highest ground in the swamp—shell mounds and storm levees. I see no bananas or oranges or limes, only buttonwoods and mangroves. Mercifully the hurricane of 1926 erased Poinciana Mainland and returned the island to fiddler crabs, which scuttle away as I approach.

As we paddle again, the wind and tide are on our side. Mangroves clip by. A large island fits like a cork in the narrows of Onion Key Bay and, beyond that, Second Bay. The tide pours gulfward and carries us into a cove in the southwest corner of Second Bay, which tapers to a point, a thin stitch of a creek hemmed in mangroves that connects to Lostmans River. Water begins to pull away from the shore. The cove, reduced to puddles, is going dry, and we are compelled to push and dig through sulfurous ooze, sinking to our knees. Eventually we hit the creek, and then the river.

Lostmans River is long, wide and deep, nowhere less than seven feet. We ride the wind and draining tide. A pair of bottle-nosed dolphins slice the surface with sharp, glistening fins. A dozen mullet panic, leaping to escape the pursuing dolphins. The dolphins chase the fish toward the shore, where the prop roots of red mangrove hold the mullet at bay. Lostmans River opens into First Bay. Beyond the mouth of the bay lies the Gulf of Mexico.

Our campsite at South Lostmans is a sand spit off an island that plugs much of the mouth of First Bay. The spit appeared after Hurricane Donna. In the early 1900s, mullet fishermen lived on the island in shacks roofed with palmetto fronds, netted mullet by the tens of thousands, dried them on racks, and shipped them in cypress barrels to Key West. The hurricane of 1910 ended the fragile reign of the fishing community.

Down the beach is the mark of a more recent hurricane, Andrew, whose eye had passed here sixteen months earlier. In a pocket the size of a football field almost every tree is down or standing gray and barkless, limbs like bones. On the rise behind the bleached lumber, the mangroves are busted but alive. Each tree wears a coif of tiny new branches that sprout from base to crown, a furry forest. (The poststorm growth pattern of the hardwood trees in the hammocks of Long Pine Key is the same.) A cadre of vultures that roosts in the dead trees flees at my approach. Big black birds against big blue sky drifting away on the wind.

The Gulf is frothing, a sea of whitecaps. An orange sun sinks in the west, settling somewhere over the Yucatán Peninsula. As the eastern sky fades to lavender, vultures settle in the bony trees. I have never seen a larger roost. Naked limbs covered by thousands of vultures.

At dawn royal terns are scouting for fish. The wind is dead and the tide rising. The January tide table lists high tide for South Lostmans at 9:35 A.M. Our only deadline is that proposed by the tide and the wind and the strength of our arms. Joshua Slocum, the first man to sail solo around the world, said that he "tried to take the offensive, relying on will power and action; to be a pilot rather than a passenger on the sea of life." We do the same. (Slocum, unfortunately, disappeared in 1909 en route to the Amazon, a fact I keep to myself.)

We're out by seven, two and a half hours before high tide, and have about five hours before the tide collapses and the Florida Plateau rises out of the sea: five hours and thirteen miles to Shark Point. With the sun comes the wind, slowly at first. We stick to a tongue of water four feet deep that spills out of the bay but hit a wickerwork of sandbars along the channel and, knee-deep in water, have to tow the canoe southward. A mile offshore the water deepens. I scan for sharks—bull or hammerhead—that lurk offshore or move into the mangroves to feed.

Off port, Highland Point is a prominent landmark to the south when seen from South Lostmans, itself a prominent landmark two miles to the north, our first sense of visible distance since we left Chokoloskee Island. Ten miles south of Shark Point, the smudge on the horizon is Northwest Cape Sable, which floats on the haze eighteen miles away. Frank calls this effect *sfumato*, the dreamlike quality where poetic vision enters art. To the west, the Gulf and sky are a featureless blue-gray.

Highland Point, on Key McLaughlin, took a direct hit from Hurricane Andrew; busted trees litter three miles of Highland Beach. Andrew's south eye wall generated a thirteen-foot storm surge that swept sand nearly fifty feet into the forest, smoothed the beach's profile to a gentle slope, and stranded millions of fish. I had passed over Highland Beach in a small plane six days after the storm, seventy thousand acres of mangroves down; an estimated seventy-five million cubic yards of splintered trees transformed a level jungle into a tortuous pile of uprooted trees and stagnant pools. The smell of rot had filled the plane and had wafted northward for thirty miles. As the hurricane's eye moved offshore, impounded water surged back to the Gulf of Mexico, gouging more than twenty ebb channels across the beach. The breach weakened the sand barrier that protects the interior mangroves against the Gulf of Mexico that in time will carve bays where forests once stood. Three miles farther down the coast, where, like the twin horns of an eland, Rodgers River and Broad River curl into an island-studded lagoon, trees have been spared by the hurricane, and green replaces gray as the dominant color. Shark Point, seven miles farther east, looks mostly green.

Frank asks me in which direction would I go if I could time travel. Pre-Columbian North America, I say, to these Everglades, to see the wild potential of South Florida, the birds, the alligators, the landscape interrupted only by the canals and the shell mounds of the Calusa, who would be paddling this very stretch of coast, half-naked. Frank wants to visit the future when everything is pristine again. For that moment, buoyed by his faith, I uncharacteristically wish to live a thousand years, to know if restoration will work, if wild South Florida will reclaim a portion of its biological wealth and survive on the fringes of urban Florida.

An hour later, we round Shark Point into Graveyard Creek, the wind hammering our backs. It is early afternoon. We have covered thirteen miles in five and a half hours, and we have not seen a shark. This is unusual, for the point is named for the young hammerheads that mill offshore fattening on the last links of the mangrove food chain.

Banked by green mangroves, Graveyard Creek is a sinuous creek that drains several square miles of coastal forest. Tannins leaking from the roots and leaves of all three species of mangroves darken otherwise clear water, which adds to the forbidding nature of the jungle, an unpredictable wetland whose dual nature—shark or dolphin—lies hidden just below the surface. A shapely white mangrove, *Laguncularia racemosa,* sits above tide line, close to the campsite. Because white mangrove grows on higher ground than either red or black mangrove and is not constantly harried by the tides, it lacks prop roots. Some specimens rooted in saturated soil may develop short pneumatophores, which is not the case with this tree. The trunk is speckled with lenticles, the white mangrove's concession to life close to the edge. The leaves are opposite, elliptic, leathery, and contain 17 percent tannin. In Brazil several million pounds of leaves are harvested annually for tanning leather. The leafstalks are red, with two conspicuous salt-secreting glands near the base of each leaf. The genus *Laguncularia,* from the Latin *laguncula,* refers to the fruits, which resemble small handblown bottles. *Racemosa* is also Latin and alludes to the flower clusters, or racemes.

Graveyard Creek is named for the murder of two thieving coon-hunters who were killed along its shore in the 1920s. We haul the canoe alongside the tree. Three men, accompanied by a twenty-four-foot powerboat, a cabin-sized canvas tent, and a huge cooler that holds enough food and liquor to cater a wedding, are not overjoyed to see us. The spokesman steps up. His name is Jack Gomez—his buddies call him Klondike—and he carries a sheathed filet knife that hangs from his hip almost to his knee. Jack dwarfs everything but the biggest trees. He is barrel-chested, and his curly blond hair falls in ringlets across wide shoulders. When he walks, his thighs ripple. "We're here to party and fish, just so you understand," he announces loud enough to ruffle the feathers of seabirds. Gomez claims to be a descendant of the pirate Juan Gomez, for whom a key in the Ten Thousand Islands is named.

According to Everglades lore, Gomez the elder was born in 1778 and served with Napoleon Bonaparte and with the pirate Gasparilla, fought in the Battle of Lake Okeechobee in Seminole War of 1837, sold slaves, and ran the blockade during the Civil War. When he drowned in his fishnet in 1900, he would have been 122 years old. So colorful was his character that the story of Juan Gomez's death and funeral appeared in Matthiessen's book *Killing Mister Watson.* His body was found, wrote Matthiessen, "hooked by his trousers in the mangroves at low tide, with his nose-warmer washed up alongside him." Jack Gomez may be one of the world's ten strongest men. Whenever he catches a fish, he kills it with his knife, a lethal blow to the head that he calls jugging. To emphasize the term, he swipes the air with his knife like a casual backhand in tennis.

Midafternoon, dead low tide, Jack and his friends go fishing. A mile offshore they leave the channel and get stuck in marl. The engine screams, plowing up bottom sediments. A gray smoke screen spews behind the boat, which goes nowhere. They spend an hour rocking and pushing the boat toward deeper water, all the while drinking. Scraps of their conversations roll shoreward like waves.

((((

The next morning, while our neighbors sleep, six royal terns and two cormorants watch the tide while idling on a snag in the mouth of Graveyard Creek. Offshore, brown pelicans plunge into deep water. As we wade toward the channel, the birds disperse. Much of the creek has drained to its lowest stage, a ribbon of water flanked by twin plains of glistening mud. As we pass a sandbar in the north end of Ponce de Leon Bay, water seeps across the bar and swirls at our feet. The sky is richly colored, a mutable canvas of tangerine that bleeds to rose, fades to lemon yellow. Eleven tributaries, themselves fed by smaller tidal creeks fed by still smaller creeks, enter Ponce de Leon Bay, creating a vascular network that swells and shrinks, clogs, reverses direction, merges, and cuts new paths. According to my chart, all the tributaries split off from two rivers: Shark River, the mother of this entire ramification, the principal distributary of the Everglades, and Little Shark River.

The shoreline here has been stabilized by thirty-two hundred years of mangrove growth. A buildup of peat and sediment has kept pace with a modest sea level rise of an inch and a half a century. I imagine that three thousand years ago the shape of Ponce de Leon Bay was similar to its shape today. Except for those damaged by the hurricanes that periodically ripped the forest asunder, trees back then, nourished by copious runoff from the Everglades, grew old and tall along Shark River. Since the 1930s, however, there has been a dramatic change: the sea has risen between seven and ten inches, stressing the entire mangrove ecosystem, which can keep pace with a rise of only about a foot per century. If the ocean rises two feet a century, as it did in the prehistoric past, the storm levees no longer separate the saltwater from the freshwater. At three feet per century South Florida would be catastrophically inundated; the Everglades would recede north, and mangroves would establish beachheads far inland. What's to blame for the changing fortunes of the world's oceans? Perhaps it is the greenhouse effect. Or maybe it is simply the will of the Earth, for glaciers keep to their own pulsating schedule, building, flowing, and melting.

I improvise a route to Shark River that will take us to our next camp at Canepatch, a Calusa mound and old Seminole site on tiny Avocado Creek. The river flows northeast. To the east all creeks peter out in blind mangrove alleys. Counting tidal rivers is futile: some radiate and enter the bay in a cloverleaf or separate like tines of a fork; others, plugged by sandbars, appear as multiple tributaries. The chart shows the first eight flowing east. I choose one, and we paddle in. For all my intense concentration, I'm never sure where we are. Three bottle-nosed dolphins escort the canoe for ten minutes, temporarily erasing the notion that we might be lost.

Eventually we blunder into Shark River, a deep, impressively wide tidal river. Before drainage, Shark River carried enough freshwater that alligators and some species of freshwater fish moved almost to the tide line. We stay on the river for seven miles. At marker 8, the first navigational aid we've seen in two days, the river splits in two. One branch veers north; the other, a jagged chevron, is more undecided—northeast one mile, southeast one mile, back northeast, and then due north. As if to confirm our proximity to freshwater, an alligator slides off the bank, and a second lolls barely at the surface, eyes and snout up like islands. We cross the east end of Tarpon Bay, through a narrow creek, and into a cove. Avocado Creek empties into the cove. Air-gulping gar dimple the surface, and schools of small sunfish nose around my paddle, both emissaries from the nearby sawgrass marshes. Windrows of dead sunfish line the shore, and a few balance on mangrove roots. Are they victims of oxygen deprivation or of increased concentrations of salt as the Gulf's influence moves farther inland during the dry season?

Prolonged cycles of rain flush salt from creeks and stagnant ponds. Then red mangroves spread into the formerly prohibitive zone of black mangrove, freshwater plants appear along the upper reaches of estuarine creeks, and sunfish enter the deep green forest. Canepatch is one and a half miles up Avocado Creek, at the edge of a small pond where red mangrove–lined tributaries peter out in the sawgrass.

A wood stork glides over the dock. Two more sail northeast toward Rookery Branch Creek, a headwater creek that merges into sawgrass. In 1934 Rookery Branch hosted a nesting colony of nearly a quarter of a million white ibis. Since the early 1970s, however, Rookery Branch has been little more than a nostalgic roost. When artificial levees and canals reduced the freshwater flow from the Everglades, the lower end of Shark Slough, which had been persistently wet, began to dry. Although white ibis and wood storks can breed successfully when commuting up to sixty miles to feed, Rookery Branch lost its appeal, because an enormous swath of the coastal jungles and southern Everglades failed to produce enough fish to sustain the birds.

The empty rookeries deprive nearby mangroves of a blizzard of guano, a localized nutrient source that is recycled for decades. The trees around the colonies are more productive than those outside and attract greater concentrations of leaf-grazing insects and schools of foraging fish. Collectively they form a nutrient-driven mosaic across the mangrove swamp. From the air, despite the passage of half a century, the mangroves around the Broad River colony site, standing out from the surrounding jungle, are still lush and vibrant.

At dawn the following morning three storks settle over Canepatch. Vultures crowd the dead mangroves directly across from the dock, perhaps attracted by the astronomical number of floating sunfish. With a falling tide and a favorable wind, we race down Avocado Creek, across the east end of Tarpon Bay, as low-level sunlight ignites the yellow-green leaves of red mangrove. In the Caribbean, red mangrove leaves are dried, smoked as tobacco, and steeped as tea. Twigs are frayed for toothpicks. How many mangroves have I seen? Trillions of trillions of trillions? Leaves beyond number.

From Shark River we paddle into Little Shark River. From a nest atop a huge dead and broken mangrove, an osprey hollers. A red mangrove propagule floats by bearing two tiny green leaves. I reach for it and almost tip the canoe. The propagule is cigar-shaped and as long as a ruler. It floats vertically, roots on bottom, leaves on top, an embryo seeking its destiny. Mangroves are viviparous, a trait they share with all but a couple of egg-laying mammals. After the flower is fertilized, the propagule germinates on the tree without a resting stage and is therefore not technically considered a seed. Red mangrove propagules can float in salt water for up to a year and may be unloosed by the very storm that killed their parent. Black mangrove propagules are several inches long and may survive 110 days afloat. White mangrove has small propagules that are more or less persistent woody fruit; when cast adrift they are viable for only a month. All three species live along the coast of West Africa, the birthplace of big weather, and their propagules probably rode the wind and waves west to the Caribbean and South Florida. If a red mangrove propagule arrives on stable sediment, it sets roots and grows. Over time an island may form with black and white mangroves establishing themselves on higher ground.

Many of the keys we've paddled past on the Wilderness Waterway began life when a propagule lodged on or next to an oyster bar. Intertidal oyster colonies grow horizontally, perpendicular to the current, often on sandbars, where they are bathed by nutrients. Their siphons suck in water; their mouths filter microscopic lunches from the tide. Oyster bars branch and merge, trapping sediments, and slowly rise to become nutritive nets for seafaring propagules Eventually trees replace oysters, shaping new islands until they are ripped by storms.

From Little Shark River we take the Shark Cutoff into Oyster Bay, past marker 2, and follow the black line on the chart labeled Wilderness Waterway through Cormorant Pass, past its jumbled green islands, and on into Whitewater Bay. We are cavalier paddlers more than two miles off course. Like the Gulf itself, the bay stretches to the horizon. Five thousand years ago Whitewater Bay was part of the freshwater Everglades, a marsh that became hollowed out by violent wind, its peat and muck spilling and splashing over the eroding shore. In the northern half of the continent, as melting glaciers fed the rising sea, saltwater moved into Whitewater Bay and mingled with the sweet waters of the Everglades. Slowly Whitewater Bay became a shallow inland bay, sometimes fresh, sometimes brackish. Seventy years ago, the free-flowing

Everglades unloaded freshwater into the bay by way of the Watson, North, Roberts, and Lane Rivers. Back then, sawgrass grew along Whitewater Bay's north shore. Canals and levees diverted freshwater away from the Everglades and invited the sea deeper into the bay. No longer do freshwater plants shade the north shore.

When Flamingo's Buttonwood Canal was completed in 1957, water from Florida Bay moved into Coot Bay and eastern Whitewater Bay, exacerbating the salt incursion. In July 1982 an artificial barrier was placed across the canal at the Flamingo Marina, and the waters of Whitewater Bay began to sweeten, a small step in the direction of regional restoration. Manatees have returned to the eastern corner of the bay; some even wander down the canal.

We retrace our strokes, and after a four-mile, two-hour detour we arrive at Oyster Bay Chickee, two days out of Flamingo. After dinner we paddle beneath a three-quarter moon, watch silver light dash across the tops of prop roots, and listen to the huff and puff of porpoises. The wind is dead; the temperature is a delightful seventy degrees. From somewhere an owl's voice rides the night currents.

❨❨❨

In the morning, we leave Oyster Bay Chickee at quarter past seven, bound for South Joe River Chickee and our last night on wilderness waters. We follow the points of the peninsulas southeast. Two enormous clouds dominate the sky: one looks like the shark we never saw, mouth agape, chasing and then finally absorbing its prey. Both are painted lavender and rose.

A pair of raccoons foraging for crabs pauses to watch us paddle by. Behind them the humped prop roots of red mangrove recede into darkness. When we enter Joe River the tide and the wind are against us. We paddle southeast, past four more miles of mangroves and itinerant dolphins, and arrive at South Joe River Chickee.

A bottle-nosed dolphin chases unseen fish around the chickee. A tour boat out of Flamingo enters Joe River and stops by. The tourists take dozens of photographs of us. I have grown accustomed to the movement of the canoe, the dripping and the swishing of our paddles, the back of Frank's head, his blue hat, the passage of trees along the shore, the sight of an island or an inlet across a bay, the chart, the compass. We've averaged about two miles an hour, day after day, our minds free to wander.

At sunset I paddle the periphery of the cove behind the chickee. Every prop root sports a dark high-tide line, and almost every one has a bouquet of coon oysters, which *A Guide to the Wilderness Waterway of the Everglades National*

Park claims are tasty but far too small to bother with. A prairie warbler flits from tree to tree before settling for the night. A mullet leaps. A dolphin snorts. To the east the blue-gray sky becomes black.

When the sun rises the next morning, we are paddling off the southwest corner of Whitewater Bay. A half-dozen powerboats and a tour boat mark the entrance to Tarpon Creek, which leads to Coot Bay. A turtle sculls past. Between the creek and Coot Bay, half a million coots once wintered before the Buttonwood Canal and its accompanying saltwater shriveled their food supply.

The canal is as straight as a razor and as boring as a Dakota interstate, a deep navigable channel beyond the noticeable influences of the moon. In addition to its predicable depth, the Buttonwood lacks the impetuous nature of a tidal creek, the potential for birds to materialize around the next bend. As if to accentuate the tedious nature of the last mile, the sky grows thick and gray and spits rain.

Within sight of the marina, on a breastwork of sandbags that protect the shore against erosion, a large crocodile basks, its mouth open in a slow-motion prehistoric pant. The reptile is the antithesis of the sandbags. It is an unrestrained messenger from the waterlogged jungle, a landscape too complicated to completely comprehend, what Anne Morrow Lindbergh called the "green silence of wilderness."

And children are just as wild about crocodilians

as they are about dinosaurs, which they lump

together into one big carnival of monsters.

DIANE ACKERMAN, 1991

12 American Crocodiles

Hearing the subterranean cries of her newly hatched young, the crocodile digs open the womb of sand, picks up a hatchling in her teeth, and ferries it to a nearby shore on Florida Bay. By dawn a knot of tiny crocodiles has formed in the beach wrack, and their mother is returning to a shallow inland bay to resume her solitary life in the Everglades.

From here the hatchlings must cross open water to the security of the mainland mangroves or the interior ponds on isolated keys. A hatchling crocodile, which wiggles like a nine-inch fishing lure, must pass a gauntlet of tarpon and snook. Once it swims several miles of Florida Bay, a baby crocodile's days are characterized by sunning and feeding and hiding. Watchful of such aquatic and aerial predators as the great white heron and the osprey, a hatchling crocodile remains bite-sized for at least six months. If it survives, and not many do these days (crocodiles are an endangered species), it may live for forty or fifty years, grow to more than fourteen feet long, weigh nearly a thousand pounds, and never lay eyes on a human being—other than Frank Mazzotti.

Mazzotti, a University of Florida wildlife scientist, has been monitoring crocodiles in Everglades National Park for more than twenty years. He has measured, weighed, poked, probed, taped, tied, tagged, and clipped more crocodiles in Florida than anyone else. He has given mouth-to-mouth resuscitation to a drowning hatchling that was pulled below the surface by a hungry blue crab (he sealed his lips around the crocodile's snout and blew gently into its lungs until it coughed up water). Mazzotti, who has eclectic reading habits, credits his knowledge of reptilian CPR to a *Mad Magazine* cartoon entitled "How to Give Artificial Respiration to a Lizard."

The American crocodile, *Crocodylus acutus,* is a dual citizen inhabiting both freshwater and saltwater, land and sea. Because hatchlings thrive in estuaries where salt levels are about ten parts per thousand (seawater is thirty-six parts per thousand), their well-being depends on the timing, location, and quantity of the freshwater flow from the Everglades into the northeast corner of Florida Bay. A rise in the Everglades crocodile population will be evidence that restoration efforts are paying off. In fact it is the Army Corps of Engineers that is funding Mazzotti's crocodile work.

"In Florida," says Mazzotti, "water flows downhill except when there's money involved."

It is about nine o'clock at night. We are wading along the edge of Cocoa Point, a spit of sand that pokes into the northeast corner of Florida Bay. Mazzotti points with informed nonchalance to an eight-foot female less than twenty feet away from me. Her eyes glow red in the beam of my flashlight. Slowly the beast rises in the water, exposing her head and tail above the surface in a territorial gesture. She sculls parallel to the beach, her eyes fixed on us. Mazzotti notes that, ferocious appearance to the contrary, the American crocodile is a timid beast. It lacks the aggression of both its cousin the American alligator and several species of Old World crocodiles, which do not fear humans and in fact consider them edible.

Frank Mazzotti's confidence notwithstanding, I feel unsettled yet thrilled as the crocodile's otherworldly eyes gleam at me. A hemisphere of stars shine in the dark sky, but none is as bright or as mysterious as the eyes of this beast in dark water.

So common was death by crocodile along the Nile that for millennia natives would not open the stomach of a dead animal for fear of liberating the spirits of their relatives or friends who may have been eaten by the beast. In *No Tears for Crocodiles,* a Victorian account of life in the African bush, Paul Potous tells of a native who fell out of his canoe and was caught by a crocodile in full view of his companions. The hapless man, unconscious and bleeding, was yanked below the surface and stuffed into the monster's lair in an undercut bank. He awoke on a carpet of bones and maggot-covered flesh, his incubus lying beside him, sleeping. When the crocodile finally slid back into the water, the man clawed his way through the roof of the cave and onto the bank. He returned to his village at night, caked white with limy mud and smelling awful. Everyone thought he was a ghost.

Most people think of crocodilians as they do of sharks, rock-hard muscle welded to bone, slimy reptiles hardwired to eat and perform a few other mindless tasks. To them crocodiles are sinister beasts that lurk in nightmares, fairy tales, and city sewers. Their toothsome grins make us flinch and shudder. Tick . . . tick . . . tick . . . goes the telltale clock in the stomach of the crocodile that so haunted Captain Hook, who himself is the embodiment of malice. The lowly crocodile is a holdover from the dinosaur past, but its incredible evolutionary journey has remained camouflaged by our irrepressible fear. I ask, "Is working with American crocodiles dangerous?" Laughing, Mazzotti sweeps a hand back toward the mangroves and says, "I'm more worried about crossing U.S. 1 on a Friday night than I am about wading in the middle of the Everglades at midnight. The hardest thing you put up with here are mosquitoes, and they never color my memories."

In Fort Lauderdale, three crocodiles live a shell skip from a popular beach. Few people know the crocodiles are there. In 1995 an eleven-foot female nested in the garden of a Sanibel Island subdivision, often resting under a condo and strolling up and down the street at night. Neighbors called her Wilma and barricaded the street after dark so that she could cross in peace. Although the risk to our lives and limbs is minimal from an American crocodile, "human stupidity has the clear ability to overcome the good common sense of wildlife," says Mazzotti. When an animal as big as a crocodile begins to rely on the largesse of dockside residents, problems are inevitable. One trio of crocodiles regularly visits a Key Largo restaurant where patrons pitch stale garlic rolls off the dock, fattening up the catfish that the jut-toothed crocodiles eat with gusto.

Several years ago I once again stood on the dock of West Lake, an inland bay bound by mangroves, ten miles northeast of Flamingo. Flashlight in hand, I scanned the dark water looking for evidence of an alligator. Well out in the water two widely spaced ruby eyes glowed. To attract the alligator, I pursed my lips and squeaked, imitating the distress cry of a young gator. The animal glided to within fifteen feet of me, scarcely disturbing the still surface, then sank out of sight, disappearing in less than two feet of water.

I touched the lake with a long, inch-thick branch, hoping the gator would rise again. Gaping jaws slammed shut and snapped the branch into three pieces. I stood stunned as my light beam held not an alligator but, for a wild instant, a crocodile, its eyes ablaze. Like a dream, it left behind a vivid after-image. Only the slightest watery imperfection lingered where the twelve-foot animal waited somewhere below. When my heart stopped racing I walked away from the dock and into a world that held infinitely more possibilities than I had previously imagined.

The crocodile wants only to be left alone. The shy mother crocodile will abandon a nest site for years if she is pestered or if her eggs repeatedly fail to hatch. A. W. Dimock, who wrote about the American subtropics a century ago, reported that a fourteen-foot crocodile had attacked his skiff only after he harpooned the beast seventeen times. John Ogden, who studied American crocodiles in the 1970s, considered them "about as dangerous to man as a fast-charging preying mantis."

Frank Mazzotti binds what's left of his gray hair in a short ponytail. He is fifty-two and as tan as a coconut. He says his interest in biology was inspired by his boyhood alter ego, Tarzan, and like the King of the Apes, he pretty much lives in a bathing suit—unless he is on a windless, mosquito-infested shoreline, in which case he leaves only his hands unprotected by layers of clothing. Mazzotti gestures constantly when he talks, and his voice still evokes the New York City suburbs. The son of a Long Island plumber, Mazzotti received a doctorate in ecology from Penn State in 1983 and has long been an authority on South Florida wetlands. After a fashion, he followed in his father's footsteps. The region's eighteen hundred miles of canals and levees are a spectacular plumbing nightmare that perhaps only God can restore.

South Florida's estuarine swamps, where the freshwater Everglades meets the sea, are the northernmost outpost of the American crocodile, whose range otherwise includes the north and east coasts of South America; the Caribbean, Gulf, and Pacific coasts of Central America north to the Yucatán Peninsula; and much of the periphery of the Greater Antilles—Cuba, Hispaniola, and Jamaica. Although crocodiles occasionally reach the Bahamas, their failure to breed there may reflect the absence of suitable streams to carry the heavy runoff that hatchlings need to feed in.

Most Americans know that alligators live in Florida, but not even many Floridians suspect that crocodiles too dwell in the saltwater swamps of their state. These relics of the Mesozoic Era are considered by biologists to be living dinosaurs. Ancient crocodilians were members of the group of giant reptiles called Archosaurs, which included the fearsome tyrannosaur. Sometime during the Ice Age, when sea levels were about three hundred feet lower than they are today, American crocodiles crossed the Florida Straits from Cuba and established a toehold on North America. Elsewhere in their range crocodiles may venture well inland—in Hispaniola, for instance, they live in freshwater lakes two thousand feet above sea level. In Florida, where alligators or their immediate progenitors have dominated the freshwater scene for twenty million years, crocodiles met a formidable obstacle to inland colonization. So the salt-tolerant crocodiles, like the mangroves that shade them, reside in brackish water, where hatchlings thrive in a biologically rich soup and grow at a faster rate than young alligators, who are intolerant of saltwater.

It was not until 1822 that the American naturalist Constantine Samuel Rafinesque guessed that the "sharp-snout alligator" of Florida was actually a crocodile. Another fifty-three years passed before William T. Hornaday and C. E. Jackson collected a pair in Arch Creek, near the head of Biscayne Bay, the first specimens taken for science. Some years later, camped on Madeira Hammock in the heart of American crocodile country, A. W. Dimock first suspected the presence of crocodiles in Florida Bay. "That night as we lay on the ground where the smoke from the campfire . . . made a barrage against the mosquitoes, Hall told me of strange monsters he had seen, which were like alligators but were not alligators. They had pointed jaws, long tusks, were larger and livelier, and were not black like 'gators. He had seen them farther from shore than alligators were ever met and he was sure he could find them again."

In 1918, thirty years after he had made their acquaintance, Dimock described how crocodiles contributed to his amusement. "It was really exciting," he wrote,

after locating the mouth of a crocodile's cave in the bank of a river, to hang the noosed end of a rope before it, while standing on the bank above. As I waited for a bite, my boatman busied himself thrusting a harpoon pole into the earth from ten to twenty feet behind me. This was followed by the outrushing crocodile and some excitement at my end of the line. The big reptile struggled and fought, he clutched at the line and rolled over and over, he swam out in the stream and he sulked in its depths, but the noose was tightly drawn and never allowed to slip, and the end found the creature facing the camera on the bank. It was a matter of ethics that the crocodile should be free when his photograph was taken, and removing the lasso called for much agility on the part of the volunteer. After a few vain attempts to escape, a crocodile would become discouraged, and our hunter boy would hold open the jaws of a very much alive reptile while the camera-man photographed them.

Crocodiles have never been common in Florida. From an historic high of about two thousand in the 1890s, their numbers dwindled during much of the twentieth century but began to rebound in the 1980s and 1990s. Crocodiles once occupied most of the creeks that flowed from the mainland into Florida Bay and Biscayne Bay and ranged as far north as Lake Worth on the east coast and Charlotte Harbor on the west. The clearing and draining of mangrove swamps along the lower east and west coasts of Florida took a heavy toll on crocodiles. They were listed as an endangered species in 1975, when they numbered about two hundred, of which only ten were nesting females. Now, in 2000, at least forty-five females nest in Florida. Mazzotti places their population at about four hundred, which doubles temporarily at hatching. (By comparison, more than a million and a half alligators live in Florida; maybe ten million lived there in the 1850s.) The animals are distributed among three main habitats, all protected: northeast Florida Bay; north Key Largo, where crocodiles nest on spoil banks adjacent to canals (and get hit by cars on U.S. Route 1); and the cooling canals of the Turkey Point Nuclear Power Plant on southwest Biscayne Bay.

They disperse freely among the three sites and have been found as far north as Fort Lauderdale on the east coast and Sanibel Island on the west. In 1978 a recalcitrant crocodile was captured in Fort Lauderdale and released on Key Largo. The animal moved sixty miles south to Big Pine Key, was returned to Key Largo, moved again, and was recaptured on a key twelve miles south. Having learned their lesson, government agents brought the crocodile back to Fort Lauderdale. After moving inland six miles, the crocodile was taken to Naples on the west coast. It was last seen ninety miles south of Naples on Cape Sable, the southernmost extension of the mainland, which separates Whitewater Bay from the Gulf of Mexico. In the course of a year the crocodile had embarked on a succession of long-distance movements (with the aid of biologists) that covered most of the species' range in Florida.

Except for a nest in Bonita Bay in 1993 and one on Marco Island in 1995, crocodiles have not been known to nest west of Cape Sable. Recently, in their never-ending search for high ground, crocodiles extended their breeding range into western Florida Bay. In April 1984 East Cape Canal, which had connected

Bear Lake to the Gulf of Mexico across the eastern end of Cape Sable, was plugged with concrete sacks to block the unnatural flow of saltwater into estuaries. That night, before the cement hardened, a crocodile climbed ashore, dug a hole in a sack, and laid her eggs. Twelve years later, the manufactured berm along the East Cape Plug supported five or six nests. Several crocodiles nest in Flamingo, and one at West Lake, all in spoil banks dredged from canals. I visited Cape Sable one summer and found that raccoons had excavated at least three nests in the berm adjacent to East Cape Canal. Eggshells were everywhere.

In the summer of 1995 six crocodile nests mingled with those of loggerhead sea turtles on the outer beaches of Cape Sable for the first time since 1898: turtle nest, turtle, turtle, crocodile, turtle, turtle, turtle, crocodile, and so on, a primeval convocation. The bayside berms of Miami Beach once hosted a thriving population of crocodiles, but now, except in the pages of Carl Hiaasen's mystery *Tourist Season,* in which a behemoth eats assorted vacationers, crocodiles have shifted south in Biscayne Bay. Crocodiles are also gone from the lower Keys; the last sighting in Key West was in 1935, and the last nest on Little Pine Key, in 1971.

For a cold-blooded, tropical reptile, warmth means health. Cold weather can be lethal to adult crocodiles that have evolved to seek the sun. During prolonged cold spells, crocodiles haul up on the banks and bask even if the air temperature is thirty degrees colder than the water temperature. A crocodile basking on a cold day loses the ability to fight infection and may succumb to septicemia, an invasion of the blood by virulent microbes. Hence its limited distribution in Florida: a tropical animal on the northern rim of its range. By contrast, alligators, which evolved in warm-temperate North America, stay submerged during cold snaps in water that is warmer than the air.

Once hatched and delivered to the water's edge by their gape-jawed mother, young crocodiles, bereft of parental care, head for nurseries in remote mangrove-lined creeks that drain the east Everglades. From mid-July to mid-August, Mazzotti checks these crocodile nests, hoping to intercept hatchlings before they disperse among the mangroves. One afternoon he takes his fifteen-foot skiff into Taylor River, a branch of Taylor Slough, the principal drainage of the eastern Everglades, which empties into Little Madeira Bay. At full throttle Mazzotti races the boat toward a wall of trees. One minute he is headed for the cleft that identifies the river, and the next he is inside deep-green, mosquito-infested shade. Half a mile upstream the river cuts an old storm bank of marl, an ancient beach that supports a forest of West Indian hardwoods—mahogany, Jamaican dogwood, pigeon plum, and sea grape—in an otherwise dense forest of mangroves. Crocodile chatter, high-pitched squeaks and grunts, wafts from a trellis of mangrove roots that rise from dark brown water.

Crocodilians are the premier vocalists of the reptile world. Besides the subterranean chorus that signals the attendant mother of an imminent hatch, males attract mates by bellowing. The bellow of an alligator carries for miles across the Everglades, where vision is obstructed by legions of sawgrass. Living in open bays and tidal rivers, however, crocodiles rely more on visual clues, like rising on the water. Mazzotti suspects that crocodiles communicate with a low sound below our threshold of hearing. When an otherwise silent crocodile produces the subsonic sound in his chest cavity, water dances above the animal's back, the very same vibrations that occur when an alligator bellows. A male crocodile may also slap its head on the water to produce a loud resounding noise.

As Mazzotti steps off the boat and onto the bank to find the nest, he sees that the mother has already dug into the nest and that there has been at least a partial hatch. Tiny crocodiles begin to appear on roots, on the bank, and sprawled on the water's surface, floating like bathtub toys. Mazzotti wants them. I reach out, catch one, two, three, four, and place the hatchlings in a nylon bag. Mazzotti steps off the boat and, submerged to his chest, brachiates through a maze of overarching mangrove roots, arm over arm, like a gibbon. He returns to the boat, three crocs in each hand. Together we catch thirteen.

In Everglades National Park most crocodiles lay their eggs in nests dug into high ground along the edge of mangrove creeks or in sand mounds on the beaches of northeast Florida Bay. Because the average clutch of thirty-nine eggs takes approximately eighty-six days to incubate and may hatch over several days, and because females nest communally, I wonder aloud whether there might be viable eggs left in the nest cavity. Mazzotti tells me that although crocodile nesting is bracketed between the close of the dry season, when desiccation is most severe, and the high water of the late wet season, creek nests dug into high ground in low-lying areas often succumb to rising groundwater, an invisible fatal threat. Sometimes the lower eggs in a nest flood, but the upper ones hatch. During a wet year, creek nests often suffer high mortality; during dry years, sand mound nests are less successful. By using both types of nests, mother crocodiles have collectively hedged their reproductive bets to maximize the number of eggs that hatch. So there is only one way to answer my question.

I scramble up the bank and tap on the trunk of a buttonwood, whose roots reach into the nest. An underground chorus rises from the marl. I tap again. The hatchlings chirp again, a passionate cacophony that crosses taxonomic lines and stirs some latent reptilian parent deep inside me. In Mazzotti, too, apparently, for he is soon digging into the hard-packed marl alongside me. "My mother used to joke about the hatchlings being my kids," he says. "Come nesting season, don't bother me. If there's a wedding or a funeral, forget it, 'cause I'm watching my kids being born. Sorry."

To reach the nest, we dig down ten inches into the marl. Of the six remaining eggs packed tightly in the gray earth, one is hatching, so, swatting mosquitoes, we remove that egg, place it on the bank, and wait it out. Then we cover the nest so that the remaining five eggs will have a chance to hatch. Slowly, the tiny crocodile's egg tooth slits its leathery eggshell. The tooth, a miniature keratin button on the upper jaw, falls off shortly after hatching; it is an anatomical character associated with birds, with whom crocodilians share a common ancestor. The baby crocodile pushes and pushes, struggles out, from one humid world into another. Once the nine-inch animal is free, I find it hard to imagine how it fit into the three-inch egg. Turtlelike, the crocodile wears a piece of shell on its back and wanders the packed marl. For the moment, food is not an issue for the little croc. Although a mother crocodile will not tend her offspring (beyond a trip to the water's edge), she does put some parental investment directly into the egg, for the yolk supplies nourishment for both the embryo and the hatchling, which absorbs the protein-rich mixture for several days before exercising its teeth.

Back at camp on Key Largo, I take one of the newly hatched crocodiles out of its temporary digs—a Playmate cooler—where it had been swarming with its siblings. They are about to be processed. Every crocodile has the same number of scales in the same position, so each of these hatchlings will have the ridge of a couple of its tail scales clipped in such a way as to leave an easily readable three-digit identification number and a birthplace code. Hundreds are indicated by clipping the right-hand row of double scales; tens, by clipping the left-hand row; and units, by clipping a single row below the double. For example, a clipped seventh scale on the right side of the raised double row of scales indicates that the croc was born in Everglades National Park.

The hatchling is rubbery. On top it is gray-brown, intricately banded, stippled and mottled with black, like a piece of hand-tooled wood. This coloring blends into a variety of backgrounds, and the crocs retain it for life. The underside of the tail is white flecked with black. The umbilicus, an opening that connects the yolk sac to the embryo, runs down the middle of the white underbelly like a surgical incision, and the frayed borders of the yolk sac hang from the scar. The animal's mustard-colored eyes have vertical black-slit pupils—night eyes. A clear membrane slides over each eye, like a goggle, and allows the crocodile to see underwater. A line of light-colored scales runs below each eye. The teardrop-shaped ear openings slant away from the eyes. When the animal submerges, valves close off the ears and the nostrils, allowing the crocodile to stay submerged for as long as two hours. With each breath the valves of the nostrils flex. There are four toes on the animal's front feet, five on the hind. Only the first three toes on each foot are clawed. Proportionally, a hatchling's snout is shorter and smaller than an adult's.

A hatchling may look nothing like a big-headed human infant, but it is almost as adorable. The lower jaw is whitish, flecked with black. The little crocs open their mouths but do not bite. I peer into maws that will one day pulverize large fish, small turtles, herons, ducks, and raccoons—perhaps even a deer—virtually anything a crocodile can overpower and drown by clamping on a limb and sinking. It is easier to see the tiny rows of salt glands on the floor of a baby croc's mouth than to see those notorious, but still nearly undetectable, teeth. I put my ear to a hatchling's chest and listen to its four-chambered heart throb: bup, bup, bup, bup; blood coursing through a reptile whose timid nature belies our own irrational fears.

《《《

Several days later, after we release the Taylor River hatchlings near their nest site, Mazzotti stops at Deer Key, an islet in Florida Bay that is shaped like Florida itself. Deer Key is a potential nesting beach that has been abandoned since the 1950s. Mazzotti cuts the engine and ties the skiff to a pole he jams in the marl. We leave the boat bobbing and walk ashore directly to a crocodile nest, recently hatched. Mazzotti thinks like a crocodile. He knows where nests are in high water and low, and where hatchlings roam. And when these snap-jawed monsters become sexually frisky, he knows where to find them.

We comb the shoreline, spot a berm that supports broad-leaved evergreens—sea grape, bay cedar, black bean, seven-year apple—and walk to it. The trees indicate that a lens of freshwater lies just below the surface, something that appeals to a mother crocodile. Inches lower on the bay side of the berm, black mangroves govern a world of salty earth. We find the crocodile nest on a large mound of pulverized shell five feet across and two feet high, backed by evergreens. Eggshells litter the sand. Some of the shells still have a thin, outer layer of calcium, which protects the eggs from drying and flooding and falls off a day or two after a hatch. The tracks of a large crocodile, a distinctive tail drag framed by star-shaped footprints, leads back and forth from the bay to the mound.

Several miles west of here two ridges of marl, Crocodile Dragover and the Dragover, frame the mouth of Madeira Bay. Perhaps when crocodiles were more common they wore grooves in the marl, hauling their bodies from one bay to the next. The same low-slung, reptilian motion that slowly wears down the substrate keeps estuarine creeks free-flowing by plowing up silt and mangrove seedlings.

An osprey cries in the southwest, and the prevailing wind howls out of the southeast, sometimes with freight-train force. A gust discharges a frigate bird, a long, thin pencil-mark of a bird that soars overhead. Waves lap the shore, tumbling seashells that fracture and gather in furrows to eventually become berms where crocodiles will dig nests. Wherever an island or peninsula blocks a shoreline from a long run of wind, mangroves fringe the coast. Because the hundred-mile-long curve of the Florida Keys softens the force of the Atlantic Ocean, the tides here in the northeast corner of Florida Bay are triggered by wind, the very element crocodiles avoid. Females enter the bay only to nest and to wait for their young to hatch. Males avoid Florida Bay altogether.

Just beyond the nest, beneath a weft of bay cedar limbs, an eight-foot crocodile idles in the sun. Mosquitoes gather around her eyes. A fly strolls across her bumpy back. I suppress an urge to touch her, to run my fingers along her tail. What's going on inside that fortress of a skull? What are crocodile thoughts—flotsam and jetsam from the age of dinosaurs? Maybe she is sated and is taking a last lounge on the beach before crossing the bay to the sodden coast. Males grow to nearly fifteen feet long, but females rarely grow to more than ten feet. Usually they begin breeding at five years old, when they reach a length of about seven feet. Although males can also start breeding at seven feet, they do not always do so. If a male is dwarfed by neighboring males, it cannot establish a territory and is left out of the breeding loop for a year or two, or even ten.

After I stare at the crocodile for fifteen minutes, her leathery countenance and her toothy grin dissolve away in my thoughts. I see her as symbolic of the edge: the edge of the continent, the edge of extinction, the edge of consciousness. My mind slows to a reptilian pace. Eventually I tear myself away and look for other nests. Mazzotti points out two false starts, little more than scrapes in the sand abandoned for reasons known only to the mother crocodile. When we return to our skiff, the dozing mother is gone. I scan the emerald chop. Somewhere nearby, hidden in less than two feet of water, lies an antediluvian reptile.

From Deer Key we travel southwest to Eagle Key, one and a half miles farther out in the bay. A crocodile nest rises above the northwest corner like an enormous ant mound. Footprints and tail drags lead from water to nest, where the female had sprawled, ear to the sand, and listened for her babies' muted grunts. I tap a red mangrove prop root, hoping to trigger another subterranean chorus. Only mosquitoes answer. Offshore a great white heron waits as patient as a tree. Did the heron find the promise of food in the crocodile nest? The ranges of both animals overlap along the western Caribbean: could this be more than a chance encounter? An osprey or a tarpon might take a hatchling, but a great white heron could ingest the entire pod.

From Eagle Key to Russell Key is a mile and a half, south by southwest. White-crowned pigeons whir past, crisscrossing the summer sky. Russell Key embraces turquoise water, a ribbon of yellowish sand, and emerald trees. Mazzotti moors the skiff fifty yards offshore, and we walk toward a berm on the east side of the key. The water is clear and refreshing. A tulip snail clutches a crown conch in its foot and slowly drills a hole in its shell, predator on predator. When the hole is finished, the tulip will begin to dissolve the conch's insides and siphon the juices. Then one more shell will roll toward the beach and line up to become sand.

Despite the lack of wind, there are no mosquitoes and no flies. There is also no sign of a crocodile. After scouring the berm on Russell Key, we head north to Black Betsy Key, an elongated zigzag of an island that had sheltered crocodile nests in the 1950s. A ten-foot female was marked on Black Betsy in 1978, an animal believed to be more than thirty years old. Mazzotti recaptured her ten years later on a nearby key, a longevity record for a wild American crocodile.

A small lemon shark moving along the shore, its dorsal fin cutting the surface, bolts in a dazzling burst of speed as I step toward it. Several shallow crocodile scrapes dimple the sand. They superficially resemble land crab burrows, which are much deeper. Mazzotti has radio-tracked hatchlings to a crab burrow, where fist-sized crabs had taken the tiny crocs apart piece by little piece. Several diamond-backed terrapin nests rise from the beach, much smaller mounds than a crocodile's. These turtles sometimes entrust their eggs to crocodile nests.

In the skiff again, racing north, we head for Madeira Beach, the most important crocodile-nesting beach in Florida. The beach, long and irregularly shaped, separates Little Madeira and Madeira bays. Walking, we find a hatched crocodile nest. Several other nests have been pillaged by raccoons. Visibly annoyed, Mazzotti dreams of the day when restoration finally sends more water through Taylor Slough. Then the estuary will move farther out into Florida Bay, increasing critical habitat for hatchling crocodiles. It is Mazzotti's hope that as the estuary spreads, crocodiles will nest on more remote keys, away from raccoons, the principle source of nest failure in Florida. When the Corps restores the flow of water through Taylor Slough, creek nests will be jeopardized by the rising groundwater, an eventuality Mazzotti accepts. Ecosystems should not be held hostage to a single species, even if it is an endangered one.

Mazzotti says that "a few crocodile nests may be flooded out, but in the end Taylor Slough will be healthier, and the enriched habitat in Florida Bay should support more hatchlings. It is important not to focus on a single aspect of the population, but rather on how the action is going to effect the whole population." During the floods of 1994 and 1995, freshwater flow into the mangroves mirrored what had naturally taken place before flood-control structures were built. In 1994 fourteen of twenty crocodile nests in Everglades National Park were built on palm keys surrounded by gorgeous water. A year later ichthyologist Jerry Lorenz, director of Audubon's Tavernier Science Center, recorded nearly pure freshwater for eight months at the mouth of Taylor Slough. "This is as close as we'll ever get to natural conditions," he told me. The vegetation, invertebrates, and fish returned. By 1997 Mazzotti had marked one hundred crocodile hatchlings in the national park. The survival rate for those animals was three to four times higher than it was the year before. Mazzotti sums up the Everglades restoration and the recovery of the American crocodile simply: "Send more clean water down Taylor Slough during the wet season."

Later that evening we enter the Taylor River to release the eighteen hatchlings. As the river narrows, I lie on the bow and push away the aerial prop roots that grow down from mangrove branches. A tarpon jumps into the boat, thudding against the engine, and Mazzotti quickly tosses it back. First a silver swirl, then gone. We release the hatchlings near their nest. Slowly they head for shore, tails sculling, hind feet paddling, treading primal water.

Taylor River flows out of a series of five brackish ponds named First Pond, Second Pond, and so on. During the dry season, when standing water in the mangroves recedes, crocodiles gather in the ponds, loiter on the limestone banks, and sulk in caves below the surface. "If you want to see big ones," says Mazzotti, "come back in the winter dry season."

Mazzotti turns the skiff around. First Pond constricts, becomes Taylor River. Stars flicker through a brooding canopy whose leafy fingers rake our scalps. The mosquitoes are relentless. This is our country's darkest corner; pooled by ink-colored water, snared by loops of mangrove roots, swarmed by biting insects.

The following morning, at a Flamingo crocodile nest, the stench of hydrogen sulfide hangs in viscid air. The nest is off the southbound lane of the main park service road, opposite the entrance to West Lake. The eggs are rotten. Crocodiles have been associated with West Lake for more than a century, when area gator hunters killed a few and brought their hides to Flamingo. (Compared with an alligator's, the hide of an American crocodile is thin, tears easily, and makes what is considered inferior leather.) Mazzotti collects the eggs while I steady my queasy stomach.

In 1978, several years after Florida Power and Light Company finished the Turkey Point Nuclear Power Plant, 32 of the plant's 168 miles of cooling canals were declared a crocodile sanctuary. The animals discovered the berms along the canals in 1975 and began nesting. In 1994 Turkey Point hosted eleven nests and hatched at least 154 crocodiles, more than a quarter of the state's production.

Surrounded by fenced-in wilderness, Turkey Point is on the southwest shore of Biscayne Bay in southern Miami–Dade County. The plant's twin towers dwarf everything in sight. To open the gate, Mazzotti punches in an electronic code. We enter then traverse a maze of roads inside a chain-link fence webbed in barbed wire, protected by electric gates, lit by spotlights, and filmed by video cameras.

On August 24, 1992, at five in the morning, Turkey Point took a direct hit from Hurricane Andrew. There was no known crocodile mortality there. The day after Andrew hit, a crocodile was killed on U.S. Route 1, near Jewfish Creek Bridge; three days later, two adults swam upstream near the mouth of Shark River, many miles from the nearest habitat.

Our guide, Joe Wasilewski, a self-employed environmental scientist and breeder of exotic reptiles, monitors the Turkey Point crocodiles and processes hatchlings in conjunction with Frank Mazzotti. Wasilewski grew up in Chicago and moved to Miami in 1979 to breed and sell reptiles. He lives with his son and dozens of pythons, boas, and iguanas. Joe wears jeans, a T-shirt, and high rubber boots. He is tall, fair-skinned, and lean. A shock of auburn hair brushes his forehead.

The cooling canals are separated from each other by berms. The canals and berms replace sixteen hundred acres of native vegetation, mostly mangroves. The canals prevent warm water effluent from leaking into Biscayne Bay. Crocodiles, often in proximity to each other, feed in the canals and nest in the berms. When rains come, weeds grow, making the nests impossible to find, even for a mother crocodile, who digs up to eight pilot holes before choosing a site. Around hatching time, she climbs out of the water, scales the berm, walks to where she thinks the nest is, bounces a few times, and then puts her ear to the ground to listen for a percussive sound, or a grunting hatchling.

Although the salinity of the cooling canals is forty parts per thousand, about 10 percent saltier than seawater, the crocodiles thrive here in the food-rich milieu, growing faster and maturing sooner than their counterparts in nearby Florida Bay. The canals also support an abundance of fish and crabs and, in winter, flocks of red-breasted mergansers. Like New England foxes trailing a hay bailer that flushes voles, some crocodiles have learned to follow bulldozers picking off panicked rats that rush into the water.

The night is as black as an alligator's back. Schools of needlefish mark the surface, driven to terror by our spacious six-passenger airboat. In my flashlight beam, everything looks like a crocodile: mats of algae, floating snags, pieces of outcropped limestone. Wasilewski sees red eye-shine near shore, disembarks, chases a four-foot animal up a berm, and catches it. Mazzotti rubber-bands the animal's snout (a standard precaution for anything larger than a hatchling), counts the clipped tail scutes—a three-year-old Turkey Point native—and begins to take measurements. To sex the beast, Wasilewski inserts his pinkie in the cloaca and probes for a clitoris or a penis, which look almost identical in immature crocodiles. Out pops a thin, hooked, pink-tipped penis. Science done, the crocodile rests in my lap, eyes locked on me, an age-encrusted stare.

Late February 1996. I am chest-deep in Davis Creek, slipping and sliding in limerock ooze, stumbling and tripping on submerged mangrove roots. Ahead of me are Frank Mazzotti and the novelist Carl Hiaasen, who has written about a rogue crocodile and now wants to see the real thing.

We reach the buttonwood embankment where I had helped collect hatchlings two summers before and slither up the steep, greasy bank. Last year's nest has been pilfered by raccoons. Dry broken shells lie scattered on the moldy earth like bits of paper-thin pottery. No creek nest hatched last year, Mazzotti says, a trace of melancholy in his voice; they all fell victim to high water and to the raccoons that had hit five of six nests on Madeira Beach.

After looking at the busted shells, we shimmy back down to Davis Creek. In the absence of crocodiles, we attend the mangrove water snakes that lay coiled and quiescent on limbs just above the water or plop right in and swim away before anyone can grab them. The mangrove water snake is a subspecies of the southern water snake, *Nerodia fasciata compressicauda*, a true estuarine snake and the only North American reptile that immigrated to northern Cuba across the Straits of Florida during the Ice Age. Perhaps the snake swimming toward Cuba and the crocodile swimming toward Florida passed each other in the night. One snake is bright copper on top and uniformly checkered black and white underneath, like a slender chess board. It has a scabbed-over eye and a growth on its snout. Another snake is midnight black; hints of white streak each side, as though someone had painted over the old pattern; a row of small white dots runs the length of the belly, bright like stars and bordered by parallel rows of copper bars. Both snakes bite the hell out of me.

Later we moor for supper off the Tern Islands. Small groups of spoonbills come to roost. After dinner we head for Joe Bay to look for big crocodiles. Inside the bay the night grows black. Crimson eyes float at the surface off the far shore. Mazzotti spins the boat toward the eyes, which seem much farther apart than a yearling's. Twenty feet away, the body below the glowing eyes resolves into a crocodile whose head is a large as a dinner plate. The boat stops, and Mazzotti steps off into the night, his crimped world lit by a headlamp. The beast holds still. Patiently it watches every step Mazzotti takes, as though deciding whether to froth the water in a burst of leather and muscle or to join us in the boat, a patsy to be fondled by naturalists who somehow feel closer to the earth when caressing antiquity. When Mazzotti is about four feet away from the croc, he slowly reaches the noose pole over its head, slips the loop back around its neck, and snares it. The crocodile is not pleased. It leaps up as though taking wing, splashes, dives, rises, sinks, rises again; then suddenly resigned to its fate, it sprawls on the surface, waiting to be processed.

Mazzotti records the animal's measurements—six feet long, forty-four pounds. The crocodile comes to my lap, kitten-calm. Like a Seminole gator wrestler, I instinctively rub the crocodile's belly to see if it falls asleep, which it doesn't. I listen to its heart purr, my ear to living leather. A mosquito settles on the crocodile's snout, finds a chink in the beast's armor, and engorges. I watch the mosquito's abdomen swell. The crocodile watches the night. A few moments later, while releasing the crocodile, I notice the pink tincture of Miami's lights staining the night sky to the northeast, luminous bridges linking the density of mangroves to the density of civilization, and the age of dinosaurs to the age of information. Less concerned about its place in the history of the planet, the crocodile swishes its tail and vanishes.

These great rookeries, aside from the fact that there
are birds in the rookeries, there is nothing more
spectacular and thrilling than to see tens of thousands
of enormous birds in trees. You can see them for a
mile before you get there, just as far as your eyes can
reach, trees laden with great birds.

HORACE M. ALBRIGHT, 1930

13 Wading Birds

The Everglades once supported the largest gathering of wading birds in North
America, perhaps in all the world. During the dry season, when declining water
levels trapped astronomical numbers of small fish and invertebrates in ever-
shrinking pools, hundreds of thousands of wading birds convened in the marl
prairies. Like combines threshing wheat, the birds slowly and methodically
combed the shallows for food. As recently as the 1930s a quarter of a million
wading birds, mostly white ibis, bred in the southern Everglades, whitening
the green mangroves for miles. Even the bison and pronghorn that populated
the pre-Columbian Great Plains could not have matched the ineffable grace
of wading birds that poured across the Everglades. If one immaculately white

egret can make me pause, what about a hundred? Or a thousand? Or ten thousand, swirling as light as air in the blue Florida sky?

Unfortunately the egret's beauty was also its undoing. By the late nineteenth century, women in major European and American cities craved feathers for their hats. Nuptial plumes, called *aigrettes,* the flowing, white feathers that grow only during the breeding season and extend like a bridal train from between a bird's shoulder blades well beyond its tail, sold for thirty-two dollars an ounce, nearly twice the price of gold. Each plume (or spray) weighs little; there are about fifty per bird. Some milliners designed hats with entire wings, even whole birds, shriveled and glass-eyed, perched on women's heads. In 1832 Audubon wrote that the wings of roseate spoonbills were sold as fans in St. Augustine. For every ounce of feathers shipped to the milliners, at least four adult wading birds were killed, which meant that eggs went unincubated and chicks were abandoned. By 1912 the price of each spray reached seventy-five cents, which netted thirty dollars per bird. Crows and vultures thrived on the carnage, gorging on abandoned eggs and hapless chicks, and alligators attracted to the gunfire snatched dead birds off the water.

Dale Gawlik, a senior environmental scientist for the South Florida Water Management District who specializes in wading birds, believes that plume hunters may not have destroyed the rookeries by killing all the adult birds. "They certainly shot for feathers—but they constantly disturbed the birds for fifteen years, which essentially shut down reproduction." According to Gawlik, a party of four or five plume hunters, each armed with a single-shot shotgun, might have killed only twenty to forty birds out of thousands. But wading-bird chicks, which have very narrow energy budgets, succumbed to heat and starvation when adults were driven off the nest.

During the first years of the twentieth century the slaughter of wading birds for the millinery trade began to arouse national sympathy. Congress passed the Lacey Act in 1900, banning the interstate shipment of birds killed in violation of state laws. It was the first effective weapon against Everglades plume hunters. The following year William Dutcher, a New York insurance company executive who would become the first president of the National Audubon Society, successfully lobbied the Florida state legislature for passage of a non-game-bird protection law, a law aimed at protecting birds from the plume trade. Although Florida had no funds to pay a game warden, Dutcher did. He arranged for the American Ornithological Union to pay the warden's salary. (Several years later the National Audubon Society took over the warden program.)

A report written to Dutcher by a member of the Florida Audubon Society declared that "the game warden, to deal with this situation, must be a resident, well acquainted with local conditions, a strong, fearless man, and one fully alive to the value of bird protection; also, he must not only be willing but anxious to serve."

In 1902 Dutcher found his man: Guy Bradley, who lived on Cape Sable, hotbed of the plume trade. Bradley was hired as Florida's first warden to protect the rookeries of Cuthbert Lake and Florida Bay. He was the perfect choice. He had grown up in Lantana, near Palm Beach, where his father and brother had once walked the mail down the coast from Lake Worth to Miami before the railroads were established, and he knew the rookeries both as a guide and as a hunter. Armed with a .32-caliber pistol, a weapon woefully inadequate against men toting rifles and shotguns, Bradley hounded his neighbors zealously, arresting some more than once.

In response to the wholesale destruction of Florida's wading birds, the National Audubon Society was incorporated in New York in January 1905. Six months later Warden Bradley, now an Audubon employee, spotted a schooner sailing toward Oyster Key, two miles south of Flamingo. Bradley recognized the boat as that of a poacher named William Smith, whose son he had arrested several times. Bradley rowed to Oyster Key, reaching the schooner as Smith's son and a friend climbed aboard. Both men carried limp egrets. When Bradley threatened to arrest the younger Smith, the elder Smith shot the warden dead. Bradley's body drifted in his skiff off East Cape Sable for more than a day, attracting clouds of turkey vultures, which in turn attracted a small search party, which found him. He was buried in a ridge of cream-colored shells, not far from bird-rich Lake Ingraham.

Three years later, Columbus MacLeod, another Audubon warden, was murdered in Charlotte Harbor. The fallen Audubon wardens became martyrs for bird protection, underscoring the evils of the plume trade, and for the most part Americans began to take note. No one was convicted of either murder.

Feathers from South Florida's birds were still being shipped illegally to Europe for several years after Bradley's death and then imported back to the United States, where more than twenty thousand sweatshop employees in New York City fixed plumes to hats. Yielding to the ongoing outcry of conservationists, the New York State legislature passed the Audubon Plumage Act in 1910, outlawing the plume trade in the state.

Unfortunately the feather market in Havana remained legal and lucrative. Florida plumes thus traveled a new route to London and Paris, where hats were legally imported back to the United States and sold. Eventually the federal government was forced to ban the importation of feathered hats. The federal law slowed the plume trade, but ultimate success was finally assured by a change in fashions. As historian Mark Derr wrote, "By 1917, prostitutes had adopted feathered hats as part of their uniform, and no respectable lady wanted to be confused with them." A few poachers continued to raid Everglades rookeries for another thirty years, often aided by unscrupulous county game wardens who would divulge the sizes and locations of the most promising wading bird rookeries for a cut in the action. Birds were still slaughtered by the hundreds, sometimes thousands; one rookery near the mouth of Shark Slough lost more than twenty thousand birds in a single raid, mostly white ibis, which were euphemistically called Chokoloskee chicken and continued to be killed for their meat and eggs well into the 1960s.

In 1927 J. V. Kelsey, a United States game management agent, wrote to his boss in Washington, "Frankly, no one is going to turn a plume hunter in, not unless such a party is ready to leave the country or wants to take a big chance on being rubbed out at the first opportunity." As wading bird numbers plummeted, the slaughter of egrets lessened, but poaching remained a problem. A memo written in May 1936 by an upper-level Audubon employee stated that instead of using cash a Naples hotel owner paid his prostitutes with plumes. He also wrote that more than twenty-five wardens would be needed in the Big Cypress country alone to stop the poaching. In another memorandum dated March 29, 1937, and stamped CONFIDENTIAL, an Audubon informant told the society's president that buyers in South Florida paid the Seminole and Miccosukee ten cents a plume and sold the feathers in Wichita, Kansas, for a dollar apiece.

On the eve of the dedication of Everglades National Park, poaching of plume birds was still a problem in remote South Florida. In a letter addressed to Audubon president John H. Baker, dated March 18, 1944, a warden named Parker, based at Cape Sable, wrote:

I proceeded on up to the head of Shark [River] where I found several alligator skeletons along the river where they had been killed and skinned four or five days past. It was too late to go to the rookery on the north prong of Shark that night. I stopped within about one mile and heard no birds and saw very few.

Early on the morning of the 15th, I made my way up to where the birds were nesting when I was there last week. I saw no birds, heard very little noise. When the sun came up, when I could see, still there were no birds but empty nests. I landed and made a careful inspection. Evidently those people who killed and skinned the alligators completely destroyed the rookery.

I saw several dead white ibis on the ground, but no shot in them. They had been killed at night with a light and stick. On the ground were several bushels of egg shells where the people had shaken the trees where the nests were, and the eggs which fell from the nests and failed to break they took with them. The broken ones they left.

It was sickening sight. The only sign of life there were the buzzards cleaning up the broken eggs and dead birds.

Lamenting the destruction of the Shark River rookery by gator hunters, Parker concluded his missive by suggesting that at least from the standpoint of serendipity, if there were no more alligators the fortunes of wading birds might improve. "Guess the sooner they kill all the alligators the better off we wardens will be."

About four miles long, Cuthbert Lake lies between West Lake and Seven Palm Lake at the southern fringe of the mainland, just north of a necklace of smaller bodies of water called lakes Long, Henry, Monroe, and Middle, and the Lungs. Like the others, Cuthbert is a shallow, fermenting bowl of mud and water, another brown spot in an otherwise green jungle. The shoreline is soft and subtle, and the surface is often agitated by wind and fish and by gases that constantly bubble up from the bottom. A narrow mangrove island about a half-mile long rises from the middle of the lake. The island, and the wading birds that once gathered there, set Cuthbert apart from the other lakes that shape the coastline of Florida Bay.

Late in the 1880s a plume hunter named Cuthbert discovered the lake, gave it his name, and immediately raided its isolated wading bird colony. At the time, New York buyers were paying twenty-eight dollars per ounce for egret plumes. Cuthbert shipped out four pounds of plumes, which sold for nearly eighteen hundred dollars, and left behind a trash heap of more than 250 great egrets.

Ornithologist Arthur Cleveland Bent, whose renowned twenty-six-volume *Life Histories of North American Birds* was originally published by the Smithsonian Institution over a period of forty years, visited Cuthbert Lake twice. In 1903, with Guy Bradley as his guide, and in 1908, he made the tortuous trip across a maze of mangrove roots, over mud banks, and across shallow lakes, where everything was connected, or disconnected, by a labyrinth of tree-choked channels, many of which were blind alleys. The trip required ten hours of poling and pushing. Although the rookery had been depleted by twenty years of plume hunting, Bent noticed that the birds had begun a modest comeback. On his first trip, he counted only eighteen great egrets and twelve roseate spoonbills; five years later, great egrets numbered three hundred or four hundred, and spoonbills, more than seventy-five. In 1908 Bent reported that the rookery supported hundreds of white ibises and several thousand tricolored herons (which had little commercial value). The outer edges of the mangroves, he wrote, were black with cormorants and anhingas.

On his second trip Bent was accompanied by Bradley's brother Louis, Frank Chapman, chairman of the department of ornithology at the American Museum of Natural History in New York City, and renowned bird artist Louis Agassiz Fuertes. Fuertes's field sketches became the source of his background painting for the Cuthbert Habitat Group, in the museum's Hall of North American Birds, a diorama that features nesting spoonbills and great egrets. Because spoonbills had become so rare in South Florida, the museum's specimens came from Pajaro Island, Mexico, where the birds were still common. By the 1930s the writings of Bent and Chapman and the museum's stunning diorama had so championed Cuthbert Lake and its wading birds that when several thousand amorous wood storks began to fill the rookery, Audubon wardens guided wealthy donors on boat tours there.

《《《

Lori Oberhoffer, a biological technician at Everglades National Park, flies part of the monthly aerial wading bird distribution survey conducted by the park and the South Florida Water Management District. The two agencies divide South Florida into ninety east-west transects, each spaced two kilometers apart. The national park flies transect 52 to transect 90, which requires three days to complete. On a February morning in 1996 Oberhoffer and an assistant sit on opposite sides of the plane, watching below. Each observer notes the number of wading birds in each of nine categories off her side of the plane for a distance of approximately 150 yards. The categories include small white heron, small dark heron, great blue heron, great white heron, wood stork, spoonbill, great egret, white ibis, and glossy ibis. Today is the third day of the survey. We'll fly transects 78 to 90, the southern tip of the peninsula, which includes Cuthbert Lake.

Oberhoffer also takes note of water conditions, which she breaks down into five categories, ranging from completely dry to completely wet. Today the Everglades is clearly drying out. From the Anhinga Trail to Little Madeira Bay, Taylor Slough appears as a series of oval pools, and the shallow depressions in the mangroves are dry and cracked like shattered ceramics. Alligator tracks radiate from puddles and mud bars, stitching together even the most obscure bodies of water. Although the leaves of red and black mangroves are green, those of white mangrove and buttonwoods have been burnt by a mid-January frost. I count four deer, none after the day heats up. A large shark patrols the shallows off Cape Sable. We fly repeatedly over Whitewater Bay, as flocks of nervous coots skitter like whirligig beetles beneath us.

Eventually I recognize Cuthbert Lake. From its center rises the famous island surrounded by murky water, guano stained and empty. The park service estimates that seventy-five great egrets and four great white herons nest here, a paltry sum compared with their numbers fifty years ago. The principal bird in the American Museum of Natural History's Cuthbert Lake diorama—the roseate spoonbill—nests elsewhere. So does the wood stork. The nesting egrets and herons are all off feeding somewhere in the shallow expanses of Florida Bay, picking, poking, and probing crabs, fish, and other edibles. Perhaps when restoration rehydrates the Everglades, and the coastal lakes fill with clean freshwater released at the proper time of year, the spoonbills will return to Cuthbert Lake.

《《《

When biologist Robert Porter Allen, author of *The Roseate Spoonbill*, began monitoring the birds for the National Audubon Society in 1939—a project that has continued for sixty-four years—he found only fifteen nests, all on Bottlepoint Key, and estimated that no more than fifty spoonbills lived in Florida Bay. Allen discovered that spoonbills, which had never recovered from the millinery trade slaughter, were still being illegally shot for food and feathers. Chicks and eggs were a local delicacy, second only to white ibis. During the peak of the millinery trade, spoonbills were never extensively hunted for their gorgeous feathers, which faded from hot pink to white shortly after being plucked. The birds themselves had been victims of their own timid nature: they deserted their eggs and chicks at the slightest provocation. Arthur Cleveland Bent noted that after concealing himself in a blind at Cuthbert Lake for parts of three days, the spoonbills abandoned the rookery altogether, and their eggs were destroyed by crows and vultures. "The ground," wrote Bent, "was strewn with broken egg shells," which led him to declare that "the egg collector, who is constantly moving about in plain sight, frightens the crows away, as well as the herons, and is therefore much less destructive than the bird photographer."

Beginning in the late 1940s, and continuing at an accelerating pace over the next thirty years, the mangrove swamps skirting the lower Keys, at the time the spoonbills' primary feeding grounds, were cut and filled for bayside developments. The birds began to shift to the northern bay, where virtually every small key and the mainland fringe were within the boundaries of Everglades National Park. Under the watchful eye of park rangers the spoonbill population doubled every decade thereafter. By 1979 at least 1,254 breeding pairs fashioned their flimsy nests in the mangroves around Florida Bay.

Three years later, the spoonbills' fortunes began to change for the worse. When the Army Corps of Engineers completed the C-111 project in 1982, the elaborate canal system in south Miami–Dade County, water from Taylor Slough destined for Florida Bay was diverted eastward to Barnes Sound. Taylor Slough, a seasonal watershed, became the most overdrained part of the national park. Without an adequate supply of freshwater, Florida Bay became saltier. Seagrass died. Fish died. Huge stinking blooms of algae turned parts of the bay pea-soup green. Not surprisingly the spoonbill population faltered. By 2001 only five hundred to seven hundred pairs nested around the bay, with varying degrees of success. According to Audubon biologist Jerry Lorenz, who has been monitoring the birds' prey base since 1989, before the construction of C-111, the spoonbills nested successfully 70 percent of the time and averaged 1.3 chicks per nest. After construction, their numbers fell to 35, with 0.6 chicks per nest. Lorenz believes that some Florida Bay spoonbills relocated to Tampa Bay and to the freshwater Everglades, where they hadn't nested for a hundred years. In fact, the first nesting ever recorded for spoonbills in Corkscrew Swamp occurred in the summer of 2000.

One February morning I join Lorenz and Frank Graham, an *Audubon* magazine field editor, for a tour of a spoonbill colony on Tern Key, in the northeast corner of Florida Bay. Graham is working on a story about Lorenz and his spoonbill study for *Audubon*'s Everglades issue. I'm along to schmooze and to see the birds that display sunset tones, even at high noon.

Lorenz looks more like a treasure hunter than a marine biologist. Thickset and nimble, he wears his strawberry-blond hair pulled straight back and tied off in a ponytail. A blue bandanna knotted around his head protects a receding hairline against the sun. A golden fish decorates one ear. The youngest of ten siblings, Lorenz grew up in Fort Thomas, Kentucky, a stone's throw from Cincinnati, where he hung out around the banks of the Ohio River, often against his mother's wishes. We depart Tavernier in a whaler, skip over the water, and enter Little Madeira Bay between Madeira Point and Eagle Key. This is crocodile country, closed to the public. Lorenz motors up Taylor River, where I collected hatching crocs with Frank Mazzotti.

South Florida is in the throes of a major drought, perhaps the worst in a century, and Lorenz wants to see whether spoonbills still feed in the series of ponds that spread out from both sides of the river. Whenever the water table in the lower Taylor Slough drainage falls below the surface, marine water moves in. The day is warm, and the water fresh, but when the drying front from the Everglades reaches Taylor River a few days hence, the tides will drive up the river's salt content. Lorenz has documented the impact of C-III on local fish populations, those species that sustain spoonbills as well as reddish egrets and great white herons. The well-being of these birds reflects the health of the bay and will eventually be used to help predict the success of Everglades restoration.

Years ago Robert Porter Allen discovered that the roseate spoonbill feeds primarily on small fish, rather than on the crustaceans and mollusks preferred by the similarly colored flamingo, and that it often feeds at night, when massive shoals of fish crowd the tidal channels and spread across the mangrove shallows. "Sometimes it appears," wrote Allen, "as if [the mangrove swamp channel] contains more animal life than water!" With this in mind Lorenz divided the mainland estuaries into three zones: fresh, lightly salty, and marine. He determined that the abundance and distribution of three species of fish—least killifish, gambusia, and sailfin molly—formed a perfect gradient from freshwater to salt. Freshwater supports more least killifish; saltwater, more mollies. Freshwater also supports a larger biomass of fish than either brackish or saltwater, but marine water supports a larger biomass than a zone of constantly fluctuating salinities, the very problem spoonbills contend with.

At the end of the rainy season, spoonbills return to Florida Bay and nest as soon as the wetlands begin to dry. Under natural drainage regimes, by the time fledglings are self-sufficient, water levels are low, and fish concentrations high. Since spoonbills feed in all three of Lorenz's salinity zones on all three species of fish, rehydrating the Everglades is essential to their survival. Although more water from the C-III system is currently routed back to Florida Bay, to drain Miami–Dade County farmland, the water management district releases water whenever the threat of rain exceeds two inches, sometimes during the nesting season. When that happens, the bay has a sudden pulse of freshwater, pools and puddles merge, and fish disperse. "If you help spoonbills recover," Lorenz reasons, "then you've helped Florida Bay. And if you help Florida Bay you have by default helped the rest of the watershed, because the only way to restore the health and vigor of the bay is to restore the Everglades."

A lone spoonbill, bent over, swinging its spatula bill to and fro, works the far side of the fourth pond. It has a bald, pale-greenish head, a white neck, pink legs, bright pink wings and body, an orange tail, and blood-red splashes on each shoulder. When the spoonbill sees us, it flushes, a pink bird in an otherwise blue sky, a sight that makes me happy to be alive. An unattributed quote on the jacket of Robert Porter Allen's book compares a spoonbill to an orchid that has taken wing, an analogy I can appreciate.

Once Lorenz has toured the ponds, which yielded only that one spoonbill and several schools of killifish, which excite him almost as much as the bird, we turn back toward Florida Bay. Out of the narrow, mangrove-pinched river, braced by the wind, we head southeast, arriving at Tern Key by midmorning. The sun is blistering. We tie the boat off by the mouth of a creek and slog through marl, which Graham has described as having "the consistency of oatmeal." Entering the creek, I sink to my knees and grope for mangrove branches to keep myself upright. A man on a mission, Lorenz wades on, leaving Graham and me to our slow, measured gaits. The creek opens into a small, shallow, brackish pond. In a dense copse of red mangroves fringing the pond are spoonbills of every conceivable age: downy nestlings and immature birds, each as clean and white as an egret; a trio of adults, red eyes piercing the dark green of the trees. Flocks of blue-winged teal rise from the shadows and whirl overhead. At any given moment there is a spoonbill or two cruising low over the treetops, neck extended and slightly drooped.

Although Lorenz has not banded or radio-collared any birds, he suspects that spoonbills circulate between the American Gulf Coast, Cuba, and the Yucatán Peninsula, one large, mobile population. I recall seeing spoonbills in the Bay of Pigs on the southwest side of Cuba. A line of four or five passed overhead, a counterpoint to the more exotic flamingoes, which combed the shallow bay for shrimp. Cuba may well have been the original source of Florida's spoonbills and may still be the birds' primary wet-season home.

The young spoonbills are tolerant of our stumbling. They lean their white-feathered heads toward me, or wander along sagging branches, wings flicking for balance. Lorenz marches deeper into the rookery, squeezing through spidery trees. He's headed for a second pond, hidden behind a screen of limbs and aerial roots. When he reaches it, a sudden burst of teal—two, three, six tiny ducks, wings whistling—rise above the jungle canopy, followed by the methodical flight of half a dozen spoonbills. For a moment I stand enchanted, birds everywhere. As quickly as Lorenz entered the rookery, he is out again, imploring us to hurry. His tally complete, he is eager to end his disturbance of the spoonbills.

The Sandy Key spoonbills, in the northwest corner of Florida Bay, had a banner year in 2000 and produced an average of three chicks per nest, a rate close to what Allen was recording each year in the 1950s. Because of the reduced supply of small fish, the birds cannot sustain that level of reproduction all the time, but there is certainly room for improvement.

❨❨❨

Peter Frederick and his colleagues at the University of Florida have a secret: the exact location of an ongoing wildlife spectacle somewhere in the Everglades. The spot is home to what Frederick calls "probably the most picturesque and beautiful bird colony in the world." Shrubs and trees festooned with blooming bromeliads host tricolored herons, great egrets, little blue herons, snowy egrets, snail kites, anhingas, and more. "It's an image nobody tells you about these days," says Frederick, who has studied ibis for fifteen years. That's because the region's wading birds have never come close to fully recovering from their population crash in the middle of the 1900s.

Hidden Colony is in a cypress strand on the border of Big Cypress National Preserve and the central Everglades. Hurricane Andrew toppled many of the cypress trees there, leaving the trunks leaning at every imaginable angle. More than eight hundred pairs of great egrets nest in Hidden Colony. To maneuver around the foliage without damaging their delicate wings and long legs, great egrets usually nest in the crowns of trees, but here in Hidden Colony the weave of toppled trunks and limbs has created open, stable nest sites lower than I imagined. Some nests are so low that I can peek in. Several of them cradle day-old chicks, white bits of fluff with rubbery bills and soft oversized feet. Nestling tricolored herons look like punk rockers; the feathers on their downy heads stand straight up. To avoid disturbing the birds excessively, Frederick monitors the colony every fifth day and stays no more than an hour each time.

Alligators lurk beneath the surface, fattening on wading-bird carcasses and chicks that fall into the water. Once Frederick watched an alligator lug itself six feet into a broken cypress and grab an ambulatory egret chick. To the benefit of the rookery, however, gators also ward off raccoons and other mammal predators. The cool air gathers mosquitoes. The water is warm, brown, and peppered with water lettuce. Green light filters through a filigree of cypress needles. Some blooming bromeliads support tricolored heron nests, perched as though on the crowns of pineapples. Wherever I go, adult birds flush, creating a cacophony of dyspeptic grunts, roars, and belches.

We visit three nests, where Frederick weighs and measures each chick and determines if any is infected with a parasitic nematode, or roundworm, called *Eustrongylides*. These three-inch worms perforate the stomach walls of wading birds to feast on the contents. An adult egret can tolerate four or five worms, but even a single worm can overwhelm a chick, which either bleeds to death or becomes so weakened and emaciated that it cannot survive. The parasite begins life as an egg in an adult wading bird. When the bird defecates, the parasite's eggs may be picked up by a tiny segmented worm that closely resembles an earthworm and lives in wetlands at the interface of earth and water, in areas of nutrient pollution often rich in human sewage. The parasite's eggs then hatch inside the segmented worm. If a small fish eats the worm, the nematode remains inside the fish until it is eaten by a wading bird. When a wading bird eats both a male and a female *Eustrongylides,* the cycle continues with reproduction of the parasite inside the bird's stomach. Without the wading bird the parasite cannot reproduce.

Frederick and his wife, Marilyn Spalding, a parasitologist and veterinarian at the University of Florida, discovered an infestation of roundworms in the Rodgers River colony, a remote wading bird rookery in the headwater mangroves. They radio-tracked adult wading birds from the colony, tracing them to a thirty-person commercial hunting camp on an island in the Big Cypress National Preserve. From the camp, called Coconuts, untreated sewage spews directly into the surrounding wetlands and supports a high population of both the segmented worm and the infected fish. (To establish Big Cypress National Preserve, the federal government had to grant existing hunting camps the right to continue operation.) Between 1989 and 1991 90 percent of the nestling herons at the Rodgers River colony died of roundworm infestation. Frederick had taken me to Coconuts several weeks before. The well-nourished aquatic vegetation that immediately surrounded the island was greener and lusher than the nearby marsh. Just off the island's boat ramp, several gambusia lurched at the surface, worm-swollen and barely able to swim, easy targets for hungry egrets.

Back at Hidden Colony, Frederick takes blood samples from several nestlings to check the percentage of freshwater in their bodies, an indication of the amount of food the birds have recently eaten. Egret chicks bleed easily. When Frederick finds a sickly one infected with *Eustrongylides,* I feel the beauty of Hidden Colony dissipate before my eyes. The tangerine sky pales, and the gorgeous wild birds passing overhead seem to vanish. I run my fingers across the nestling's gut and feel the coiled worm encased in a hard tube the nestling has secreted in a desperate attempt to wall off the parasite.

Saddened that wading birds face this extra hurdle, Frederick reminds me that local, typically human-generated, nutrient sources in the oligotrophic, nutrient-poor, Everglades favor the segmented worm over the birds. No segmented worm, no parasite infestation. "I worry about the forty-thousand-acre retention pond that will be built to clean the runoff from cane fields," Frederick says. "We may be creating an ideal habitat for an *Eustrongylides* infestation."

《《《

There are better records for wading birds than for any other animal in the Everglades. In the late 1920s Robert Porter Allen developed a survey that Audubon wardens filled out each week, answering questions that included the location, the size, the species composition, and the timing of colony formations. After I studied these surveys, several facts became clear: although wading birds nested every year, the supercolonies, the ones the Everglades is famous for, formed approximately two out of every ten years, always in the headwaters of tidal rivers at the interface of the mangroves and the freshwater Everglades. These colonies were named for their parent rivers: East River, Lane River, Broad River, and Rookery Branch. Great egret, snowy egret, tricolored heron, and white ibis composed 90 to 100 percent of each supercolony, but the white ibis alone accounted for 80 to 90 percent of these.

Logic persuaded me that the supercolonies formed after three or four wet years, when fish populations should increase exponentially. My logic, however, was wrong. John Ogden, of the South Florida Water Management District, believes that the opposite is true, that drought was the trigger: "although there was very little nesting during a severe multiyear drought, the big colonies almost always formed the very next wet year." This bears repeating for the umpteenth time: the Everglades is a low-nutrient, low-productivity wetland that does not produce a high number of prey species per square meter. "Drought," says Ogden, "killed the big predatory fish like bass and gar and organized energy pulses." The desiccating masses of periphyton released stored phosphorous, and fires liberated nutrients bound in the marsh plants and peat. When the rains finally came, the pulses of phosphorous in the Everglades produced trillions of small animals—crayfish, grass shrimp, killifish, gambusia—that prospered in the absence of bass and gar and fed the great clouds of birds. In 2001 a paper published in the journal *Wetlands* by Frederick and Ogden demonstrated the pattern statistically. Since the 1930s there have been eight supercolonies and eight severe droughts; the supercolonies have occurred after every one of the severe droughts. "A couple of years after the drought," says Ogden, "when the pulse of nutrients had moved through the system and the predatory fish had returned, the supercolonies began to break up."

Although white ibises eat crabs, frogs, and an occasional snake, including young water moccasins, their cue to breed is concentrations of aquatic invertebrates, particularly crayfish (or fish as in 1992). In fact, because white ibis were so much more common than all other species of wading birds combined, the Everglades was truly an invertebrate-dominated system, which sets it apart from most other wetlands. One biologist estimated that a white ibis supercolony would consume more than 800,000,000 pounds of crayfish in a year. Ibis readily gorged on fish as well. Several years ago I watched dozens work a pool blackened with fish; shoulder-to-shoulder, the ibis crowded in among lilies, shoving and bumping like children on a playground. Virtually every time a bird put its red sickle bill in the water, it caught a killifish. After it had eaten ten or twenty fish, the ibis flew onto one of the many overhanging limbs and digested its meal. The birds were in constant flux, moving between tree and water. Pasty lines of guano stained the surface of the pool.

The white ibis is a nomadic breeder. At the turn of the twentieth century almost the entire North American population nested in Florida, mostly in the southern Everglades. Perhaps a million or more ibis nested in the Everglades in the years before plume hunting. In 1932 an Audubon warden reported, "Looks like a million birds feeding in the marsh above Harney [River]." The following year he wrote, "estimated 2 million young from 6 rookeries." In 1934 Robert Porter Allen reported in *Bird Lore* that a million birds nested in Rookery Branch. (Warden reports for that year offer a more conservative estimate of 225,000.) Then, for three out of the next five years, virtually no white ibis nested in the Everglades. White ibis shifted their breeding population at least four times between 1930 and 1993: first to the Gulf Coast of central Florida, then to South Carolina and Georgia, and most recently to Louisiana. The presence or absence of food appears to trigger these shifts. Ever since the 1960s, by which time nearly the entire system of canals and levees was in place, white ibis virtually ceased to nest in the coastal Everglades. In the late 1980s large numbers of ibis colonized Louisiana, attracted by the bounty of numerous crayfish farms.

The Everglades, unlike most other estuarine systems, has little freshwater sediment or nutrient load. Its estuarine productivity may derive from the increase in available nutrients resulting from chemical changes inherent in the mixing of freshwater and saltwater; some nutrients simply become more available as salinity changes in the marine zone. When canal construction redirected the flow of water out of the Everglades, reducing the mixing of waters in the estuarine mangrove swamps, fewer nutrients were available in the food chain, which meant fewer prey for the birds. As the flow of freshwater into the mangroves diminished, salinity levels began to fluctuate widely. Although fish are osmoregulators (their tissues are fresher than the outside seawater), crustaceans, a favorite ibis food, are osmoconformers (the salt content of their tissues is closer to that of seawater). Adult ibis are tolerant of salty food, but juveniles are not. Chicks fed a steady diet of crustaceans expend energy trying to rid their systems of excess salt, depleting their energy reserves needed for growth. Although the small fish that also sustained the supercolonies—such as sheepshead minnow, marsh killifish, gulf killifish, sailfin molly, and rainwater killifish—can tolerate sudden, even dramatic, changes in salinity, they cannot tolerate the absence of their own food sources and the aquatic plants they use for cover. No cover, no fish. Eventually, no birds.

Ibis and wood storks left South Florida, and great egrets, snowy egrets, and tricolored herons moved their rookeries to interior areas, such as Hidden Colony, where water levels and fish populations are somewhat more stable. The spectacular coastal rookeries that inspired the creation of Everglades National Park have fallen silent.

Many biologists believe that to help establish a national park in the Everglades the 1930s Audubon wardens might have routinely exaggerated their counts of nesting birds in the coastal rookeries. "What we've really lost in the Everglades," says Frederick, "is not so much a head count of wading birds, we've lost a phenomenon, a gathering of birds that leaves you so blown away you can hardly speak." Asking someone like Robert Porter Allen if he actually saw a million birds, continues Frederick, is "sort of like asking a poet, 'Did you really mean it?'"

The Everglades experienced four record wet years between 1994 and 1999. The freshwater flow in the mangroves mirrored what had naturally taken place before the region's flood-control structures were built. The vegetation, the invertebrates, and the fish returned. The birds did not. In 2000, the park's wading bird survey in the traditional coastal rookeries counted only 330 nests, mostly wood storks and great egrets, but no white ibis.

Peter Frederick predicts that there will be a time lag before white ibis respond—if they do at all—to an increase in freshwater, the primary goal of Everglades restoration efforts. "Ibis may never return in great numbers. Louisiana crayfish farms may be too much of a good thing," he laments. "What if you throw the party and nobody comes?"

《《《

Dale Gawlik monitors wading birds' response to hydrologic change. Using artificial feeding ponds, in which he manipulates water level, Gawlik documents the optimal foraging depths for various species of birds. A distillation of his work reveals that an equal number of prey at varying depths are not equally available. Stated another way: some species of wading birds are more sensitive to water depth than others. According to Gawlik, in approximately four inches of water, when fish are abundant, all bird species feed until virtually every fish is gone. When fish are densely packed in four inches of water, white ibis and wood stork, feeders that locate their food by touch, are as successful as such visual feeders as great egrets and great blue herons.

When the water depth approaches eleven inches, however, even if prey density remains extremely high, white ibises, wood storks, and snowy egrets do not feed, although other species keep feeding. For these three species to prosper, he tells me, they require both shallow water and a dense prey base. If one or the other is missing, the birds suffer, because the cost of feeding, in terms of expended energy, becomes too high.

Unlike ibises and storks, snowy egrets are active, visual feeders, fish specialists par excellence. When prey are particularly dense, and the water is particularly shallow, I've watched snowies fly back and forth, yellow feet dimpling the surface, chumming for gambusia and killifish. Whenever a fish rises to the disturbance, the bird strikes, swift and lethal, then feeds on the wing, all the while fluttering above the water. When the density of fish drops, the egrets disperse. A little blue heron, which is about the same size as a snowy egret, works the shallows long after snowies leave. When fish are scarce, a little blue will shift to aquatic insects and frogs, something snowy egrets are loath to do. I have often seen little blue herons feeding along the edge of Eco Pond several days after the last snowy has left the area. One particular little blue was adept at spiking giant water bugs, which it worked in its bill, turning, positioning, and pressing them, as the big insects' legs flailed. Tilting its head back, the bird swallowed the bugs, then sipped water as though washing down a vitamin pill.

Since the 1930s the populations of snowy egrets, white ibis, and wood storks have seriously declined throughout South Florida. The draining and development of the marl prairies eliminated one of the most productive foraging sites for wading birds. The white ibis and wood stork, which feed by touch, depended on concentrations of prey along the prairies to cue their breeding season. Historically storks begin nesting in early December, snowy egrets in late February, followed in early March by ibis. Because the debased wetlands now offer such conflicting cues, nesting has been pushed later into the dry season, which often leaves chicks and fledglings susceptible to rising water levels and dispersal of their food supply.

Despite the jury-rigging of the Everglades, every once in a while an astronomical number of fish and invertebrates still get trapped in shallow, shrinking pools. Then wood storks and ibis gorge, shoulder to shoulder with great egrets, great blue herons, and spoonbills. Snowy egrets and little blues work the edges; green herons, the snags. Wood storks move slowly, methodically stirring the bottom with pale pink legs; a stretched wing canopies the water, creating shade that attracts luckless fish. The storks progress open-beaked; their bald, flinty heads rock side to side as they move. When a bill touches a fish, the beak clamps shut like a sprung trap. One biologist claimed that a wood stork could close its mouth in a twenty-five thousandth of a second, the fastest-known reflex in the animal kingdom. After witnessing a stork feeding frenzy (they were known as wood ibis then), John James Audubon wrote:

> As soon as they have discovered a place abounding in fish, they dance as it were all through it, until the water becomes thick with mud stirred from the bottom by their feet. The fishes, on rising to the surface, are instantly struck by the beaks of the ibises and, on being deprived of life, they turn over and so remain. In the course of 10 or 15 minutes, hundred of fishes, frogs, young alligators, and water snakes cover the surface, and the birds greedily swallow them until they are completely gorged, after which they walk to the nearest margins, place themselves in long rows, with their breasts all turned toward the sun, in the manner of pelicans and vultures, and thus remain for an hour or so.

I have never seen storks litter the water surface with disabled prey, but I have seen them catch flagfish and shiners, one after the other. When the birds were sated they flew high into the air, circled, and drifted off to a distant rookery. Storks are so dependent on concentrations of fish during the nesting season that they often travel forty or more miles to feed, and then return each evening to regurgitate the day's catch down the gullets of their young. Corkscrew Swamp, the National Audubon Society's old-growth cypress swamp east of Naples, hosts a large colony of nesting wood storks. When conditions are perfect, the glades slowly drying, more than two thousand pairs fix their nests in the canopy, then, as a friend notes, it becomes Stork Screw Sanctuary. If water levels are high the following year, the sanctuary's cypress will be bereft of storks. Nesting is an all or nothing proposition.

Each winter, wood storks arrive in the Everglades and make "a go, no go" decision, says John Ogden. If they stay and nest, which happens less frequently, they are not always successful. The dry year 2000 following a very wet 1999 was an exception: more than seventeen hundred nests in southwest Florida fledged twenty-five hundred chicks. Nearly sixteen hundred pairs nested in Everglades National Park, mostly away from the coast in a large colony near the Tamiami

Trail. Many colonies began in mid-December, the more traditional time. By April the park service and water management district's monthly reconnaissance flights tallied more than eighty-five hundred storks in and around the national park, numbers that approached historic proportions.

《《《

I am the guest of Julie Heath, a doctoral student of Peter Frederick. Julie, who rocket-nets white ibis in the central Everglades, is trying to understand why birds aren't breeding—too little food, too much mercury? Hormones tell the tale. By half past four in the morning, we are in an airboat inside the central Everglades, somewhere between the North New River Canal and the Miami Canal. We reach an open area in the marsh, cut the loud engine, and wade out fifty yards to set a flock of thirty-four lawn ornaments—white plastic flamingos, wire legs jammed into the peat. The crude decoys attract white ibis. We set the net, fix three rockets, trail the ignition wires back to the boat, turn on the firing mechanism, and wait.

A little more than an hour later the first of hundreds of white ibis appear on the horizon; livening the sky, dozens of lines of four and five birds radiate from an unseen point. More than five thousand roost five miles to our west, but the Everglades is too dry for us to go farther. So the birds come to us. High overhead is a pair of spoonbills. The eastern sky is grapefruit-pink. Hanging in the west, the moon, a shave off full, slides in and out of the clouds.

Four birds are lured in; just out of firing range, all circle the plastic flamingos, then leave. Finally at quarter past six, an ibis lands. Julie fires the rockets, shattering the morning silence. Caught and retrieved, the female ibis weighs 735 grams. She has a pink decurved bill and pink legs. The bill of a male ibis is much longer than that of a female. As courtship progresses, the skin and faces of all wading birds turn bright colors. An aroused white ibis turns fire engine red, then, within days of pairing, fades to various shades of pink. Using Pittsburgh Paint chips, Julie approximates the color of the bird's face, bill, and legs. Lobster Bisque. (A second female caught later in the morning is Strawberry Ice.) The ibis is snow white, with iridescent green-black wing tips. Her eyes are powder blue. After weighing the bird, Julie measures the bill length, angle of bill curve, and fat deposit—very little. She also determines that the ibis holds eggs.

By nine o'clock we pack the net, take down the plastic flamingos, and head back. A thousand ibis rise out of the marsh. As birds fill the sky I begin to think about something Audubon biologist Alexander Sprunt III wrote in 1940 after estimating that seventy thousand nests filled the mangroves in the Broad

River rookery: "It is, of course, quite impossible to describe it. There are no words or certainly none in my power to give the impression of an observer in the midst of that feathered metropolis. It was as if humanity had ceased to exist, and that we were intruders in a world which was peopled entirely by birds, birds which ruled the country and which regarded us as interlopers to be ejected as soon as possible."

A stranger to these waters could only assume
he was traveling in authentic wilderness, pure
and thriving. If only it were so.

CARL HIAASEN, 1995

14 Florida Bay

Brian Mealy was on the dock at the Flamingo Marina before the sun had risen in the February sky. I didn't recognize Mealy by his appearance (we had never met), but I did recognize him by his paraphernalia: a three-man, inflatable boat and outboard engine, an aluminum ladder, a centrifuge, a toolbox. All the gear he needs to cross Florida Bay, scale a couple of trees, and take blood samples from four bald eagle chicks.

I introduce myself to Mealy and to his assistant, Greta Parks, who, after raising her children, decided that she wanted a life close to wildlife, an opportunity Mealy provides in spades. We load the boat, which is loosely tethered to the dock. The tide and the sun are slowly rising. Once the boat is loaded and the gear secured, I step in and sit on the air-cushioned gunwale next to Mealy, who, in quick succession, unties the boat, pushes off, and then fires the engine. Because manatees swim in Buttonwood Canal, we proceed at a snail's pace, which stirs green herons hunched on the bank. At the mouth of the canal, water spreads across the mudflats from the long, gray lips of the deeper channels. Between the rising tide and the wind, which teases each accompanying wavelet into a tiny whitecap that folds back on itself, I imagine that our boat is a basketball being dribbled across Florida Bay, a sensation that rhythmically moves from the hull up my legs.

Although the bay has been ill, and its well-being is a vital component of Everglades restoration, birds are everywhere: on the mud, in the gray channels of water, in the air, and far out to sea. Because of our constant bouncing, I can get only glimpses of the action. Long-legged birds in the channels appear oblivious to the rising water. Flocks of tiny sandpipers, driven from the flats by an incoming tide, pirouette above the bay, their ranks alternately loosening and tightening, giving the more distant flocks the look of restless smoke. A line of black skimmers flies low over the water. Terns hover. Brown pelicans and white pelicans crowd a mudflat in front of Joe Kemp Key, an isle of a dozen red mangroves.

We are on our way to Sandy Key, the island visited by John James Audubon in 1832, where Mealy will climb to the first eagle nest. Sandy Key is a mile or so inside the boundary of Everglades National Park, seven miles southwest of Flamingo. Except for a fish or a porpoise at high tide nothing crosses Florida Bay in a straight line. Our route covers twelve miles.

Florida Bay is North America's largest subtropical estuary, remarkably shallow for a body of water covering more than 850 square miles of torturous channels and sprawling mudflats often hidden beneath a thin skin of water. Eighty-five percent of Florida Bay is within the boundaries of the national park. The northern border of the bay is the tip of peninsular Florida, a petering maze of creeks and lakes and a bulwark of mangroves; arcing from the southeast, the Florida Keys separate the bay from the Atlantic; on the west lies the Gulf of Mexico. Nutrient-rich water from brackish Florida Bay flowing through the passes between the keys helps fertilize the coral reefs on the Atlantic side.

Mealy threads the boat carefully toward Sandy Key. He has no choice; Florida Bay is a subdivision of basins cut by mudbanks and channels. They are easily visible from the air—the deeper the water, the darker the color—but from the surface (at least in the western half of the bay), all are a single shade of milky gray. The average depth of the bay is three feet, and nowhere is it deeper than nine feet. At high tide much of Florida Bay is boat-scrapingly shallow. At low tide it is an endless run of glistening, bird-busy mudflats. And the wind has been known to blow the water out of the bay and to send it sometimes miles inland.

Several years ago I co-led an Everglades tour attended by fourteen people. One night a park service naturalist warned me that a rising tide near high and a driving rain accompanied by thirty-mile-per-hour winds out of the Caribbean might push Florida Bay into the campground around midnight. Not wanting to relocate in the dark, and finding the warning difficult to believe, I ignored the ranger and kept us tented in the palms close to shore. Shortly after one in the morning, water began to rise through the floor of my tent. Although the bay had never breached its two-foot-high marl embankment, the wind had pounded it against the shore, pushing water up from the already-rain-saturated earth. Eventually eight inches of water collected in the swales (our campsite), and a sheet several inches deep covered the campground to the edge of the parking area, 150 yards behind us. Drenched and grumpy, we abandoned camp, crammed into a rented cottage, and waited several days for both the campground and our gear to dry. I learned to respect the bay and the people who dispense the local forecast.

More than two hundred mangrove keys punctuate Florida Bay, some so small and so new that they do not appear on nautical charts; others are long and convoluted. All rise from mudbanks. Unlike tree islands in the Everglades, which obey a predictable current and are uniform in both shape and direction, the keys in Florida Bay have been forged by the vagaries of unstable currents and are a medley of shapes and sizes that line up in every conceivable direction. Some of their names evoke images of wild America: Dead Terrapin Key, Curlew, Man of War, Calusa, Buttonwood, Whipray, and so on. Others— Dildo, Umbrella, Topsy, Cluett, the Arsenickers—do not. Mealy bounces the inflatable past Curry Key and Bradley Key, named for Guy Bradley, the Audubon warden murdered by plume hunters in 1905; past Murray Key and Upper and Lower Oyster keys, where Bradley was killed. Looking northeast, I see Frank Key, which Red Smith, the sports columnist for the *New York Times,* once called the Grand Central Station of Everglades bird life, a tribute to the spoonbills, cormorants, brown pelicans, and assorted wading birds that crowd the outer branches of the island.

Eventually Sandy Key appears in the distance, lean and green. On the chart it is shaped like a golf club, head pointing east. From the water the isle is a shimmering line of trees and a bevy of hyperactive birds. In 1960 Hurricane Donna tore through Sandy Key, severing the tip of the handle (now named Carl Ross Key) from the shaft of the club. Four dolphins slice the narrow channel separating the two islands.

High tide on Sandy Key is about two hours earlier than at Flamingo. Mealy cuts the engine and lets the wind push us into a tiny cove, where he ties the boat to a leaning mangrove. Sandy Key's western beach is a jumble of shells and shelly sand brought by the Gulf of Mexico; the eastern edge of the key is more marl than sand, a tapered coastline that blends into extensive flats at low tide. Just beyond the wave line, where the sea oats grow, the bones of a sea turtle bake in the sun. Fifteen feet beyond the oats we cross a band of yellow-green coastal prairie bordered by a wall of mangroves. A great white heron flushes from a snag, grunts, and belches, its long neck slowly curving back on itself in flight. Inside the woods it is moist and dark; the floor of the forest is a soft carpet of rotting leaves. I pause at the edge of a spoonbill rookery and look up at incubating birds, bouquets of pink, red, and orange. At the far end of the rookery a cluster of spoonbill feathers is all that remains of an eagle's kill.

Mealy finds the eagle nest in a twisted black mangrove slightly taller that its neighbors. He visits each nest three times: in the beginning of the nesting cycle to gage when the chicks will be ready to handle; when they are old enough to be banded and bled; and after they've fledged to see how they're doing. I tote the toolbox, which contains pliers and bird bands, into a small prairie on the eastern shore within sight of the nest.

As soon as I step out of the woods, an adult eagle, with its seven-foot wing-span, begins to cut reckless loops above the trees. Its hot yellow eyes are fixed on me. While Mealy climbs, Parks gives moral support. Mealy reaches the nest, a huge pile of sticks and seaweed anchored to a radial platform of thick branches, reaches in, and removes the first of two huge eaglets, as dark and uniform brown as a chocolate bar. The five- or six-pound chicks are thirty-five to forty days old; their toes and scimitar talons fold in a knot of yellow, scaly feet, as though the young birds are unaware of their own power.

Mealy, who holds a master's degree in zoology from the Florida International University, is the director of the Miami Museum of Science Falcon Batchelor Bird of Prey Center, where he supervises the treatment and rehabilitation of raptors and conducts research on area birds and reptiles. For nearly a decade he has reached into Florida Bay eagle and osprey nests to collect blood samples and bacterial cultures from more than 150 nestlings, and for more than five years he has studied the bay's diamond-backed terrapins, the region's resident estuarine turtles. Mealy is soft-spoken and considerate to both humans and birds. He wears a neatly trimmed full beard and has a compact muscular physique, like a collegiate wrestler's, but appears even smaller when he holds a six- or seven-pound eagle chick, its feathers puffed in distress. After the second bird is down, Mealy brings the first into the prairie opening. Cackling like a hen, a distressed mother eagle passes repeatedly and swiftly overhead, chasing her shadow across the ground.

Mealy profiles eagle and osprey blood chemistry because, he says, blood is a window into the health of an animal and its habitat. He has found fluctuating traces of mercury and pesticides in the blood of both eaglets and osprey. If an eaglet is anemic its red blood cell count is low; if it is dehydrated the count is high. If its immune system is compromised, the white blood cell count is low. And so on. Mealy also examines the bird's blood-borne bacteria to determine the normal level of infestation. When a bird is stressed by the environment, its bacteria often multiply, sometimes to lethal levels.

In collaboration with Everglades National Park, Brian Mealy wants to see whether the birds have been affected by the shifting fortunes of Florida Bay, which has suffered from restricted circulation and from unnatural shifts in salinity. The bay is a nursery for more than sixty species of fish, including twenty-two of commercial importance—snook, bonefish, tarpon, and redfish, for instance—and for several species of tasty crustacean—spiny lobster, blue crab, stone crab, pink shrimp. It is the bottom of the watershed, the end of the line, where the area's problems of water quantity, quality, and timing of flow are amplified. If you restore Florida Bay, you have restored the rest of the Everglades.

Until recently the bay had been a game-fishing Mecca. Ernest Hemingway, Zane Grey, and Ted Williams have lived on the Florida Keys, lured by the Keys' legendary tarpon, bonefish, and sea trout. And Dwight Eisenhower and George Bush senior repeatedly wet their lines in Florida Bay. According to Audubon biologist Jerry Lorenz the bay's aquatic plant communities, which support a pyramid of food, do not do well in rapidly fluctuating salinities. During the floods of 1999 Lorenz found purple-flowered bladderwort growing in tidal creeks along with a rapidly expanding fish population. When the rains stopped, the water management district restricted the flow to Florida Bay. Then, as the salinity level approached five parts per thousand, bladderwort died, and fish thinned out. "Unnatural changes in salinity, which often occur monthly, devastate both salt- and freshwater plants," according to Lorenz.

In 1905 Henry Flagler, who had brought the East Coast Railroad from Daytona to Homestead, was ready to tackle the last 128 miles of track from the mainland to Key West. Flagler planned to fill the southeast Everglades to Key Largo and most of the passes between the Keys. But federal engineers feared that blocking the flow of water between Biscayne Bay, Florida Bay, and the Atlantic Ocean would move the Gulf Stream away from the coast. They also worried that the constricted passes would increase the voracity of storm surges between the Keys. Flagler compromised and agreed to put in eleven miles of concrete viaducts and seventeen miles of bridges, mostly over deep water, and in 1912 the Overseas Railroad reached Key West.

The railroad's construction restricted the flow of water between Florida Bay and the Atlantic Ocean, affecting both the bay and the chain of coral reefs off the eastern shore of the Florida Keys. The Overseas Railroad was destroyed when the Labor Day hurricane of 1935 ripped across the middle Keys and knocked out forty miles of track. The federal government had wanted to connect Key West with the rest of Florida with something more than the Overseas Railroad. Once the railroad was destroyed, the state purchased the remaining causeway, right of way, trestles, and arches and constructed the Overseas Highway, a continuation of U.S. Route 1, which reached Key West on July 4, 1938.

Although the filling of portions of the passes between the Keys never drove the Gulf Stream away, it did reduce the mixing and flushing of the waters, the first step in the conversion of Florida Bay from an estuary of seasonally shifting salinities to a salty marine lagoon. Between 1987 and 1990 a severe drought reduced the already diminished flow of freshwater from the Everglades, creating a hypersaline condition in the bay. A salinity high of eighty parts per thousand (more than twice that of seawater) was recorded in the central portion of the bay. Hypersalinity stressed young fish and favored a slime mold that began to kill the beds of turtle grass that had carpeted nearly 80 percent of the bay. Nutrients released by decaying sea grass triggered blooms of algae, which turned gin-clear water into something closer to pea soup. Cloudy water blocked sunlight, further choking sea grass. As more sea grass died, the water grew even cloudier. Caught in this negative feedback loop, tens of thousands of acres of turtle grass died as the health of Florida Bay spiraled downward.

More than fifty pairs of bald eagles nest on Florida Bay, about as many as were there in the 1950s. Because of the bird's catholic feeding habits, Mealy believes that the bay's eagle population has recently fared better than populations of more strictly fish-eating species. In South Florida, eagles eat birds—egrets, pelicans, herons, spoonbills, and cormorants—which is why bird-crowded mudflats often desert whenever an eagle sails over. Mealy has found as many as seven terrapin shells in an eagle nest. Today the Sandy Key nest is littered with ibis and spoonbill feathers, as if the big birds had gone grocery shopping in the rookery next door.

Mealy sets to work. To get bacterial samples, he gently wipes a sterile swab around the bird's throat and another around its cloaca. Then he draws blood from a vein in the wing. Finally he bands the bird with a band large enough to fit a human baby's wrist. A second adult eagle joins the first, their wings almost touching, and together the birds tighten their circles; the tips of their primary wing feathers strum the air. Intent on his work, Mealy barely notices.

After the second chick is processed, he returns both birds to the nest. We gather our gear and retrace our route back to the boat, where Mealy spins the blood samples in a centrifuge wired to the boat's battery. From Sandy Key we head northeast to Rankin Key, a long, thin isle off the mouth of Rankin Bight. On the chart Rankin Bight appears circular, a two-mile-wide cove inside the curved spits of Shark Point and Mosquito Point, which extend from the mainland like the pinchers of a beetle.

A trip across Florida Bay is a trip back in time. Sediment corings reveal a patina of freshwater peat sandwiched between the bedrock limestone and the marl. On a key close to the mainland the remains of pines lie beneath mud and mangrove. Beginning about five thousand years ago, and lasting for approximately the next two thousand years, the sea rose about a foot a century, flooding what is now Florida Bay. Over the next thousand years the freshwater wetland became increasingly more saline. Mangrove keys replaced bay heads, and sea grass replaced sawgrass as freshwater wetlands retreated north. Radiocarbon dating of peat reveals that Everglades marshes existed in southwestern Florida Bay about five thousand years ago, in central Florida Bay about four thousand years ago, and in northeastern Florida Bay, about twenty-five hundred years ago.

The topography of the floor of Florida Bay is an afterimage of the shapes of lakes and bays inside the coast. Several thousand years ago the rising sea, driven by hurricanes, flooded the mangrove forest and the brackish lake system that had replaced the bay's original freshwater wetlands. The tidal surges gutted the shallow bodies of water, widening, enlarging, and hollowing them. The scattered mangrove forests drowned in rising seawater, leaving behind the keys, which survive on the highest mudbanks. Old lake bottoms were colonized by sea grass. Gradually freshwater creeks gave way to tidal channels. Mangroves spread north along the channels and along alligator trails gouged in the peat. Hurricane tidal surges flushed out the freshwater marshes, leaving behind a necklace of shallow tidal lakes and bights, including Rankin.

Mealy ties off on a prop root within sight of the second nest, another monster pile of sticks in a black mangrove, then lugs his ladder across the prairie. Two chicks peek over the rim of the nest, both big. While Mealy and Parks bleed the birds, I stand in the scorching sun and watch the parents swoop past. Mine are not the only eyes watching. An osprey leaves its perch and vexes the bigger of the two eagles, the female; she rolls over, slowly flapping upside down; her legs extended and her knife-sharp talons pointed skyward, she engages her neighbor in ritualistic combat. Just above the eagle, the osprey brakes its dive, rises, and then stoops again. And again . . . and again . . . fourteen times. And each time the big bird flies upside down, dignified and indifferent.

《 《 《

A week later I join Mealy and Parks back at the boat ramp at the Flamingo Marina. Today's quest is osprey chicks. The boat loaded, we enter Florida Bay, catch a channel that runs due east, and aim for Rankin Key, where Mealy has two low osprey nests he wants to check, not far from last week's eagle's nest. For much of the trip we remain outside Snake Bight, the largest curve along Florida Bay coastline and one of the finest birding sites in Everglades National Park. At low tide the sprawling mudflats are regularly patrolled by peregrines and bald eagles that harry hundreds, sometimes thousands, of shorebirds and waders gathered to feed. Almost always the rare and animated reddish egret is among them, lurching and teetering along some oblique channel. And once I saw a flock of forty-seven flamingos, shimmering through distant waves of heat. If the waters of Snake Bight are particularly sweet, alligators come; when the tide recedes, they loiter on the flats caked in gray marl.

The tide drops quickly, the marl glimmering in the sun. This is not the time to be caught outside a channel, where the emerging flats can leave you a mile or more from navigable water. The first time I kayaked on Florida Bay, my late wife Linny and I didn't buy a nautical chart. As the tide receded, western sandpipers, willets, marble godwits, and dunlin swarmed around us. Mesmerized by the moment, we lost track of both time and tide and found ourselves more than a hundred yards from water. As the sun set, mosquitoes found us. Forced out of my boat, I began to drag the two kayaks, Linny still sitting in hers, through the shelly ooze, sinking to my knees, occasionally to my thighs. When the sunset-cruise ship from the Flamingo Marina passed into view, the captain, speaking on the PA system, called everyone's attention to the majesty of the birds and to the folly of our situation. "Unless you're a bird, you need to have a chart to paddle Florida Bay," he broadcast, our progress marked by half a hundred pairs of eyes.

We reach the west side of Rankin Key, tie off, and cross the prairie. Two osprey nests within a hundred yards of each other sit on stumps, three feet off the ground. The first nest has three small nestlings, big-footed bits of fluff hatched a day or so apart, much too young to process. The second nest has a pair of grown chicks. Mealy removes the first bird and works beneath the shadows of four ospreys and a bald eagle.

According to national park records, there were 221 osprey nests in Florida Bay in 1973. By the early 1990s, when the bay's productivity had collapsed because of the sea grass blight, the number of nests had fallen to less than 70. During the early 1990s, another obligate fish-eater, the brown pelican, had gone from 861 nesting pairs to 350. Both birds catch prey by plunging into the water, sometimes from considerable heights. The osprey hooks fish on sharp talons; the pelican engulfs them in its outlandish bill. To be successful both birds must be able to see the fish they catch. The opaque broth of an overly saline bay reduced visibility.

What plagues Florida Bay is not entirely the result of restricted circulation and reduced inflow of freshwater from the Everglades, which in 1989 was less than a fifth of the predrainage rate. Until Hurricane Irene, the bay had not been hit by a deluge since Hurricane Betsy in 1965 and not by a gargantuan hurricane since Donna in 1960. Historically storms that affect the bay's bottom and coastline have occurred on three- to five-year intervals, and hurricanes have struck every seven years. During the thirty-nine-year absence of a major storm (Andrew passed too far north and too fast to affect Florida Bay), undisturbed turtle grass beds became dense shags of vegetation. Unusually warm fall temperatures during the late 1980s kept the grass beds metabolizing near summer rates, even though the length of daylight and the amount time available for photosynthesis was decreasing. During the warm fall days, the grass "literally starved to death," wrote park interpreter Peter Allen.

With little to secure the soft bay bottom, waters became murky, blocking sunlight and killing yet more grass. Coupled with the severe drought that began in 1987 and lasted for five years, Florida Bay became both hotter and saltier, which triggered the growth of a naturally occurring slime mold *Labyrinthula*. The slime mold attacked stressed sea grass, particularly in western Florida Bay, where salinities were highest. By 1989 even black mangroves along the edges of the bay had begun to die.

Scientists began to focus more attention on Florida Bay, began to search for the reason behind the bay's collapse. By 1995 nearly six million dollars was spent on more than seventy research projects that looked at everything from eagles to spiny lobsters, from algal blooms to circulation models and contaminants. To maintain his objectivity, one biologist, who studied sea grass, swam in his research plots in random directions with his eyes closed. Several times he bumped heads with a lemon shark, and once he opened his eyes to find himself directly over an alligator, which he stared down. Theories about the bay's decline surfaced. One popular theory claimed runoff from the sugarcane fields around Lake Okeechobee poisoned the water. Another claimed that the River of Sand, a prehistoric tunnel in the bedrock, channeled phosphorous-rich water from central Florida into Florida Bay, a sort of pollution pipeline. After much research, both theories proved false.

The health of the Florida reef tract—a 220-mile-long, semicontinuous necklace of coral reefs that arcs along the Florida Keys from south Miami all the way beyond the Dry Tortugas—is entwined with the Everglades and Florida Bay. In 1997 scientists found that disease on Florida's coral reefs had increased nearly threefold. Although the reefs follow the curve of the Florida Keys, the largest reefs are off the upper and lower Keys. Historically the reefs off the middle Keys have been affected by Florida Bay, whose waters pour through wide passes and bathe coral with water that at various times of the year is either too hot, too cold, too silty, or too salty to promote vigorous reef growth.

One night in 1977, for example, a cold front chilled Florida Bay to fifty-four degrees. Cold water flowing out of the bay killed branching coral all the way to the Dry Tortugas. In recent years the bay's massive algal blooms, driven by tidal cycles and the wind, have moved eastward across the reefs. Studies suggest that bay sediment and algal blooms may have killed some of the already stressed coral colonies off the middle Keys.

Rain provided the answer and has given everyone from scientists to fishing guides hope for Florida Bay's future. Since 1994 South Florida has had six years of above average rainfall. Salinities have returned to normal, averaging twenty-six parts per thousand for the entire bay and between two and eighteen parts per thousand in its northeast and western sections, leaving Florida Bay in its best condition in twenty years. In 1995 ninety-two thousand acre-feet of freshwater passed under the Taylor Slough bridge (along the main park service road) on its way to northeastern Florida Bay, the greatest volume since record-keeping began 1961. (By contrast less than eight thousand acre-feet passed under the bridge in 1989.) By 2001 more than 150 pairs of osprey were nesting in Florida Bay.

Spreading from underground stems called rhizomes, rarely from seed, turtle grass is slowly and steadily recovering. Widgeon grass, *Ruppia maritima,* a long, stringy sea grass that prefers water that is fresh to slightly brackish, has reappeared in places it had not grown in twenty years. Widgeon grass was so common in Florida Bay in the 1940s that commercial netters claimed that it rolled up like hay bails in their nets. Ducks love widgeon grass. In the 1930s Flamingo supported a commercial duck-harvesting operation on the northern bay. As Florida Bay became saltier, dabbling ducks left. For the first time in a decade small flocks of mottled ducks have returned to the bay.

Finished on Rankin Key, Mealy heads due southwest to Buoy Key, five miles off the eastern rim of Snake Bight, where several hundred white pelicans huddle out of the wind in a cove on the south side. On the island two osprey nests, located about a hundred feet apart, rise like muskrat lodges from the floor of the prairie. The parent ospreys nest confidant that the island is absent of predatory mammals; to reach Buoy Key a raccoon would have to negotiate wind and tide and defy alligators, crocodiles, sharks, and eagles, a formidable task indeed. A forlorn white pelican stands in the middle of the prairie. At three feet tall, the bird is much bigger than I had imagined. Unable to fly, the pelican waddles off, and Mealy, Parks, and I pursue and catch it. I hold its bill, Parks stretches out the wing, and Mealy draws blood. Tests later confirm that the pelican, which depends on fish for both sustenance and water, was severely dehydrated. We release the bird, which I assume will die before the sun goes down.

The first osprey nest holds two eggs and a hatchling; the second, three large chicks, all annoyed at our intrusion. Osprey chicks are gorgeous: orange eyes, russet nape merging to fawn, and brown mottled wings. While Mealy completes his sampling, I scan for the parents, which are nowhere to be found. High overhead a frigate bird glides over and disappears in the blue haze of the noon sky.

《《《

The following morning, Mealy, Parks, and I assemble on the dock at the Key Largo Ranger Station and then head southwest to Nest Key to search for diamond-backed terrapins, *Malaclemys terrapin,* once prized for food and sold in seafood stores from Massachusetts to Texas, which greatly reduced their numbers. The water in northeast Florida Bay is a mix of turquoise and deep blue and very clear, entirely different from the turbid waters of the western and central bay. We fasten the boat to shore, walk through a screen of stunted chest-high mangroves, and begin to comb the flooded salt pans and drying pools for signs of terrapins. The turtles gather in interior ponds on the keys to feed on snails, to breed, and when the dry season comes, to sleep in the marl, much the way northern turtles hibernate in pond mud. At eight to nine inches across the carapace, female terrapins are twice the size of males. Thus far Mealy has marked twelve hundred terrapins, all adults. He catches many more females than males. Perhaps, he says, the smaller males bask more to stay warm and are picked off by bald eagles. Adult female terrapins are too large for eagles to pick up. For the past several years the number of male terrapins Mealy has caught on the island has risen, possibly because the island's resident eagles have not nested and presumably hunt elsewhere.

I see plenty of fish, some two or three inches long, but no swimming terrapins. The soft, slippery marl, which is not shelly, oozes over my feet and ankles, making walking difficult. On the drying fringe of a salt pan, turtle tracks baked into the marl lead us to a slight depression in the ground where the tracks stop. Gently Mealy pokes a rod into the marl. Tap. Tap. Tap. He strikes something hard, reaches into the mud, and pulls out two female diamond-backed terrapins, one on top of the other. At the base of the nearby depression Mealy pulls up a third turtle. (With the help of college students, he has caught as many as sixty-eight on Nest Key.) The faces of all three terrapins are thickly covered in marl, their dark, moist eyes beaming out of the mud pack.

Over the years Mealy has recaptured 45 percent of his terrapins, a phenomenal rate of recovery he attributes to the turtles' fidelity to nesting and feeding sites. Using radio transmitters and satellite tracking, he has never caught a terrapin that moved more than three miles away from its initial capture site. (Two females had moved approximately three miles.)

We take the turtles back to the boat and dip them in the surf to wash off their marl compresses, clouding the otherwise clear water. The turtles have a hand-tooled look. A low, wide keel runs down the center of the nearly black carapace, and each scute is marked by contoured and concentric growth rings; the plastron (belly) is yellowed ivory, smudged here and there by black. The head is smoky gray, blotched with dark vermiculations, and the eyes are black. Excess salt drains from glands near the eyes; sea turtles have the same mechanism.

Mealy weighs and measures each animal, takes a bacterial culture from the cloaca, and finally draws blood from a leg. When he is through, we release the terrapins, which wander across the salt pan and disappear into the mangroves. Terrapins have survived the shifting of continents, the thawing of many Ice Ages, and more recently the gustatory habits of coastal Americans. When South Florida faces another prolonged drought, will the terrapins survive the rising salinities? Will Florida Bay itself survive?

Restoration of Taylor Slough, which is almost entirely protected by state and federal lands, is under way. In 1995 the water management district purchased from a consortium of tomato farmers the headwaters of the slough, a fifty-four-hundred-acre swale called Frog Pond. Now the farmers, who chose to lease Frog Pond back from the state, wait for the fields to naturally drain before they plant; no longer will there be an artificial dry down. And the Army Corps of

Engineers has removed the east-west levee on the C-III canal, the largest canal in south Miami–Dade County, allowing freshwater that had been pirated from Shark Slough and Taylor Slough for Barnes Sound to spread out across the southeastern Everglades and into Florida Bay. By 2001 the single bridge over the slough had been replaced by two bridges and a series of culverts on the main park service road. Now during the wet season the delta of Taylor Slough pushes toward the middle of Florida Bay, well away from the mangrove jungles, where the water flows fresh.

(((

I say good-bye to Mealy and Parks, thank them for letting me tag along, drive two hours to Flamingo, and spend the night in the home of friends who work for Everglades National Park. Their house is raised on cinder block stilts. The living space is on the second floor, above the carport and screened porch, a hedge against an angry bay that has been known to walk across the coastal prairie—though not recently.

The next morning, while I settle into the upstairs verandah organizing my notes, I eavesdrop on a prairie warbler and a cardinal and on a young couple paddling a red canoe close to shore.

Woman: "Why aren't there any canoes out there? Everyone must know something that we don't."

Man: "Stop complaining and keep paddling. This isn't any fun. Do you want to go back? Tell me now, and we'll just turn around."

Woman: "I'm stressed. Can't you tell I'm stressed."

Man (greatly annoyed): "What the hell is your problem?"

Woman: "I don't want to get bitten by a shark."

Woman (after a few minutes of silence): "There's something out there. See! No. No, you're paddling toward it. Don't go toward it."

Consumed by the breaching of her own irrepressible fear, the young woman and her callous, impatient partner do not see the flights of myriad shorebirds across the bay, nor the plunge of a nearby a osprey. The palm-clad islets, wild, green shores, and the wintering birds seem to elude the strained couple.

Florida Bay has been denied its promise as a cradle for game fish, shellfish, and wading birds by a century of water-diversion projects. It depends on the whims of the weather cycle, upon rain alone, to supply its annual budget of freshwater, but as sure as the sun rises in the east, the skies will dry again.

Human Impact

We stand today in an unbroken line that stretches back almost a century to 1905 when a brave group of women stood against the prevailing political winds of the age, which called for the development of the Everglades from coast to coast.

J. ALLISON DEFOOR II, 2000

15 Lots of People

Its sharp fin cutting the surface, its thick tail swishing back and forth, dull-eyed and hungry, the shark swam in the shallow waters of Biscayne Bay. Behind the five-foot shark two Tequesta fishermen paddled a dugout canoe. The boat approached within fifteen feet of the shark; then the bowman stopped paddling and stood up, a harpoon in his right hand. The morning sun lit the bone point, which shone white until it was buried in a gray curve of the shark's flesh. For a couple of minutes the big fish thrashed violently, red blood spilling into blue water. Then it tired. Chanting to the sea below and to the sky above, the fishermen paddled home, towing their catch by a rope made from the fibrous interior of a tree.

Though the Tequesta ate sharks, this one was not to be consumed. It was an offering to something or someone that time has erased. For more than a thousand years, from their main village by the mouth of the Miami River, the Tequesta had watched the sun rise over Biscayne Bay and set over the Everglades. The river was a link between the freshwater interior and the bay, the beautiful center of the Tequesta's watery world.

In downtown Miami, atop the Brickell Avenue drawbridge, stands a statue of a bare-chested Tequesta warrior and his family. His bow arched, his arrow pointed skyward, he is a sentinel guarding the sacred mouth of the Miami River. Until recently, this image was the only connection most Miamians had with the Tequesta, who disappeared more than two hundred years ago, well before the city was founded. Then, in the summer of 1998, a construction crew for a large apartment building unearthed a garage-sized oval made up of dozens of holes carved in the limestone bedrock. Nothing like it had been found before in North America. Called the Miami Circle, the carving is estimated to be more than nine hundred years old. Shaped like an eye with a stone pupil, one of the circle's holes faces due east toward Biscayne Bay, unblinking and resolute. Stone tools, some made of exotic rock, two-thousand-year-old pottery shards, beads and shells, and the skeleton of a five-foot shark were also found.

A possible North American Stonehenge, the Miami Circle's perfect east-west axis marked the equinox. Whatever the significance of the circle—spiritual, astronomical, or practical—it has fired the imagination of Miami–Dade County residents, who have stopped construction of the condominiums and sought formal historic preservation status for the inner city site, perhaps as an addition to Biscayne National Park. The developer offered to move the site somewhere else so that his $126 million project could proceed. His offer was not accepted.

Now that Miami has begun to embrace the people of its distant past, the time has come for it to also embrace its natural heritage. How do you preserve and restore a functional remnant of the Everglades? No matter how talented and committed the team of engineers, hydrologists, and biologists, no matter how vocal and persistent the activists, no matter how generous the philanthropists, no matter how eloquent the artists and helpful the politicians, the bulk of urban South Florida has no sense of what lies beyond its threshold. The fate of the Everglades is, and has always has been, determined by the conflict between wilderness and city and farm. After all, this is not Yosemite or Yellowstone, anchored firmly and safely in the sparkling unpopulated headwaters of their watersheds; it is "the park at the end of the pipe." The Everglades needs the sympathy of its human neighbors, whose population has expanded exponentially during the twentieth century and is projected, some say encouraged, to crest at twelve million by 2050. By then urban water demand alone will exceed two billion gallons a day. Of course there is the agricultural demand for water, specifically Big Sugar's big thirst. Rather than place a limit on growth, acknowledging that the landscape can support only so many people—the concept of carrying capacity is as valid for us as for egrets or soft-shelled turtles—the Army Corps of Engineers originally drafted restoration plans to accommodate an eventual twelve million people. A second version, more sympathetic to the environment, was signed by President Clinton on December 11, 2000.

《《《

On July 28, 1896, twenty years after Custer's Last Stand, ten years after the Wild West was no longer wild, 344 voters incorporated the city of Miami. In the 1500s it was the site of a Spanish mission; more recently, it was Fort Dallas, a military post and trading village at the mouth of the Miami River that sat squarely and atop the Tequesta ruin. Built in the late 1830s during the second of three Seminole Wars, Fort Dallas was one of a series of isolated military outposts along Florida's east coast. In 1855 Captain Abner Doubleday, who according to legend had already invented baseball, was stationed at Fort Dallas, where he spent the next three years overseeing the cutting of the first road north to Fort Lauderdale. The forts remained wilderness outposts until the 1890s. Then, during the winters of 1893, 1894, and 1895, terrible freezes crippled the citrus industry in central Florida, attracting the attention of railroad magnate Henry Flagler. After much encouragement from Julia Tuttle, who owned a trading post at the mouth of the Miami River, Flagler was convinced that Fort Dallas lay at the heart of Florida's true fortunes. He brought the East Coast Railroad to Miami in 1896.

Twenty years earlier, Harriet Beecher Stowe, the author of *Uncle Tom's Cabin,* who had been living in Florida since the end of the Civil War, was appalled by the wholesale destruction of native wildlife, particularly birds, and feared for the overcrowded future of her adopted state. In 1877, writing in *The Semi-Tropical,* a popular and influential monthly magazine that extolled the virtues of, and offered advice on aspects of, living and vacationing in Florida, she expressed her feelings:

Florida has been considered in all respects as a prey and a spoil to all comers. Its splendid flowers and trees, its rare and curious animals have been looked upon as made and created only to please the fancy of tourists—to be used and abused as the whims of the hour dictate. Thousands of idle loungers pour down here every year, people without a home or landed interest in the State, and whose only object seems to be to amuse themselves while in it without the least consideration of future results to the country.

The decks of boats are crowded with men, whose only feeling amid our magnificent forests, seems to be a wild desire to shoot something, and who fire at every living thing on shore, careless of maiming, wounding or killing the living creatures which they see, full of life and enjoyment. But to shoot for the mere love of killing is perfect barbarism, unworthy of any civilized man, and, unless some protection shall be extended over the animal creation, there is danger that there may be a war of extermination waged on our forests.

Besides the guns of hunters, the birds of Florida are exposed to the incursions of bird trappers, who come regularly every year and trap and carry off by the thousands and tens of thousands the bright children of our forest. These birds die by the hundreds in the passage to New York and Europe. It is a perfect slave trade over again, and it is slowly and surely robbing our beautiful State of one of its chief attractions.

The protection that Stowe sought came in 1905 from a most unlikely source—the women of the Coconut Grove Women's Club. Although they were deprived of the right to vote at the time, the women stood against the prevailing political winds and whims of the day and agitated for the creation of a state park on Paradise Key, a botanical gem and gateway to the vast marshes of the southeastern Everglades. The club had several prominent allies: Mrs. Henry Flagler persuaded her husband to donate the key, which would become the seed that would grow into Everglades National Park; May Mann Jennings, president of the state Federation of Women's Clubs and wife of the development-oriented governor, William S. Jennings, joined the campaign to protect Paradise Key. Jennings enlisted an in-law, Ruth Bryan Owen, daughter of William Jennings Bryan, three times the democratic nominee for the United States presidency. Owen, the first congresswoman from the south, eventually became a powerful and spirited voice for the creation of a "tropical Florida national park." (To the horror of many of her colleagues, she once draped a corn snake over her shoulders to emphasize a point on the floor of Congress.) Jennings and Owen's most lasting contribution to the preservation of the Everglades, however, was the recruitment of the young Marjory Stoneman Douglas to their cause.

In 1915, when twenty-five-year-old Marjory Stoneman Douglas arrived from New York City, Miami's population was less than ten thousand, living mostly around Coconut Grove, the highest point on the coastal ridge, and the mouth of the Miami River. Between Jacksonville and Miami, Douglas's nearly empty train passed through endless pinelands, as wild and desolate as the northern Rocky Mountains. "I kept looking out and seeing pine trees go by," she wrote. "Pine trees for hour after hour, an infinity of pine trees." Between 1920 and 1923 the population of Miami doubled. By 1942 the *Miami Herald*, where Douglas's father had served as first editor and where she had served in a variety of capacities ever since her arrival, in a veiled reference to Latin American immigration, reported that "political, economic and geographic factors slowly are swinging Miami into a position that will make the Indian wars, the coming of the railroad, the land boom and the ever present military cauldron look like a quiet Sunday afternoon on a Swiss Alp."

The 2000 census showed the population of Miami–Dade County (greater Miami) to be more than two million. To the north Broward County had one and a half million residents, and Palm Beach County, just over a million. In other words four and a half million people pressed against the eastern ribs of the Everglades, all dependent upon a finite supply of freshwater.

Leveled by Hurricane Andrew in 1992, Homestead Air Force Base, or what's left of it—an American flag fluttering over rows of empty barracks and guardhouses—sits eight and a half miles from Everglades National Park and two miles from Biscayne National Park. The federal government reversed its position in 2000 and, taking pity on the two parks, rejected a locally sponsored plan that would have rebuilt the base into an international airport that would have accommodated 236,000 flights a year and triggered a surge of industrial development. Local politicians and influential developers still want the airport; citizens concerned about rampant growth do not. Across the glades to the west, Collier County, one of the fastest growing counties in the United States, spawns golf courses and upscale communities at such a rate that the growth will reach the edge of Big Cypress National Preserve by 2020 unless it is halted by the state or federal government.

A 1998 Sierra Club report, *The Dark Side of the American Dream: The Costs and Consequences of Suburban Sprawl*, defines sprawl as low-density housing where people have to drive to work and to schools, recreation, shopping, and other such services. For cities in the United States with a population of more than one million, the report ranked Fort Lauderdale as the ninth most sprawl threatened. For cities between five hundred thousand and a million, West Palm Beach, which expanded its urban area 75 percent between 1990 and 1996, was ranked fourth. Between 1990 and 1996 Fort Lauderdale's metropolitan area grew 27 percent to cover 415 square miles. According to the city's *Sun-Sentinel*, the state has approved an additional eighty-five thousand housing units in southwest Broward County. The only remaining place for Fort Lauderdale to expand is west—into the Everglades.

The stated mission of the South Florida Regional Planning Council is to bridle the region's chaotic growth, to stop suburban sprawl in favor of downtown revitalization. Yet in what amounts to an epitaph for the council's mission of growth management, the *Miami Herald* reported that of the twenty-seven developments of regional impact that came before the council between 1988 and 1998, including a proposed new city of seventeen thousand, all twenty-seven projects were approved.

In a most perverse form of suburban mitosis, the city of Weston was developed by the Arvida Corporation on the western flank of Fort Lauderdale. When finished, the model community will support eight schools, at least three shopping centers, and nearly eight million square feet of industrial, office, or commercial space. More than one thousand people will commute to Weston to staff a variety of suburban stores and offices or to trim the lawns and prune the bushes of the area's wealthy residents.

Only one parcel of wetland was spared. A 120-acre vestige of the Everglades located in western Broward County was slated for development as an employment center for Weston. It was saved from the bulldozers when the town canned the project and voted, instead, to have the land preserved for aquifer recharge. The water management district wants to acquire this land, in 1998 valued at $30,000 an acre, for Everglades restoration. The owner of the land thinks $150,000 an acre is more appropriate. The Tequesta watched the sun set over the Everglades; now people can watch the sun set over what's left of the Everglades.

《《《

Southern Miami–Dade County has been a hotbed of agricultural and suburban development for decades. When electric lines were brought from Florida City into Everglades National Park in 1947, the park's superintendent, Daniel Beard, had the poles set in an extensive pineland well off the road, hidden from visitors approaching from Homestead. Today the poles rise out of fields of tomatoes and yellow squash and bear witness to the increasing transformation of South Florida.

On the eastern apron of the Everglades, within sight of tomato fields, is the northeast corner of Shark Slough and the fire-abused marl prairies of the Rocky Glades. The region is called the East Everglades. In 1989, to increase the flow of water into the eastern side of Everglades National Park, the federal government authorized the purchase of 109,000 acres of the East Everglades. Thirteen years later, at the dawn of 2002, the parcels designated for purchase had not all been acquired. There are thousands of landowners to deal with, many of whom are victims of real estate scams who have never seen their sodden pieces of paradise. This land includes the northeast Shark Slough, the last vestige of floodplain in the East Everglades.

"Protect home and business with Curtain Wall Technology," read a full-page newspaper ad tacked up on Bob Johnson's office bulletin board in Everglades National Park. Johnson is the park's director of natural resources and the superintendent's advisor and indispensable spokesman. The ad was paid for by the First National Bank of Homestead, which holds mortgages on many of the homes and farms that crowd the marshland. A vocal and extremely influential minority—farmers, bankers, developers, and local politicians—wanted to wall off the Everglades from its suburban and agricultural neighbors by building an impermeable barrier, as though wrapping a leaky landfill in plastic.

Curtain-wall technology would have protected homeowners, but more significantly, it would have allowed development to the very edge of the national park. Its price tag was between $3.6 million and $6.3 million per mile, at least two and a half times what it would have cost to buy all the low-lying, flood-prone lands. Ecological costs, of course, would have been far greater: the curtain wall would have cut off groundwater flow east to Biscayne Bay, making the bay hypersaline and prone to destructive algae blooms like those plaguing Florida Bay. It would have stifled the underground water flows to Miami–Dade County's water wells and caused Everglades National Park to flood.

A few miles away, tentative efforts are being made to expand the Everglades rather than to constrict it. The history of the Frog Pond, the headwaters of Taylor Slough, which still sustains more tomatoes than amphibians, represents the quintessential history of the forces that have nursed South Florida's growth. Although some private land supported winter vegetables grown at the mercy of the water table, most of the Frog Pond had been state-owned Everglades adjacent to the national park. In the 1960s Aerojet General, a division of General Tire, persuaded the state to sell the Frog Pond as a site for testing solid rocket fuel. To oblige Aerojet the Army Engineers dredged and expanded the C-111 system, originally to have been a small drainage canal, to accommodate barges carrying the giant rockets Aerojet hoped to ferry north to Cape Canaveral. Environmentalists prevented the water management district from installing locks on C-111, which in turn prevented Aerojet from using the canal as a waterway for industrial transportation, a blow to other industrial developers in southern Miami–Dade County.

The solid rocket fuel program fizzled. But because C-111 had created more drainage potential than originally planned, farmers planted on drained land then asked for additional water for their winter crops at the expense of water deliveries to Everglades National Park. Aerojet leased a portion of the Frog Pond to farmers; then, in 1988, while negotiating a sale to the South Florida Water Management District, General Tire sold the land to the South Dade Land Corporation, an agribusiness, for $6.8 million. The corporation continued farming.

Hydrologists from the water management district determined that a five-inch rain during the dry season would raise the groundwater in the Frog Pond twelve inches. To prevent crop flooding, the C-III system rerouted the excess water from the Taylor Slough drainage and dumped it in Barnes Sound rather than in Florida Bay, often with disastrous results. To keep the farms dry, extension canals were dug around the Frog Pond.

In Bob Johnson's company, when I stood at the edge of the Frog Pond in the spring of 1995, I was unable to discover Taylor Slough's headwaters—no gushing springs, no river issuing from a lake. Instead what I found in the tomato fields was a slight swale filled with willows and tall reeds, and a canal with a small pump station that shoved water into Everglades National Park. The canal separated the park from the tomatoes and cut through Taylor Slough, keeping its water permanently low to drain the farmland. Unfortunately the canal also drained the national park.

The slough was in a one-in-ten-year drought cycle, having been drained to protect the Frog Pond; the rest of South Florida was swamped by the wettest year on record. By the time water reached this corner of the park, Taylor Slough had already lost 60 percent of its volume. As a result the park received less water, and Florida Bay became too salty. During a wet year, if your fields are flooded until January, why expect the state to drain off the water so that you can plant crops? Elsewhere in the country farmers live with the vagaries of the weather and plant accordingly. Why in South Florida are farmers encouraged by both local and state governments to plant marginal farmland, often at the expense of the national park, which is deprived of vital water?

To correct the environmental injustice, the South Florida Water Management District condemned the Frog Pond as poor agricultural land and began the process of legal acquisition. After President Clinton implemented the North American Free Trade Agreement, cheaper tomatoes began moving across the Mexican border, which prompted the South Dade Land Corporation to strike a deal with the state to sell the Frog Pond for twelve and a half million dollars. Despite a nearly 100 percent return on the company's investment, James Humble, the loquacious vice president and CEO of the land corporation, preferred the curtain wall to the state's buyout. He eventually sued for more money, and a jury will decide the final price; if they are sympathetic to the South Dade Land Corporation, the amount could come close to thirty million dollars.

As soon as the water management district took possession of the Frog Pond, claiming that the state had no money to manage the land, it leased the land back to the very farmers it had planned to evict. This allowed the farmers to farm according to the natural rhythms of the land and thereby prevented an invasion of exotic vegetation that would surely have overrun the otherwise abandoned farmland.

((((

Stranger and sadder than the story of the Frog Pond is what happened to an unincorporated section of Miami–Dade County called the 8.5 Square Mile Area (8.5 SMA), a community of 365 homes, a hundred trailers, and more than a thousand small ranches, orchards, and other parcels west of Homestead. Developed more than thirty years ago in violation of county building and zoning codes, while politicians looked the other way, the 8.5 SMA sits on the west side of federal canals and flood control levees meant to separate Everglades National Park from its suburban and agricultural neighbors in southern Miami–Dade County.

The 8.5 SMA has become the center of a controversial dispute that has divided South Florida's environmental community and created alliances that include the area's Latino residents, some environmental sympathizers, the Miccosukee, and a national Latino organization. The 8.5 SMA exists because water is held back north of the Tamiami Trail, and a crushed limerock levee blocks the west-to-east flow of lower Shark Slough, which otherwise would flood the 8.5 SMA. The levee, however, keeps almost seven times more water on the west side of the slough than would naturally be there, whereas the northeast side, historically the deeper, often wilts. To return water to northeast Shark Slough and to drain water away from the flooded western end, the Corps of Engineers has to grapple with several alternatives for the 8.5 SMA, which happens to sit on the sodden northeast floodplain, one good storm away from submersion. All or part of the community could be walled off, an expense that would be paid by federal, state, or local taxes; or, as in the instance of the Frog Pond, the state could condemn the land and buy it at fair market value; or the residents could continue to fend for themselves, something they have done for thirty years.

Because the Cape Sable seaside sparrow nests only along the shoulders of lower Shark Slough, its habitat is imperiled. One half of its range is underwater; the other, artificially drier, half is burning. Discussions of the fate of the sparrow and the 8.5 SMA are explosive. To keep the residents reasonably dry and to prevent further flooding to the western population of sparrows, the flow gates on the Tamiami Trail have been closed, which backs water up in Water Conservation Area 3A. Because the Everglades Agricultural Area routinely pumps its excess water into the conservation areas, and because excess water is not permitted to flow into the national park, this marshland to the north has become an organic killing tub, drowning ancient tree islands and jeopardizing the cultural and ceremonial life of the Miccosukee.

To discuss these issues (and others related to Everglades restoration) the Sierra Club sponsors Everglades Commons, an Internet mailing list where more than a hundred participants either voice their opinions or eavesdrop on often spirited e-mail discussions. The sparrow and the community have become magnets for hostile, sometimes thoughtless, comments. One subscriber wrote, "I'm sorry about the bird, but if you put the handle of the sluice gate in my hand, I'd open it." Another suggested bombing the 8.5 SMA. And residents of the 8.5 SMA flooded the Everglades Commons, railing against "the ideological stances of eco-Nazi groups like the Nature Conservancy, Sierra Club, and Friends of the Everglades," the organization founded by Marjory Stoneman Douglas, "for ruining the lives of thousands of people they don't even know."

Because most of the residents are Cuban exiles who fled Castro, local supporters of the 8.5 SMA have painted environmentalists as bigots, more concerned about sparrows than Latinos. In 1999 a national Hispanic organization voted to make the 8.5 SMA's plight their human rights issue. While the battle rages, the East Everglades lies gasping for water, and the central Everglades drowns.

The most logical (and least expensive) solution to the sparrow and 8.5 SMA dilemma is for the government to take the property by eminent domain, pay the landowners a fair market value, poke holes in the L-67 extension levee, and then open the gates on the Tamiami Trail. As a result, northeast Shark Slough would be rehydrated, and the western side would drain; the conservation areas would not be perpetually flooded, and the hydroperiods in the sparrow's floodplain habitat would be returned to normal. The Everglades itself would be one step closer to whole.

Why should a community of 365 homes built on flood-prone marshland in violation of county codes be allowed to prevent the restoration of a world-class Natural Heritage Site? Why should a community of any ethnicity be allowed to stand in the way of a reunited Everglades? The national park remains one of the top ten tourist destinations in North America, and its waters are vital to the future of South Florida, which could not exist without the Everglades and its Biscayne Aquifer as its source of freshwater.

In 1998 the South Florida Water Management District finally decided to buy out the 8.5 SMA for $120 million. The alternative plan of flood protection would have cost approximately $200 million, including road building and mitigation (almost $200,000 per house), $2 million a year for municipal services—fire, police, trash collection—and another $2 million for maintenance of the flood control system, far more than the residents of the 8.5 SMA contribute in taxes. In addition, two thousand more acres would be squandered in the name of flood protection. The buyout cost would be about half as much.

Unfortunately, when the South Florida Water Management District's staff began the condemnation meetings, they failed to notify the residents of the 8.5 SMA, a violation of Florida's Government-in-the-Sunshine Law. Fearing that a string of lawsuits and negotiations would keep the courts humming and the tribal lands flooded for years, the Miccosukee zeroed in on the district's failure to comply with the Sunshine Law and filed a lawsuit with several home-owners.

The Miccosukee had gained legal rights to Big Cypress National Preserve after the federal government bought property from private landowners, many of them unwilling sellers. It is ironic that in its 8.5 SMA lawsuit the tribe objected to condemning and confiscating private property. The issue of condemnation was so controversial that the president of Friends of the Everglades resigned rather than support her organization's position in favor of buying out the residents of the 8.5 SMA. She felt that people should not be victims of ecological restoration. Meanwhile an editorial in the *Palm Beach Post* accused the Miccosukee of "rapidly becoming the worst enemies of the environment in Florida." Mike Collins, chairman of the governing board of the South Florida Water Management District, accused Colonel Terry Rice, formerly the district commander of the Army Corps of Engineers, now an advisor to the Miccosukee, of "shipping off e-mails from Mars to churn people up." According to environmental activist Joe Browder:

If agencies have decided that's the best option [buying the 8.5 SMA], it is sad for people with homes in the area. It is sad whenever anyone is forced to give up a home or farm for highways, for parks and schools and water management. But regardless of how shocked or opposed some people are because of this, that kind of government taking of private property for pub-lic purposes has been part of our society from the beginning, and remains so. And where the people whose farms or homes or investment lands are taken believe they aren't getting a price that equals the value of the land, the courts decide.

In February 1999, faced with mounting criticism over the Sunshine Law viola-tion, the South Florida Water Management District backed off its request for preliminary funds to purchase the 8.5 SMA. Of course the issue of what to do with the 8.5 SMA did not go away. When I asked Collins about the district's reversal, he said, "My feeling is rather than take a baseball bat to their heads and tell them they're leaving, put an offer on the table and buy the land. Build the project and see what happens." By 2001 the Army Corps of Engineers settled on a plan, called alternative 6D: the 8.5 SMA will be split down the middle; the eastern half would get flood protection, and the western half, mostly farm and pasture land, would be bought out and reflooded.

When I visited the 8.5 SMA in 1999, a week after the district's concession, several of the residents with whom I spoke were rabid in their denouncement of Everglades National Park and its superintendent, Dick Ring, who they felt was at the heart of South Florida's environmental ills, claiming he had scuttled the Modified Water Delivery plan approved by Congress in 1989, which would have spared their community. Modified Water Delivery has not been implemented because, across the board—from the park to the Corps to the water management district—hydrologists concluded that the plan was inadequate to resolve the Everglades' problems. Now, for restoration of the Everglades to continue, the eastern residents of the 8.5 SMA must be protected from rising water.

The residents also scoffed at what they called the "imaginary" plight of the Cape Sable seaside sparrow and vilified Stuart Pimm, the birds' chief defender. But they praised their own good fortune to live in a natural area like the Everglades, where exotic trees—melaleuca, Australian pine, and Brazilian pepper—rise from the battered earth like unkempt hair.

One February afternoon several dozen residents gathered trash along the main road, built in 1936 by the Works Progress Administration. Part of the agricultural community—lemons, winter vegetables, and nursery plants—dates back to the 1930s. "See, our community has old roots. We should get historic status. That would piss off the park!" says Madeleine Fortin, a pas-sionate defender of the 8.5 SMA who gravitates to my tape recorder like a fish to bait.

Fortin had recently completed a master's thesis on the 8.5 SMA's history. She is a four-year resident of the area, but she does not hold anywhere near the community's longevity record; many have lived in the 8.5 SMA since the 1960s. The landowners collectively pay $1.2 million in taxes each year, she tells me, and receive nothing for their money. Of the fifty-five miles of roads, none are paved. Children walk to the nearest paved road to meet the school bus. Miami–Dade County provides no trash pickup. Three generations of lawyers have been feasting off their plight, says Fortin, so the seventeen hundred property owners and their supporters formed the United Property Owners and Friends of the 8.5 Square Mile Area. Contrary to newspaper reports that claim that residents are lining up to sell, she says, very few are willing sellers. "Our whole . . . situation is mediated by middle-aged white guys in suits that have never been here."

She continues:

> One of the saddest things about all this, it used to be people interacted with the environment in a real way in their daily lives. You knew when the nighthawks came back and started their aerial displays; when it was going to rain; when to plant. Direct interaction. Now our interaction with the environment is being dictated by bureaucrats who have never been here. These people at these meetings like the Task Force, the Southern Everglades Restoration Alliance, the Restudy, the Working Group, none of these people actually come here. They don't know what it's like. I could show them a chicken turtle shell, and I know for a fact they don't know what kind of turtle it is. They think it's a gopher tortoise.

When I mentioned Fortin's contention of political isolation and neglect, J. Allison Defoor II, the former Everglades policy coordinator for Jeb Bush, replied: "Isn't she a piece of work. I have been there, all the water management board members have been there, and many legislators have been there."

In 1999 Hurricane Irene rejuvenated Florida Bay but turned the 8.5 SMA into a knee-deep lake. Firing guns in the air, hoodlums in airboats roared down flooded dirt roads. Drowned farm animals began to rot, prompting owners to kill dying livestock and burn the bodies. The sickening odor of burning hair and singed flesh wafted through the neighborhood. In a desperate attempt to alleviate the flooding, the United Property Owners and Friends of the 8.5 Square Mile Area began dredging a drainage ditch into Everglades National Park. The destruction of federal wetlands and the pollution from raw sewage outraged both national park officials and the South Florida Water Management District, which ordered the group to stop digging, threatening a fine of up to ten thousand dollars a day for each day of unauthorized work.

Although the National Guard delivered freshwater and supplies to the stranded residents, the water lingered in their yards for weeks, which prompted the Federal Emergency Management Agency and the state Department of Community Affairs to promise to raise roads, install culverts, and build a sewage treatment plant. Meanwhile, residents of the 8.5 SMA took their travails directly to environmentalists, flooding the Everglades Commons with furious e-mails, pointing out that their community is six feet, nine inches above sea level, higher in fact than Kendell, a sprawl south of Miami, which is protected from flooding.

"We have been made into pariahs," wrote Madeleine Fortin. "Through no fault of our own we have been placed on the politically incorrect side of an ideological boundary in an effort to justify twenty years of institutionalized neglect, discrimination and abuse at the hands of almost everyone who could profit from our misery." Some responses from environmentalists were uglier. "With the way you are presenting your case," wrote a member of the Everglades Commons, "you have just about convinced the rest of us that the best thing to do is to nuke the 8.5 SMA to keep the rabid ones from breeding." To which Fortin replied, "It looks like eco-cleansing is just around the corner."

One contributor to the Everglades Commons, a biologist who has worked with Stuart Pimm on the Cape Sable seaside sparrow for many years, left the list in disgust. When the list's moderator threatened to delete those who made offensive comments or those who could not keep to the subject of Everglades restoration, e-mails complained about censorship and denial of First Amendment rights.

"If you think that Everglades restoration is some genteel issue to be debated with our pinkies in the air, . . ." wrote a subscriber, "you are sadly mistaken." Unfortunately, while everyone rants about the fate of the 8.5 SMA, the Cape Sable seaside sparrow, the drowning of the central glades, and the responsibility of Big Sugar toward restoration, a plan that would promote the ecological salvation of the Everglades waits for someone to finally take charge.

Between 1990 and 2000 the population of Broward County increased by 280,000; Miami–Dade County, by 240,000; and Palm Beach County, by 186,000—another more than 700,000 people who need to wash cars and flush toilets. If no one is willing to limit South Florida's growth, the sodden miles of sawgrass and lily will be buried by the hubris of our culture.

The Ever Glades are now suitable only for the
haunt of noxious vermin, or the resort of pestilent
reptiles. The statesman whose exertions shall cause
the millions of acres they contain, now worse than
worthless, to teem with the products of agricultural
industry . . . will merit a high place in public favor.

BUCKINGHAM SMITH, 1846

16 Big Sugar

Staining an otherwise cerulean sky, black oily smoke billows a mile high from
more than half a dozen fires south of Lake Okeechobee. You can see lines of
smoke from West Palm Beach, like the exhalations of detonated bombs. It is
eerily quiet. No sirens.

From the highway around the lake, from the outskirts of towns called
Canal Point, Pahokee, South Bay, Belle Glade, Clewiston, Moore Haven,
and Harlem, where they hold the Miss Brown Sugar Contest, sugarcane runs
to the horizon, a ghostly replacement of what was once sawgrass marshes.
Flames rush through patches of cane, burning off extraneous tassels and
blades, leaving only the sucrose-rich stalks, which line up straight and tall,
like an army of stunted bamboo. You can hear the fires cackle from the streets

of Clewiston, "America's Sweetest Town." Since 1931 it has been home to the U.S. Sugar Corporation, one of the oldest and largest players in the sugar industry, an industry that survives on our insatiable appetite for things sweet and on political largesse. It is in fact the industry that dictated the direction of the eight-billion-dollar Everglades restoration project.

A region larger than the state of Rhode Island, the upper quarter of the original Everglades is more than seven hundred thousand acres of cane fields, winter vegetables, and a few sod farms. It is officially called the Everglades Agricultural Area (EAA), but it is known simply as Big Sugar, and every fourth teaspoon of sugar consumed in the United States is grown here. "Big" stands for the industry's political power, hard to explain, given the industry's relative insignificance on a global economic stage that includes steel, automobiles, oil, chemicals, and pharmaceuticals. Between 1988 and 1994 Big Sugar made more than five and a half million dollars in campaign contributions, far out of proportion to its size; in 1999 sugar baron Alfonso Fanjul Jr. hosted a twenty-five thousand-dollar-a-plate dinner to support the Florida Democratic Party; sixty guests attended, including Bill Clinton. In the agricultural sector, only the tobacco industry spends more on campaign contributions and lobbying efforts then sugar barons, but then tobacco companies are global giants. During a 1994 Florida statehouse debate on an environmental referendum that would have taxed farmers a penny for every pound of sugar milled in the EAA, more than thirty industry lobbyists convened in Tallahassee.

《《《

Alfy and Pepe Fanjul never intended to farm in Florida. After four generations in Cuba, where their family empire included 150,000 acres of cane, ten sugar mills, and three alcohol distilleries, their businesses were nationalized by Fidel Castro in 1959. (Castro uses the Fanjuls' childhood home as one of his residences.) When the United States embargoed Cuban sugar in 1960, the stage was set for the Florida sugar boom and for the Americanization of the Fanjuls. Moving from Cuba to Palm Beach in 1960, Alfonso Fanjul Sr. and some fellow exiles bought a four-thousand-acre parcel of farmland in the EAA for $640,000. Florida offered low taxes for land and water, and at an annual expense of more than $50 million to the American taxpayers, Washington kept the EAA drained in the wet season and irrigated in the dry. In 1970 the Fanjuls created Flo-Sun, Inc. After the death of their father ten years later Alfy and Pepe inherited the business. In 1985 the company borrowed $240 million to purchase the holdings of Gulf and Western, a floundering sugar rival, which netted the Fanjuls an additional 90,000 acres of cane in Florida and 110,000 in the Dominican Republic. Whenever they wanted to expand they simply pushed back the fences. By 1990 the Fanjuls farmed 180,000 acres in the EAA and 160,000 acres in the Dominican Republic. Today their farms and four mills produce about a million tons of raw sugar a year; their refinery markets white sugar directly to consumers under the name Florida Crystals. The Fanjuls also own a rice mill and Casa de Campo, one of the Caribbean's most lavish resorts.

So pronounced is the Fanjuls' effect on regional politics and Everglades issues that the movie *Striptease,* a satirical account of the sugar industry, based on Carl Hiaasen's novel, lampoons brothers Joaquin and Wilbur Rojo, whom people acquainted with South Florida politics recognize as Alfy and Pepe. The Fanjuls allegedly were incensed and offended by any comparison to the fictional Rojos, who attempted murder to protect their business empire. Says environmental activist Joe Browder, "It's unfortunately part of a long history that reinforces ethnic stereotypes of Cubans in South Florida." Stereotyping reached a nadir several years ago when the *Miami Herald's Tropic Magazine* used a cocainelike pile of sugar on the cover of an issue featuring a profile of the Fanjuls.

United States tariffs and price controls keep domestic sugar prices around twenty-two cents a pound. Most of the rest of the world sells sugar for eight cents a pound. In 1998 sugar-grower price supports in effect cost Americans $1.4 billion in higher prices for candy, cookies, soda, ice cream, gum, and a host of other sweet things from cereal to catsup. That same year, the Fanjuls enjoyed more than $60 million in subsidies, which led *Time* to suggest that they may be the "first family of corporate welfare."

And that is only part of the story. The federal government finances sugar farmers each year by guaranteeing low-interest loans, basing the loan amount on the projected sale price. If supply exceeds demand, sugar prices generally fall below the projected sale price. Then farmers may either attempt to sell the surplus, and make good their loans, or forfeit the surplus to the government in lieu of paying off their loans, which also eliminates interest payments and the expense of marketing the crop, an additional savings that amounts to about two and a half cents a pound. When foreign sugar flooded the American market in 1985, domestic prices plunged, which prompted the forfeiture of 430,000 tons of sugar. The federal government eventually sold the sugar to China for five cents a pound, a seventy-million-dollar loss absorbed by American taxpayers. With so much help, it is no wonder that the Fanjuls are one of the wealthiest families in the United States and that cane farms have spread across marginal land, wetlands better left to alligators and anhingas and to the preservation of the region and its long-term water regime.

According to James Bovard of the Cato Institute, a conservative public policy research foundation, "Paying lavish subsidies to produce sugar in Florida makes as much sense as creating a federal subsidy program to grow bananas in Massachusetts." According to Bovard, the only thing that will make EAA cane farmers competitive would be massive global warming.

Robert Kennedy Jr., whose father and uncle had befriended the Fanjuls, lambasted the owners of Flo-Sun on the television show *Politically Incorrect*, questioning the sugar barons' environmental policy and immigration status. A letter Kennedy wrote Pepe Fanjul in response to an angry rebuttal, in which Fanjul reminded Kennedy that the Fanjuls were legal aliens, was published in the *Palm Beach Post* in May 1997.

> Under the current system, individuals like yourself can pilfer America's natural wealth and heritage, destroy publicly owned resources, garner subsidies in the form of below cost natural resources and artificial price controls, poison our rivers and streams, mistreat workers and then protect their place at the public trough by sharing their loot with public officials with payoffs disguised as campaign contributions.
>
> What is the difference if democracy is distorted by American citizens, resident aliens or by foreign nationals? Does a man whose home is burgled fret about the immigration status of the thief? What does it matter if the corrupt officials are Democrat or Republican? All people of good-will should oppose a system that favors the special interest over the public interest. Such a system will inevitably lead to the destruction of community and individual dignity, human health, and the environment.

Once again the environmental community had inadvertently turned a discussion of the effect of sugarcane on the Everglades into inflammatory anti-Cuban rhetoric. In an ill-advised effort to make the Fanjuls bend to the demands of Everglades repair, leading environmentalists either dismissed the Cuban-American population in Miami as a potential constituency or supplied the *Miami Herald* with anti-Cuban quotes.

❨❨❨

Modern sugarcane is a complex hybrid of towering perennial grasses in the genus *Saccharum*. Of the six known species, four are domesticated, and two are wild. Sugarcane was discovered in Southeast Asia about ten thousand years ago, when Florida was a wide, arid Ice Age landscape. It has been boiled for syrup for more than two thousand years. *Saccharum officinarum*, the most widely grown of the industry, was first cultivated in New Guinea, and its rigorous hybridization and backcrossing have led to the establishment of cane sugar in 127 tropical and subtropical countries, including some areas that would otherwise have been unfit for production of any monocrop. Florida, for instance, is a far cry from being prime cane habitat. Restricted by a frostier climate and wetter, nutrient-poor soils, farmers in the EAA spend $150 more to produce a metric ton of raw sugar than do farmers in Australia.

Remember the miraculous equation for photosynthesis, where green plants produce sugar from carbon dioxide, water, and sunlight? Let's take a closer look at photosynthesis. The sugar that the plant manufactures is glucose, a six-carbon simple sugar, part of a group of sugars called monosaccharides. Written in scientific shorthand as $C_6H_{12}O_6$, each molecule of glucose consists of six carbon atoms, twelve hydrogen atoms, and six oxygen atoms. In the words of molecular biologist Mahlon Hoagland, glucose is the fuel "that drives the engines of life, and the basic material from which much of life is constructed." Metabolized glucose provides the energy for respiration, growth, reproduction, and movement, and is the building block for assembling the amino acids and nucleotides from which all proteins and DNA are made. The production of glucose is at the heart of virtually every food chain, which in the Everglades includes creatures as disparate as indigo snakes and the transparent grass shrimp. When wading birds crowded South Florida, their bewildering numbers where supported by the photosynthetic activity of sawgrass, turtle grass, manatee grass, and periphyton, and from the decomposition of mangrove leaves, themselves the product of photosynthesis. Says Hoagland, "Each year, Earth's green plants make enough glucose to fill a freight train 30 million miles long."

Surprisingly, for all its importance, glucose cannot be stored by plants. Instead, what plants do not use for their own metabolic process is converted into either starches or more complex sugars, one of which, sucrose ($C_{12}H_{22}O_{11}$) —a disaccharide, meaning "two sugars"—is created by the combination of glucose and fructose. Better known as table sugar, sucrose is chemically stable and perhaps the single most abundant pure organic molecule in the world, one of the most widely known and popular foods. Whereas neither glucose nor fructose can be manufactured in sufficient quantity for wide commercial use, sucrose is readily available from sugarcane, sugar beets, and sugar maples.

Of the three, sugarcane accumulates the highest concentrations of sucrose and is considered by agronomists to be one of the most energy-efficient plants in the world. On average 20 percent of the weight of cane is sucrose, and from each milled stalk comes approximately six teaspoons of molasses, thirty teaspoons of sugar, two and a quarter pints of water, and six ounces of pulverized stem, called bagasse, which in the EAA is burned as solid fuel for processing cane. It is a good thing that sugarcane yields so much sucrose, for we cannot seem to do without it. According to *Harper's* the average American consumes the equivalent of a pound of sweetener every sixty hours. (Chocolate makers in Europe add more sugar for the American export market than for any other of their world markets.)

Shortly after Columbus reached the New World, the commercial growth of cane became extremely important in the Caribbean, where African slaves were brought in 1503 to toil in the fields. In the shameless "triangle of trade," raw sugar from the British Caribbean colonies was shipped to England for refining, then the ships went to Africa to exchange goods for slaves, who were shipped across the Atlantic and sold to Caribbean plantation owners to produce sugar. Sugar became the economic lifeline for the British colonies of Barbados and Jamaica, the Spanish colonies of Cuba and Hispaniola, and Martinique and Guadeloupe, the French West Indies.

The Seminole grew cane on secret hammocks in the Everglades, and pioneer families from Homosassa to Flamingo grew small plots of cane. Florida's interest in growing sugar in a region that is not suitable without subsidies and tariffs remained a homegrown affair until 1920. Though it did not really take off until the Fanjuls arrived. First grown in North America in the Spanish settlement of St. Augustine in 1572, sugarcane failed as a commercial crop in Florida several times in the eighteenth century. Hamilton Disston, the first entrepreneur to drain a large section of the Everglades, organized the Florida Sugar Manufacturing Company in 1890, a precarious venture that employed Louisiana tenant farmers. Using his political connections Disston persuaded the federal government to establish an agricultural research station near Lake Okeechobee that introduced thirty types of cane to Florida. Despite Disston's prodigious hopes, by the early 1900s only thirteen thousand acres of cane were grown in the entire state, mostly for syrup.

Then came large-scale draining. On July 4, 1906, the *Everglades*, which the *St. Augustine Record* lauded as "the largest and finest dredge boat south of Philadelphia," moved up the New River, near Fort Lauderdale, and began wresting muck from the glades, the first step in the creation of the North

New River Canal, a fifty-eight-mile conduit that would eventually unplug Lake Okeechobee. The following year, a second dredge, the *Okeechobee,* began excavating the South New River Canal west from Fort Lauderdale, which would eventually link the North New River Canal and the Miami Canal, also under construction.

Large land companies, such as Florida Fruit Lands and Everglades Plantation, bought tracks of undeveloped wetlands and then sold more than eighteen thousand parcels to unsuspecting buyers, mostly in ten-acre chunks, usually sight unseen. Many buyers planned to resell when their investments were drained and cleared. Factless slogans declared the muck soil richer than that in the Nile Valley and ten times more productive than the soil of northern farmland. Some companies encouraged pioneer families to take a tent, a bag of beans, and a hoe onto their land; telling them that after they cleared a few rows of sawgrass and planted some seeds they would have income in eight weeks.

Though the crescent of pond apple muck that rings the southern end of Lake Okeechobee is the most fertile soil in the Everglades, settlers found that clearing the thick swamp vegetation was an arduous task that involved sawing, chopping, hacking, pulling, rooting, cutting, prying, yanking, splitting, and finally burning. Decent progress was an acre a week. After ten weeks of labor, by the time a man had cleared his last acre, a vigorous new growth of elderberry had sprouted on the first acre cleared. Clearing sawgrass proved more difficult. Fifty square feet a day was considered good. At that rate, three and a half months was required to clear a little more than an acre. Plowing, too, was torturous. Draft animals sank into the soft, wet muck. Eventually someone designed a snowshoelike steel boot that allowed mules and oxen to stay on the surface.

Once their land had been plowed, settlers faced more problems. Lacking such essential micronutrients as copper and molybdenum, sawgrass peat in the northern Everglades grew sawgrass and little else. Crops would not mature. Cattle weakened and died. Those that survived suffered from foot rot and from the hordes of insects that drank their blood and clogged their nostrils. Large-scale farming in the northern Everglades remained an illusion happily sold to suckers.

By 1917 the four large muck-dredged canals that dissected the Everglades, together with the Caloosahatchee River, dropped Okeechobee from about twenty-two feet above sea level to between seventeen and nineteen. Water receded below the surface of the Everglades along the canals, until finally the land was ready for cultivation by large politically connected corporate-scale farms. This was the dream envisioned in 1847 by Buckingham Smith, a St. Augustine lawyer who had been sent by the federal government on a scientific reconnaissance through South Florida's watery interior. When the Atlantic Coast Line Railroad reached the southwest side of Lake Okeechobee in 1918, farming the Everglades began in earnest.

Sugarcane was one of the first crops grown on large parcels. The Pennsylvania Sugar Company planted a thousand acres along the Miami Canal in 1919, sixteen miles from Miami, a project that swiftly failed. In 1925 Bror Dahlberg, a wallboard manufacturer from Chicago, bought the ailing Southern Sugar Company, mainly as an investment, but used the pulverized cane for wallboard. By 1929 Southern Sugar owned a hundred thousand acres along the western and southern shores of Lake Okeechobee and had helped create the town of Clewiston. Two years later, the company collapsed—a result of the stock market crash and the plummeting price of sugar. Charles Stewart Mott, retired executive vice president of General Motors and a prominent philanthropist, and Clarence Bitting bought Southern Sugar at a land insolvency sale and renamed the company United States Sugar. By 1940 U.S. Sugar was producing 86 percent of the sugar grown in the Everglades.[1]

In 1930, several years after a pair of deadly hurricanes hurled Okeechobee over its earthen corset and drowned more than twenty-five hundred people, mostly field-workers and their families, a federal flood control project disguised as a navigation project was signed by President Hoover (the federal government was leery about appropriating funds for flood control during the depression). The spoils from dredging a navigable canal around the southern end of Lake Okeechobee were then used to build Hoover Dike, which disconnected the lake from the Everglades. After nearly half a century of false hopes, Lake Okeechobee was finally "harnessed" and serious development of the northern Everglades began.

Like every other plant except sawgrass, sugarcane struggled to grow in the nutrient-starved soil. Once farmers began to fertilize their fields with phosphorous, however, their harvests improved, and the industry slowly expanded. By the 1933–34 season approximately fifteen thousand acres of cane grew in the northern Everglades. By the 1939–40 season, thirty-eight thousand acres.

Then came the rains of 1947 and 1948. After hurricanes left farmland on the lower east coast underwater for more than six months, Congress authorized

---

1. The Charles Stewart Mott Foundation, a generous supporter of environmental causes—they spent eight hundred thousand dollars in the 1990s to protect a South American wetland—still has financial and managerial control of U.S. Sugar, which in 1996 spent three million dollars to defeat amendments to protect the Everglades. Why won't the environmental community target the Mott family with the same intensity it takes on the Fanjul clan?

massive flood control. In 1947 the Corps of Engineers deepened and widened those four 1917 canals, which soon became the cornerstone of the Central and Southern Florida Project for Flood Control and Other Purposes. Between 1952 and 1954, the Corps dug the eastern perimeter levee from Palm Beach to Miami–Dade County, lopping off the eastern flank of the glades and effectively blocking total development of the interior of South Florida. (Miami–Dade County's 8.5 Square Mile Area, however, is the notable exception, having developed on the west side of the levee.) Suburban development fostered by the Central and Southern Florida Project occupies the deepest part of the former Everglades, thus removing much of the storage capacity of the system. Gated retirement communities, subdivisions, and malls have replaced sawgrass and tree islands, and avocado plantations and palm and orchid nurseries subdivided the prairies and pinelands of the former eastern sector of the glades. Even the Miami International Airport sprawls across former Everglades.

In 1963, a few years after the Fanjuls arrived in Palm Beach, the Corps completed its balkanization of the Everglades, parceling off the national park, the EAA, and the three water conservation areas, which function as reservoirs that protect the EAA and the lower east coast of Florida from floods. Afterward, sheet flow, one of the most distinctive and ecologically important features of the Everglades, was disrupted. Pumps, which kept the EAA dry in the wet season and irrigated in the dry season, created an environment beneficial to cane-growing. Because the waters of the Everglades no longer flowed in a great, saturating arc, pumps along the Tamiami Trail provided minimum water delivery schedules for Shark Slough and Taylor Slough, drenching or parching the national park, often in opposition to natural cycles. Today, on the southern border of the EAA, the monster S-5 pump can move 365,000 gallons of water a minute, enough to fill a swimming pool in one second. Much of this water either goes to sea or stagnates in the conservation areas, flooding tree islands and drowning wetland plants.

Sugarcane cultivation is out of sync with South Florida's natural cycles. Because Big Sugar must remain dry in the wet season, every day more than a billion gallons of water is diverted away from the Everglades. By a year's end three to four million acre-feet—enough to submerge Connecticut beneath a foot of water—have been stolen from their natural destination, the Everglades itself. Starved for freshwater, Florida Bay has turned dangerously saline, and the central Everglades remains perpetually flooded. Although Big Sugar uses only two hundred thousand acre-feet a year (about seventy billion gallons) for irrigation in the dry season, ironically, during the wet season rain must be diverted for the EAA to grow sugar and vegetables instead of sawgrass.

《《《

An important point that bears repeating is that the Everglades is a nutrient-poor, though not unproductive, oligotrophic wetland. Sawgrass thrives in the glades because low levels of phosphorous inhibit the growth of more aggressive species, like cattails. Ron Jones, a microbiologist at Florida International University who for years has testified against Big Sugar, claimed that the Everglades' natural level of phosphorous is a measly 5 to 7 parts per billion, with a maximum of 10, equivalent to about fifty drops in an Olympic swimming pool. Scientists employed by Big Sugar claimed that pristine phosphorous levels were closer to 50 parts per billion and that the average rainfall in Florida contains twice that amount. In a 1996 research project, Herbert Grimshaw, a South Florida Water Management District senior environmental scientist, concluded that the phosphorous level in rainfall was only 1.3 parts per billion, which meant the state had underestimated how polluted the EAA runoff was. The district refused to publish Grimshaw's study and then fired him in 1998, claiming that his work was substandard. The following year Grimshaw won a legal settlement against the district and was reinstated. His rainfall paper was sent out to a peer-reviewed scientific journal without further hassle from his bosses.

Spreading phosphorus on the cane fields is a common practice in the EAA, which uses as much as thirty-three pounds per acre, depending on soil tests. When peat dries, and the wind blows away the recently oxidized organic matter, native phosphorous that had been stored for centuries beneath the surface of the Everglades also washes into canals. Jones, who found that farm runoff contains phosphorous levels of two hundred to five hundred parts per billion, believes that each year approximately two hundred metric tons of phosphorous flows off the EAA.

Phosphorous-rich water from the EAA was regularly back-pumped into Lake Okeechobee until 1979, exacerbating the lake's nutrient overload. To reduce the lake's nutrient level, the South Florida Water Management District began pumping untreated farm runoff into the central Everglades. The phosphorous infusion at first caused sawgrass to grow rapidly and abnormally large; then it died and gave way to cattails (*Typha* species), which usurp fifty acres of sawgrass a day. Today more than fifty thousand acres of cattails have spread across the water conservation areas, filling in portions of the central Everglades, crowding out willow and bay, excluding fish. Wading birds have no place to feed, no place to land. The composition of algal species that make up periphyton has changed. Dissolved oxygen has decreased, crippling delicate food webs.

Normally a benign and localized native, the cattail was formerly restricted to sites with natural pulses of nutrients: the edges of alligator holes, downstream from heron rookeries, and in recent burns. But now, says Jones, "Cattails are the grave marker" of a dying ecosystem.

In 1988 United States attorney Dexter Leitinen filed a lawsuit against the South Florida Water Management District and the Florida Department of Environmental Regulations for not enforcing the state's water quality standards—for looking the other way as phosphorous poured out of the EAA. Two and a half years later Florida's newly elected governor, Lawton Chiles, walked into a federal court saying, "I've brought my sword. Who do I surrender to?," conceding that the state needed to enforce its own laws. By the summer of 1991 Governor Chiles and Dick Thornburgh, the United States attorney general, began working on a timetable to clean up the Everglades. Thornburgh claimed, "Today marks a new day for the Everglades. Today's settlement represents a model for bold protective action." A new state law gave the South Florida Water Management District the power to impose taxes on sugar farmers to pay for their cleanup costs. But the farmers fought the tax in court, and the water managers must pay for most of the forty-thousand-acre artificial marsh to filter EAA runoff. The law was to be called the Marjory Stoneman Douglas–Everglades Forever Act.

The settlement allowed for future expansion of the artificial marsh, if needed, and set preliminary water standards to be met by 1997, when farmers would be required to cut phosphorous discharge by 10 percent. Long-term goals called for a further reduction of 25 percent. The water quality lawsuit had cost Florida six million dollars and exhausted ten thousand hours of federal time.

Sugar fought back, filing more than a dozen lawsuits. During the 1992 presidential campaign, the Fanjuls split their political allegiances: Pepe chaired the Bush-Quayle Finance Committee, and Alfy led Clinton into the heart of the Cuban-American community, a Republican stronghold. Four months after Clinton's victory, Alfy Fanjul gave a blueprint for Everglades restoration that had been prepared by Flo-Sun scientists to Bruce Babbitt, the secretary of the interior. Two years later, at the urging of Fanjul, Babbitt turned the Everglades cleanup over to the state legislature, where Big Sugar held all the trump cards. The coterie of three dozen lobbyists they employed to represent them in Tallahassee included two former state house speakers and Governor Chiles's former campaign manager and chief of staff. Sugar blitzed the media, downplaying the phosphorous problem, claiming disingenuously that rainwater had far more phosphorous than the goal set for EAA runoff.

In 1994, to the dismay of Florida legislators, Marjory Stoneman Douglas, then 103 years old, publicly demanded that her name be stricken from the Marjory Stoneman Douglas–Everglades Forever Act of 1994 because she felt that the state had retreated from its commitment to restore the Everglades. Later that year, in the company of Bruce Babbitt at an Everglades National Park ceremony, Governor Chiles signed an amended version of the Everglades Forever Act that suspended state water quality standards until 2003 and empowered state officials, not federal scientists, to determine allowable phosphorous levels. The act also capped Big Sugar's cleanup costs at $320 million. Once again taxpayers would pay the difference, estimated at more than $400 million.

If Big Sugar were a manufacturing company, it would have been forced to clean up its act years ago. But until recently, no one wanted to move against agriculture. Nonetheless sugar is grown in the Caribbean at lower cost and with less environmental disruption without jeopardizing a vast, almost incomprehensible, wilderness.

(((

With her book *The Everglades: River of Grass,* which distilled the marsh into elegant and vivid prose, Marjory Stoneman Douglas forever changed the way Americans view the Florida Everglades. "The clear burning light of the sun pours daylong into the sawgrass," she wrote, "and is lost there, soaked up, never given back. Only the water flashes and glints. The grass yields nothing."

For much of the last century, Douglas had been associated with the Everglades. In the 1920s she wrote editorials opposing its draining and urging its protection. In the 1930s and 1940s she served on a committee seeking to form a Florida national park and lobbied at the federal and state levels for its creation. In 1947, the year she wrote *River of Grass,* she sat on the dais with President Harry S. Truman during the dedication of Everglades National Park. Despite her previous efforts, however, Douglas once said that she did not become truly involved with the Everglades and the effort to save it until 1967, when she wrote *Florida: The Long Frontier* and became one of the country's leading environmental activists.

In 1969 Douglas founded the Friends of the Everglades, now a five-thousand-member group pledged to the protection and restoration of the South Florida wetland. She traveled all over the state speaking on behalf of the Everglades and railing against its enemies—land-hungry developers, the sugar corporations, the Army Corps of Engineers, and compromising politicians. In

1992 Douglas appeared on television opposite Bob Buker Jr., a vice president and spokesman for U.S. Sugar. After Douglas gave a rousing condemnation of Big Sugar's effect on Everglades water, Buker said, "I thought I would show you what it feels like this evening" and held a paper bull's-eye over his heart. Then, to punctuate his point that phosphorous-rich farm runoff was as safe as mother's milk, he drank a jar of brown swamp-water, declaring that the Marjory Stoneman Douglas–Everglades Forever Act would ruin farmers. Replied Douglas: "Sugarcane doesn't belong in the Everglades, period."

Douglas was feisty and tireless. The Army Corps of Engineers, the agency whose canals and levees make cane-growing possible, was one of Douglas's favorite targets. One evening, while attending an Everglades forum, she sat next to the district colonel who oversaw Everglades waterworks. The audience, decidedly pro-environment, eagerly awaited her trademark lambasting of the Corps. Approaching the podium, Douglas dropped her handkerchief, and the colonel stooped to retrieve it. Reaching the podium, microphone in hand, Douglas turned to the colonel and said, "Getting on your knees, Colonel, will not change what I have to say one whit."

《《《

Driving through the town of Belle Glade, along the southeastern side of Lake Okeechobee, I notice a sign that proudly announces, "Her soil is her fortune." Someone ought to change the wording of the sign from *is* to *was*, for in the past seventy-five years more than six feet of peat has disappeared from the EAA. Farmers may soon strike bedrock. The organic soils of the Everglades were formed underwater, in the absence of oxygen and oxygen-loving microorganisms, whose voracious appetites would have consumed the gathering mess of stems, leaves, roots, and rhizomes. Because periodic and often prolonged flooding held aerobic microbes at bay, peat deposits built up, and the ridge of pond apple muck around the southern end of Lake Okeechobee, broached here and there by eight short rivers (the regulator valves), governed the lake's spillover during all but the most violent weather.

Geologists have determined that without the veneer of freshwater marl that was deposited about six thousand years ago, the Everglades could not have developed. Like a weatherproof shield, the marl sealed the northern limestone. Water that would otherwise have percolated into the rock, dissolving cavities and tunnels (as in the southern Everglades), stayed on the surface, allowing peat to develop, and produced a great, slow-moving arc of southward-flowing water. A positive feedback loop was created: peat, covering the irregular surface of the limestone, built deep even deposits that were supported, and in turn nourished, by an inland sea of sawgrass, dense enough in the northern glades to keep out alligators.

When canals dropped the water table below the surface, and the sawgrass was painstakingly cleared, the peat dried, shrank, and blew away, or burnt like a cigar, smoldering for months and years, filling the blue sky with black smoke. Worse, the dry soil oxidized, as hungry aerobic bacteria gorged. Already the rate of soil subsidence in the EAA has reached one inch a year. Because sugarcane needs the water table well below the surface, peat subsides faster on sugar farms than on pastures, rice paddies, or some types of vegetable farms.

The first land to be farmed adjacent to the canals was also the first to subside, and it remained drier longer than neighboring wetlands, until the higher wetlands themselves began to drain into it. To irrigate, farmers had to dig more canals. More land subsided. Eventually the water table along the eastern rim of the Everglades was so low that freshwater springs in Biscayne Bay and along the coast stopped flowing. No longer held back by a full aquifer, heavier saltwater entered the porous limestone from below and flowed farther up coastal rivers and transverse glades. The lower east coast grappled with its own environmental disaster as saltwater contaminated shallow wells.

According to geologist Garald Parker, who began studying South Florida saltwater intrusion in 1939, to avoid saltwater intrusion the shallow Biscayne Aquifer had to be kept at least two and a half feet higher than sea level. On the basis of Parker's recommendations, Miami built saltwater-control dams near the mouths of metropolitan canals. The first dam was finished in November 1953. In the 1960s, after the Corps had almost completed the Central and Southern Florida Flood Control Project, saltwater intrusion contaminated more wells. As a hedge against further well contamination, the walled-off water conservation areas often have been kept at abnormally high levels, their cycles closely reflecting the cycles of cane farming, and plant communities in the central Everglades have shifted from sawgrass to slough.

The path of the surplus water draining from the EAA is so crucial to the health of the Everglades that Vice President Al Gore promised that restoration would include the recovery of at least an additional one hundred thousand acres of cane fields to be used mostly for water storage. But after one phone call from Alfy Fanjul to the White House, the purchase of more land from the EAA was dropped from the Everglades restoration plan.

Guided by the principle that lawsuits take time, the Miccosukee have joined Big Sugar in demanding that no more sugar lands be used for water storage. In an effort to protect tribal land in the central Everglades from chronic flood, the Miccosukee now insist that Everglades National Park absorb Big Sugar's surplus water. Although the park and the dun-colored sparrow it protects have become lightning rods for the advocates of draining the conservation areas, Big Sugar remains dry and prosperous and insulated from southern water issues.

《《《

I am at the Okeelanta sugar mills, a guest of Flo-Sun. Jorge Dominicus, the vice president in charge of public relations, has arranged my day. My first stop is the conference center, called the hacienda, where the late Peter Rosendahl, a hydrologist, Raul Perdomo, an agronomist in charge of sugar products, and Dominicus field my questions. They unequivocally believe that the Everglades Forever Act was an excellent compromise between farming and environmental concerns. If the state were to lower the limit of phosphorous permitted to flow out of the EAA, the final cleanup costs would have escalated. And Flo-Sun has already agreed to pay its fair share, they tell me.

As part of the agreement, Flo-Sun will pay up to one hundred million dollars over twenty years to help finance a four-thousand-acre farm runoff retention pond, a fact that Dominicus repeats seven times this morning. "Just because the industry is here," says Rosendahl, "we shouldn't pay for everything. Environmentalists should step back. They have no financial stake in this, even though they are considered stakeholders." Adds Dominicus: "Never once has it been proven in a court of law that the industry caused any damage to the adjacent Everglades. The issue with sugar is phosphorous, and we believe the portion that Flo-Sun has agreed to pay reflects the farmers' contribution to the system." He concludes with, "How many years do we want to fight? We want to be sustainable. So, we settled this and have gotten on with our business."

But the sugar giant got off easy, and everyone else will pay the lion's share. Taxpayers sold public land cheaply, financed its drainage, subsidized its land and water taxes, provided cheap loans, and bought its price-controlled product. Now we are being asked to pay for most of the cleanup of EAA's wastewater.

Rosendahl then reminds me that the Everglades Forever Act wants the phosphorous level down to fifty parts per billion: "That's two orders of magnitude less than the effluent from a typical treatment plant in New England." Adds Domincus, "We're talking parts per billion. Bottled water you buy in the store has more phosphorous than is allowed by the Everglades Forever Act. You'd have to drink fourteen hundred gallons of the stuff to get your daily recommended allowance."

Because the Fanjuls began farming in the 1960s, thirty years after the more fertile land closer to Lake Okeechobee had been claimed by other farmers,

Flo-Sun's cane fields are at the very edge of the EAA, where the shallower peat deposits are disappearing quickly. If anyone strikes bedrock, surely it will be Flo-Sun. Then what will be the fate of the lower EAA? Subdivisions and malls? Racetracks and theme parks? Ecologically speaking, once the veneer of marl is scraped off the limestone of the EAA, the northern Everglades will be beyond repair.

Save Our Everglades (SOE) is a group headed by Mary Barley, widow of George Barley, a wealthy and passionate environmentalist who died when his small plane went down on the way to an Everglades conservation meeting. By her own admission Barley's a "conservative Republican." In 1996 SOE placed three amendments on the Florida ballot. Amendment 4 would have required farmers to pay a penny for each pound of sugar produced in the Everglades Agricultural Area in order to fund an Everglades cleanup; amendment 5 made polluters responsible for cleaning up their own mess; and amendment 6 created an Everglades trust fund primarily financed by the penny-a-pound tax.

Fighting back, sugar industry lawyers filed thirty-eight lawsuits challenging everything from misplaced commas to potentially unconstitutional language in the amendments. They spent more than thirty-five million dollars to defeat amendment 4, including newspaper, radio, and television ads, most of which promulgated false claims and outright lies. Industry analysts estimated that the big sugar companies made about 5.2 cents profit on every pound of sugar, a profit furthermore guaranteed by the federal government. Barley claimed that the penny-a-pound tax would generate thirty million dollars a year, nine hundred million dollars over the life of the program. Big Sugar said the tax would cripple the industry and eliminate forty thousand jobs. On behalf of the sugar interests, Jesse Jackson told an outdoor rally, "We should never have a showdown between people and alligators. We should always choose people."

On Election Day alone the sugar lobby spent more than a million dollars fighting the amendments. The results were mixed: amendment 4 lost in what a Fort Lauderdale *Sun Sentinel* editorial called "a triumph of disinformation"; amendments 5 and 6 won. Polluters would pay to clean up the Everglades, but without the penny-a-pound tax, how was the money going to be raised? "We've already agreed to pay our fair share," Dominicus tells me again, "a sales tax wasn't necessary."

In May 1999 Big Sugar's fortunes changed drastically. The Miccosukee, citing the Clean Water Act, won federal approval for a ten parts per billion phosphorous limit on their seventy-five thousand acres of reservation in the Everglades. Six months later scientists at the Florida Department of Environmental Protection advocated limiting the average phosphorous level for Water Conservation Area 2 to eight and a half parts per billion, noting that phosphorous levels in unpolluted stretches of the Everglades were even lower. Thus far, the water managers who run the cleanup do not have a clue as to how to meet the new state standards. Although environmentalists want to reach the eight and a half parts per billion level as soon as possible, sugar representatives like Dominicus are opting for inertia. Déjà vu.

After a Cuban lunch at the hacienda, Perdomo hands me a piece of raw sugarcane for dessert. Like bubblegum, the cane is a flavor burst that fades in minutes. In Florida, cane requires ten to twelve months to mature and usually flowers by mid-September but does not produce seeds under commercial conditions. To plant cane, freshly cut stalks—each containing two or three nodes, an axillary, or "eye," bud and root primordia—are placed in the bottom of furrows. Fertilizer follows. Roots develop from the root primordia, and the stalk grows up from the eye. The new shoots emerge in fifteen to sixty days. "We're on the fringe of where cane can be grown," says Perdomo. "If the stalks aren't cut by fourteen or fifteen months, new sprouts develop, fueled by the stored sucrose. Flowering is a natural message: 'I'm done. If you don't cut I will begin to dry out.' We harvest before that point." Sugarcane can sustain two or three cuttings before the stalk's sucrose content trails off significantly.

Next I watch a public relations video that describes how well the migrant Jamaican cane cutters are treated, how their dingy gray barracks were repainted an upbeat white. "They're better than soldiers' barracks," claims Dominicus. The happy-cutters video was made in response to Alec Wilkinson's book *Big Sugar*, an exposé of the industry's notoriously poor labor record. In 1942 U.S. Sugar was indicted for peonage at the federal district court in Tampa, and until recently, migrant workers were treated like indentured servants on lease from their home countries. "The book was popular because slavery sells," Dominicus tells me. "No one ever heard of a cutter losing a body part [from an errant machete swing] at our company. Our cane cutters had workers' compensation. They had health insurance." Flo-Sun no longer frets over the media's portrayal of its workers' conditions, for the cutters have been replaced by machines, which, from a distance, look like mechanical dinosaurs lauding over the fields.

Later in the afternoon I tour Okeelanta, the largest of Flo-Sun's three sugar mills. The plant is so noisy that I wear ear protectors and so steamy that everything feels sticky, even the air. Rivers of mud-brown sucrose squirt out as cane is shredded and pressed. Swirling tendrils of sweet steam rise above caldrons of boiling liquid that will be refined and stored as tan sugar crystals called turbinado. Sixty feet overhead a conveyor transports sugar crystals to feed a tan mountain of sugar six hundred yards long. A continuous drizzle of crystals tinks against my yellow plastic hard hat.

My long day as Flo-Sun's guest ends at half past seven. The following morning the *Miami Herald* reported that five convicted killers had escaped from a nearby prison and hidden in the mill while I merrily toured. Under a coif of darkness, several hours after I left Okeelanta, the fugitives slipped a dragnet and vanished into the cane fields like so many tax dollars.

Fish do best where there is water.

BILL LOFTUS, Everglades National Park biologist,

1996

17 Reviving the Everglades

Although no one has a precise map of what the future Everglades will look like, there is an overwhelming commitment to begin the restoration process. The Comprehensive Everglades Restoration Plan (CERP) will cost nearly $8 billion to build, plus another $172 million a year to operate; it will take almost half a century to complete, and there are a multitude of uncertainties that could derail it along the way. But every one of the dozens of scientists who had a hand in shaping the plan agrees on one thing: it could not have come any sooner.

Redeeming the Everglades involves sixty-eight massive engineering projects that divide roughly into three major challenges: water storage, the most expensive aspect of the ecological rescue; seepage control; and the reassemblage of some of the separated parts of the original ecosystem. "Ten years ago restoration was a pipe dream," says Stuart Strahl, president and CEO of Audubon of Florida, the Florida State Office of the National Audubon Society. "Now here we are with a plan crafted by the environmental community, the Army Corps of Engineers, the sugar industry, the Florida Chamber of Commerce, and the water utilities. If you had told people in 1996, the year I started with Audubon, that we'd have fifty thousand acres of sugar land bought, that we'd have a water preserve area designed that went beyond our wildest dreams in 1992, that the state had approved condemnation to acquire those lands, and that only three people in Congress would have voted against the eight billion dollar restoration bill, they would have said, 'Man, we want what you're smoking.'"

The main objective of restoration is to recapture trillions of gallons of freshwater currently flushed out to sea and to eventually redirect that lost water back to the ailing wetlands without flooding South Florida's corporate farms and booming cities. To review: Eighteen hundred miles of canals and levees have already drained half the Everglades and chopped up the other half, rendering the landscape habitable for people and vegetables but untenable for alligators, egrets, and dozens of other Everglades-dependent species; the disruption of seasonal water flows has wreaked havoc on the ecosystem's delicate balance; phosphorous runoff from the sugarcane fields has severely diminished water quality; and invasive species are replacing natives at a rapid pace.

As we saw earlier, wildlife has suffered the most harm: alligators have moved off the edge and into the bowels of the Everglades, fish numbers have dropped precipitously on the marl prairies, and populations of white ibis, wood storks, and snowy egrets have plummeted by more than 90 percent in the past fifty years.

Eight billion dollars to restore the Everglades is a lot of money, enough to make many scientists believe that they can reverse the decline. According to estimates by Conservation International, just over half of the project's cost would be enough to buy and protect all the world's rain forests. Still, no one is guaranteeing success. "Our understanding of the Everglades is based almost entirely on information collected after it became a disturbed ecosystem," says John Ogden, a senior ecologist for the South Florida Water Management District, one of the principal agencies carrying out restoration. "We don't know what the natural system really is, so we're basing these projects on a set of predictions on how we think it will respond."

CERP will eliminate some 240 miles of canals and levees, allowing more natural flows of clean, freshwater to course through the liquid land. The plan also calls for the construction of new filtering marshes that will cleanse the runoff from the seven hundred thousand acres of adjacent farms and sugarcane fields, and the construction of artificial reservoirs and underground water-storage facilities designed to ensure a steady supply of water for South Florida's thirsty (and ever-increasing) residents. The water stored in the reservoirs and underground aquifers is to be released periodically, to mimic the historical wet-dry cycle.

No one knows, however, whether any of this will really work, whether the wildlife will actually rebound, or whether the three hundred wells drilled a thousand feet underground will be able to hold enough of the water now being shunted out to the Atlantic Ocean and the Gulf of Mexico. Six pilot projects to be implemented between 2000 and 2012 will address each uncertainty. Scientists admit that there are no ironclad guidelines for the restoration. Some of the technology will have to be worked out along the way. "Maybe it's premature to implement a plan," says Stuart Applebaum, chief of ecosystem restoration for the Army Corps of Engineers Jacksonville office, "but the Everglades is in dire straits and I don't want to do a postmortem."

It bears repeating: To supply the clouds that bring rain to the Everglades there must be oceanic moisture and onshore winds and thousands of square miles of water that moves so slowly you can't tell it is moving at all. Nearly everything south of Disney World in Orlando was once covered by a low-lying, seasonally flooded wetland. For more than one hundred miles, the change in elevation from Lake Okeechobee to Florida Bay is less than the slope of some city blocks in San Francisco. During wet periods, when the sloughs spilled over their banks and flooded the limy, rock-studded earth, the marl prairie became a biological mecca. Every winter the fish and crawfish, marooned in drying potholes and depressions, attracted thousands of wading birds. Everglades mink and gray fox also followed the drying front from the prairies toward the central slough, feasting on fish and frogs as well as on round-tailed muskrats and marsh rabbits. Sadly, much of the marl prairie is already gone, buried beneath tract housing and malls, invaded by exotic trees, and laced by highways whose names—Sawgrass Expressway, Palmetto Expressway—are the only hint of the obliterated landscape.

Water once used exclusively by turtles, snakes, and other creatures is today used by large-scale agriculture, golf courses, and swimming pools; it is also a hedge against drought. "Regaining the system's ability to store vast quantities of water is both the most expensive and the most challenging aspect of restoration," says Mark Kraus, deputy director of restoration science at Audubon of Florida. Where do you store the water, those uncountable trillions of tide-borne gallons, when half the Everglades is gone, and Lake Okeechobee, tight against Hoover Dike, is managed at a lower than natural water level?

CERP will be a new challenge, because large-scale aquifer storage and recovery, where water is stored in rock formations deep below the earth's surface, has never been done. "Pumping water of dubious quality under high pressure into the upper Floridan Aquifer [which underlies most of Florida and holds more water than all of the Great Lakes combined] is a gamble," says Kraus. Florida has injected chemical waste and treated sewage into the lower portion of the aquifer. There is an assumption that the upper and lower aquifers are not connected. "We don't know that for sure," says Kraus. If the pressure of the pumped water cracks the bedrock, then the upper aquifer may become polluted. South of Lake Okeechobee, saline water underlies the Floridan Aquifer's freshwater. Engineers expect the pumped freshwater will settle as a bubble on top of the saltwater. If it doesn't, minerals from the saline portion might contaminate drinking water—or introduce pathogens with unknown consequences.

In a region that receives sixty inches of rainfall a year but loses fifty-eight to evapotranspiration, storing water underground seems to be a logical alternative to either raising the water level of Lake Okeechobee, which would drown the lush wetlands inside Herbert Hoover Dike, or buying undeveloped land. "The reason we're putting a whole lot of money into aquifer storage is because it would take half a million acres to store the water on land. And that would affect growth," said the national park's Bob Johnson. Assuming that aquifer storage and recovery can be shown to work, as much as 1.7 billion gallons a day will be injected below the surface. If it does not work, an act of Congress will not be necessary to amend CERP, for the blueprint for restoration authorizes what Applebaum calls adaptive assessment, the ability of CERP's managers to correct mistakes without congressional intervention.

Adaptive assessment is the cornerstone of Everglades restoration, an ecological work-in-progress. That all but three out of more than 450 members of Congress voted for the legislation, thereby relinquishing control over a complex and expensive long-term project of national, and even international, import, was a political miracle. The journey from bill to law, however, was not smooth. The death of stalwart supporter Senator John Chaffee, a moderate Republican from Rhode Island and chairman of the critically important Senate Environment and Public Works Committee, left CERP mired in political squabbles and interagency backstabbing. When Bob Smith succeeded Chaffee as committee chairman, environmentalists grieved. Smith, from New Hampshire, had a reputation as a skinflint and had voted against

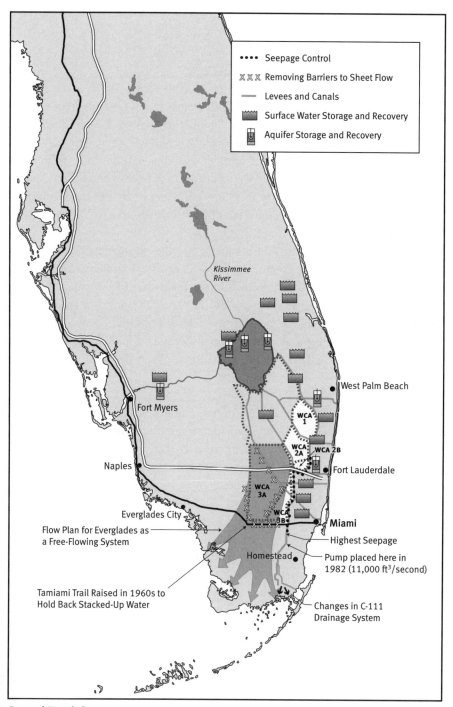

Legend:

- •••• Seepage Control
- ✕✕✕ Removing Barriers to Sheet Flow
- —— Levees and Canals
- Surface Water Storage and Recovery
- Aquifer Storage and Recovery

Kissimmee River

West Palm Beach

Fort Myers

WCA 1

Naples

WCA 2A

WCA 2B

Fort Lauderdale

WCA 3A

Everglades City

WCA 3B

Flow Plan for Everglades as a Free-Flowing System

Miami

Highest Seepage

Homestead

Pump placed here in 1982 (11,000 ft³/second)

Tamiami Trail Raised in 1960s to Hold Back Stacked-Up Water

Changes in C-111 Drainage System

Restored Everglades

environmentalists 87 percent of the time since 1989, when he was first elected to the United States Senate. "We looked at Smith and saw a guy that was pretty much right of Attila the Hun," recalls Stuart Strahl. "The reaction was 'Oh God, how are we going to work with this guy.'"

Then to everyone's surprise, including his own staff's, Smith made Everglades restoration his top priority, declaring that there was no daylight between his position and that of John Chaffee. "Smith fell out of the sky clutching restoration to his breast," remembers Audubon biologist Jerry Lorenz. "We were stunned." He played hardball with all who dragged their feet, from the sugar industry to fellow senators. When Senator Max Baucus called Everglades restoration "a treacherous money pit," Smith threatened to feed the Montana Democrat to an alligator. A month later Smith had signed on Baucus as one of the bill's cosponsors.

"We assumed that adaptive assessment was like motherhood. It would make everyone feel better," reflects John Ogden. But several environmental organizations, including the Sierra Club, the Defenders of Wildlife, and the Natural Resources Defense Council, did not trust the political future and opposed the plan, preferring instead that a rock-solid plan be written into law. For them a conceptual plan that evolved as you learned more might be hijacked by, in Ogden's words, "evil forces." Even the park service was skeptical.

Once water that would be otherwise lost has been stored and becomes available for both the Everglades and the municipalities, replumbing will be aimed at keeping the suburbs dry. The eastern perimeter levee, which runs more than one hundred miles from West Palm Beach to Homestead, separates the unruly reptilian denizens of Florida from the genteel suburbs. The levee does not follow the natural contours of the land and for most of its length separates contiguous, low-lying flood-prone areas—the lowest areas are actually on the residential side of the levee. (In other words, the deepest side of the Everglades is protected from flooding, and the shallower side is used for water storage.) Without flood control, water added to the park would pool against the eastern perimeter levee, seep through the spongy limestone, and rise in the suburbs, where residents of Kendall and Hialeah might find a canoe more useful for running errands than a sport utility vehicle.

Along with aquifer storage and seepage control, the third, and most visible, feature of restoration is the removal of the more than two hundred miles of levees and canals. To re-create some portion of the historic sheet flow, much of the central Everglades will be reconnected to both Big Cypress National

Preserve and the national park. To achieve this reconnection, sections of the Tamiami Trail will be raised, forty-five miles of the Miami Canal will be filled, and the levees that divide Water Conservation Area 3 will be partially breached. Unfortunately Loxahatchee National Wildlife Refuge and Water Conservation Area 2 will remain orphaned. Corseted by levees and higher than the more southerly marshes, both areas would drain dry if reconnected to the rest of the Everglades. If the levees that enclose Loxahatchee and Conservation Area 2 were removed and Lake Okeechobee provided the dry season water supply, the lake would drain down to a mere six feet, compared with its current elevation of fifteen feet above sea level (originally it was twenty-two feet above sea level). Hundreds of square miles of lake bottom would be exposed.

Even if the two artificially isolated areas could be incorporated without threatening Lake Okeechobee, water would flow southeast and pile up to unacceptable depths against the eastern perimeter levee. Tree islands, bowers of life in the Everglades, a thousand years in the making and already stressed from unnaturally deep water, would drown. Steve Davis, a lead scientist for the South Florida Water Management District and an authority on water chemistry, has warned that restoring complete sheet flow "is not the end-all some people think, particularly with today's water quality." In fact, agricultural runoff is believed to be the ten-foot alligator chomping at everyone's heels. New water quality standards have curtailed the amount of phosphorous being dumped into the marshes, but there is still plenty of polluted water getting spewed out by Big Sugar, and all that sugarcane sitting at the top of the eco-system is not going anywhere else for the foreseeable future. As I've mentioned before, because the Everglades is nutrient-poor, sawgrass thrives without competition from other species of wetland plants. But until phosphorous levels drop to ten parts for every billion parts of water, polluted agricultural runoff will continue to promote growth of plumes of phosphorous-loving cattails, which are already a taking over parts of Water Conservation Area 2. A borrow canal takes polluted runoff from the cane fields away from the refuge and into Water Conservation Area 2, sparing Loxahatchee.

In 1984, when the Corps had completed the water conveyance project for south Miami–Dade known as the c-III system, a pump capable of delivering a flow of eleven thousand cubic feet per second sent lake water south toward Florida Bay from Okeechobee in a matter of days, a hundred-mile journey that once required months. The gate on the c-III system is not supposed to open unless there is an extreme high-water event, defined as the threat of two or more inches of rain. Because the threat of two inches of rain is an almost daily occurrence during six months of the year in South Florida, the Corps and the water management district can open the gate virtually anytime they want.

In December 2000, for example, fifteen inches of rain fell on Lake Okeechobee. Two months later a portion of the lake bottom was dry and caught fire, and premier bass-fishing holes were a mile from the nearest water. "South Florida is the only place in the world where, when it rains, somebody sues the government," says Audubon's Jerry Lorenz. "If you can't tolerate the inconvenience of rain, why move to Florida? It's insane. If you live in Vermont, can you sue because it snowed and the roads aren't plowed?"

Ernest Coe, father of Everglades National Park, whom Marjory Stoneman Douglas called a prophet, pleaded that the boundaries of a tropical Florida Park ought to follow natural flow-ways and should be drawn north of the Tamiami Trail to include portions of the central Everglades and Big Cypress Swamp. In 1938 Daniel Beard, a biologist at the Department of the Interior, who would eventually become the park's first superintendent, recommended that the park service acquire at least 250 square miles north of the Trail as a buffer against drainage. Beard reasoned that because parkland would be off-limits to hunting, there would be no way to reach land beyond the northern boundary, which would also stay remote. No one listened. When the Corps unveiled its flood-control design in 1951, its own engineers worried that if the central Everglades north of the Tamiami Trail became a sump, the national park would dry up. Unfortunately, the Corps acted against its own concerns.

For the millions who have flocked to the Sunshine State in the past fifty years the Corps' Central and Southern Florida Flood Control District has worked. For the region's plants and animals, of which sixty-eight species are either federally or regionally endangered or threatened, it has been a disaster. Unfortunately the Corps built a system that cannot accommodate the ecological extremes of flood and drought inherent to the Everglades. Because the Everglades has lost storage capacity, water is drained away in the wet season and stored in the dry season. To provide both flood protection and a steady supply of drinking water for South Florida's six million residents, natural resource managers are forced to stack excess water in the conservation areas, affording those areas little chance for their natural and necessary dry-down cycle. As a result, parts of the northern and southern Everglades remain bone-dry, and for unnaturally long periods. Too many intense peat fires, triggered by lightning strikes and arson in unusually dry conditions, have devastated large swaths of the wetlands. Many areas of the Everglades now either drown or burn, and the national park is on life support. "What we have out there now is Everglades in name only," says John Ogden. "It may look like the Everglades, but it doesn't function like the Everglades."

Although some people envision successful restoration in hydrologic terms—on the basis of volume and flow patterns—and others see success in ecological terms—the sky alive with wading birds, and the estuaries roiling with life—every one of the hundreds of scientists, engineers, politicians, sportsmen, activists, and businesspeople who have been involved imagines a healthy Everglades that flashes some semblance of its original vibrancy and subtropical lushness, that pulsates to the rhythms of flood and drought and fire and frost, that bends but does not break in big weather. And an Everglades that coexists with farming, commerce, and growth.

How will the success of Everglades restoration be measured? Should the Everglades look like it did circa 1900, before the marsh was drained? Or perhaps it should be the 1947 version, the year President Truman dedicated Everglades National Park. Or maybe a more recent vintage, say, the mid-1970s, the last good years for nesting wading birds. Maybe it will be different from anything it has ever been before. "Restoration will provide ecological surprises," says Steve Davis, "and anyone who thinks otherwise is foolish." What everyone hopes is that the Everglades does not remain the ecological debacle it now is.

To understand how restoration will eventually be graded, I visit John Ogden, who chairs Recover, a team of one hundred interagency and multidisciplinary scientists charged with monitoring the results of Everglades restoration. His home, a refurbished two-story farmhouse replete with gothic columns and mahogany floors, is recessed from the road and immured by tropical trees. When viewed from the corner of Krome and Avocado avenues, Ogden's property looks like a luxuriant hardwood hammock growing in the middle of south Miami-Dade farmland. Royal palms line the driveway. Orchids bloom on the porch.

Ogden's round face supports a close-cropped beard, which merges into a coif of neatly trimmed hair, both more white than gray. He is barefoot, dressed in shorts and a Hawaiian shirt. He speaks with a Tennessee lilt. Ogden's informal charm belies an encyclopedic knowledge of the Everglades acquired during the thirty years he, at one time or another, worked for the National Park Service, the National Audubon Society, and the South Florida Water Management District. He has studied everything from crocodiles to short-tailed hawks and is an authority on the history and ecology of Everglades wading birds.

In 1996 Ogden was part of a team of scientists who designed a restoration plan by first listing the features that marked the predrainage landscape. But the original Everglades was a lost world, a landscape they could never fully comprehend. Eventually it dawned on Ogden that people refer to the region as unique. In fact, Marjory Stoneman Douglas begins her book *Everglades: River of Grass* by stating that "there are no other Everglades in the world." Once Ogden and his colleagues agreed on what made the region singular, they had a restoration target. They described the Everglades as a nutrient-poor marsh that covered a vast area; a broad, shallow flowing sheet of water, largely underscored by peat, that had the dynamic ability to store vast quantities of slowly moving water. The recovery of these defining characteristics of the Everglades became the goal of the restoration. Because water cues the nesting and distribution of so many species, ecologists hope the replumbed system will once again become a working ecosystem.

The litmus test for the success of restoration will be the combined achievements of 150 "performance measures" (pared down from an initial 1,200). These measures include the abundance and distribution of fish, wading birds, and alligators; the absence of exotic vegetation; the health of tree islands; the quantity, quality, and flow patterns of freshwater; and after the slow creep of time, the building of peat. "We started listing every performance measure everybody suggested," says Ogden. "Then, if we couldn't link a measure's response to restoration, it was eliminated as a performance measure." Loggerhead sea turtles, which nest on the milk-white beaches of Cape Sable, were eliminated from the list because their Gulf Coast nest sites do not depend on the health of the Everglades. So were black bears, whose wide-ranging habits and catholic appetites take them in and out of the watershed. Although they are currently on the list, panthers, which depend more on uplands than wetlands, may eventually be removed.

To develop a good monitoring plan it is necessary to select the proper parameters that would enable one to evaluate how the Everglades responds to CERP. Not too many items. Not too few. The single biggest reason that a plan fails is that scientists try to monitor too many factors, Ogden tells me. Although Everglades restoration has allocated one hundred million dollars for a ten-year monitoring program, the amount is not enough to cover the salaries, equipment, and plane flights necessary to track 150 performance measures. "How many can we adequately monitor at $10 million a year?" Ogden rhetorically asks. "Maybe a hundred."

Some performance measures, such as the growth and composition of periphyton, may take only a few weeks to respond, but anyone with even a casual acquaintance with wild Florida takes a longer view and sees successful restoration in terms of the region's megafauna, the feathered and scaled wild animals, irrefutable symbols of the Everglades. It was the shear abundance of alligators and wading birds that persuaded the federal government to establish the first park in the world based on perishable biologic resources.

Dimwitted and mud-encrusted, alligators were once a keystone species whose excavations attracted a festival of aquatic life to the marl prairies. To reiterate a previous point, one hundred years ago alligators nested in every creek in the mangroves, in every pothole on the marl prairie, and throughout the western cypress country. In response to water management, however, they have substantially redistributed themselves. When normally wet areas are deprived of water, the gators are forced to move off the marl edges and into the deeper central Everglades and the labyrinthine canal system, where prey is hard to come by. Today the marl prairies, once ruled by alligators, are mostly barren of life.

I recall traveling by airboat several years ago across the watery heart of the central Everglades. The night eyes of alligators shone red like smoldering bits of coal. Little knowing, I thought the world was just perfect. But in the days before drainage, alligators ruled the periphery of the Everglades, where their prehistoric voices filled April mornings. In his autobiography, *Gladesman: Gator Hunters, Moonshiners, and Skiffers,* Glen Simmons writes about gator hunting on the marl prairies from a flat-bottom skiff and about waiting along the rim of a prairie gator hole with the patience of stone. The shallow mangrove creeks that fed the fertile estuaries were also a favorite haunt of gator hunters. Simmons never mentions hunting the deep-water interior.

"The marl prairies are biologically dead," says Ogden. "They're the most degraded region in the system." To restore the Everglades, alligator numbers in the interior sloughs and canals must be significantly reduced. If the marl prairies and mangrove creeks can once again accommodate alligators in an ecologically meaningful way, "then we've gone a long way toward restoration," Ogden asserts.

During the last decades of the nineteenth century, before the demands of the feather trade crippled Florida's wading bird populations, some biologists speculated that as many as 1,500,000 waders nested in the mangrove-lined rivers that fed Whitewater Bay at the southern end of Everglades National Park. Ogden thinks that number may be inflated. The high-end estimate he favors is 250,000—most of them white ibis—a number recorded in both the 1933 and 1934 breeding seasons by Audubon wardens whose job it was to patrol the waterlogged backcountry during the first half of the past century (a job the state of Florida was loath to do).

Again, today Florida Bay's mangrove rookeries stand silent in testimony to engineering gone awry. Populations of wood storks and white ibis, both tactile feeders, and snowy egrets, immaculate little herons that comb the shallows as if they are wired on caffeine, have either crashed or moved elsewhere. All three depended on seasonally low water on the marl prairies.

But the marl prairies are now either too dry or too wet, and wading birds are forced to feed in the central Everglades. When the water depth approaches ten inches, it is too high for the tactile feeders. In contrast, the population of great egrets in the Everglades has not appreciably changed since the 1930s. Great egrets, which are not dependent on prey density and can feed alone, are doing fine in the degraded wetlands, dining on a wide variety of food, from salamanders and frogs to snakes and baby alligators to fish. Consequently the health of their population is not a performance measure for restoration.

The predrainage Everglades was like a huge grocery store where shelves were always restocked. In the modern version, entire aisles are deserted. Although more than twenty-three thousand pairs of white ibis nested in 2000 in the central Everglades, food in the conservation areas goes quickly, and colonies with chicks often collapse. The solution is simple, Ogden says: if you send more freshwater down Shark Slough you will flood the marl prairies and rejuvenate the coastal mangrove-lined creeks.

But scientists are split on exactly how much water should be put back into the Everglades. One camp, which consists mostly of biologists and hydrologists from Everglades National Park, insists that anything less than 80 percent of historical water-flows will be insufficient to kick-start the ecosystem on its road back to health. The current plan calls for about 70 percent of those flows to be spread out across the Everglades. "But it isn't as if you get 70 percent of the biological functions back with 70 percent of the water," says Tom Van Lent, a hydrologist with Everglades National Park. On the basis of computer modeling, park scientists have determined that 80 to 90 percent of the historical water volume is necessary to trigger conditions that would be favorable to the marl prairies, the southern estuaries, and nesting wading birds.

Other scientists, mostly from the Army Corps of Engineers and the South Florida Water Management District, contend that less water will be adequate as long as certain depths are restored in most of the decimated parts of the ecosystem. Given that half the original Everglades has been swallowed up by houses, macadam roads, and sugarcane, these scientists say that the Everglades ecosystem cannot absorb the same amount of water it did a hundred years ago. Recent studies by the Environmental Protection Agency, which reveal substantial peat loss in the drier parts of the Everglades, seem to back up their claim. "Our information shows that these areas have lost 39 to 69 percent of their soil," says Dan Scheidt, a senior scientist with the EPA.

The construction of levees and the slightly flatter landscape—owing to the loss of peat—changes the whole water equation, says Lorraine Heisler, a biologist with the United States Fish and Wildlife Service. "We can put all the water back in there, but with a different topography, we're not going to have the same watershed," she says. "It's like restoring a river in a different channel." The impact of the extra water would be greatest on the eroded central Everglades, north of the park, in WCA 2, where 90 percent of the tree islands stressed by unnaturally deep water have already drowned. To get the Everglades to start making peat again and build the land back up naturally will take centuries.

The national park staff contends that CERP fell short in two ways: first, the volume and timing of water delivery to downstream estuaries does not mimic the computer model that shows natural conditions; second, there are still too many levees and canals in the conservation areas that will obstruct flow. Today Shark Slough carries less than 50 percent of its original volume of water. Modified Water Delivery, part of the 1989 Everglades Expansion Act and currently under construction, will increase Shark Slough's flow to about 65 percent. CERP bumps it up to 70 percent. The park's Bob Johnson is quick to point out that Modified Water Delivery costs three hundred million dollars, while CERP costs eight billion dollars. "We're not getting the bang for our buck with CERP," says Johnson. "Clearly, the focus is not on the downstream estuaries because the incremental improvement over Modified Water Delivery is not that great."

During CERP's initial planning phase two basic restoration strategies were proposed. The first was to identify the priority areas in the Everglades (for instance the national park) and plan a restoration model that maximizes the benefits to these areas, even at the expense of other parts of the system (such as the water conservation areas). The second strategy, the one that was ultimately selected, plans for maximum benefits uniformly across the system. With the first approach you might get 90 to 100 percent restoration of the national park but only 60 percent in the central Everglades. The second approach might give you 70 percent across the entire system. For Shark Slough, that means the difference between a flowage of seven thousand cubic feet of water per second and the approximately fifty-five hundred cubic feet the current plan will deliver.

"The national park was the Lone Ranger during the conceptual stages of CERP," says Ogden. "Dick Ring [then superintendent] thought he could get what he wanted for the park without bringing them in as science partners. I don't think Dick trusted the multiagency democratic process. He didn't want to risk his cards to a strong science consensus process." Mike Collins, appointed by Governor Jeb Bush to be chairman of the governing board of the South Florida Water Management District, called Ring an "unbelievably corrosive individual" and railed against what he called the "territorial imperative" of Everglades National Park managers. During the initial planning phase a single team of scientists evaluated the water conservation areas and the national park. Members of the team were mostly from the park staff. "After a month or two, it became obvious that the only way we could get equal treatment for both areas was to set up two teams," says Ogden.

National park officials argue that water levels in the central and northern Everglades were originally deeper than presumed and that restoration targets are not deep enough. "From a scientific point of view," says Ogden, "pumping extra water into the Everglades causes as many problems as it solves." Nonetheless, the park's concerns have not gone unheard: the Army Corps of Engineers has agreed to consider adding more water to the restoration plan, which park biologists say will get them closer to the necessary 80 percent.

Though Steve Davis and Bob Johnson offer differing prescriptions for fixing the Everglades, both have long been enchanted by the wilds of subtropical Florida. When the veteran scientists are asked to name the image that best expresses their fondness for the Everglades, both identify water, not wildlife. Davis, of the water management district, recalls racing a monster thunderhead back toward Florida Bay after watching the sky blacken over Cape Sable one afternoon. Johnson, of the national park, speaks of shutting off his airboat and sitting in the rain, alone, at peace in the middle of a sawgrass marsh. But water, the thread that binds heaven and earth, also separates these two scientists.

Steve Davis helped lay the groundwork for Everglades restoration by coediting (along with John Ogden) *Everglades: The Ecosystem and Its Restoration,* a tome that featured the work of fifty-seven scientists representing twenty-five agencies and universities. When the book was published in 1994, restoration efforts were bogged down in lawsuits and scientific turf battles. The book helped resolve many of those disputes, issuing a clarion call for restoration. It also articulated the basis for former Secretary of the Interior Bruce Babbit's "ecosystem approach" to solving environmental problems.

After completing the text, Davis worked with farmers, politicians, and fellow scientists to help build support for Everglades restoration. "We began holding workshops on everything in the book," said Davis. In essence, he added, "that compilation was the latest science on the Everglades, and it wound up being the basis for all the policy and management meetings that led to the restoration plan."

Bob Johnson, while no less passionate an advocate for the Everglades, nearly derailed the restoration plan shortly after it was unveiled in October 1999. As Everglades National Park's chief scientist, Johnson claimed in a counterplan that the park was getting the short end of the deal, because not enough water was going to be returned to its ailing marshes and estuaries. The pronouncement caught nearly everyone off guard, including Davis.

For months, facing scathing criticism, Johnson called attention to the park's most pressing need: more water for its parched habitat. The way to move that water, claimed Johnson, was through the marsh, not through canals. He asserted that a greater depth upstream in Water Conservation Area 3 was needed to push more water into the estuaries. "We have a mandate to keep the natural ecosystem intact. But we're just as concerned with what's happening north of the Park." Because there is a correlation between pumping massive amounts of water from the canefields and chronic flooding in Water Conservation Area 3, Johnson believes that tree islands drown because both state and federal policies keep the Everglades Agricultural Area dry. "The Everglades is one watershed, and you can't manage the Park without looking at the entire system."

Johnson is pushing hard to remove as many barriers as possible, to let the Everglades flow more freely. The Tamiami Trail, for instance, a crossstate highway opened in 1928, chokes off Shark Slough, blocking the flow of its water into the southern Everglades and separating Water Conservation Area 3 from Everglades National Park. The Trail itself is a levee, called L-29. To keep water moving south into the national park, the Corps of Engineers has built four gates, each with six gated spillways that both Davis and Johnson agree are not enough to either drain the flooded central Everglades or rehydrate the park itself.

CERP will transform portions of a thirty-mile stretch of the Tamiami Trail into a series of bridges and causeways. Scientists will create hydrological models to determine how much roadbed to remove. "Unfortunately, it won't be all thirty miles," says Davis. "It's too costly. But when we're through we'll have complete hydrologic connection." Yet Johnson contends that hydrologic reconnection may not be ecological reconnection. "Engineers want the hydrologic equivalent of making the Tamiami Trail disappear," says Johnson. "But what does it mean to remove the effect of the road versus actually removing the road? You've solved the hydrologic problem, but what about the ecological problems?" The national park, of course, wants ecological reconnection—the full movement of energy, the full movement of animals, the full movement of organic matter through the water column from one side to the other. Engineers suggest building six one-thousand-foot bridges, for approximately $30 million; the national park prefers an eleven-mile causeway priced at $160 million. Describing his ideal vision of restoration, Johnson says, "In our minds you have to have a very strong justification to leave any levees and canals inside public land."

In response to Johnson's concerns, the hydrologists reexamined their plan and found for the ecosystem an additional 245,000 acre-feet of water that was being lost to tide through the area's network of canals in Broward and Palm Beach counties. Concerns over the quality, storage, and transportation of the extra water prohibit returning it to the Everglades immediately. "It's a changed system," says Davis. "We have 100 percent of the rainfall collecting on 50 percent of the land. Because of soil subsidence deeper water would drown tree islands. If we can restore peat, we can gradually restore the depths and heads of water."

Although the restoration of peat will take centuries, there is at least a commitment to try. To many advocates, this means a vastly improved plan. "Johnson's dogged persistence ensured that the southern part of the Everglades, including the national park, received its fair share of water, which was the original intent of the plan," says Mark Kraus.

Davis and Johnson admit that because of a deadline for submitting the restoration plan to Congress, the blueprint was cobbled together quickly. "Restoration is a process, not a product," says Davis. "I'm not defending the plan we have, but the longer we wait the more problems we'll create. Declines are still going on. We're losing sloughs, we're losing birds, we're losing just about everything that's a performance measure. I just want to get started." Johnson agrees, but he doesn't want the sense of urgency to be used as an excuse not to do the best restoration possible.

The indicator species that most worries Ogden is the Cape Sable seaside sparrow. In the 1920s the sparrows nested in the brackish marshes of Cape Sable. Several years ago when Ogden visited the old colony sites he discovered that open marshes had ceded to dense tangles of black mangrove, the result of rising sea level, hurricane storm surges, and canals siphoning away freshwater. As conditions changed, the birds abandoned Cape Sable. They were first reported on the southern marl prairies in the 1950s, where their nests are built close to the ground in clumps of *Muhlenbergia* grass. "The sparrows," says Ogden, "may be running out of options."

For restoration to succeed on an ecosystemwide basis, the duration of flooding on the marl prairies must increase to a period of six to nine months from the current one to two months. Muhly grass itself is an artifact of drainage and may vanish when CERP lengthens the hydroperiod on the prairies. Biologist Taylor Alexander, who had surveyed the region in the 1930s and 1940s, first sighted muhly grass in the Everglades in the late 1940s. Indeed, Cape Sable seaside sparrows were fortunate that muhly grass arrived on the marl prairies when it did.

During the 1990s, the sparrow controversy that pitted the Miccosukee Indians, whose land north of the Tamiami Trail was flooded, against Everglades National Park, where parts of the park were either too dry or too wet—often simultaneously—grew to include other adversaries: the Miami–Dade County farm bureau against the state, the park and the state against the residents of the 8.5 Square Mile Area. A pair of dueling sparrow biologists, one representing the Miccosukee, the other, the park service, regularly issued press releases denouncing each other's findings.

In 1999, when litigation in the controversy had become common, the American Ornithological Union was called in to mediate. Unfortunately and unintentionally, the increased volume of water that will be sent down Shark Slough may eliminate the debate. "In twenty-five years, if muhly grass disappears, where will the sparrow go?" Ogden laments.

What the Everglades needs is a King Solomon to consider all the water politics—the encased self-interests—and tease out the trade-offs. "Everyone wants their piece of the system to be fixed now," says Bob Pace, a biologist with the U.S. Fish and Wildlife Service. "But it's not easy to please everyone." In the end success will be measured by how well the ecosystem and all its creatures bounce back.

On an airboat, under a wide sky and a blazing sun, I close my eyes and imagine that it is late January 2050—about a dozen years after the target date for completion of Everglades restoration. Shoals of tiny fish gather in depressions on the marl prairies, waiting. Tens of thousands of puddles. Millions of fish. Day by day, the pools shrink, and the fish—mostly gambusia, tiny sunfish, marsh killifish, least killifish, sailfin mollies, elegant dorsal fins rippling like curtains in a breeze—wait for death, pinioned by lances of sunlight or speared by squadrons of the birds I picture gathering here each morning. Along the apron of the Everglades time has always been measured by the presence or absence of water. Now in 2050 it's the middle of the dry season, and this bumper crop of ill-fated fish, crayfish, and grass shrimp, themselves three or four years in the making, may well trigger one of North America's most awesome pageants: a convocation of wading birds.

Add water and stir.

WALT DINEEN, South Florida Water Management
District scientist, 1994

18 Downstream

In 1973 Archie Carr began his book *The Everglades,* for Time-Life's American Wilderness series, searching for the source of the watershed. Using discordant maps and native intuition, he settled on Turkey Lake, a small body of water at the head of central Florida's chain of lakes, as "the real beginnings of the Everglades." The lake lies in the drainage of Shingle Creek, the northernmost tributary of the Kissimmee-Okeechobee-Everglades drainage basin. Following Carr's lead, in 1995 I drive to Turkey Lake Park to see the birthplace for myself.

The entrance attendant, a buoyant woman who is not a connoisseur of Orange County geography, unflinchingly says, "Nope. No. No Everglades here." I ask where I can find Shingle Creek. "Shingle Creek? Never heard of it." I head in the direction of the lake, following a loggerhead shrike from orange tree to orange tree, past pocket gopher mounds, which rise from the lawn like formidable anthills. Leaving the bird behind, I enter an oak woods and emerge on the shore of Turkey Lake. A bass fisherman casting a plug into the grassy surface tells me that during high water Shingle Creek begins as a spring west of the lake and that, except for leaks in the limestone, Turkey Lake and Shingle Creek meet only during floods.

To see Shingle Creek I drive to the outskirts of Orlando, to an Aerobic Sewage Treatment Plant on McLeod Street. Here a thin, methane-reeking tributary passes through a culvert beneath the road. The creek unhinges my sense of natural order. Contrary to other wilderness watersheds in North America, which begin in snow-capped mountains or pristine lakes, the Everglades drainage begins in the suburbs and becomes wilder the farther it travels from its inauspicious source. Gambusia, however, find something to recommend the creek; they dimple the surface like raindrops. A green heron and a great egret wait with glacial patience for the fish to swim by.

Six miles south, on the north side of Route 482, Shingle Creek is wider, blacker, and banked by cypress. As if to proclaim the creek's healthier appearance, a great blue heron poises in midstream. For the next eleven miles Shingle Creek keeps to itself, curling through wetlands and pastures well away from roads. Outside Kissimmee, where strip development blends miles of commerce, Shingle Creek passes under Space Coast Highway. Not far away, a grotesque pink building, the Shell Factory Outlet, announces the week's bargains.

Several miles south of Space Coast Highway is the Pleasant Hill Elementary School. Three sandhill cranes roam the school yard, and overhead is a Snoopy blimp. Nearby, Shingle Creek unloads into Lake Tohopekaliga, the northernmost of the big lakes in the Kissimmee Valley. A state hydrologist who is working near the mouth of Shingle Creek tells me that two other tributaries, Boggy Creek and Canoe Creek, drain lakes and cypress swamps west of Turkey Lake and eventually empty into Lake Kissimmee. They are therefore part of the Everglades watershed. He also reiterates that Florida south of Orlando is one gigantic fossil sponge, where water seeps, leaks, and flows through punky limestone from one wetland to the next, making South Florida a family of marshes, swamps, and shallow lakes threaded together above and below the surface by creeks.

((((

River Woods, approximately seventy miles southeast of Lake Tohopekaliga, is the quintessential Kissimmee Valley housing development, a complex that rises from a former wetland. Here a pink-carpeted, excessively mirrored ranch house built by a bass-fishing retiree from Ohio becomes my temporary home. I am the guest of the new owner, the South Florida Water Management District. Recently purchased by eminent domain, River Woods sits on the old floodplain of the Kissimmee River, a good cast from a stagnant oxbow slated for resuscitation. When the water management district reconnects the river to its oxbow, the house will be torn down. Until then, visiting scientists and journalists sleep on the moss-soft carpet.

The grounds around River Woods are sandy, the grass sparse. Several live oaks festooned with Spanish moss flank the driveway. Resembling impressions made by big raindrops, the funnel-traps of ant lions, a predatory larval insect that captures unsuspecting ants, indent the sand. A cardinal flashes past, appearing all the more vivid against the cooler greens and blues that dominate wild Florida. Beyond the front yard, on a wooden dock, a fisherman wets a line. In his bucket are a pickerel, a largemouth bass, and a bluegill.

In 1971, as part of the Central and Southern Florida Flood Control Project, the Army Corps of Engineers redirected the flow of the Kissimmee River, Lake Okeechobee's largest tributary. The shallow river, which had wandered a mile east or west for every mile it flowed south, was straightened into a fifty-two-mile-long, 30-foot-deep canal. Renamed c-38, and nicknamed "The Ditch" by environmentalists, the Kissimmee project proved to be an ecological fiasco. Forty-five thousand acres of swamplands withered, causing a decline in evaporation, which accounts for 70 to 90 percent of South Florida's summer rainfall, and increasing the ferocity of droughts. Before the death of the swamps, more than a million ducks wintered on the Kissimmee. One January day in 1985, a biologist surveying the river tallied just eight ducks.

Now, after years of lobbying by environmental organizations, the Corps and the water management district have begun to restore approximately forty miles of the Kissimmee's original oxbows, including the one down the road from River Woods. Neighboring cattle ranchers, who stand to lose thousands of acres of pasture, oppose the plan.

The Kissimmee Valley drains about three thousand square miles of wet prairie and pineland, the heart of central Florida's cattle industry. Between 1958 and 1972, more than half of the unimproved pasture was drained and planted in imported Bahia grass at the expense of native forage. After a series of big freezes in central Florida in the earlier 1980s, citrus plantations moved into the region from ridge towns to the north, places called Winter Haven and

Frostproof. Land that once spawned bobcats and sandhill cranes now grows cattle and oranges.

A dozen miles northeast of River Woods lies the National Audubon Society's Ordway-Whittell Kissimmee Prairie Sanctuary, a vestige of the former valley, eight thousand acres of wire grass interspersed with oak and cabbage palm hammocks, marshes, and ponds. This island in a sea of exotic grasses is what remains of what was once the extensive Kissimmee Prairie. The prairie existed because of wildfire. The lightning that comes with the wet season would torch a knot of wire grass and fire would spread, killing shrubs and small trees that would have otherwise choked the prairie. Steam and smoke would sprout in its wake.

Scott Hedges, a graduate of the University of Maine and then the director of the Kissimmee Prairie Preserve, waits for me at the front gate. Hedges sets controlled burns at the refuge and afterward monitors population trends of grasshopper sparrows and eastern meadowlarks, both prairie species favored by periodic fire. After a burn flowers bloom in profusion, as they must have in 1513, when Spanish explorer Ponce de León named North America's most familiar appendage *La Florida,* "Land of Flowers." Ponce de León did not find the Fountain of Youth, nor did he find streets of gold in Florida; instead he found only the fierce and proud Calusa, who mortally wounded him on a subsequent visit.

The preserve is seventy-two feet above sea level. Although this is not an ear-popping altitude, it is high enough to drain water away from the coast toward the Kissimmee River, which cuts a swath through the valley, ten miles to the west. We get in Hedge's swamp buggy and drive down the sanctuary's dirt road, where bleached horse conch shells poke above the surface. The shells are an affirmation that central Florida was beneath the sea only a hundred thousand years ago.

We veer off the shell-pocked road onto an off-road-vehicle trail. Muddy puddles fill the ruts. Hedges is six feet, eight inches tall, raw-boned, and full of conversation. His is a one-man show. There are no facilities at the prairie, not even an office. Besides lighting fires and tracking the fortunes of song-birds, he guides school groups, creates an annual budget and administers the funds, testifies at local restoration hearings, repairs fences, and cozies up to the neighbors. The local residents, all rural Floridians, were at first suspicious of the preserve when the National Audubon Society purchased the land in 1981, but now, in part because of Hedges's easy-going style, they have accepted the society as part of their community.

We park, and Hedges strides west toward a shallow pond. Tufts of sun-dried wire grass and patches of fire-stunted palmettos meet the eastern horizon. The lee side of the pond, beyond the western shore, holds a fire shadow of oak and palm, an artifact of the prevailing wind. Repeatedly, wind-driven flames have passed around the pond and the band of trees, converged with one another, and moved on, scorching the prairie. The pond is spattered with water lilies and spike rush. Frogs splash at our approach. Half a dozen oval, plate-sized muskrat lodges accent the water. These are the homes of the round-tailed muskrat, a small rodent endemic to Florida and southern Georgia. Each lodge is a tight weave of sedges and rushes fastened to dead stems. Water laps the foundation. I break open a lodge. No one's home. Fine grass lines the interior cavity, which is snugly surrounded by three-inch-thick walls, an ideal nursery for infant muskrats. Two escape hatches lead below the surface.

The soft mud in our path displays a montage of animal tracks: bobcat, spotted skunk, striped skunk, round-tailed muskrat, gray fox, various species of frogs, beetles, and snails. A young water moccasin, its yellow-tipped tail twitching to lure a frog within striking distance, lies coiled along a lane of tracks. The spoor of wild hog, descended from feral Spanish pigs that have been rooting up Florida for more than four centuries, penetrates the mud. To control the beasts, Hedges contracts with twins from the local high school, large boys from the cheerleading squad. The twins run down the hogs, wrestle them into submission, slit their throats, and take pork home for their family's table.

Down the road from the Audubon preserve, Hedges introduces me to several native Floridians who are harvesting and grinding sugarcane by hand. I pitch in and quickly tire. These lifelong residents hunt the Kissimmee Valley, fish Okeechobee, grow their own vegetables and fruit, make molasses, attend revivals, and are as much a manifestation of unalloyed Florida as the sandhill cranes that bugle in the distance. They wish the Army Corps of Engineers would go home. "Them engineers shoulda left the Kissimmee alone in the first place, and they sure as hell can't fix it now. The government don't live here," says one, and a half a dozen wizened heads nod. Yet they have a canal when they need a river, and only the Corps is capable of undoing a problem as grand as the one it created.

Two shaggy, half-grown wild hogs caught as piglets lounge in a pen in the backyard. Like Hansel and Gretel they are being groomed for the pot. The hogs are rough-hewn, more like European wild boars than domestic pigs; their russet tones are dappled with black and white. Although the state manages hogs as game animals, most regional biologists prefer a swine-free wild Florida because the animals uproot young plants and trample vegetation. It is unlikely their wish will come true.

Florida is so flat that United States Geological Survey topographic maps of the state are marked in five-foot contour intervals. If traditional twenty-foot contours were used, only two intervals would appear along the entire length of the Kissimmee River, which drops only forty feet in as many miles between lakes Kissimmee and Okeechobee, and none would mark the Everglades. Leaving Hedges and his neighbors, I visit a Kissimmee River restoration site, where plugs and weirs along c-38 send water back into a series of oxbows. The force of the water pushes the accumulated debris out of the oxbows and into c-38, filling sections of the canal. The estimated price for restoring less than half the river is five hundred million dollars—fourteen times what it cost to obliterate it.

On the river late in the afternoon, it is sunny and warm. Clouds drift by, silhouetting the foraging flight of thousands of tree swallows come south for the winter. My guide, Al Goldstein, head of the water management district's Okeechobee office, fires his airboat, and we head north on c-38, a straight, wide aquatic highway, then enter a functioning oxbow, where water can rise over the banks and spill across the surrounding wetlands. An alligator slides off a fallen cypress. Moss-covered oaks line the higher banks. Verdant marsh plants spread from the shore. At the far end of the oxbow, after several serpentine miles of travel, our beautiful twisting, turning, curving course represents a net gain of about three hundred yards north.

《《《

If peninsular Florida were the outstretched neck of a turtle, Lake Okeechobee, the state's most recognizable natural feature, would be its troubled blue eye: 733 square miles of freshwater fermenting in a shallow, wedge-shaped depression inland from West Palm Beach. In the late 1920s, a pair of hurricanes whipped the lake into a froth, overwhelming an earthen dam that protected towns along its southern margins. More than twenty-five hundred people died, and many more were left homeless. In response the Corps cinched Okeechobee behind a lime-rock levee called Herbert Hoover Dike. Before that, the lake would expand during wet years to perhaps 850 square miles and shrink during a drought. Now a stand of cypress and red maple a half mile north of the lake marks the former northern shoreline; to the south, the opposite shore, which once merged into the Everglades, has become part of the Everglades Agricultural Area.

Like the Everglades, Okeechobee is relatively young, about sixty-three hundred years old, but unlike the Everglades it is eutrophic, a shallow, nutrient-rich broth with little dissolved oxygen. Formerly, when water overflowed the lake's southern rim during flood years, the pulse of nutrients fed the swamp and the northern glades, growing sawgrass ten feet tall and building a peat bed twelve feet deep. Forty years ago the lake had such large hatches of mayflies, a species whose aquatic larvae require sandy bottoms and clean, oxygen-rich water, that snowplows were used to push their delicate cadavers off nearby roads. But Okeechobee was given a death sentence when the Kissimmee River became "the Ditch," and the agricultural area began to back-pump fertilized water into the lake. Today mayflies have been replaced by pollution-tolerant segmented worms, which account for 80 percent of the bottom fauna. I scoop a handful of muck and watch small, dark worms writhe between my fingers.

Thirty-five miles southwest, along the lake's western shore, an Australian import transforms the littoral zone. A jungle of melaleuca saplings, their white papery bark peeling and glinting in the morning light, thrive in the altered wetlands. Well mannered while at home in Australia, the fast-growing and water-hungry tree was imported to Florida in 1906 as an ornamental and was later planted to help drain the Everglades. In the late 1930s the Army Engineers planted melaleuca lakeward along the southwest periphery of Hoover Dike as a hedge against wind and wave erosion. Prospering in the absence of natural enemies—Australian insects and microbes—melaleuca now infests more than half a million acres in South Florida, forty-seven thousand of which support little else, and has spread across a quarter of the lake's hundred-thousand-acre littoral zone. It grows everywhere, tolerates flood, drought, and fire, flowers up to five times a year, casts millions of airborne seeds when disturbed, and sprouts when felled. Not surprisingly, the control of melaleuca has become one of restoration's principal goals.

By airboat from the town dock in Moore Haven it takes less than ten minutes to cross several miles of spike rush and water lilies to the edge of the melaleuca wall. This morning the air temperature is forty-six degrees, and the wind hustles out of the northeast at twenty-five miles per hour. The lake hisses in my face. I dress optimistically—shorts, sandals, T-shirt under a windbreaker, which sticks to my body like Saran Wrap.

Escorted by representatives of four government agencies, our flotilla roars up to three Guatemalan laborers wearing waders and baseball caps in the cool, waist-deep water, their machetes hacking melaleucas. Chop . . . chop . . . chop—the metronome of the morning. The hackers' foreman, a Florida native, serves as interpreter and is the representative of the company that was hired by the district to tackle the lake's melaleuca problem. "I'm their nursemaid and mother. I take them to the doctor, patch them up. I'm like a drill sergeant in the army. I'm all they need, except their paycheck on Friday, and somebody else sends that to them. We have no problems physical or spiritual." I ask the foreman what the laborers' hourly wage is. "None of your business."

When a sufficient number of trees have been girdled, the workers paint the exposed cambium blue with Arsenal, a biodegradable herbicide originally developed as an antihistamine. Beyond the cutters looms a dark wall of melaleuca. Thus far, two crews of six to eight men have treated two and a half million trees and pulled five and a half million seedlings on Lake Okeechobee alone.

Handling melaleuca is the most laborious and tedious part of ecological restoration. Yet if left unchecked the tree would turn much of the Everglades into a dark, aromatic woodland. To keep the severed branches from sprouting, the men carefully drape them in the standing trees. In November 1994, when Hurricane Gordon brought eight inches of rain, Lake Okeechobee rose two and a half feet, and any of the pruned branches that had a leaf or two touching the raised water grew roots. A sprig with just twelve leaves can flower. "How long does it take to reach flowering age?" I ask no one in particular. "About fifteen minutes," comes a reply from three airboats to my right.

The good news is that melaleuca seeds are viable for only a year, and high water greatly reduces successful germination—further encouragement for those promoting the restoration of natural water flows in the lake basin and across the remaining Everglades. Even so, Dan Thayer, the water district's director of vegetation management, hopes only to contain this invader. Eradicating it is out of the question.

The foreman, his deeply tanned face compressed as he turns toward the sun, announces that Florida is losing land because developers convince politicians that marshes degraded by melaleuca are suitable for drainage and development rather than restoration. "Half the state legislature calls Havana home, and the other half is from New York. What do they know?" he says, arms spinning. "Too many damn people here. There should not have been anybody living south of Saint Petersburg and Fort Pierce. Very little down there besides fishing along the coast. Interior-wise you can raise a few cows here and yonder—beef cows, scrub cows. That's it. People come down here and they say, 'Oh, that's a pretty site. I think I'll build here.' Wouldn't you ask in a state as flat as Florida where the high floodplain was before you built?"

"What would your solution be?" I ask, knowing the foreman has given the subject some thought.

"If you shut the water off right here at the end of the lake, everybody would head north. They wouldn't have no water to drink, or flush johns, or mix bourbon, or nothing. Then I'd build a Great Wall, 350 miles long from Fernandina to Pensacola, across the Florida state line. There'd be two types of entries: for five hundred dollars you get a driver's license and go to Disney World; or for two dollars and fifty cents you get a fishing license and room to roam."

Bibliography

SCIENCES

Ackerman, Diane. *Moon by Whale Light.* New York: Random House, 1991.

Allen, Robert Porter. *The Roseate Spoonbill.* New York: Dover, 1966.

Altman, Mara B. "Nurseries of the Sea." *Sanctuary* 30, no. 1 (1990).

Alvarez, Ken. *Twilight of the Panther.* Sarasota: Myakka River Publishing, 1993.

Ashton, Ray E., Jr., and Patricia Sawyer Ashton. *Handbook of Reptiles and Amphibians of Florida.* Part 1, *The Snakes.* Miami: Windward Publishing, 1981.

———. *Handbook of Reptiles and Amphibians of Florida.* Part 2, *Lizards, Turtles, and Crocodilians.* Miami: Windward Publishing, 1985.

———. *Handbook of Reptiles and Amphibians of Florida.* Part 3, *The Amphibians.* Miami: Windward Publishing, 1988.

Austin, Elizabeth S., ed. *Frank M. Chapman in Florida: His Journals and Letters.* Gainesville: University of Florida Press, 1967.

Bancroft, G. Thomas. "Status and Conservation of Wading Birds in the Everglades." *American Birds* 43, no. 5 (1989).

Bancroft, G. Thomas, Allan M. Strong, Richard J. Sawicki, Wayne Hoffman, and Susan D. Jewell. "Relationships among Wading Birds' Foraging Patterns, Colony Locations, and Hydrology in the Everglades." In *Everglades: The Ecosystem and Its Restoration,* edited by S. M. Davis and J. C. Ogden. Delray Beach, Fla.: St. Lucie Press, 1994.

Barbour, Thomas. *That Vanishing Eden: A Naturalist's Florida.* Boston: Little, Brown, 1944.

Bartram, William. *The Travels of William Bartram.* New York: Macy-Masius Publishers, 1928.

Blatchley, W. S. *My Nature Nook; or, Notes on the Natural History of the Vicinity of Dunedin, Florida.* Indianapolis: Nature Publishing, 1931.

————. *In Days Agone: Notes on the Fauna and Flora of Subtropical Florida in the Days When Most of Its Area Was a Primeval Wilderness.* Indianapolis: Nature Publishing, 1932.

Beard, Daniel. *Wildlife Reconnaissance: Everglades National Park Project.* Washington: U.S. Department of the Interior, National Park Service, October 1938.

Beissinger, Steven R. "Nest Failure and Demography of the Everglades Kite." End-of-year report. Washington, D.C.: U.S. Fish and Wildlife Service, Endangered Species Division, 1981.

————. "Nest Failure and Demography of the Snail Kite: Effects of Everglades Water Management." End-of-the-year-report. Washington, D.C.: U.S. Fish and Wildlife Service, Endangered Species Division, 1983.

————. "Demography, Environmental Uncertainty, and the Evolution of Mate Desertion." *Ecology* 67, no. 6 (1986).

————. "Anisogamy Overcome: Female Strategies in Snail Kites." *American Naturalist* 129, no. 4 (1987).

————. "A Faithful, Fickle Hawk: The Fluctuating Everglades Influences the Nesting Behavior of an Endangered Bird." *Natural History* 97, no. 1 (1988).

Beissinger, Steven R., and Noel F. R. Snyder. "Mate Desertion in the Snail Kite." *Animal Behavior* 35 (1987).

Bell, C. Ritchie, and Bryan J. Taylor. *Florida Wildflowers and Roadside Plants.* Chapel Hill: Laurel Hill Press, 1982.

Bennetts, Robert E., Michael W. Callopy, and James A. Rodgers Jr. "The Snail Kite in the Florida Everglades: A Food Specialist in a Changing Environment." In *Everglades: The Ecosystem and Its Restoration,* edited by S. M. Davis and J. C. Ogden. Delray Beach, Fla.: St. Lucie Press, 1994.

Bennetts, Robert E., and Wiley M. Kitchens. "Estimation and Environmental Correlates of Survival and Dispersal of Snail Kites in Florida." Annual progress report. Prepared for U.S. Department of the Interior, Fish and Wildlife Service, and U.S. Department of the Interior, National Park Service, Everglades National Park, 1993.

Bent, Arthur Cleveland. *Life Histories of North American Marsh Birds.* New York: Dover, 1963.

Bernardino, Frank S., Jr., and George Dalrymple. "Seasonal Activity and Road Mortality of the Snakes of the Pa-hay-okee Wetlands of Everglades National Park, U.S.A." *Biological Conservation* 62, no. 2 (1992).

Bidlingmayer, W. L. "The Effect of Moonlight on the Flight Activity of Mosquitoes." *Ecology* 45, no. 1 (1964).

Bidlingmayer, W. L., and D. G. Hem. "Sugar Feeding by Florida Mosquitoes." *Mosquito News* 33, no. 4 (1973).

Bottcher, A. B., and F. T. Izuno, eds. *Everglades Agricultural Area (EAA): Water, Soil, Crop, and Environmental Management.* Gainesville: University Press of Florida, 1994.

Brockman, C. Frank. *Trees of North America: A Guide to Field Identification.* New York: Golden Press, 1968.

Buck, Sharon V. "Florida's Herp Trade: A Collector's Paradise . . . and a Land Exploited." *Reptile and Amphibian,* no. 45 (January–February 1997).

Campell, Howard W. "Ecological or Phylogenetic Interpretation of Crocodilian Nesting Habits." *Nature* 238, no. 5364 (1972).

Carpenter, Betsy. "A Panther by Another Name." *U.S. News and World Report,* 17 June 1991.

Carr, Archie Fairly, Jr. *A Contribution to the Herpetology of Florida.* Gainesville: University of Florida Publications, 1940.

———. *A Naturalist in Florida: A Celebration of Eden.* New Haven: Yale University Press, 1994.

Catesby, Mark. *The Natural History of Carolina, Florida, and the Bahama Islands.* 2 vols. 1754. Reprint, Savannah: Beehive Press, 1974.

Chabreck, Robert H. 1971. "The Foods and Feeding Habits of Alligators from Fresh and Saline Environments in Louisiana." In *Proceedings of the 25th Annual Conference of the Southeastern Association of Game and Fish Commissioners.* 1971.

Chenoweth, Michael. "Evapotranspiration: The Forgotten Key to Everglades Restoration." Position paper of Friends of the Everglades, 2001.

Coe, Ernest F. *The Story of the Everglades National Park Project.* Prepared for Everglades National Park. Coconut Grove, Fla., 1950.

Colt, George Howe. "The Frail Future of an Alligator Hole." *Life,* September 1995.

Cope, Edward D. *Crocodilians, Lizards and Snakes.* Washington: U.S. National Museum, 1900.

Craighead, Frank C. *Orchids and Other Air Plants of the Everglades National Park.* Coral Gables: University of Miami Press, 1963.

———. *The Trees of South Florida: The Natural Environments and Their Succession.* Vol. 1. Coral Gables: University of Miami Press, 1971.

———. "Hammocks of South Florida." In *Environments of South Florida: Present and Past,* edited by Patrick J. Gleason. Memoir 2. Miami: Miami Geological Society, 1974.

Cruickshank, Helen Gere, ed. *John and William Bartram's America: Selections from the Writings of the Philadelphia Naturalists.* New York: Devin-Adair, 1957.

Curnutt, John L., Audrey L. Mayer, Thomas M. Brooks, Lisa Manne, Oron L. Bass Jr., D. Martin Fleming, and Stuart L. Pimm. *Population Dynamics of the Endangered Cape Seaside Sparrow.* South Florida Biologic Research Center Special Publication. Everglades National Park, 1998.

Dalrymple, George H. "The Herpetofauna of Long Pine Key, Everglades National Park, in Relation to Vegetation and Hydrology." In *Proceedings of Symposium Management of Amphibians, Reptiles, and Small Mammals in North America, Flagstaff, Ariz., July 19–21, 1988.*

Dalrymple, George H., William F. Loftus, and Frank S. Bernardino Jr., eds. *Wildlife in the Everglades and Latin American Wetlands: Abstracts of the Proceedings of the First Everglades National Park Symposium, Held in Miami, February 25–March 1, 1985.* [Miami, Fla.]: Florida International University, the State University of Florida at Miami, 1988.

Davis, John H., Jr. *The Natural Features of Southern Florida: Especially the Vegetation and the Everglades.* Tallahassee: Florida Geologic Survey, 1943.

Davis, Steven M. *Growth, Decomposition, and Nutrient Retention of Sawgrass and Cattail in the Everglades.* South Florida Water Management District Technical Publication 90-03. West Palm Beach, 1990.

Davis, Steven M., and John C. Ogden, eds. *Everglades: The Ecosystem and Its Restoration.* Delray Beach, Fla.: St. Lucie Press, 1994.

Day, Jonathan F. "Opportunistic Blood-Feeding on Egg-Laying Sea Turtles by Salt Marsh Mosquitoes." *Florida Entomologist* 66, no. 3 (1983).

———. "Epidemic Proportions." *Natural History* 100, no. 7 (1991).

Day, Jonathan F., and G. A. Curtis. "When It Rains, They Soar and That Makes *Culex nigripalpus* a Dangerous Mosquito." *American Entomologist,* fall 1995.

Day, Jonathan F., E. E. Storrs, L. M. Stark, A. L. Lewis, and S. Williams. "Antibodies to St. Louis Encephalitis Virus in Armadillos from Southern Florida." *Journal of Wildlife Disease* 31, no. 1 (1994).

DeAngelis, Donald L., and Peter S. White. "Ecosystems as Products of Spatially and Temporally Varying Driving Forces, Ecological Processes, and Landscapes: A Theoretical Perspective." In *Everglades: The Ecosystem and Its Restoration,* edited by S. M. Davis and J. C. Ogden. Delray Beach, Fla.: St. Lucie Press, 1994.

Deneen, Sally. "The Panther's Last Stand." *E Magazine,* September–October 1994.

Dimock, A. W. "The Florida Crocodile." *American Museum Journal* 18, no. 6 (1918).

Ditmars, Raymond L. *The Reptiles of North America.* Garden City, N.Y.: Doubleday, Doran, 1936.

Duever, Michael J., John E. Carlson, John F. Meeker, Linda C. Duever, Lance H. Gunderson, Lawrence A. Riopelle, Taylor R. Alexander, Ronald L. Myers, and Daniel P. Spangler. *The Big Cypress National Preserve.* New York: National Audubon Society, 1986.

Dunkle, Sidney W. *Dragonflies of the Florida Peninsula, Bermuda, and the Bahamas.* Gainesville: Scientific Publishers, 1989.

Dunson, A. William, and Frank J. Mazzotti. "Some Aspects of Water and Sodium Exchange of Freshwater Crocodilians in Fresh Water and Sea-water: Role of the Integument." *Comparative Biochemical Physiology* 90A, no. 3 (1988).

Edman, J. D. "Dragonflies Attracted to and Selectively Feeding on Concentrations of Mosquitoes." *Florida Entomologist* 57, no. 4 (1974).

———. "Host-Feeding Patterns of Florida Mosquitoes IV. Deinocerites." *Journal of Medical Entomology* 11, no. 1 (1974).

———. "Orientation of Some Florida Mosquitoes toward Small Vertebrates and Carbon Dioxide in the Field." *Journal of Medical Entomology* 15, no. 3 (1979).

———. "Biting the Hand That Feeds You." *Natural History* 100, no. 7 (1991).

Edman, John D., and W. L. Bidlingmayer. 1969. "Flight Capacity of Blood-Engorged Mosquitoes." *Mosquito News* 29, no. 3 (1969).

Edman, John D., and H. W. Kale II. "Host Behavior: Its Influence on the Feeding Success of Mosquitoes." *Annals of the Entomological Society of America* 64, no. 2 (1971).

Edman, John D., and D. J. Taylor. "*Culex nigripalpus*: Seasonal Shift in the Bird-Mammal Feeding Ratio in a Mosquito Vector of Human Encephalitis." *Science* 161, no. 3836 (1968).

Edman, John D., L. A. Webber, and H. W. Kale II. "Effect of Mosquito Density on the Interrelationship of Host Behavior and Mosquito Feeding Success." *American Journal of Tropical Medicine and Hygiene* 21, no. 4 (1972).

Edman, John D., L. A. Webber, and A. A. Schmid. "Effect of Host Defenses on the Feeding Pattern of *Culex nigripalpus* When Offered a Choice of Blood Sources." *Journal of Parasitology* 60, no. 5 (1974).

Ellis, Tamir M. "Tolerance of Sea Water by the American Crocodile, *Crocodylus acutus.*" *Journal of Herpetology* 15, no. 2 (1981).

"Everglades Ecosystem Restoration and the C & SF Project Restudy." Position paper. Everglades Coalition, 1998.

Ewan, Joseph, ed. *William Bartram: Botanical and Zoological Drawings, 1756–1788.* Philadelphia: American Philosophical Society, 1968.

Ewel, Katherine C. "Swamps." In *Ecosystems of Florida,* edited by Ronald L. Myers and John J. Ewel. Orlando: University of Central Florida Press, 1990.

Feduccia, Alan, ed. *Catesby's Birds of Colonial America.* Chapel Hill: University of North Carolina Press, 1985.

Fenneman, N. M. *Physiography of Eastern United States.* New York: McGraw-Hill, 1931.

Fergus, Charles. "The Florida Panther Verges on Extinction." *Science* 251, no. 4998 (1991).

———. *Swamp Screamer.* New York: North Point Press, 1996.

Fernald, Edward A., and Donald J. Patton. *Water Resources Atlas of Florida.* Tallahassee: Florida State University Press, 1984.

Florida Mosquito Control Handbook. Vero Beach: University of Florida Medical Entomological Laboratory, 1994.

Florida Panther (Felis concolor coryi) Recovery Plan. 2d rev. Atlanta: U.S. Fish and Wildlife Service, Southeast Region.

Fogarty, Michael J., and J. David Albury. "Late Summer Foods of Young Alligators in Florida." In *Proceedings of the 21st Annual Conference of the Southeastern Association of Game and Fish Commissioners,* 1967.

Foster, Melissa L., and Stephen R. Humphreys. "Use of Highway Underpasses by the Florida Panther and Other Wildlife." *Wildlife Society Bulletin* 23, no. 1 (1994).

Fourqurean, James W., Ronald D. Jones, and Joseph C. Zieman. "Process Influencing Water Column Nutrient Characteristics and Phosphorous Limitation of Phytoplankton Biomass in Florida Bay, Florida, U.S.A.: Inferences from Spatial Distribution." *Estuarine, Coastal and Shelf Science* 36 (1993).

Frank, J. H., and G. A. Curtis. "On the Bionomics of Bromeliad-Inhabiting Mosquitoes." Part 4, "Egg Mortality of *Wyeomyia vanduzeei* Caused by Rainfall." *Mosquito News* 37, no. 2 (1977).

Frank, J. H., G. A. Curtis, and H. T. Evans. "On the Bionomics of Bromeliad-Inhabiting Mosquitoes." Part 2, "The Relationship of Bromeliad Size to the Number of Immature *Wyeomyia vanduzeei* and *W. medioalbipes.*" *Mosquito News* 37, no. 2 (1977).

Frank, J. H., and G. F. O'Meara. "The Bromeliad *Catopsis berteroniana* Traps Terrestrial Arthropods but Harbors Wyeomyia Larvae." *Florida Entomologist* 67, no. 3 (1984).

Frederick, Peter C., Keith L. Bildstein, Bruce Fleury, and John Ogden. "Conservation of Large Nomadic Populations of White Ibises (*Eudocimus albus*) in the United States." *Conservation Biology* 10, no. 1 (1996).

Frederick, Peter C., and William F. Loftus. "Responses of Marsh Fishes and Breeding Wading Birds to Low Temperatures: A Possible Behavioral Link between Predator and Prey." *Estuaries* 16, no. 2 (1993).

Frederick, Peter C., and George V. N. Powell. "Nutrient Transport by Wading Birds in the Everglades." In *Everglades: The Ecosystem and Its Restoration,* edited by S. M. Davis and J. C. Ogden. Delray Beach, Fla.: St. Lucie Press, 1994.

Frederick, Peter C., and M. S. Spalding. "Factors Affecting Reproductive Success of Wading Birds (Ciconiiformes) in the Everglades Ecosystem." In *Everglades: The Ecosystem and Its Restoration,* edited by S. M. Davis and J. C. Ogden. Delray Beach, Fla.: St. Lucie Press, 1994.

Funk, Ben. "Hurricane!" *National Geographic* 158, no. 3 (1980).

Gaby, Ronald, Mark P. McMahon, Frank J. Mazzotti, W. Neil Gilles, and J. Ross Wilcox. "Ecology of a Population of *Crocodylus acutus* at a Power Plant Site in Florida." *Journal of Herpetology* 9, no. 2 (1985).

Gantz, Charlotte Orr. *A Naturalist in Southern Florida.* Coral Gables: University of Miami Press, 1971.

Gawlik, Dale E., ed. *1995 Summary and Mid-Season Wading Bird Status Report for the*

Everglades. South Florida Water Management District Publication 1, no. 1. West Palm Beach, 1995.

————. *1995 Summary and Late-Season Wading Bird Nesting Report for the Everglades.* South Florida Water Management District Publication 1, no. 2. West Palm Beach, 1995.

————. *South Florida Wading Bird Report.* South Florida Water Management District Publication 3, no. 1 West Palm Beach, 1997.

————. *South Florida Wading Bird Report.* South Florida Water Management District Publication 4, no. 1. West Palm Beach, 1998.

————. *South Florida Wading Bird Report.* South Florida Water Management District Publication 5, no. 1. West Palm Beach, 1999.

————. *South Florida Wading Bird Report.* South Florida Water Management District Publication 6, no. 1. West Palm Beach, 2000.

————. "The Effects of Prey Availability on the Feeding Tactics of Wading Birds." *Ecology* (forthcoming).

Gawlik, Dale E., and John C. Ogden, eds. *1996 Mid-Season Wading Bird Nesting Report for South Florida.* South Florida Water Management District Publication. West Palm Beach, 1996.

————. *1996 Late-Season Wading Bird Nesting Report for South Florida.* South Florida Water Management District Publication. West Palm Beach, 1996.

Gawlik, Dale E., and Deborah A. Rocque. "Avian Communities in Bayheads, Willowheads, and Sawgrass Marshes of the Central Everglades." *Wilson Bulletin* 110, no. 1 (1998).

Gentry, R. Cecil. "Hurricanes in South Florida." In *Environments of South Florida: Present and Past,* edited by Patrick J. Gleason. Memoir 2. Miami: Miami Geological Society, 1974.

George, Jean Craighead. *Everglades Wildguide.* Washington: U.S. Government Printing Office, 1972.

Gerberg, Eugene J., and Ross H. Arnett. *Florida Butterflies.* Baltimore: Natural Science Publications, 1989.

Gleason, H. A. *New Britton and Brown Illustrated Flora of the Northeastern United States and Adjacent Canada.* Vol. 1. Hafner Publishing Company for the New York Botanical Garden, 1963.

Gleason, Patrick J., ed. *Environments of South Florida: Present and Past, II,* 2d ed. Coral Gables: Miami Geological Society, 1984.

Goldstein, Alan L., and Gary J. Ritter. "A Performance-Based Regulatory Program for Phosphorus Control to Prevent the Accelerated Eutrophication of Lake Okeechobee, Florida." *Science Technology* 28 (1993).

Graham, Frank, Jr. "Kite vs. Stork." *Audubon* 92, no. 3 (1990).

————. "Portrait in Red and White." *Audubon* 102, no. 4 (2000).

————. "A Wing and A Prayer." *Audubon* 103, no. 4 (2001).

Gunderson, Lance H., and William F. Loftus. "The Everglades." In *Biodiversity of the Southeastern United States: Lowland,* edited by Eugene Odum. New York: John Wiley, 1993.

Haeger, James S. "Behavior Preceding Migration in the Salt-Marsh Mosquito, *Aedes taeniorhynchus* (Wiedemann)." *Mosquito News* 20, no. 2 (1960).

Hall, David. *Pond-Apple Zone South of Lake Okeechobee.* Prepared for Tetra Tech, Inc. Lafayette, Calif., 2000.

Hanning, G. M. "Aspects of Reproduction in *Pomacea paludosa* (mesogastroda: Piliade)." Master's thesis, Florida State University, 1978.

Harper, Francis, ed. *The Travels of William Bartram.* New Haven: Yale University Press, 1958.

Harper's Index. *Harper's Magazine* 292, no. 1743 (1995).

Harrar, Ellwood S., and J. George Harrar. *Guide to Southern Trees.* New York: Dover, 1946.

Harrington, R. W., Jr., and E. S. Harrington. "Food Selection among Fishes Invading a High Subtropical Salt Marsh: From Onset of Flooding through the Progress of a Mosquito Brood." *Ecology* 42, no. 4 (1961).

Hay, Oliver P. *The Pleistocene of North America and Its Vertebrate Animals from the States East of the Mississippi River and from the Canadian Provinces East of Longitude 95.* Washington, D.C.: Carnegie Institution of Washington, D.C., 1923.

Heald, E. J., W. E. Odum, and D. C. Tabb. "Mangroves in the Estuarine Food Chain." In *Environments of South Florida: Present and Past, II,* 2d ed., edited by Patrick J. Gleason. Coral Gables: Miami Geological Society, 1984.

Henry, James A., Kenneth M. Porter, and Jan Coyne. *The Climate and Weather of Florida.* Sarasota: Pineapple Press, 1994.

Herndon, Alan, Lance Gunderson, and John Stenberg. "Sawgrass (*Cladium jamaicense*) Survival in a Regime of Fire and Flooding." *Wetlands* 11, no. 1 (1991).

Hiaasen, Carl. "The Last Days of Florida Bay." *Sports Illustrated* 83, no. 12 (1995).

———. *Team Rodent: How Disney Devours the World.* New York: Library of Contemporary Thought, 1998.

Hiestand, Emily. *The Very Rich Hours.* Boston: Beacon Press, 1992.

Hillis, D. M., M. T. Dixon, and A. L. Jones. "Minimal Genetic Variation in a Morphologically Diverse Species (Florida Tree Snail, *Liguus fasiatus*)." *Journal of Heredity,* 82 (1991).

Hirschfeld, S. E. "Vertebrate Fauna of Nichol's Hammock, a Natural Trap." *Quarterly Journal of the Florida Academy of Science* 31 (1968).

Hoffman, Wayne, G. Thomas Bancroft, and Richard J. Sawicki. "Foraging Habitat of Wading Birds in the Water Conservation Areas of the Everglades." In *Everglades: The Ecosystem and Its Restoration,* edited by S. M. Davis and J. C. Ogden. Delray Beach, Fla.: St. Lucie Press, 1994.

Hoffmeister, John Edward. *Land from the Sea: The Geologic Story of South Florida.* Coral Gables: University of Miami Press, 1974.

Holloway, Marguerite. "Nurturing Nature." *Scientific American* 270, no. 4 (1994).

Hornocker, Maurice G. "Learning to Live with Mountain Lions." *National Geographic* 182, no. 1 (1992).

Howell, A. H. *Florida Bird Life.* New York: Coward-McCann, 1932.

Hurdee, Marvin T. "Life History Studies and Habitat Requirements of the Apple Snail at Lake Woodruff National Wildlife Refuge." In *Proceedings of the 27th Annual Conference of Southeast Association of Game and Fish Commissioners.* 1973.

In South Florida, the Environment Is the Economy. Produced by Environmental Economics Symposium Committee, Greater Miami Chamber of Commerce, Environmental Affairs Group & Environmental Economics Council, National Audubon Society, Everglades Conservation Office, in conjunction with South Florida Water Management District. Miami: Greater Miami Chamber of Commerce, 1999.

Jewell, Susan D. *Exploring Wild South Florida.* Sarasota: Pineapple Press, 1993.

———. "Restoring South Florida's Future." *People, Land and Water* 6, no. 4 (1999).

Johns, Grace M. "Status and Preservation of the Agricultural Industry in South Florida." Report to the National Audubon Society–Everglades Conservation Office prepared by Hazen and Sawyer: Environmental Engineers and Scientists (1998).

Johnson, Kenneth G., and E. Darrell Land. "Genetic Restoration of the Florida Panther." *Florida Wildlife,* January–February 1996.

Johnson, Kenneth G., Darrell E. Land, and Mark A. Lotz. *Annual Performance Report: Statewide Wildlife Research: Florida Panther Genetic Restoration and Management.* Florida Game and Freshwater Fish Commission, 1995.

———. *Annual Performance Report: Florida Panther Genetic Restoration and Management.* Florida Game and Freshwater Fish Commission Study 7508. 1996.

———. *Annual Performance Report: Florida Panther Genetic Restoration and Management.* Florida Game and Freshwater Fish Commission Study 7508. 1997.

King, Jonathon. "From the Wings of Eagles: Can Birds of Prey Save Florida Bay?" *Sunshine Magazine,* 16 April 1995.

Kloor, Keith. "Forgotten Islands." *Audubon* 103, no. 4 (2001).

Klowden, Marc J. "Tales of a Mosquito Psychologist." *Natural History* 100, no. 7 (1991).

Kreitman, Abe, and Leslie Wedderburn. "Hydrology of South Florida." In *Environments of South Florida: Present and Past, II,* 2d ed., edited by Patrick J. Gleason. Coral Gables: Miami Geological Society, 1984.

Kurten, Bjorn, and Elaine Anderson. *Pleistocene Mammals of North America.* New York: Columbia University Press, 1980.

Kushlan, James A. "Population Changes of the Apple Snail *Pomacea paludosa* in the Southern Everglades." *Nautilus* 89, no. 1 (1975).

———. "Predation on Apple Snail Eggs (*Pomacea paludosa*)." *Nautilus* 92, no. 1 (1978).

———. "Design and Management of Continental Wildlife Reserves: Lessons from the Everglades." *Biological Conservation* 15, no. 4 (1979).

———. "Prey Choice by Tactile-Foraging Wading Birds." In *Proceedings of the Colonial Wading Bird Group 3.* 1979.

———. "Feeding Ecology and Prey Selection in the White Ibis." *Condor* 81, no. 4 (1980).

―――. "Population Fluctuations of Everglades Fishes." *Copeia,* no. 4 (December 1980).

―――. "The Sandhill Crane in the Everglades." *Florida Field Naturalist* 10, no. 4 (1982).

―――. "Freshwater Marshes." In *Ecosystems of Florida,* edited by Ronald L. Myers and John J. Ewel. Orlando: University of Central Florida Press, 1990.

Kushlan, James A., and Frank J. Mazzotti. "Historic and Present Distribution of the American Crocodile in Florida." *Journal of Herpetology* 23, no. 1 (1989).

―――. "Population Biology of the American Crocodile." *Journal of Herpetology* 23, no. 1 (1989).

Lake Okeechobee Advisory Committee. *Melaleuca Management Plan for Lake Okeechobee.* 1994.

Land, E. Darrell, Sharon K. Taylor, and James A. Kushlan. *Annual Report: Florida Panther Genetic Restoration and Management.* Naples: Florida Game and Fresh Water Fish Commission, Bureau of Wildlife Diversity Conservation, 1998.

Laroche, Francois B. ed. *Melaleuca Management Plan for Florida.* Exotic Pest Plant Council, 1990.

Lazell, James D., Jr. *Wildlife of the Florida Keys: A Natural History.* Washington, D.C.: Island Press, 1989.

Leopold, Luna B., et al. *Environmental Impact of Big Cypress Swamp Jetport.* Washington, D.C.: U.S. Department of the Interior, 1969.

Levin, Ted. "Survival of the Wettest." *Audubon* 94, no. 6 (1992).

―――. "The Croc Doc." *Sports Illustrated* 81, no. 26 (1994).

―――. "A Singular Swamp." *Audubon* 96, no. 4 (1994).

―――. *Everglades National Park.* New York: Abbeville Press, 1995.

―――. "Wanderer in Search of Escargot." *Living Bird* 14, no. 2 (1995).

―――. "Whither the Snail Kite?" *Wildlife Conservation* 98, no. 1 (1995).

―――. "The Mosquito Coast." *Sports Illustrated* 84, no. 25 (1996).

―――. "A Night in East Everglades." *Florida Wildlife and Nature* 1, no. 1 (1996).

―――. "Listening to Wildlife in the Everglades." *National Wildlife* 36, no. 4 (1998).

―――. "Everglades: The Tenuous Tropics." *Audubon* 100, no. 6 (1998).

―――. "Florida's Coral Reef: A Wonderful World of Color" *Audubon* 101, no. 6 (1999).

―――. "To Save a Reef." *National Wildlife* 37, no. 2 (1999).

Line, Les. "One Picture." *Audubon* 103, no. 4 (2001).

Lodge, Thomas E. *The Everglades Handbook: Understanding the Ecosystem.* Delray Beach, Fla.: St. Lucie Press, 1994.

Loftus, William F. "Distribution and Ecology of Exotic Fishes in Everglades National Park." Paper presented at Conference on Science in the National Parks 5, 1986.

Loftus, William F., and Oron L. Bass Jr. *Mercury Threatens Wildlife Resources.* Park Science: A Resource Management Bulletin 12, no. 4. 1992.

Loftus, William F., Oron L. Bass Jr., and Joel C. Trexler. "Long-term Fish Monitoring in the Everglades: Looking Beyond the Park Boundary." In *Proceedings of the*

9th Conference on Research and Resource Management in Parks and on Public Lands. 1997.

Loftus, William F., and Anne-Marie Eklund. "Long-term Dynamics of an Everglades Small-Fish Assemblage." In *Everglades: The Ecosystem and its Restoration,* edited by S. M. Davis and J. C. Ogden. Delray Beach, Fla.: St. Lucie Press, 1994.

Loftus, William F., Robert A. Johnson, and Gordon H. Anderson. "Ecological Impacts of the Reduction of Groundwater Levels in Short-Hydroperiod Marshes of the Everglades." Paper presented at First International Conference on Groundwater Ecology, U.S. Environmental Protection Agency, 1992.

Loftus, William F., and James A. Kushlan. *Freshwater Fishes of Southern Florida.* Bulletin of the Florida State Museum. Biological Sciences 31, no. 4. Gainesville: University of Florida, 1987.

Long, Robert W., and Olga Lakela. *A Flora of Tropical Florida.* Coral Gables: University of Miami Press, 1971.

Lorenz, Jerome J. "The Response of Fishes to Physiochemical Changes in the Mangroves of Northeast Florida Bay." *Estuaries* 22, no. 2B (1999).

Lorenz, Jerome J., John C. Ogden, Robin Bjork, and George V. N. Powell. "Nesting Patterns of Roseate Spoonbills in Florida Bay, 1935–1999: Implications of Landscape Scale Anthropogenic Impacts." *Ecology* (forthcoming).

Lounibos, L. P. "The Mosquito Community of Treeholes in Subtropical Florida in Phytotelmata: Terrestrial Plants as Hosts for Aquatic Insect Communities." Medford, N.J.: Plexus Publishing, 1983.

Loveless, Charles M. "A Study of the Vegetation of the Florida Everglades." *Ecology* 40, no. 1 (1959).

Luer, Carlyle A. *The Native Orchids of Florida.* New York: New York Botanical Garden, 1972.

Luoma, Jon R. "Born to Be Wild." *Audubon* 94, no. 1 (1992).

MacGonigle, John W. "The Geography of the Southern Peninsula of the United States." *National Geographic* 1, no. 7 (1896).

Maehr, David S. "The Florida Panther on Private Lands." *Conservation Biology* 4, no. 2 (1990).

———. "Tracking Florida's Panthers." *Defenders* 65 (September–October 1990).

———. "Florida Panther." In *Rare and Endangered Biota of Florida.* Vol. 1, *Mammals,* edited by Stephen R. Humphreys. Gainesville: University Press of Florida, 1992.

———. *The Florida Panther: Life and Death of a Vanishing Carnivore.* Washington, D.C.: Island Press, 1997.

Maehr, David S., and Chris Belden. "The Endangered Florida Panther." *Florida Wildlife,* May–June 1991.

Maehr, David S., and James R. Brady. "Food Habits of Bobcats in Florida." *Journal of Mammalogy* 67, no. 1 (1986).

Maehr, David S., and Dan Decker. "What Happened to Cat #12?" *Telonics Quarterly* 2, no. 3 (1989).

Maehr, David S., E. Darrell Land, and Jayde C. Roof. "Social Ecology of Florida Panthers." *National Geographic Research and Exploration* 7, no. 4 (1991).

Maehr, David S., E. Darrell Land, Jayde C. Roof, and J. Walter McCown. "Day Beds, Natal Dens, and Activity of Florida Panthers." *Proceedings of the Annual Conference of Southeastern Association of Fish and Wildlife Agencies* 44 (1990).

Maehr, David S., Jayde C. Roof, E. Darrell Land, and J. Walter McCown. "First Reproduction in a Panther (*Felis concolor coryi*) in Southern Florida, U.S.A." *Mammalia* 53, no. 1 (1989).

Maehr, David S., Jayde C. Roof, E. Darrell Land, J. Walter McCown, Robert C. Belden, and W. G. Frankenberger. "Fates of Wild Hogs Introduced into Occupied Panther Home Ranges." *Florida Field Naturalist* 17, no. 2 (1989).

Maehr, David S., et al. "Food Habits of Panthers in Southwest Florida." *Journal of Wildlife Management* 54, no. 3 (1990).

Maltby, E., and J. P. Dugan. "Wetland Ecosystem Protection, Management, and Restoration: An International Prospective." In *Everglades: The Ecosystem and Its Restoration,* edited by S. M. Davis and J. C. Ogden. Delray Beach, Fla.: St. Lucie Press, 1994.

Martin, Thomas, Paul W. Sykes Jr., Alexander Sprunt Jr., and Lovell E. Williams Jr. *The Everglades Kite: Recovery Plan.* Atlanta: U.S. Fish and Wildlife Service, Region 4, 1983.

May, Peter G., Steven T. Heulett, Terence M. Farrell, and Melissa A. Pilgrim. "Live Fast, Love Hard, and Die Young: The Ecology of Pigmy Rattlesnakes." *Reptile and Amphibian* no. 45 (January–February 1997).

Mazzotti, Frank J. "Factors Affecting the Nesting Success of the American Crocodile, *Crocodylus acutus,* in Florida Bay." *Bulletin of Marine Science* 44, no. 1 (1989).

———. *Status and Trends of Nesting of the American Crocodile in Everglades National Park, Florida.* A report prepared for the U.S. Army Corps of Engineers and National Park Service, 1994.

Mazzotti, Frank J., James A. Kushlan, and Ann Dunbar-Cooper. "Desiccation and Cryptic Nest Flooding as Probable Causes of Egg Mortality in the American Crocodile, *Crocodylus acutus,* in Everglades National Park, Florida." *Quarterly Journal of the Florida Academy of Sciences* 51, no. 2 (1988).

McClary, Andrew. "Surface Inspiration and Ciliary Feeding in *Pomacea paludosa* (Prosobranchia mesogatropoda: Ampullaridae). *Malacologia* 2, no. 1 (1964).

McCown, James W., Melody E. Roelke, Donald J. Forrester, Clinton T. Moore, and John C. Roboski. "Physiological Evaluation of Two White-Tailed Deer Herds in Southern Florida." In *Proceedings of the Annual Conference of Southeastern Association of Fish and Wildlife Agencies.* 1991.

McIver, Carole C., Janet A. Ley, and Robin D. Bjork. "Changes in Freshwater Inflow from the Everglades to Florida Bay: A Review." In *Everglades: The Ecosystem and Its Restoration,* edited by S. M. Davis and J. C. Ogden. Delray Beach, Fla.: St. Lucie Press, 1994.

McMullen, James P. *Cry of the Panther.* Englewood, Fla.: Pineapple Press, 1984.

Melvin, Stefani L, Dale E. Gawlik, and T. Scharff. "Long-term Movement Patterns for Seven Species of Wading Birds." *Waterbirds* 22, no. 3 (1999).

Milleson, James F., Robert L. Goodrick, and Joel A. Van Arman. *Plant Communities of the Kissimmee River Valley.* South Florida Water Management District Technical Publication 80-7. West Palm Beach, 1980.

Milner, Richard. "The Mosquito Fish's Checkered Career." *Natural History* 100, no. 7 (1991).

Missimer, Thomas M. "Geology of South Florida." In *Environments of South Florida: Present and Past, II,* 2d ed., edited by Patrick J. Gleason. Coral Gables: Miami Geological Society, 1984.

Moore, J. C. "The Crocodile in the Everglades National Park." *Copeia,* no. 1 (1953).

Morris, C. D., and K. B. Clanton. "Comparison of People Who Request Mosquito Control Services and Their Non-requesting Neighbors." *Journal of the American Mosquito Control Association* 8, no. 1 (1992).

Morton, Julia F. *Wild Plants for Survival in South Florida.* Miami: Fairchild Tropical Garden, 1982.

Myers, Ronald L., and John J. Ewel, eds. *Ecosystems of Florida.* Orlando: University of Central Florida Press, 1990.

Nabhan, Gary Paul. *Lost Gourds and Spent Soils on the Shores of Lake Okeechobee in Enduring Seeds: Native American Agriculture and Wild Plant Conservation.* San Francisco: North Point Press, 1989.

National Audubon Society Everglades Ecosystem Restoration Campaign. *Lake Belt Lands: Their Role in the Restoration and Sustainability of the Everglades and the South Florida Ecosystem.* Miami, 1996.

———. "Water Preserve Areas: Defining Biological Functions and Spatial Extent." Workshop report. Miami, 1997.

———. "Comments of the National Audubon Society to the Central and Southern Florida Project Comprehensive Review Study." Everglades Conservation Office, Miami, 1998.

———. "Maximizing Water Storage for Everglades–South Florida Ecosystem Restoration and Sustainability." Prepared for the Environmental Economics Council Office, 1998.

———. "Comments of the National Audubon Society regarding FDEP Discharge Permit #FLA-183504-001-IW8A Lake Okeechobee Structures." Everglades Conservation Office, Miami, 1999.

———. "Water Preserve Areas: Acquisition Status and Future Directions." Everglades Conservation Office, Miami, 1999.

Nayar, J. K., ed. *Bionomics and Physiology of* Aedes taeniorhynchus *and* Aedes sollicitans: *The Salt Marsh Mosquitoes of Florida.* University of Florida. Agricultural Experiment Station Bulletin 852. Gainesville: Florida Agricultural Experiment Stations, Institute of Food and Agricultural Sciences, University of Florida, 1985.

Neil, Wilfred T. *The Last of the Ruling Reptiles: Alligators, Crocodiles, and their Kin.* New York: Columbia University Press, 1971.

Nelson, Gil. *The Trees of Florida*. Sarasota: Pineapple Press, 1994.

Newmand, Charles J., Brian R. Jarvinen, and Arthur C. Pike. *Tropical Cyclones of the North Atlantic, 1871–1986*. Washington: U.S. Department of Commerce, NOAA, 1986.

Nielsen, Erik Tetens, and James S. Haeger. "Swarming and Mating in Mosquitoes." *Miscellaneous Publications of the Entomological Society of America* 1, no. 3 (1960).

Nielsen, Lewis T. "Mosquitoes, the Mighty Killers." *National Geographic* 156, no. 3 (1979).

———. "Mosquitoes Unlimited." *Natural History* 100, no. 7 (1991).

Nott, M. Philip, Oron L. Bass Jr., D. Martin Fleming, Stephen E. Killeffer, Nancy Fraley, Lisa Manne, John L. Curnutt, Thomas M. Brooks, Robert Powell, and Stuart L. Pimm. *Water Levels, Rapid Vegetational Changes, and the Endangered Cape Sable Seaside Sparrow*. South Florida Biologic Research Center Report. Homestead, 1998.

O'Brien, Stephen J., et al. "Genetic Introgression within the Florida Panther *Felis concolor coryi*." *National Geographic Research* 6, no. 4 (1990).

Ogden, John C. "Night of the Crocodile." *Audubon* 75, no. 3 (1973).

———. "Status and Nesting Biology of the American Crocodile, *Crocodylus acutus* (*Reptilia, Crocodilidae*) in Florida." *Journal of Herpetology* 12, no. 2 (1978).

———. "Nesting by Wood Storks in Natural, Altered, and Artificial Wetlands in Central and Northern Florida." *Colonial Waterbirds* 14, no. 1 (1991).

Ogden, John C., James A. Kushlan, and James T. Tilmant. *The Food Habits and Nesting Success of Wood Storks in Everglades National Park in 1974*. Natural Resources Report 16. U.S. Department of the Interior, National Park Service, 1974.

———. "Prey Selectivity by the Wood Stork." *Condor* 78, no. 3 (1976).

———. "A Comparison of Wading Bird Nesting Dynamics (1931–1946 and 1974–1989) as an Indication of Ecosystem Conditions in the Southern Everglades." In *Everglades: The Ecosystem and Its Restoration*, edited by S. M. Davis and J. C. Ogden. Delray Beach, Fla.: St. Lucie Press, 1994.

Ogden, John C., Donald A. McCrimmon Jr., G. Thomas Bancroft, and Barbara W. Patty. "Breeding Populations of the Wood Stork in the Southeastern United States." *Condor* 89, no. 4 (1987).

Ogden, John C., and Steven M. Davis, eds. *The Use of Conceptual Ecological Landscape Models as Planning Tools for the South Florida Ecosystem Restoration Programs*. West Palm Beach: South Florida Water Management District, June 29, 1999.

Olmsted, Ingrid C., Lloyd L. Loope, and Robert P. Russell. *Vegetation of the Southern Coastal Region of Everglades National Park between Flamingo and Joe Bay*. Report T-620. Homestead: National Park, South Florida, Biological Research Center, 1981.

O'Meara, George F. "Gonotrophic Interactions in Mosquitoes: Kicking the Blood-Feeding Habit." *Florida Entomologist* 68, no. 1 (1985).

O'Meara, George F., and David H. Cook. "Facultative Blood-Feeding in the Crabhole Mosquito, Deinocerites cancer." *Medical and Veterinary Entomology* 4 (1990).

O'Meara, George F., and John D. Day. "Autogenous Egg Production in the Salt-Marsh Mosquito, *Aedes taeniorhynchus*." *Biological Bulletin* 149, no. 3 (1975).

O'Meara, George F., and David G. Evans. "Blood-Feeding Requirements of the Mosquito: Geographical Variation in Aedes taeniorhynchus." *Science* 180, no. 4092 (1973).

O'Reilly, John. "South Florida's Amazing Everglades." *National Geographic* 77, no. 1 (1940).

O'Shea, Thomas J. "Manatees." *Scientific American* 271, no. 1 (1994).

Ownby, Miriam Lee. *Explore the Everglades*. Kissimmee: Teakwood Press, 1992.

Palmer, Thomas. *Landscape with Reptile: Rattlesnakes in an Urban World*. New York: Ticknor and Fields, 1992.

Parker, Gerald. "Hydrology of the Pre-drainage System of the Everglades in Southern Florida." In *Environments of South Florida: Present and Past, II*, 2d ed., edited by Patrick J. Gleason. Coral Gables: Miami Geological Society, 1984.

Pesnell, Gary L., and Robert T. Brown III. *The Major Plant Communities of Lake Okeechobee, Florida, and Their Associated Inundation Characteristics as Determined by Gradient Analysis*. South Florida Water Management District Technical Publication 77-1. West Palm Beach: Resource Planning Department, South Florida Water Management District, 1977.

Peterson, Roger Tory, and James Fisher. *Wild America*. Boston: Houghton Mifflin, 1955.

Post, William, and Jon S. Greenlaw. "The Present and Future of the Cape Sable Seaside Sparrow." *Florida Field Naturalist* 28, no. 3 (2000).

Potous, Paul. *No Tears for Crocodiles*. London: Hutchinson, 1956.

Powell, George V. N., Robin D. Bjork, John C. Ogden, Richard T. Paul, A. Harriett Powell, and William B. Robertson. "Population Trends in Some Florida Bay Wading Birds." *Wilson Bulletin* 101, no. 3 (1989).

Proby, Kathryn Hall. *Audubon in Florida: With Selections from the Writings of John James Audubon*. Coral Gables: University of Miami Press, 1974.

Provost, M. W. "The Zoogeography of Mosquitoes in Florida." In *Proceedings and Papers of the Forty-second Annual Conference of the California Mosquito Control Association, Inc., and the Thirtieth Annual Meeting of the American Mosquito Control Association, Inc.*, 24–27 February 1974.

Raloff, Janet. "The Gender Benders." *Science News*, 8 January 1993.

Rich, E. P. "Observation of Feeding by *Pomacea paludosa*." *Florida Scientist* 53 (supplement 1), no. 13 (1990).

Richardson, John R., Wade L. Bryant, Wiley M. Kitchens, Kevin R. Pope, and Jennifer E. Mattson. *An Evaluation of Refuge Habitats and Relationships to Water Quality, Quantity, and Hydroperiod*. Florida Cooperative Wildlife Research Unit, University of Florida. Gainesville: University of Florida, 1990.

Ring, Richard G. "Florida Bay." Paper presented to the Interagency Marine Commission, 15 September 1993.

Robertson, William B., Jr. *A Survey of the Effects of Fire in Everglades National Park*. Washington, D.C.: U.S. Department of the Interior, National Park Service, 1953.

Robertson, William B., Jr., Lorraine L. Breen, and Barbara W. Patty. "Movement of Marked Roseate Spoonbills in Florida with a Review of Present Distribution." *Journal of Field Ornithology* 54, no. 3 (1983).

Robertson, William B., Jr., and Peter C. Frederick. "The Faunal Chapters: Contexts, Synthesis, and Departures." In *Everglades: The Ecosystem and Its Restoration,* edited by S. M. Davis and J. C. Ogden. Delray Beach, Fla.: St. Lucie Press, 1994.

Robertson, William B., Jr., and James A. Kushlan. "The Southern Florida Avifauna." In *Environments of South Florida: Present and Past,* edited by Patrick J. Gleason. Memoir 2. Miami: Miami Geological Society, 1974.

Roelke, Melody E., Janice S. Martenson, and Stephen J. O'Brien. "The Consequences of Demographic Reduction and Genetic Depletion in the Endangered Florida Panther." *Current Biology* 3, no. 6 (1993).

Roman, Charles T., Nicholas G. Aumen, Joel C. Trexler, Robert J Fennema, William F. Loftus, and Michael A. Soukup. "Hurricane Andrew's Impact on Freshwater Resources." *BioScience* 44, no. 4 (1994).

Roof, Jayde C., and David S. Maehr. "Sign Surveys for Florida Panthers on Peripheral Areas of Their Known Range." *Florida Field Naturalist* 16, no. 4 (1988).

Roy, Sujoy, and Steven Gherini. *An Overview of the Historical Everglades Ecosystem and Implications for Establishing Restoration Goals.* Lafayette, Calif.: Tetra Tech, 2000.

Schortemeyer, James L., David S. Maehr, Walter McCown, Darrell E. Land, and Philip D. Manor. "Prey Management for the Florida Panther: A Unique Role for Wildlife Managers." *Transactions of the North American Wildlife and Natural Resources Conference* 56 (1991).

Schultz, Gwen. *Glaciers and the Ice Age.* New York: Holt, Rinehart and Winston, 1963.

Schwartz, Albert, and Robert W. Henderson. *Amphibians and Reptiles of the West Indies: Descriptions, Distributions, and Natural History.* Gainesville: University Press of Florida, 1991.

Schweigart, Joseph A., Christian Flierl IV, and Jo Ann Hyres. "Hurricane Irene: South Florida Water Management District After-Action Assessment." West Palm Beach: South Florida Water Management District, 1999.

Scott, Peter. "An Affair with a 'Mermaid,' Florida 1980." In *Travel Diaries of a Naturalist.* Vol. 2. London: Collins Sons, 1985.

Simpson, Charles Torrey. *Florida Wild Life.* New York: Macmillan, 1932.

Small, John Kunkel. *Flora of Miami.* New York: Published by the author, 1913.

———. "Exploration in the Everglades and on the Florida Keys." *Journal of the New York Botanical Garden* (1914).

———. "Coastwise Dunes and Lagoons: A Record of Botanical Exploration in Florida in the Spring of 1918." *Journal of the New York Botanical Garden* 20 (October 1919).

———. "The Everglades." *Scientific Monthly* 28 (1929).

———. *Ferns of Florida.* New York: Science Press, 1931.

Smith, Andrew T. *An Environmental Study of Everglades Mink.* South Florida Biological

Research Center Report T-555. Homestead: Everglades National Park, South Florida Biological Research Center, 1980.

Snyder, G. H., and J. M. Davidson. "Everglades Agriculture: Past, Present, and Future." In *Everglades: The Ecosystem and Its Restoration,* edited by S. M. Davis and J. C. Ogden. Delray Beach, Fla.: St. Lucie Press, 1994.

Snyder, James R., Alan Herndon, and William B. Robertson. "South Florida Rockland." In *Ecosystems of Florida,* edited by Ronald L. Myers and John J. Ewel. Orlando: University of Central Florida Press, 1990.

South Florida Water Management District. *Executive Summary: Everglades Consolidated Report.* Vols. 1 and 2. West Palm Beach, 1999.

———. *Executive Summary: Everglades Consolidated Report.* West Palm Beach, 2000.

———. *Executive Summary: Everglades Consolidated Report.* West Palm Beach, 2001.

Spalding, Marilyn G. "Antemortem Diagnosis of Eustrongylidosis in Wading Birds (Ciconiiformes)." *Colonial Waterbirds* 13, no. 1 (1990).

Spalding, Marilyn G., G. Thomas Bancroft, and Donald J. Forrester. "The Epizootiology of Eustrongylidosis in Wading Birds (Ciconiiformes) in Florida." *Journal of Wildlife Diseases* 29, no. 2 (1993).

Spalding, Marilyn G., and Donald J. Forrester. "Pathogenesis of *Eustrongylides ignotus* (Nematoda: Dioctophymatoidea) in Ciconiiformes." *Journal of Wildlife Diseases* 29, no. 2 (1993).

Stap, Don. "The Crocodile's Power Play." *National Wildlife* 40, no. 2 (2002).

Stevenson, George B. *Trees of the Everglades National Park and the Florida Keys.* Miami: Banyan Books, 1979.

Steward, Kerry K., and W. H. Ornes. *The Autecology of Sawgrass* (Mariscus jamaciensis) *in the Florida Everglades.* Prepared for the National Park Service. 1973. Distributed by the U.S. Department of Commerce, National Technical Information Service, Springfield, Va.

———. *Investigations into the Mineral Nutrition of Sawgrass Using Experimental Culture Techniques.* Agricultural Research Service, Ecological Report Number DI-SFPL-74-105. 1973.

Stoneburner, D. L., and James A. Kushlan. "Heavy Metal Burdens in American Crocodile Eggs from Florida Bay, U.S.A." *Journal of Herpetology* 18, no. 2 (1984).

Sykes, Paul M., Jr. "Evening Roosts of the Snail Kite in Florida." *Wilson Bulletin* 97, no. 1 (1985).

Sykes, Paul M., Jr., James A. Rodgers Jr., and Robert E. Bennetts. "Snail Kite." In *The Birds of North America,* edited by Peter Stettenheim and Frank Gill. Washington, D.C.: American Ornithological Union, 1995.

Tabb, Durbin C. *A Summary of Existing Information on the Freshwater and Marine Ecology of the Florida Everglades Park.* Miami: Marine Laboratory, Institute of Marine Science of the University of Miami, 1963.

Tabb, Durbin C., David L. Dubrow, Raymond B. Manning. *The Ecology of Northern*

Florida Bay and Adjacent Estuaries. Technical Series, no. 39. Miami: Marine Laboratory, Institute of Marine Science of the University of Miami, 1962.

Tarboton, Kenneth C., Calvin J. Neidrauer, and E. Ray Santee. "Application of the South Florida Water Management Model to Develop the Comprehensive Everglades Restoration Plan. Specialty Symposium: Integrated Surface and Ground Water Management." Paper presented at World Water and Environmental Resource Congress, Orlando, 2001.

Taylor, D. Scott. "The Swarms of Summer." *Natural History* 100, no. 7 (1991).

Tebeau, Charlton W. "Past Environments from Historical Sources." Washington, D.C.: U.S. Department of the Interior, National Park Service, South Florida Environmental Project, 1973.

Toops, Connie M. *The Alligator: Monarch of the Everglades.* Homestead: Everglades Natural History Association, 1979.

Toth, Louis A. *Effects of Hydrologic Regimes on Lifetime Production and Nutrient Dynamics of Sawgrass.* South Florida Water Management District, Technical Publication 87-6. West Palm Beach, 1987.

Truslow, Frederick Kent, and Frederick G. Vosburgh. "The Threatened Glories of Everglades National Park." *National Geographic* 132, no. 4 (1967).

Turner, Richard L. *The Effects of Hydrology on the Population Dynamics of the Florida Apple Snail.* Palatka: St. Johns River Water Management District, 1994.

Tveten, John. "In Search of the Florida Panther." *Exxon U.S.A.,* third quarter, 1984.

U.S. Army Corps of Engineers. *Central and Southern Florida Project Comprehensive Review Study.* Vols. 1–9. Washington: U.S. Government Printing Office, October 1998.

———. *Central and Southern Florida Project Comprehensive Review Study: Final Integrated Feasibility Report and Programmatic Environmental Impact Statement.* Washington: U.S. Government Printing Office, April 1999.

U.S. Department of the Interior. *See* Beard, Daniel

Van Handel, Emile, and Jonathan F. Day. "Nectar-Feeding Habits of *Aedes taeniorhynchus.*" *Journal of the American Mosquito Control Association* 6, no. 2 (1990).

Van Meter, Victoria Brook. *The Florida Panther.* Miami: Florida Power and Light Company, 1988.

Villano, David. "New Hope for the Panther." *Defenders* 68 (spring 1993).

Walters, Jeffrey R., Steven R. Beissinger, John W. Fitzpatrick, Russell Greenberg, James D. Nichols, H. Ronald Pulliam, and David W. Winkler. "The AOU Conservation Committee Review of the Biology, Status, and Management of Cape Sable Seaside Sparrows: Final Report." *Auk* 117, no. 4 (2000).

Wanless, Harold W. "Mangrove Sedimentation in Geologic Perspective." In *Environments of South Florida: Present and Past, II,* 2d ed., edited by Patrick J. Gleason. Coral Gables: Miami Geological Society, 1984.

Weaver, James, and Bradford Brown. *Report of the South Florida Management and Coordination Working Group: Federal Objectives for South Florida Restoration by the Science Sub Group.* Washington: U.S. Government Printing Office, 15 November 1993.

Webb, S. David, ed. *Pleistocene Mammals of Florida.* Gainesville: University Presses of Florida, 1974.

Webber, L. A., and J. D. Edman. "Anti-mosquito Behavior of Ciconiiforme Birds." *Animal Behavior* 20, no. 2 (1972).

White, William A. *The Geomorphology of the Florida Peninsula.* Geological Bulletin 51. Published for the Bureau of Geology, Division of Interior Resources, Florida Department of Natural Resources, Tallahassee, 1970, by Designers Press, Orlando.

Wilson, Edward O. *Naturalist.* Washington, D.C.: Island Press, 1994.

Wilson, Larry David, and Louis Porras. *The Ecological Impact of Man on the South Florida Herpetofauna.* Lawrence: University Press of Kansas, 1983.

Wilson, Samuel M. "Pandora's Bite." *Natural History* 100, no. 7 (1991).

Wolkomir, Richard, and Joyce Wolkomir. "In Search of Sanctuary: American Wood Storks." *Smithsonian* 31, no. 11 (2001).

Wood, John M., and George W. Tanner. "Graminoid Community Composition and Structure within Four Everglades Management Areas." *Wetlands* 10, no. 2 (1988).

Zaffke, Michael. *Plant Communities of Water Conservation Area 3A; Baseline Documentation Prior to the Operation of S-339 and S-340.* Technical Memorandum DRE-164. South Florida Water Management District Publication. West Palm Beach, 1983.

Zavaro Perez, Carlos, and Ramona Oviedo Prieto. "Etnobotánica y Ecología de *Cladium jamaicense* Crantz (Cyperaceae) en la Ciénaga de Zapata, Cuba." *Fontqueria* (1993).

Zieman, Joseph C., James W. Fourqurean, and Richard L. Iverson. "Distribution, Abundance and Productivity of Seagrasses and Macroalgae in Florida Bay." *Bulletin of Marine Science* 44, no. 1 (1989).

POLITICS AND HISTORY

Allen, Paul. "Come On, Hunters, Help Save the Panther." *St. Petersburg Times,* 1 December 1985.

Allen, Peter. "Florida Bay: Downstream from the Everglades, Upstream from the Florida Keys." *National Parks and Preserves of South Florida* 5, no. 2 (1993).

Balz, John, and Craig Pittman. "Glades Restoration Plan Passes House." *St. Petersburg Times,* 20 October 2000.

Barlett, Donald L., and James B. Steele. "Sweet Deal." *Time* 152, no. 21 (1998).

Benedick, Robin. "Census: South Florida Is Younger, More Diverse and Rapidly Changing." *Fort Lauderdale Sun-Sentinel,* 20 October 2000.

Bernstein, Jacob. "Deep Well Injection: A Sordid Tale about Rule Number One: Don't Shit Where You Drink." *Miami New Times,* 5 October 2000.

Blake, Nelson M. *Land into Water—Water into Land: A History of Water Management in Florida.* Tallahassee: University Presses of Florida, 1980.

Bohlen, Larry, and Tim Frank. *The Dark Side of the American Dream: The Costs and Consequences of Suburban Sprawl.* College Park, Md.: Sierra Club, [1999].

Boucher, Norman. "Everglades Journey." *Boston Globe Magazine,* 21 January 1990.

———. "Smart as Gods." *Wilderness* 55, no. 195 (1991).

Boyle, Robert H., and Rose Mary Mechem. "Anatomy of a Man-made Drought." *Sports Illustrated* 56, no. 11 (1982).

Brenner, Mary. "The Battle against Florida's Powerful Sugar Kings." *Vanity Fair,* no. 486 (2001).

Brown, Loren G. Totch. *Totch: A Life in the Everglades.* Gainesville: University Press of Florida, 1993.

Browning, Michael. "Sinkhole Reveals an Ice Age Prize." *Miami Herald,* 20 June 1993.

Campbell, James. "Paddling a Watery Wilderness." *Audubon* 103, no. 4 (2001).

Carr, Archie Fairly, Jr. *The Everglades: The American Wilderness Series.* New York: Time-Life Books, 1973.

Carter, Luther. *The Florida Experience: Land and Water Policy in a Growth State.* Baltimore: Johns Hopkins University Press, 1976.

Chang, Chris. "Go with the Flow." *Audubon* 103, no. 4 (2001).

Clark, Lesley. "Glades Restoration Fuels Panel Debate." *Miami Herald,* 17 December 1999.

Clary, Mary. "The Once-Reclusive Miccosukees Will Open a $50-Million Resort in the Park's Fragile Ecosystem." *Los Angeles Times,* 3 June 1999.

"Conflicts and Controversy over 8 1/2 Square Miles." Editorial. *Miami Herald,* 2 November 1998.

Craighead, Frank. "Is Man Destroying South Florida?" In *The Environmental Destruction of South Florida,* edited by W. R. McCluney. Coral Gables: University of Miami Press, 1969.

Crum, Robert. "American Xanadu." *Sierra* 78, no. 6 (1993).

Cummings, Tina. "Poll: Burgeoning Growth Worries Floridians." *Miami Herald,* 17 February 2000.

Cushman, John H., Jr. "Clinton Backing Vast Effort to Restore Florida Swamps." *New York Times,* 18 February 1996.

Dasmann, Raymond F. *No Further Retreat: The Fight to Save Florida.* New York: Macmillan, 1971.

de Hart, Allen. *Adventuring in Florida: The Sierra Club Travel Guide to the Sunshine State.* San Francisco: Sierra Club Books, 1991.

Derr, Mark. *Some Kind of Paradise: A Chronicle of Man and the Land in Florida.* New York: William Morrow, 1989.

———. "Redeeming the Everglades." *Audubon* 95, no. 5 (1993).

Dewer, Helen. "Everglades Project Is Approved." *Washington Post,* 20 October 2000.

Dillingham, Maud. "Everglades Escape among the Alligators." *Christian Science Monitor,* 12 March 1997.

di Vise, David. "Broward Suburbs Exploding in Size." *Miami Herald,* 21 October 2000.

Douglas, Marjory Stoneman. *The Everglades: River of Grass.* Covington, Ga.: Mockingbird Books, 1947.

———. "The Forgotten Man Who Saved the Everglades." *Audubon* 73, no. 5 (1971).

Douglas, Marjory Stoneman, with John Rothchild. *Marjory Stoneman Douglas: Voice of the River.* Englewood, Fla.: Pineapple Press, 1987.

Ericson, Edward, Jr. "Sugar's Bittersweet Victory." *Weekly Planet*, 5 December 1996.

Fiedler, Tom. "Everglades National Park Born Thanks to a Poker Game." *Miami Herald*, 21 May 1998.

Finefrock, Don. "Miami–Dade Is Growing, But Not That Much." *Miami Herald*, 21 October 2000.

Flicker, John. "Audubon View." *Audubon* 103, no. 4 (2001).

Florida Bay News. Everglades National Park, fall 1995–summer 1997.

Flowers, Charles. "Starting Over in the Everglades." *National Wildlife* 23, no. 2 (1985).

Foster, John T., and Sarah Whitmer Foster. *Beechers, Stowes, and Yankee Strangers: The Transformation of Florida*. Gainesville: University Press of Florida, 1999.

Gallagher, Peter B. "Alligator: A Special Report on a New Industry." *St. Petersburg Times*, 29 May 1983.

———. "Mrazek Pond." *St. Petersburg Times*, 16 November 1983.

———. "Wild Panthers: A Time to Live or a Time to Die?" *St. Petersburg Times*, 20 May 1984.

Gifford, John C. *The Everglades and Other Essays Relating to Southern Florida*. Miami: Everglade Land Sales Co., 1912.

———. *On Preserving Tropical Florida*, compiled by Elizabeth Ogren Rothra. Coral Gables: University of Miami Press, 1972.

Gorman, Stephen. "Trekking Tropical Trails." *Audubon* 103, no. 4 (2001).

Governor's Commission for a Sustainable South Florida. *A Conceptual Plan for the Central and South Florida Project Restudy*. Coral Gables, 28 August 1996.

Graham, Frank, Jr. "The Audubon Arc." *Audubon* 80, no. 1 (1978).

Grosso, Richard. "More People, Less Land: How to Manage Our Growth." *Miami Herald*, 30 January 2000.

Grunwald, Michael. "In Everglades, a Chance for Redemption." *Washington Post*, 14 September 2000.

Harney, W. W. "The Drainage of the Everglades." *Harper's New Monthly Magazine*, March 1884.

Helmuth, Laura. "Can This Swamp Be Saved?" *Science News* 155, no. 16 (1999).

Hiaasen, Carl. "Time to Ground Jetport Scheme." *Miami Herald*, 12 August 1999.

———. "Thou Shalt Not Go West." *Miami Herald*, 20 October 1999.

———. "Politicians, Sincere or Not, Save the Everglades." *Miami Herald*, 25 October 2000.

Hinrichsen, Don. "Waterworld: A Hundred Years of Plumbing, Plantations, and Politics in the Everglades." *Amicus* (summer 1995).

Hollman, Laurie. "State Cuts Speed Limit in Everglades to Protect Panthers." *St. Petersburg Times*, 17 January 1985.

Hurchalla, Maggy. "Laying Off the Sparrow." *Palm Beach Post*, 19 December 1999.

Ingham, John. "The Gator Doc on a Mission to Save Wild Wetlands." *Express Micro-edition*, 3 October 1999.

Jackson, Derrick Z. "The Birds' Warning." *Boston Globe*, 22 April 1992.

Kaye, Russell. "Cat Fight." *Discover* 13, no. 7 (1992).

"Keep the Everglades Out of Politics." Editorial. *Miami Herald,* 19 October 2000.

King, Robert P. "Kennedy, Fanjul Feuding over Everglades." *Palm Beach Post,* 19 May 1997.

———. "Everglades a Prize, Pawn in Presidential Race." *Palm Beach Post,* 29 January 2000.

Klingener, Nancy. "Florida Bay Hit by Dirty Water, Irene's Overflow Spreads Trouble." *Miami Herald,* 26 October 1999.

———. "The Actists: Richard Grosso and Shannon Estenoz." *Audubon* 103, no. 4 (2001).

Klinkenberg, Jeff. "45 Miles of Bad Road Imperils Florida Panther." *St. Petersburg Times,* 1 May 1983.

———. "Searching for the Ghost of the 'Glades." *St. Petersburg Times,* 21 February 1988.

———. "Clyde's World." *St. Petersburg Times,* 7 November 1993.

———. "Big Sugar: A Way of Life." Part 2. *St. Petersburg Times,* 16 May 1994.

———. "Through His Eyes: Clyde Butcher." *St. Petersburg Times,* 30 November 1997.

Kloor, Keith. "Everglades Restoration Plan Hits Rough Waters." *Science* 288, no. 5469 (2000).

———. "A Fork in the River." *Audubon* 103, no. 4 (2001).

———. "Good News, Bad News." *Audubon* 103, no. 4 (2001).

Knickerbocker, Brad. "Sugar Firms Asked to Pay for Everglades Damage." *Christian Science Monitor,* 20 January 1994.

Levin, Ted. "Cuba's Sea of Grass." *Audubon* 96, no. 2 (1994).

———. "Immersed in the Everglades." *Sierra* 81, no. 3 (1996).

———. "Defending the 'Glades': Marjory Stoneman Douglas." *Audubon* 100, no. 6 (1998).

———. "Forever Glades: Ebbs and Flows of the Great American Wetland." *Audubon* 103, no. 4 (2001).

———. "Reviving the River of Grass." *Audubon* 103, no. 4 (2001).

———. "The Scientists: Steve Davis and Bob Johnson." *Audubon* 103, no. 4 (2001).

Lorente, Rafael, and Joe Kollin. "Florida Sprawl Worst in Nation Sierra Club Study Says." *Fort Lauderdale Sun-Sentinel,* 9 September 1998.

Luoma, Jon R. "The Big Thirst." *Wildlife Conservation* 95, no. 4 (1992).

———. "Blueprint for the Future." *Audubon* 103, no. 4 (2001).

MacLeish, William H. "From Sea to Shining Sea: 1492." *Smithsonian* 22, no. 8 (1991).

Mairson, Allan. "The Everglades: Dying for Help." *National Geographic* 185, no. 4 (1994).

Marine, Gene. "Algae and Arojet." In *The Environmental Destruction of South Florida,* edited by W. R. McCluney. Coral Gables: University of Miami Press, 1969.

Matthiessen, Peter. "The Long River." In *Indian Country.* New York: Viking Press, 1984.

McCally, David. *The Everglades: An Environmental History.* Gainesville: University Press of Florida, 1999.

McCluney, William Ross, ed. *The Environmental Destruction of South Florida*. Coral Gables: University of Miami Press, 1969.

McPhee, John A. *Oranges*. New York: Farrar, Straus and Giroux, 1967.

Merzer, Martin. "Circle Makes Archaeologist Overnight Celebrity." *Miami Herald*, 10 February 1999.

Merzer, Martin, and Alfonso Chardy. "Developer Gets Tough about 'Dig.'" *Miami Herald*, 10 February 1999.

"Miamians Watch, Help Dig at Tequesta Ruins." Associated Press. *Tampa Tribune*, 3 January 1999.

"Miccosukees Sue District, County under Sunshine Law." Associated Press. *St. Petersburg Times*, 2 February 1999.

Morgan, Curtis. "Cold Weather Cuts Number of Exotic Fish That Invade Everglades National Park." *Miami Herald*, 27 January 2001.

Morgenthaler, Eric. "What's Florida to Do with an Explosion of Melaleuca Trees?" *Wall Street Journal*, 8 February 1993.

Muir, John. *A Thousand-Mile Walk to the Gulf*. San Francisco: Sierra Club Books, 1991.

"No Friend of the Everglades." Editorial. *Palm Beach Post*, 12 February 1999.

O'Brien, Stephen J., and Ernst Mayr. "Bureaucratic Mischief: Recognizing Endangered Species and Subspecies." *Science* 251, no. 4998 (1991).

Olinger, David. "Gators on Lake Apopka Altered." *St. Petersburg Times*, 21 August 1994.

Orlean, Susan. *The Orchid Thief*. New York: Random House, 1998.

"Osprey, Pelican Numbers Tumble in Florida Bay." Associated Press. *St. Petersburg Times*, 29 October 1993.

Pacenti, John. "Experts, Amateurs Unite at Dig in Downtown Miami." *Detroit Free Press*, 5 January 1999.

"Panther Cousins Threaten Purebred." Associated Press. *St. Petersburg Times*, 26 November 1980.

"The Panther vs. Seminole Ritual." Editorial. *St. Petersburg Times*, 8 December 1983.

Parks, Arva Moore. *The Forgotten Frontier: Florida through the Lens of Ralph Middleton Munroe*. Miami: Banyan Books, 1977.

Pittman, Craig. "Some Call Everglades Board 'Bushwhacked.'" *St. Petersburg Times*, 30 November 1999.

———. "The Wanderer." *St. Petersburg Times*, 19 November 2000.

———. "Mosquito Spray Deadly to Birds." *St. Petersburg Times*, 28 January 2001.

Plunkett, Judy A. "Gator Kills 10-Year-Old Boy." *Miami Herald*, 20 June 1993.

Raeburn, Paul. "Everglades Law Leaves Sugar Growers with Bitter Aftertaste." *Indianapolis Sentinel*, 16 June 1994.

Rawlings, Marjorie Kinnan. *Cross Creek*. New York: Collier Books, 1942.

"Region Must Pay Share to Rebuild Water System." Editorial. *Palm Beach Post*, 31 January 2000.

Rhodes, Richard. "The Killing of the Everglades." *Playboy*, January 1972.

Rice, Terry, and Robert H. Buker Jr. "Blame Won't Save Sparrow; Plan May." *Palm Beach Post*, 29 January 2000.

Rich, E. R. "The Population Explosion in Dade County, in *The Environmental Destruction of South Florida*," edited by W. R. McCluney. Coral Gables: University of Miami Press, 1969.

Roberts, Paul. "The Sweet Hereafter." *Harper's* 299, no. 1794 (1999).

Rodgers, David K. "The Everglades under Pressure: Dying Sea Grass Points to Trouble Ahead for the Wetlands Wilderness." *St. Petersburg Times*, 12 February 1989.

Rozsa, Lori. "Farmers Agree to Sell Frog Pond for Flooding." *Miami Herald*, 22 February 1995.

———. "Irene's Rainfall Temporarily Restores Glades' Water Glory." *Miami Herald*, 23 October 1999.

Samson, Jack. "Crisis in Florida Bay." *Fly Rod and Reel* 17, no. 1 (1995).

Schmidt, Eric, and David Stouts. "House Passes $7.8 Billion Plan to Save the Florida Everglades." *New York Times*, 19 October 2000.

Schrope, Mark. "Save Our Swamp." *Nature* 409 (2001).

"Scientists Pin Hopes on Insect to Save the Everglades." Associated Press. *Orlando Sentinel*, 24 September 1996.

Seideman, David. Editor's Note. *Audubon* 103, no. 4 (2001).

Silva, Mark. "Cleanup Plan Is a Mess, Glades Champion Declares." *Miami Herald*, 3 March 1994.

Simmons, Glen. "Does Anyone Care about Filling Up Water Pits?" *South Dade News Leader*, 13 October 1999.

Simmons, Glen, and Laura Ogden. *Gladesmen: Gator Hunters, Moonshiners, and Skiffers*. Gainesville: University Press of Florida, 1998.

Small, John Kunkel. *From Eden to Sahara: Florida's Tragedy*. Lancaster, Pa.: Science Press Printing, 1929.

Smiley, Nixon. "Poker Game Helped Found Everglades National Park." *Miami Herald*, 3 December 1967.

Smith, Buckingham. "The Everglades of Florida." In *Acts, Reports and Other Papers, State and National, Relating to the Everglades of the State of Florida and Their Reclamation*. U.S. Congress. 62d Cong., 1st sess., 1848. S. Doc. 89.

Stamper, Judith Bauer. *Save the Everglades*. New York: Steck-Vaughn, 1993.

Stap, Don. "Gliding Through the Glades." *Audubon* 103, no. 4 (2001).

Stevens, William K. "A Bay Is Sick: Will the Cure Make It Worse?" *New York Times*, 15 April 1997.

Stewart, Doug. "The Madness That Swept Miami." *Smithsonian* 31, no. 10 (2001).

"Stop Everglades Intrusion, Buy 8 1/2-Square-Mile Area." Editorial. *Miami Herald*, 10 November 1999.

Stowe, Harriet Beecher. "Protect the Birds." *Semi-Tropical* 3 (January 1877).

"Study Shows No Increase in Florida Bay's Salinity." *Citizen* staff report. *Key West Citizen*, 31 January 1996.

Tebeau, Charlton W. *Florida's Last Frontier: The History of Collier County*. Rev. ed. Coral Gables: University of Miami Press, 1966.

———. *Man in the Everglades: 2000 Years of History in the Everglades National Park.* Coral Gables: University of Miami Press, 1968.

Terry, Carl. "EPA Approves Tough Phosphorous Limit for Tribal Waters in Everglades." Press release, EPA Press and Media Relations, 26 May 1999.

Tomalin, Terry. "Wet and Wild: A Week in the Everglades." Parts 1–6. *St. Petersburg Times,* 26–31 January 1992.

———. "Runnin' the Outside." Parts 1–3. *St. Petersburg Times,* 23–25 February 1993.

Truesdell, William G. *A Guide to the Wilderness Waterway of the Everglades National Park.* 1969. Rev. ed. Coral Gables: University of Miami Press, 1985.

Vick, Karl. "Big Sugar." Part 1, "Can Growers Afford the Tax? It Depends." *St. Petersburg Times,* 15 May 1994.

———. "Big Sugar." Part 2, "A Sweet Deal under Fire." *St. Petersburg Times,* 16 May 1994.

———. "Big Sugar." Part 3, "Lobbyists Add Political Sweetener." *St. Petersburg Times,* 17 May 1994.

Volfer, Al. "There Is More to the Glades Than Meets the Eye." In *The Environmental Destruction of South Florida,* edited by W. R. McCluney. Coral Gables: University of Miami Press, 1969.

Wallace, David Rains. *Bulow Hammock: Mind in a Forest.* San Francisco: Sierra Club Books, 1988.

Walters, Mark Jerome. *A Shadow and a Song: The Struggle to Save an Endangered Species.* Post Mills, Vt.: Chelsea Green, 1992.

Weinstock, Maia. "Peril in Paradise." *Science World* 56, no. 4 (1999).

White, Randy Wayne. *Batfishing in the Rainforest: Strange Tales of Travel and Fishing.* New York: Lyons Press, 1998.

Whitehead, Charles E. *The Camp-Fires of the Everglades, or Wild Sports in the South.* 1891. Reprint, Gainesville: University Press of Florida, 1991.

Whoriskey, Peter, "Development Unbridled by Council." *Miami Herald,* 28 November 1998.

Wilkinson, Alec. *Big Sugar.* New York: Alfred A. Knopf, 1989.

Williams, Joy. "The Imaginary Everglades." *Outside,* January 1994.

Williams, Ted. "Big Water Blues." *Audubon* 103, no. 4 (2001).

Willoughby, Hugh L. *Across the Everglades.* Port Salerno, Fla.: Florida Classics Library, 1898.

Yakutchik, Maryalice. "The 'Glades Beyond the Gators." *Los Angeles Times,* 25 March 2001.

Zaneski, Cyril T. "Destruction of Wetlands May Silence Forever a Tiny Everglades Songbird." *Miami Herald,* 28 May 1996.

———. "Land Swap Adds to Big Cypress Swamp." *Miami Herald,* 19 December 1996.

———. "Napoleon Bonaparte Broward Probably Would Have Approved of This News." *Miami Herald,* 10 September 1998.

———. "Tribe Will Help Residents Fight to Save Homes." *Miami Herald,* 9 February 1999.

———. "Water District Says Residents Extended Ditch into Glades." *Miami Herald,* 10 November 1999.

———. "Sparrow Plan May Aid Farms, Everglades." *Miami Herald,* 18 December 1999.

———. "Biscayne Bay Partnership Launch Points Up Environmental Conflicts." *Miami Herald,* 29 January 2000.

———. "William B. Robertson II, Glades Scientist." *Miami Herald,* 2 February 2000.

———. "Anatomy of a Deal." *Audubon* 103, no. 4 (2001).

———. "The Philanthropists: Mary Barley and Paul Tudor Jones II." *Audubon* 103, no. 4 (2001).

———. "The Politicians: Bob Graham and Jeb Bush." *Audubon* 103, no. 4 (2001).

POETRY AND FICTION

Asch, Frank, and Ted Levin. *Sawgrass Poems: A View of the Everglades.* New York: Harcourt Brace, 1996.

Berry, Wendell. "The Farm." *Audubon* 97, no. 6 (1995).

DeFelice, Cynthia. *Lostman's River.* New York: Macmillan, 1994.

Eberhart, Richard. *Florida Poems.* Gulfport, Fla.: Konglomerati Press, 1981.

George, Jean Craighead. *The Talking Earth.* New York: Harper Collins, 1983.

———. *The Missing 'Gator of Gumbo Limbo: An Ecological Mystery.* New York: Harper Collins, 1992.

Hemingway, Ernest. *To Have and Have Not.* New York: Scribner's, 1937.

Hiaasen, Carl. *Tourist Season.* New York: Warner Books, 1986.

———. *Double Whammy.* New York: Warner Books, 1987.

———. *Skin Tight.* New York: Fawcett Crest, 1989.

———. *Native Tongue.* New York: Fawcett Crest, 1991.

———. *Strip Tease.* New York: Warner Books, 1993.

———. *Stormy Weather.* New York: Alfred A. Knopf, 1995.

———. *Lucky You.* New York: Alfred A. Knopf, 1997.

Hurston, Zora Neale. *Their Eyes Were Watching God.* New York: Lippincott, 1937.

Kallen, Lucille. *C. B. Greenfield: The Piano Bird.* New York: Ballantine, 1984.

Matthiessen, Peter. *Killing Mister Watson.* New York: Random House, 1990.

———. *Lost Man's River.* New York: Random House, 1997.

———. *Bone by Bone.* New York: Random House, 1999.

Oliver, Mary. "Postcard from Flamingo." In *American Primitive.* Boston: Little, Brown, 1984.

———. "Vultures." In *American Primitive.* Boston: Little, Brown, 1984.

———. "Alligator Poem." In *New and Collected Poems.* Boston: Little, Brown, 1992.

Porter, Donald Clayton. *Seminole.* New York: Bantam Books, 1986.

Powell, Richard. *I Take This Land.* St. Simons Island, Ga.: Mockingbird Books, 1962.

Robson, Lucia St. Clair. *Light a Distant Fire.* New York: Ballantine Books, 1988.

Smith, Patrick D. *A Land Remembered.* Englewood, Fla.: Pineapple Press, 1984.

VIDEOS

Everglades: Secrets of the Swamp. National Geographic Society, Washington, D.C., 1997.

Florida Panther. Travel Florida 4. International Video Projects. 1993.

Lost Man's River. Mystic Fire Video, New York, 1992.

Realm of the Alligator. National Geographic Society, Washington, D.C., 1986.

Sugar Scandal. National Audubon Society, New York, 1995.

We Can Save the Everglades. National Wildlife Federation, Vienna, Va., 2000.

Wood Stork—Barometer of the Everglades. National Audubon Society, New York, 1987.

Acknowledgments

I am grateful and indebted to the individuals with whom I traveled in South Florida and beyond. To Rob Bennetts, who showed me the central Everglades and shores of Lake Okeechobee while introducing me to the snail kite. To Frank Mazzotti, who led me through the mazes of northeast Florida Bay and the southern mainland while introducing me to the American crocodile. To Archie Jones, who, in pursuit of tree snails, showed me the hammocks of the southern Everglades. David Maehr took me into Fakahatchee Strand; Mike Owen brought me back. Deb Jansen showed me a red-cockaded woodpecker colony in Big Cypress Swamp; Jack Moller took me to his camp on the northern end of the swamp. With Peter Frederick I visited wading bird colonies in Big Cypress and in the central Everglades. Russell Yates allowed me to get in his way most of one night in East Everglades. Skip Snow and Jim Meeker led me through Long Pine Key on the trail of bark beetles and pine weevils and then answered my questions about Hurricane Andrew. I am indebted to Bill Platt, of Louisiana State University, for flying me to Lostmans Pines and showing me the effects of fire in an old-growth pine woods. To Peter Allen, who shared his love of Florida Bay; and to Brian Mealy and Greta Parks, with whom I searched the Bay for bald eagles, osprey, and diamond-backed terrapins. To Larry Richardson for introducing me to the Florida Panther National Wildlife Refuge and for answering my questions about big cats. To Jerry Lorenz, who led me into a spoonbill colony on Tern Key. To Mike Duever, who, several days after the passage of the Hurricane Andrew, flew the path of the storm with me and interpreted its effects. To Richard Coleman, who took me into the upper reaches of the Kissimmee River. To Duane Kolterman, of the biology department at the University of Puerto Rico, and to Ramona Oviedo Prieto, curator of the herbarium of the Cuban Academy of Sciences, in Havana, for leading me into the jungles of Ciénaga de la Zapata. To Steve Miller, University of North Carolina at Wilmington, who took me snorkeling around the reefs off Key Largo. And to Stuart Pimm and Phil Nott, who introduced me to the marl prairies and the precarious world of the Cape Sable seaside sparrow.

I am equally grateful to the Florida Panther Recovery Team—Darrell Land, Mark Lotz, Roy McBride, Mark Cunningham, and formerly Ken Johnson—for letting me tag along with them for several weeks. And to Everglades National Park—Larry Bely, Bob Johnson, Sonny Bass, Sue Perry, Tom Van Lent, Bill Loftus, Lori Oberhoffer, Stuart Pimm, Angelina DeGregorio, Robert Brock, Alan Scott, Pat Tolle, Sandy Dayoff, Marty Fleming, Bob Sholler, Frankie Aranzamendi, the late Bill Robertson, Judy Visti, and Peter Allen—for answering my questions and lending scientific reprints to me, as well as for guiding me in the field. Bob Johnson was particularly helpful, explaining the park's position on the original and final draft of the Restudy. I owe a special thanks to the park's spokesperson, Rick Cooke, for arranging interviews and field sessions and for providing me with comfortable places to stay; to Vivie Thuie for opening the doors to the park's Beard Center Library; and to Deb Nordeen for allowing me to borrow a crucial book.

To the South Florida Water Management District I owe a large debt. Al Goldstein introduced me to the restored oxbows on the lower Kissimmee River and to Davey Dairy's sewage retention pond; Dan Thayer escorted me to a melaleuca treatment project on Lake Okeechobee. District scientists—John Ogden, Steve Davis, Christopher McVoy, Fred Skliar, Dale Gawlik, and Ken Tarboten—granted me extensive interviews and later graciously fielded my telephone questions. Mike Collins, chairman of the governing board, gave me a very candid interview. On several occasions, I was an overnight guest of the district at the River Woods Center on the Kissimmee River. Cynthia Polockman and Pat Ohrn, who curate the district's reference library, found obscure books and articles and allowed me to use the copying machine and microfiche printer.

The National Audubon Society provided invaluable assistance. When I began this project in 1992, Bernie Yokel shared his knowledge and expertise; then the staff at the Corkscrew Swamp Sanctuary—Ed Carlson, Joel Rhymer, Mike Duever, Jean

McCollum, Larry Riopelle, and Ted Below—pointed me in the right direction. On several occasions Ed Carlson made Corkscrew's guest cottage available to me. Over the years, Jerry Lorenz faithfully answered my questions and arranged for me to use the library at Audubon's Tavernier Science Center. Scott Hedges and Paul Gray taught me about the natural history of the Kissimmee River valley. Stuart Strahl and Mark Kraus endured long interviews, while making Audubon's Everglades restoration headquarters in Miami accessible to me.

Stuart Applebaum of the United States Army Corps of Engineers and Col. Terry Rice, formerly of the Corps, were also generous with their time, as was the Corps' Ron Miedema, with whom I toured the southern end of Herbert Hoover Dike on Lake Okeechobee. Gary Warren, of the Florida Fish and Wildlife Conservation Commission, showed me the insects of Lake Okeechobee. Joe Wasilewski, an environmental scientist with Florida Power and Light, showed me the crocodiles of the Turkey Point Nuclear Power Plant. Mike Duever taught me about the hydrology of Big Cypress Swamp, while Pat Kenney explained the national preserve's complicated management issues. Representatives of the Miccosukee Nation, J. K. Jones and Steve Terry, answered my questions about the Miccosukee's relationship to the Everglades and to the status of several water-quality lawsuits. Joe Browder recounted the history of environmental activism in South Florida for me. The late Jim Webb, of the Wilderness Society, entertained me in his Coral Gables office, where he spoke at length about political logjams on the road to Everglades restoration. Tom MacVicar and James Humble showed me the Frog Pond and answered my questions about tomato farming and its effect on Taylor Slough and northeast Florida Bay.

The University of Florida Medical Entomology Laboratory in Vero Beach provided lodging in their research center while I interviewed mosquito authorities George O'Meara and Jonathan Day and worked in the research library. Peter Frederick and Marilyn Spalding, both of the University of Florida, Gainesville, answered my questions about wading birds. Julie Heath, Peter's graduate student, took me in the field to band white ibis. Harry Slater, a doctoral candidate at Louisiana State University, taught me about the hammock trees of Long Pine Key, while Jeff Baylis, a biologist at the University of Wisconsin, taught me about exotic fish. The other John Ogden, of Florida Institute of Oceanography, and Billy Causey, superintendent of the Florida Keys Marine Sanctuary, answered my questions about coral reef ecology. Brady Barr, then a graduate student at the University of Miami, and Laura Brandt, a biologist at Loxahatchee National Wildlife Refuge, told me everything I wanted to know about alligators, while George Dalrymple, formerly of Florida International University, spoke about the plight of snakes and frogs in the Everglades. Mahlon Hoagland answered my questions about photosynthesis. Connie Rinaldo, director of the Ernst Mayr Library at Harvard's Museum of Comparative Zoology, completed literature searches for me. I am also grateful for use of the Baker Library Special Collection Room and the Dana Bio-Medical Library, both at Dartmouth College, and to Manley Fuller of the Florida Wildlife Federation for lending "Land into Water, Water into Land" to me. Bill Weyrick solved my computer troubles, which were many.

At the U.S. Sugar headquarters in Clewiston, John Dunkleman introduced me to the biology of sugarcane and the economics of farming in the northern Everglades. While I was at Flo-Sun's Okeelanta headquarters, the late Peter Rosendahl, Raul Perdomo, and Jorge Dominicus generously gave me their time and attention. Although they sensed my sympathies lay elsewhere, they unflinchingly answered tough questions about the effects of cane growing on the health of the Everglades and about the history of labor problems in the fields. Their tours of the fields and mill were most appreciated.

Through the years, friends joined me on numerous outings in the Everglades. Together with my late wife, Linny, and our eldest son, Casey, I camped, canoed, and hiked in the national park, Fakahatchee Strand State Preserve, and Collier-Seminole State Park. With Frank Asch I paddled the Wilderness Waterway. With John Douglas, Ben Moore, and Denny Donahue I walked across Big Cypress National Preserve from Loop Road to the Oasis Visitor Center. At one time or another, I traipsed across South Florida with Joan Waltermire, Donna Nelson, Delia Clark, Kalmia Traver, Tim Traver, Jesse White, Sandra Miller, Joey Lopisi, Brown Dobyns, David Brooks, and the butter-eater.

My graduate students at Antioch New England, who studied the issues behind Everglades restoration and traveled the watershed from Lake Kissimmee to Florida Bay, asked questions I never thought of, made connections I never dreamt of. Many students, particularly Jesse White, nurtured my love of South Florida. With John Douglas, I led numerous expeditions into the Everglades for the Hulbert Outdoor Center in Fairlee, Vermont, and for Lebanon College in Lebanon, New Hampshire. On each trip I saw something I had never seen and learned something I had never known.

I am indebted to many editors. At *Audubon,* Bruce Stutz, Linda Perney, Pat Crow, David Seideman, Sydney Horton, and Keith Kloor worked with me on various stories that appear here in different form. Likewise, I wrote about mosquitoes and crocodiles for Myra Gelband at *Sports Illustrated,* coral reefs and Everglades animals for Lisa Drew and Mark Wexler at *National Wildlife,* snail kites for Tim Gallagher at *Living Bird,* and the watershed for Reed McManus at *Sierra.* Their insights and deft editorial suggestions enrich my writing. A small portion of the preface first appeared in *The Curious Naturalist,* published by the National Geographic Society in 1991. I appreciate Jennifer Ackerman's editing and director William Gray's permission to rework a small portion of the material. I respectfully thank Liz Van Doren, my editor at Harcourt Brace, and Susan Costello, my editor at Abbeville, for their fine efforts on *Sawgrass Poems: A View of the Everglades* and *Everglades National Park* in the Tiny Folio series. Several paragraphs from both books were reshaped for this project. Several stories were distilled into four-minute commentaries for Vermont Public Radio; the suggestions of audio editors Betty Smith and Bob Merrill were eventually incorporated into the manuscript.

For five years I was a regular on the Everglades Commons, an electronic mailing list operated by the Sierra Club. I would like to thank Joe Browder, the late John

DiNunzio, Peter Rauch, David Guggenheim, Joe Podgor, Alan Fargo, Roderick Tirrell, Charles Lee, Peter Gallagher, Madeleine Fortin, Gene Duncan, Jack Moller, Brad Sewell, Jim Harvey, Stuart Pimm, and Bob Mooney for debating issues and posting relevant newspaper articles.

Many people read, reviewed, and criticized portions of this manuscript. Thank you David Dobbs, Jim Schley, Ian Baldwin, Alexis Jetter, Frank Asch, Terry Osborn, Ned Perrin, Ginny Barlow, John Hay, Donna Nelson, Tim Traver, Delia Clark, Ginger Wallis, Sandra Miller, Joan Waltermire, and John Douglas. Members of the Everglades scientific community commented on specific areas: Peter Allen and Judy Visti (chapter 1 and the preface), Christopher McVoy (predrainage wetlands), Robert Brock (Florida Bay), Laura Brandt (alligators), Rob Bennetts (snail kites), George O'Meara (mosquitoes), Deb Jansen (Florida panthers), Joe Browder (Big Sugar), and Allison Defoor (geology and population). Ian Baldwin read the entire manuscript and provided carefully detailed suggestions. Errors that appear in the final draft are regrettably my own.

Peter Allen and Judy Visti shared their home overlooking Florida Bay with me, fed me redfish and snapper, and encouraged this project in so many ways, including helping me flesh out the theme of the book and introducing me to key people in Everglades National Park. (Judy also made great margaritas for my birthday.) Rob Bennetts, Mike Wilson, Sue Wilson (now McDonald), and Joe and Gigi Lopez gave me shelter and warm meals when I needed them most. On many occasions I used the home of my parents, Betty and Mel, as a base camp. Rob Bennetts introduced me to Peter Frederick, who introduced me to Russell Yates. Skip Snow suggested that I call Archie Jones.

I wish to thank my agent, Nina Ryan, and my editor, Barbara Ras, for their support and encouragement during the long period this project took to complete and for their editorial guidance during the many stages of the manuscript's preparation. Although at times I wavered, they always saw the big picture.

Without the love and support of my late wife, Linny, who died in November 2000, this project would not have been started and certainly would not have been finished. She faithfully kept the family afloat whenever I headed south, which was often, read every draft of nearly every chapter, and cheerfully kept me on track, even though she was fighting a three-year battle against cancer. Several months after Linny's death, the very thought of her enabled me to finish this book. To my friends Jeannie and Amos Kornfeld and Diane Roston and David Plaut—thank you so much for stepping in as surrogate parents when I returned to Florida. My two boys, Casey and Jordan, with whom I have shared many Florida adventures, now have their papa's undivided attention.

I am deeply and humbly grateful for a decade's worth of support and encouragement. If I have omitted anyone in these acknowledgments I am truly sorry.

Index

Barr, Brady, 95
Bartram, William, 92
bass, large-mouthed, 165
Bass, Oron "Sonny," 116
bats, vampire, 27
bay cedar, 146
Beard, Daniel, 62, 95, 100, 192, 226
bears: black, 228; Florida spectacled, 27
Bennetts, Rob, 75–86, 88
Bent, Arthur Cleveland, 157–58, 159
Big Cypress Jetport, 101
Big Cypress National Preserve, 47, 99–102,
   191, 197; establishment of, 100–101, 164.
   See also Big Cypress Swamp
Big Cypress Swamp, 28, 99, 100–102. See also
   Big Cypress National Preserve
Big Sugar. See Everglades Agricultural Area
   (EAA): sugar industry and
birds, blood samples from, 176, 177–78.
   See also rookeries; wading birds; and
   individual species
Biscayne Aquifer, 30–31
Biscayne Bay, 142, 193
Biscayne National Park, 188
black bean, 146
Black Betsy Key, 148
bladderwort, 176
bluebirds, xiv, 46
bluefin killifish, 33
bonefish, 176
Bovard, James, 204
Bradley, Guy, 155, 157, 174
Broerman, Fred, 84–85
bromeliads, 57, 58
Broward, Napoleon Bonaparte, 8
Broward County, 191, 192, 200
Browder, Joe, 197, 203
Brown, Loren G., 95
bryozoans, 29
Buker, Bob, Jr., 213
buttonwood, 128
Buttonwood Canal, 136, 173

C-111 canal system, 32, 160, 161, 184, 193–94,
   225–26
cacti, 28
calcium carbonate, 28–29
Caloosahatchee River, 9, 103

Calusa Indians, 4, 120, 121–22, 128, 132, 239
canals, 3, 6, 133, 214, 231; alligators and,
   96–97; American crocodiles and, 142–43,
   150–51; early use of, 9, 31–32, 206–9;
   panthers and, 103, 106; removal of, 120,
   220, 224–25; water salinity and, 135, 166.
   See also specific canals and canal systems
Canepatch, 132, 133
Cape Sable seaside sparrows. See sparrows,
   Cape Sable seaside
caracara, 28
Carr, Archie, 60, 91, 94, 236
Castro, Fidel, 202
cattails, 82, 210–11, 225
Central and Southern Florida Flood Control
   District, 9, 226
Central and Southern Florida Flood Control
   Project, 32, 52–53, 209, 238
Chaffee, John, 222
Chapman, Frank, 158
Chatham River, 124
Chevalier Bay, 124
Chiles, Lawton, 211, 212
Chokoloskee Island, 122
Clewiston, 201–2
Clinton, Bill, 189, 194, 202
Coconut Grove Women's Club, 190
Coe, Ernest, 226
Collier County, 120, 191
Collins, Mike, 10, 197–98
Comprehensive Everglades Restoration
   Plan (CERP), 11, 219–21, 231, 233; adaptive
   assessment and, 222–23; performance
   measures for, 228, 230
coots, 136
coral bean, 28
coral reef, 173, 177, 181
Corkscrew Swamp, 169
Cory, Charles, 114
Craig, George, 52, 57
Craighead, Frank, 95
crayfish, 32, 165–66; blind, 31
crocodiles, American (crocodilians), 39,
   41–42, 137–52; compared to alligators,
   93, 138, 141, 142, 143, 150; nests and
   hatchlings of, 137–38, 140, 143–46, 147–51;
   range of, 139–40, 142–43; restoration
   and, 11, 138

rabbits, marsh, 55
raccoons, 55
Rafinesque, Constantine Samuel, 141
rainfall, 5, 29, 133, 181, 210
Rankin Bight, 178
rattlesnakes. *See* snakes
red-cockaded woodpeckers, xiv
redfish, 176
Rice, Colonel Terry, 197
ridge and slough, 16, 17–18
Ring, Dick, 198, 231–32
River of Sand, 181
River Woods, 238
Robertson, Bill, 5
Rocky Glades, 26–27, 28, 30–33, 192
rookeries, 133, 157–58, 167; alligators and,
    89–90, 96, 163; poaching and, 154, 155,
    156–57. *See also* Hidden Colony; Rookery
    Branch Creek
Rookery Branch Creek, 133, 166
Rosendahl, Peter, 215
Royal Palm Hammock, xiv

Sagittaria, 81–82
St. Augustine, 206
Sandy Key, 173, 174–75
Save Our Everglades (soe), 216
sawgrass, 16–18, 81, 210; agriculture and, 207;
    germination of, 5
sawgrass plains, 16–18
Scheidt, Dan, 230
sea grape, 146
sea level, 13, 27, 29, 132, 141, 178
seasons, wet and dry, 5, 35–38; gator holes
    and, 87–88; mosquito proliferation and,
    52; pig frogs and, 73; snail kites and, 38,
    77–78; wading birds and, 38, 153, 161
Seminole Indians, xvi, 4, 47, 101–2, 123,
    132; plume trading and, 156; resistance
    to disease among, 59; sugarcane farming
    and, 206
seven-year apple trees, 38, 146
Shark River, 132–34
Shark Slough, 8, 18, 19, 230, 231; alligators in,
    96; 8.5 sma and, 195–96; formation of, 29;
    levees and pumps in, 21, 135, 195, 209; as
    part of East Everglades, 912–93; snail kites
    in, 78–79

Shingle Creek, 236–37
Sierra Club, 11, 196, 224
Simmons, Glen, 22, 95, 229
skunks, hog-nosed, 27
slash pine, 32, 45, 46–47
Slater, Harry, 46
slime mold, 180
Slocum, Joshua, 129
sloths, ground, 29
sloughs, 6, 13; defined, xv. *See also* Shark
    Slough; Taylor Slough
Small, John Kunkel, 14, 47, 64
Smith, Bob, 222–23
Smith, William, 155
snail kites, 5, 36, 38, 40, 74–86; breeding
    and nesting of, 75–76, 77, 82; habitat of,
    77–78, 79, 82; predators of, 83; restoration
    and, 11, 78–79, 86
snails: apple, 38, 77, 78, 82; *Euglandina rosea,*
    66; tulip, 148. *See also* tree snails
Snake Bight, 179
snakes, 28; eastern diamondback
    rattlesnakes, 54, 67, 96; pygmy
    rattlesnakes, 61; water moccasins, xiv, 99;
    water snakes, xiii, 151–52
Snapper Creek, 30
snook, 176
solution holes, 32, 33, 60
South Dade Land Corporation, 194–95
Southern Sugar. *See* U.S. Sugar Corporation
South Florida Regional Planning Council,
    192
South Florida Water Management District,
    9, 40, 77, 158, 192; c-111 and, 161, 226; 8.5
    sma and, 197–98, 199; farm runoff and,
    210, 211; Florida Bay and, 176; Frog Pond
    and, 183, 193–95; Loxahatchee and, 19;
    River Woods and, 238
South Lostmans, 128–29
South New River Canal, 207. *See also* New
    River
Spalding, Marilyn, 164
sparrows: Cape Sable seaside, 21–22, 23–25,
    234–35; ——, 8.5 sma and, 195–96, 198;
    grasshopper, 239
spoonbills, roseate, 154, 158, 159–62
sprawl, 191–92
Sprunt, Alexander, III, 6, 170–71

State Road 94 (Loop Road), 100, 102
Stowe, Harriet Beecher, 189–90
Strahl, Stuart, 219–20, 224
strand, defined, xv
sugarcane, 204–6, 217; phosphorus and, 208,
    210, 215, 216–17, 220, 225
sugar industry, 201–18; farm runoff, 181,
    210–12, 216–17, 220, 225; history of,
    202–4, 206–9; legal and political disputes
    regarding, 202, 210, 211–12, 216–17, 214–17

tamarind, wild, 46–47
Tamiami Trail, 21, 196, 225, 233
tarpon, 176
Taylor River, 143, 149
Taylor Slough, 8, 19, 67, 143, 160, 209;
    American crocodiles in, 148–49; Frog Pond
    and, 183–84, 193–94; previous name for, 67
Ten Thousand Islands, 118
Tequesta Indians, 188
Thayer, Dan, 243
Thornburgh, Dick, 211
tidal creeks, 132; alligators and, 89
trees. See specific species
tree snails, 36, 62–63, 64, 66, 67; conser-
    vation of, 63, 65; population decline of,
    62, 64, 65; variation of, 61–62, 66
tulip snails, 148
Turkey Lake, 236–37
Turkey Point Nuclear Power Plant, 142, 150
Turner River, 120, 121
turtle grass, 180, 181
turtles, 93, 94, 97; diamond-backed
    terrapins, 148, 175, 182–83; Florida
    softshell, 97; loggerhead, 143, 228;
    tortoise, 28, 29

United States Army Corps of Engineers: 9,
    78–79, 138, 232, 242; C-111 and, 160, 183–
    84, 193, 225–26; construction of canals,
    levees, and dikes by, 21, 160, 209, 238, 241;
    8.5 SMA and, 195, 198; Loxahatchee and, 19

United States Fish and Wildlife Service, 19,
    78–79, 113
U.S. Sugar Corporation (Southern Sugar),
    202, 208, 213, 217

Van Lent, Tom, 31, 230

wading birds, 5–6, 153–71, 229–30; flooding
    and, 38; parasites and, 163–64; poaching
    of, 154–57, 159; seasonal changes and, 38,
    153, 161. See also rookeries; and individual
    species
warblers, pine, 46
Wasilewski, Joe, 150–51
Water Conservation Areas (WCA), 10, 209,
    214; WCA 2, 217, 225, 231; —, snail kites
    in, 77; WCA 3 (3A and 3B), 77, 78–79, 196,
    225, 233
water storage, 214–15, 219, 221–22
Watson, Edgar, 124
wax myrtle, 19, 81
West Lake, 149–50
Weston, 192
West Palm Beach, 191
West Palm Beach Canal, 32
wet prairie, 20, 88
White, William A., 18
Whitewater Bay, 134–35
widgeon grass, 181
Wilderness Waterway, 119, 122
Wilkinson, Alec, 217
Williams, Joy, 10
willows, 81
wolves: dire, 29; red, xiv
woodpeckers, ivory-billed, xiv
wood storks, xv, 5, 86, 133, 168, 169–70;
    departure of, from Everglades, 167, 220,
    229

Yates, Russell, 68–73
Young, Stanley P., 114
yucca, 28